WARHEAD

WARHEAD

How the Brain Shapes War and War Shapes the Brain

Nicholas Wright

MACMILLAN

First published in the US 2025 by St Martin's Press
an imprint of St Martin's Publishing Group

First published in the UK 2025 by Macmillan
an imprint of Pan Macmillan
The Smithson, 6 Briset Street, London EC1M 5NR
EU representative: Macmillan Publishers Ireland Ltd, 1st Floor,
The Liffey Trust Centre, 117–126 Sheriff Street Upper,
Dublin 1 D01 YC43
Associated companies throughout the world

ISBN 978-1-0350-1398-2 HB
ISBN 978-1-0350-1399-9 TPB

3 5 7 9 8 6 4 2

A CIP catalogue record for this book is available from the British Library.

Text design by Steven Seighman

Printed and bound in India by Thomson Press India Ltd

Dedicated to my great-uncle Sydney Spiers; my wife, Marsha; and my children, Ceci and Hugo. During World War II, Sydney survived years of fighting against Nazi Germany and its allies in North Africa and Italy, receiving the Military Cross for bravery in combat. Here, Sydney was at his hundredth birthday party in 2016, in Brighton, with Marsha and Hugo. Hugo had a tiny brain then. But brains grow. Hugo's generation might know a little more about itself than Sydney's, or Marsha's and mine—and that makes me optimistic.

CONTENTS

PREFACE

Outside, it was a dark, chilly evening in late 2021. I sat in a warm, comfortable pub in North London, with two friends I'd first met while we researched the brain together at the Institute of Neurology in London's Queen Square. We hadn't seen each other for a few months. After a couple of beers, one of my friends—a psychiatric doctor—turned to me and asked what I was working on. I told him I was writing a book on war and the brain.

Rick laughed out loud. "Nobody's going to go to war! Not a big one anyway."

I mentioned Ukraine or Taiwan as potential flash points.

"Why on Earth," Rick replied, "would the Russians or Chinese bother going to war over either of them?"

I replied that they might—and they might win, too. Not everyone, I told him, sees the world as we do.

Rick looked skeptical. "Anyway, America has so many high-end ships, planes, missiles, and everything else that actually *losing* seems very unlikely. And it's irrelevant because there just won't be a war over Ukraine or Taiwan. So it doesn't matter. It's not going to happen."

Three months later Russia launched a large-scale invasion of Ukraine, the biggest war in Europe since World War II's end. Tanks, planes, infantry, and artillery. Backed by enough nuclear weapons to destroy the world many times over. Tens of thousands died on both sides.

Even moderate, restrained analysts no longer view it as unlikely that

Taiwan, or something else, could lead to war between China and the United States. And China might win. That evening over beers with my psychiatrist friend, I knew that eighteen successive war games about Taiwan by U.S. military planners had shown American forces losing.

Wars happen. Individuals get into conflict. So do groups and entire nations. And today the stakes are higher than in Afghanistan or Iraq, which had smaller populations than the leading democracies and obsolete technology. For the first time since the Cold War, democracies must compete, without huge material superiority.

What are we supposed to *do* with this realization?

Recoil? Say war is bad, and disarm ourselves? Disarm the people who feel threatened in countries bordering aggressive authoritarians? Or build ever more powerful militaries and go around thumping anyone who looks suspicious? Neither extreme option worked out well in the past.

We must respond more wisely, and to do that we need to better understand why and how humans fight. What happens inside our heads, whether we are frontline soldiers, civilians, or leaders like China's President Xi Jinping? The reason I—a neuroscientist—have worked with the Pentagon Joint Staff for years is because they know that the human brain is pivotal to conflict, and they want to understand the remarkable new discoveries about the brain.

The Pentagon understands something that my neuroscientist friends in London, New York, and Beijing never see. Human brains weren't built only for comfortable lives. I believe both perspectives can learn from each other.

The latest cognitive neuroscience gives us better self-knowledge to answer the question: Why do humans fight, lose, and win wars? I hope you come to believe, as I do, that the human capacity to think about the world outside us—and to think about our own thinking—can save civilization. Because self-knowledge is power.

INTRODUCTION

Two armies faced each other in May 1940. The German side had fewer trained men, guns, tanks, and planes.[1] They had lost a world war two decades earlier. Their opponents' leaders—and many independent observers—believed that material inferiority meant the Germans couldn't win this time either.

But in the 1920s and '30s, German military professionals had asked how they could harness the human brain's capacities for shock, creativity, guile, will, daring, and skill, alongside the technologies of their time, to win wars. One idea was to use tanks en masse to surprise an enemy, and radio communications to think and decide faster than the enemy. And in May 1940, as we all know, their *Blitzkrieg*, or lightning war, catastrophically defeated the British and French forces.

German effectiveness created the initial opening. But there was more to it: German troops advanced so far in 1940 through an enemy with more trained men, guns, tanks, and planes because French will collapsed. And French capitulation handed Germany vast armaments that enabled their June 1941 Russian invasion. What's more, collaboration meant that by 1942 fewer than three thousand German police were needed to handle all of occupied France.[2]

Happily for us, Germany's democratic enemy had also combined brains and machines. British commanders in the 1930s had looked ahead to build new air forces that would win the Battle of Britain, Hitler's first major defeat.

Russians, unlike the French, had the resolve to withstand an almost unimaginable number of deaths. Hitler foolishly decided to declare war on the United States. The Allies skillfully nurtured the cooperation that enabled their fight back—seen so powerfully in the exquisite trust built between the British and Americans who planned D-Day and fought through to German soil. If the Germans and Japanese had worked together even a fraction as well, they could have won the war. After all, German soldiers were beaten back from Moscow's outskirts by Soviet troops who no longer needed to face Japan.

The story of World War II is often told as one in which, after a rocky start weathered by British courage, victory was inevitable through overwhelming Russian manpower and American manufacturing. But Germany almost won; Britain didn't lose; Russian will didn't collapse; and Americans learned from ingenious and effective adversaries. None of that can be understood without the central weapon of war, the human brain.

In the previous paragraphs, while reading about history, your eye passed over terms that have much to do with the brain: courage, cooperation, learning, deciding, foolishness, creativity, trust. All are fundamentally psychological.

Harnessing human brains for war, given the technologies and societies of the time, has always provided an advantage—from the eras of Alexander the Great and Sun Tzu to Shaka Zulu, Heinz Guderian, and Dwight David Eisenhower. This is no less true in our time.

Cognitive neuroscience gives us better self-knowledge of why humans fight, lose, and win wars—to better understand our past, anticipate our future, and, in the process, know ourselves better as humans. The brain provides a new perspective, and a new source of evidence, to help us understand war.

And war gives a new perspective on the brain, because every human brain is built to win—or at least survive—a fight. Human against nature; human against human.

In this book, we will journey through ten brain regions, each the focus of a chapter. We start at the base of the brain, at the brainstem, from which dopamine can compel us, pain can cripple us, and arousal floods our brain. From there we climb step by step until we reach that most distinctively human region at the other end of the brain: the frontal pole that helps us think about our thinking, explore, and change our minds. This approach emphasizes specific brain regions and also weaves in the broader neural networks in which they operate—so that you can see both the forest and the trees.

The picture of the brain that emerges may be unlike the one you're used to. It challenges our common understanding of perception and reality; turns what you thought you knew about yourself upside down; and grounds us in the basic biology of life. How does hunger work? Why do we experience life in the first person? How do you become *you*?

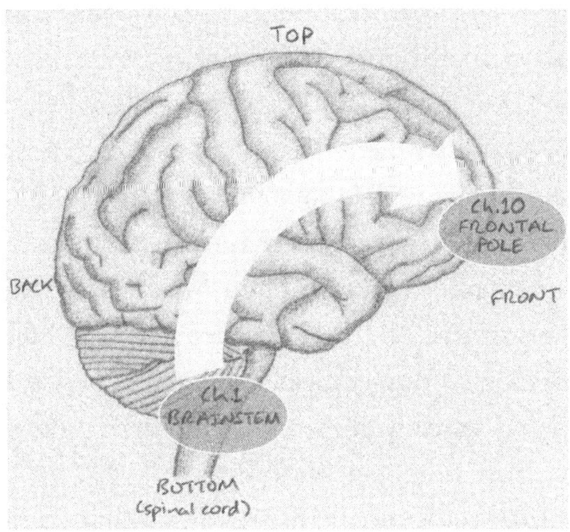

FIGURE 1: A journey through ten brain regions, each the focus of a chapter.

Brain anatomy provides the book's framework, and each chapter also frames a critical question about war. For a foot soldier: What is it like to fight? And, indeed, why stand to fight at all? For commanders like Shaka Zulu: How can they see through the fog of war, make better decisions, and communicate with those who must pull off their plans?

To view such questions in context, we follow war as it unfolded over the past eight decades. We begin with the more than 2,174 days[3] of World War II, proceed through the Cold War's hot conflicts, through the U.S. unipolar moment, and on into our current era. As you'll see, many choices that seem clear with hindsight (what idiot would appease Hitler!) were often foggier for folk living history forward. As you must.

Technology will also affect how every brain system manifests in our era. Brains in battle will perceive and act through artificial intelligence, quantum, and bioengineering. Drugs, implants, sensors, and genes will mold new generations of warriors. Moreover, because technologies that start in the military often later revolutionize everyday life—like the internet or GPS—they can show us our technological futures. But although technology changes how war is fought, war's essence remains the same because war is a clash between humans with brains.

Those brains were themselves shaped by war. Fighting is fundamental to how we evolved. Nonhuman primates build coalitions and strategies for violence—using alliances, bluff, and raw combat in life-and-death conflicts. We are primates ourselves, carrying with us a prehistory full of violence. Much that seems irrational in everyday life, or national politics, becomes more comprehensible when we take that into account. An analogy is obesity: many people today overeat even though no threat of food shortage looms and they know that obesity can kill. Similarly, even in objectively safe places the brain often makes snap judgments, reacts tribally, or sees conspiracies. The ingredients of our life's stories—such as hunger, exhaustion, courage, loyalty, creativity, stress, fear, deception, leading, or following—are always with us, and in our journey through the brain we can step back to see them afresh.

Zooming out from the tumult of day-to-day events, we must see war and national politics afresh—because we have begun a new historical era. For twenty-five years after winning the Cold War in 1989, nothing threatened western democracies' overwhelming military superiority. That's changed.

Democracies can no longer afford oversimplistic ideas that are not so much wrong—but are dangerously *incomplete*. That includes incomplete ideas from liberal thinkers like Steven Pinker, who say that it's all going to be okay because the arc of history tends toward peace and war is irrational.[4] The same arguments were made in the run-up to World War I, after nearly a century without a general European war. "Peace," wrote the Nobel Peace Prize winner Bertha von Suttner, "is a condition that the process of civilization will bring about by necessity . . . It is a mathematical certainty that in the course of centuries the warlike spirit will witness a progressive decline." She was one of many before World War I. "There will be no war in the future," opined Ivan Bloch, a financier whose massive study of war showed the advanced powers would be mad to fight, "for it has become impossible, now that it is clear war means suicide."[5] Fact-filled, passionately argued, and dangerously incomplete for thinking about war—because even if the trend is toward peace, major wars *can* (and did) break out.

Such ideas don't help us prepare to fight better if we must. Neither do incomplete, simplistic ideas that decry overweening experts and planning. Nor pacifist homilies that go little beyond the truth that war is bad. Nor military innovators too focused on machines alone rather than brains plus machines—the Taliban did not win through superior tech. As a captured Taliban warrior reportedly said: "You have the watches, we have the time."[6]

Who, in our time, is most diligently exploiting the human brain's possibilities for war? Russia is pioneering the use of social media and artificial intelligence to exploit its enemies' cognitive vulnerabilities. As for China, its vast new armament programs—its navy is the world's largest—place superior human decision-making at their heart.[7] China is the world's sole manufacturing superpower, producing more in 2020 than the nine next largest manufacturers combined.[8] A single human—President Xi Jinping—is the most powerful Chinese leader since Mao Zedong. If Xi's brain decides to invade Taiwan, an invasion will launch.

The arc of history may bend toward peace and democracy. But wars happen and don't win themselves. Unless the democracies adapt fast enough as the world changes, we will lose. We must see ourselves, and improve how we use our brains.

Part I
Life and Death in the Everyday

Throughout history and prehistory, many humans faced violence, starvation, and other nastiness. To navigate such life-threatening emergencies, our brains use models of the world that are, in effect, survival-grade neural machinery.

But much of our life is spent in the everyday, and our brains' models must succeed here, too. Even during war or revolution people spend long periods waiting, sleeping, or getting from point A to point B (and possibly trying to sneak some food, or sex, at unscheduled point C).

The next four chapters begin our tour of the brain. We start at the base and travel upward through the brain's fundamental and internal regions, on which the brain's fancier parts will build in later chapters. Step by step, we will weave together a picture of how our brains' models are built.

These primal brain regions control much that is reflexive and instinctual. Even here, knowing ourselves better can improve performance—in everyday life, as well as in conflict. But perhaps the most important thing these "lower" parts of the brain teach us is how the brain actually works, because the same essential principles will help us understand more sophisticated brain systems later on.

Why look at ourselves through the prism of war? Because the

stakes could hardly be higher, as I am frequently reminded in my work with the Pentagon.

If one of your friends or a neighbor died suddenly tomorrow, that would likely be bad. You might be sad for some time. Several such deaths would be devastating. And if death wiped out your whole street or neighborhood, you would be numbed. But what if thousands—or millions—of people in your area died?

And what if that single death of your friend was not an accident, but deliberate? What if several people were deliberately murdered? Or thousands or millions? With nuclear weapons that could happen tomorrow, whether deliberately or by accident. How would that affect our thinking?

Such questions seem almost impossible to grasp without becoming callous or glib, or just burrowing our heads into comfortable sand to avoid thinking about big things. It can seem frightening. But every generation *before* us had to think in some ways about some of these questions. Now, so must we—and we can benefit from sciences that help us know ourselves better.

To begin to grasp life and death, we can start very simply.

1

STAYING ALIVE

THE WORK OF THE BRAINSTEM AND CEREBELLUM

Imagine a fighter, entering an arena. It could be any fighter, male or female, at any time in history, anywhere in the world. Anyone facing death. It could be you. But let's be specific. Let's say he is a captive warrior, captured in battle and imprisoned by his Aztec enemies six hundred years ago in their capital city, Tenochtitlan.

He strides into the square, led by his Aztec captors. They'd dressed him colorfully for the festivities. He walks toward a circular stone, 6 feet across and raised high enough for the crowd to see whatever happens on top.

All turn toward him. Small children stand wide-eyed.

Four Aztec champions wait for him by the platform. The captive's mouth is dry, his heart pounds. As he climbs onto the platform, somebody takes hold of a rope around his waist and tethers him to the center of the stone.

Living six hundred years ago, the captive warrior can hardly know that the stone beneath his bare feet—its texture, solidity, and coolness—is sensed by tiny nerve endings in his toes that send messages through nerves in his feet and legs up to his brain. Nor can he know that those same nerves carry commands to his muscles as he shifts his weight, readying himself to fight those four champions.

The Aztec champions will come at him in turn, one after the other.

We know this happened. We know this kind of ceremonial fight took place,[1] and that Aztec champions would seek to prolong the spectacle for the crowd. To cut the captive warrior delicately, tenderly, with narrow blades. To lace his living skin with blood, until, finally—exhausted—he would fall.

But he is not dead yet. He has a chance.

An Aztec hands weapons to the captive warrior. Four pine clubs, for throwing. Then a warrior's wooden sword, although his is not edged with razor-sharp flint but with feathers.

Nerves from his hands sense the oak sword's weight and balance, and his brain sends commands to his hands to adjust their grip. He stands atop the raised stone, ready to strike at his enemies' heads.

To stay alive, every part of the brain of this living, breathing human will be called upon. But much depends on the slender, 3-inch-long stalk at the base of the brain called the brainstem, and the cerebellum nestled in behind. Let's slow down and look.

This fundamental brain region grounds our tour of the brain in the biological basics of life itself. In these opening chapters, we'll find life has two defining features. Here's the first: an organism acts to keep its internal conditions within acceptable ranges. The brainstem can save us from bleeding to death and numb what would otherwise be crippling pain. Powerful chemicals surge up from the brainstem to gird us for a fight, and others—like dopamine, known from addiction—can compel us.

This brain region helps us to grasp in a practical way: *How do we stay alive?*

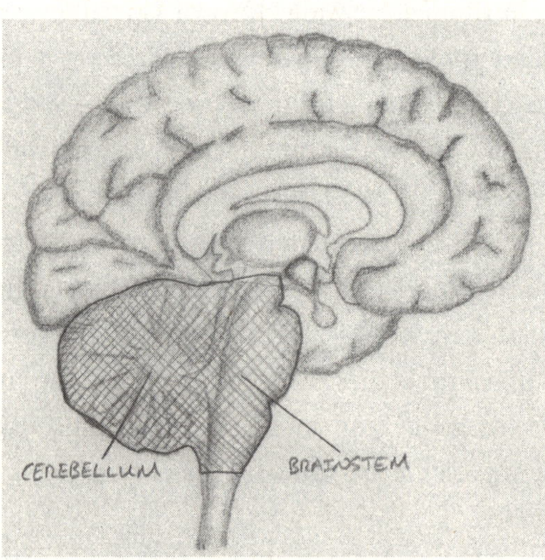

FIGURE 2: The spinal cord becomes the brainstem as it enters the skull. Part of the brainstem is buried within the brain, so here we show the brain cut down the middle. Chapter 1 explores the 3-inch-long brainstem, and the cerebellum that sits behind.

MODELS OF OUR WORLDS

The human brain can seem dauntingly complicated. So let's begin by contemplating something far simpler.

Any organism that acts in the world—from a single-celled organism, to a nematode worm, to a human—often benefits from having a *model* to guide its actions. The concept of a model may seem a little abstract, but bear with me because this concept is central to understanding any brain. *Think of a model as a process that describes how senses can be linked to actions that help the organism achieve its goals.* The links can be supremely simple: "If I sense *x*, then I should do *y*." The links can become more complicated: "If I sense *x* and remember that *p* recently happened, then I should do *q*." And the links can become massively more complicated. But the basic idea of a model remains the same.

In a way, you could think of an organism's model as the internalized scheme it uses to get along in the world. As organisms become more complicated, their models become more complicated, and their models can even become contained in a dedicated part of the body called a brain.

Consider, for example, the model that a small bird might have, which helps it stay alive over winter by foraging for food among the trees and shrubs in my suburb of North London. From my windows I often see a robin. These jolly little birds with red breasts are famous from Christmas cards. But to stay alive such small birds must eat between one-quarter and one-third of their body weight every day. That's tough: although robins can live for almost two decades, few survive longer than two years. By the end of a winter, the majority die.[2]

Robins are ground feeders, who hop around beneath trees and shrubs. In these often dim conditions, they need excellent models to process the data coming in from their large eyes to sense their invertebrate prey—and then link that to the actions needed to catch the bug. Again and again. Robins' models can also exploit more sophisticated patterns in what they sense. The robin in my garden follows me while I dig, because that often unearths tasty worms. Their models must also contain knowledge of local geography—a map—because robins are fiercely territorial.

In some populations, up to 10 percent of adult robins die from clashes over territory. Jolly-looking birds, sure. And they need effective models that link *senses* to *actions* that help them achieve their *goal* over the winter: staying alive.

Yet even such a bird is still very complicated, compared to a single-celled organism such as an *amoeba.* And despite having no brain at all, single-celled organisms can also possess models that enable astonishing actions like hunting. Such a single-celled organism senses its world and has a model that links those senses to actions that help the organism achieve its goals. The models in such very simple organisms are, consequently, very simple; but as we get to more complicated animals, such as fruit flies, robins, mice, or humans, the models that link senses to actions become more complicated.

Once we get up to the complexity of an organism like a mouse or a human, its model can even simulate potential courses of action "offline" in its imagination. A mouse or human, for example, has a detailed model of the physical world's geography—a map—that it can safely explore in its brain to choose the best route to navigate in potentially dangerous environments. We humans have many layers of neural machinery in our brains that give us ever more sophisticated models of ourselves and of the world around us. Every chapter of *Warhead* explores new ways that our models operate. We humans use our models to see, hear, act, think creatively, know others, reason, strategize—and we even use them for self-knowledge.

Throughout the book we will come back again and again to this idea of a model, because it's fundamental to how our brain works at every level. And to make clear that we are discussing something very specific, we'll call it a Model with a capital "M."

Now we've seen what a Model *is,* we can look at the very simplest organisms to see basic features of these Models that will serve as guideposts throughout our journey in the brain. Let's watch single-cell organisms in their natural environment, hunting for prey.[3]

Diving into their watery world, we can see that these single-celled beasts don't exist passively: they sense and they act, guided by their Models. We first see a sleek, powerful cell called an *amoeba*, which can sense other cells by detecting chemicals they release. These senses are linked to the amoeba's movements. Like a lion chasing a zebra, the amoeba catches and devours an unfortunate *Paramecium*. Their Models are tested in life-and-death competition.

Single-celled plants like the green algae *Chlamydomonas* have an "eye-spot" containing the same light-detecting rhodopsin molecules found in the human retina. Signals from the eyespot are linked by its Model to whiplike tails on the cell's surface that can beat in different ways, so that it swims toward brighter light but away from light that is too bright. Light energy is a harsh reality. To survive, the organism's Model must be anchored closely enough to this reality.

Anticipating life-threatening change is another crucial function of our Models, and single-celled organisms show this, too. *Dendrocometes* lives attached to a freshwater shrimp's gill plates. Shrimp molt regularly, which means that the *Dendrocometes* risks being left behind on an empty shell—and if that happened it could starve to death by losing the constant water flow over the gills that brings it prey. Remarkably, *Dendrocometes* can sense the earliest stages of molting (possibly via a molting hormone) and then its Model triggers it to metamorphose, developing motorized hairs so it can move to new gill plates. Its Model helps it respond flexibly to a changing world.

It's worth emphasizing that these single-celled organisms have no brains (they use clever chemical processes and structures). But even here we see three key aspects of our brains' Models that recur throughout the book, and help us survive life-and-death competition. The Models must be close enough to *reality* to help, not hinder, the organism; *anticipate* potential problems; and help us respond *flexibly* enough to change as the world changes.

After a couple of billion years of life on Earth with just single-celled organisms, multi-celled organisms appeared about 1.6 billion years ago[4]—and even organisms like plants also act in order to survive. The naturalist David Attenborough used speeded-up film to show that for a few months each year the Earth's largest inland water world, South America's Pantanal, provides ideal conditions for a beautiful ballet of water plants. Until, as he describes, something stirs from the depths:

> **It's a monster. It's well armed. It clears space for itself by wielding one of its buds. Like a club . . . This is a leaf of the giant water lily . . . Competitors are pushed aside . . . Eventually, its immense leaves press their margins against one another, totally cutting off the light from the plants beneath them. The battle is over. And victory is total.[5]**

Within these multi-celled plants, cells can signal to each other to coordinate and build an organism containing many cells. But plants don't have what we would normally call a brain.

Animals are multicellular organisms that appeared some 600 million years ago[6]—and within an animal, chemical signaling between cells can construct a nervous system. In some animals a mass of these cells concentrates into something new: a *brain.*

What is a brain? A brain is a bunch of nerve cells that serves the organism's whole body (not only a segment of the organism) and sends wiring out to target effects on the organism.[7]

As organisms get more complicated, the Models get more complicated: from single-celled organisms, to plants, to ever more complicated animals. But the basics remain familiar from the robin in my garden. The *Model* describes how *senses* are linked to *actions* that help the organism achieve its goals.

* * *

A few years ago, I attended a dinner in Washington, D.C., near the White House. Finding my seat, I sat next to a recently retired U.S. general. Only nine U.S. officers have ever risen to five-star rank. This man had four.

Neat, restrained, and courteous, he struck up a conversation over our appetizers. I peppered him with questions about technological subjects like nuclear weapons and cyber threats, which he thoughtfully answered. When he learned that I was a doctor and neuroscientist, he peppered me with questions.

It has been my enormous good fortune to spend years helping people with neurological problems, and studying the brain. My hands have touched and held human brains. I was part of brain surgery teams who worked on patients who were fully awake while probes sank deeply into precise areas of the patients' brains. And while the probes moved inside their brains, the patients told us how this radically altered their world.

I described some of these experiences, and gradually I realized that what animated the general most was something very basic that concerned life and death itself: how to save his wounded troops, out in the field, from bleeding to death.

I told him about the powerful Models we rely on to stay alive—to cope if we lose blood or lack oxygen. And I told him how they rely on the brainstem, where the spinal cord enters the skull.

LIFE-AND-DEATH MODELS

The lowest part of the brain is the slender 3-inch-long brainstem, and the lowest third of the brainstem is the medulla. The medulla's tidy, ordered little groups of cells control heart rate, breathing, and swallowing. If the medulla dies, the body dies.

Destroying areas higher than the medulla can be devastating but won't necessarily kill you. If the area just above the medulla is destroyed, that can cause "locked-in" syndrome, a condition made famous by the book *The Diving Bell and the Butterfly*. A stroke gave its author, Jean-Dominique Bauby, just such an area of damage that left him conscious—although he could only move his left eyelid. He moved that eyelid to make himself understood and, eventually, painstakingly, dictated his book.[8] But if his damage had been a fraction lower, in the medulla, he'd have been dead.

The medulla constantly monitors and adjusts our life support systems. It receives inputs from sensors measuring blood pressure, uses Models to determine what actions to take, then sends out messages to control heart rate and blood vessels. Like the robin's Model linking senses to actions, it does much of this automatically. Yours is doing it now, while you read this book.

Even seemingly helpless human babies have these lifesaving Models, as you'll know if you've ever seen a baby dunked underwater. All mammals have the diving reflex to prevent death. Sensory signals from wetting the face and nose cause commands to lower the heart rate, stop breathing, and reduce peripheral blood flow—so the baby can preserve its oxygen stores.

Our Models also help us respond flexibly—as we see if we move just above the medulla to an area called the periaqueductal gray, which is crucial in the network for pain.[9]

We need pain. Tissue damage can be dangerous, and if the alarm system of pain fails us, consequences can be dire. I have treated patients who, without pain, developed serious problems they didn't even notice. But we must also sometimes rise above pain. If a Spitfire pilot hit by a bullet was instantly overwhelmed by pain, that might not enable the best reaction.

Pain illustrates how the brain's Models sit *between* sensation and action. From there, if necessary, this Model can dial down pain so that we can choose flexibly from among a repertoire of responses. Not just shriek "Owwww!" Instead: fly the Spitfire to bring down the enemy bomber; or fly back from over enemy territory; or bail out; or warn comrades; and so on.

That's why people who've been hit by a projectile such as a bullet often liken it to being struck by a stone or lump of mud or "a prodding finger."[10] As the ancient Roman philosopher Lucretius described, when "the scythed chariots, reeking with indiscriminate slaughter, suddenly chop off the limbs," the "eagerness of the man's mind" means that "he cannot feel the pain" and "plunges afresh into the fray and the slaughter."

During World War II, the American physician Henry Beecher interviewed wounded men near the front lines. One-third claimed to feel no pain, while a quarter said the pain was slight.[11] To be clear, the wounded men still had the capacity to feel pain: even when badly wounded and reporting no pain, they would still curse medics who gave them injections roughly. Their Models could dial pain up and down flexibly.

And our brains' Models for pain can be as powerful as morphine. Replacing morphine with saltwater can treat pain, and Beecher researched such placebo effects.[12] How do placebos work? If our Model anticipates that a medicine will relieve pain, that anticipation can in itself be enough to cause analgesia. Unfortunately, this effect works both ways, and we may feel pain only because our Model anticipates it: sometimes long after someone's limb is amputated, a phantom limb can go on hurting.

* * *

When we anticipate pain and death, for ourselves or others, it can affect our decision-making.

In September 1939, seven out of twenty-two members of the British Cabinet had won the Military Cross—a high award for bravery—on World War I's Western Front.[13] They were part of a generation that had lost 880,000 British military dead, as commemorated on war memorials in every town.

In France, too, the Great War cast a terrible shadow: 1.3 million Frenchmen had died, leaving more than 600,000 widows and more than 750,000 orphans.[14] During the interwar years France built a vast "Maginot Line" of steel and concrete fortifications, in the hope that technology could protect lives.

This backdrop helps us understand why so many among the British and French populations—and among their leaders—had little appetite to risk lives by opposing Germany. Not in 1936, when Hitler remilitarized the Rhineland. Not in March 1938 when Germany united with Austria. Not in September 1938 when Germany threatened the Sudetenland in neighboring Czechoslovakia: a region that British and French leaders gave away in the infamous Munich Agreement. Now infamous as appeasement, that deal was popular among the British and French publics—and much of the German public wanted to avoid another great power war, too.[15]

Only in March 1939, when Hitler reneged on the Munich deal and occupied the rest of Czechoslovakia, did appeasement become widely discredited in Britain. And when Hitler invaded Poland on September 1, 1939, British and French decision-makers overcame their reluctance. On September 3 they declared war.

Yet still Britain and France did almost nothing that would risk lives on land or in the air. The French commander-in-chief, General Maurice

Gamelin, had guaranteed that the bulk of his forces would launch an offensive to help Poland[16]—but instead during eight months of "Phoney War" the British and French did little except at sea.

Hitler and Stalin, on the other hand, invaded three smaller democracies that had failed to join Britain and France. Russia attacked the vastly outnumbered Finns, who fought bravely but eventually conceded. On April 9, 1940, Germany invaded Norway and Denmark, with the latter doing almost *nothing* to fight back.[17]

Of course it would be foolish to suggest that French and British policy in the 1930s was entirely driven by raw memories of First World War pains and deaths. The leaders of those countries were sophisticated thinkers. But it's important to acknowledge that the human brain is strongly influenced by elementary drives located in the brainstem. Later we will see that the brain is like an orchestra. When threat is banging loudly in the percussion section, it's hard to listen to the subtleties of the violins.

PREDICTION AND SURPRISE

In the upper part of the brainstem a group of cells manufacture a molecule that is sent up through much of the brain to deliver hits far and wide. In recent years, this molecule's name has become familiar as something we crave, a reward: dopamine. The *New York Times* bestselling book *Dopamine Nation* describes the smartphone as a modern-day hypodermic needle, delivering digital dopamine 24-7.

The classic view of dopamine as a "pleasure" chemical largely sprang from pioneering 1950s work by scientists who implanted electrodes into rats' brains. The rats could press a lever to activate the electrode. Some rats went crazy for the lever, because in those rats the electrodes activated their dopamine system.

Many Germans in World War II ended up taking the methamphetamine Pervitin for similar reasons.[18] German forces received more than 35 million Pervitin doses between April and July 1940 alone. As the young German soldier (and later Nobel laureate) Heinrich Böll explained to his family, one pill kept him as alert as several cups of coffee. And when Böll took Pervitin, he could be happy. For many soldiers this became addictive, and addiction began to take its toll—psychosis, exhaustion, suicide. Consumption only declined from 1941–42, after the medical establishment acknowledged this addiction.

But dopamine doesn't simply equal reward; the story is more important than that.

In 1997 my former Ph.D. supervisor Peter Dayan published a paper with his colleagues that revolutionized our understanding of dopamine.[19] In fact, the principle they described had much wider implications—and much research since then has shown that this principle is fundamental for how much of the rest of the brain works, too.

Dayan and his colleagues saw that our Models of the world face a massive challenge—the world changes, often unpredictably. So, when the world *changes*, how can our Models *change* flexibly, too?

They discovered a measurable quantity in the brains of humans and other animals that changes our Models, as and when necessary. They called this *prediction error.*

"Prediction error" is a basic principle of how the brain works and the concept recurs throughout the book, so it's worth taking a little time over.

We've seen how the brain uses Models to process incoming data and send out commands. Now we can add the idea that these Models include *predictions* about the data they will receive. If the Models' predictions are wrong, then the brain uses these errors (*prediction errors*) to update the Models and improve them.

We can call this *learning.*

Prediction error is the measurable difference between what the brain's Model had anticipated and what was actually identified. The impact an event has on our decision-making is amplified by the event's associated prediction error. The bigger the associated prediction error, the bigger the event's psychological impact.

Dayan's pioneering work on prediction error looked specifically at recordings of dopamine neurons in the brainstem of monkeys, while they received rewards of tasty juice. His team showed that dopamine levels neatly reflected the prediction errors as the monkeys did (and did not) get the tasty juice.

Since then, dopamine's relationship to prediction errors has been shown extensively, and causally, in numerous animals, by many labs.[20]

I emphasize that the findings were shown again, using multiple methods that reinforce and complement each other, because that is crucial for the rest of the book. If you desire to, you can almost always find some interesting neuroscience or psychology study that supports almost any point you fancy making. But as many as half of all single scientific studies—in fields from psychology to cancer biology—arise by chance.[21] Running the experiment again often fails to reproduce the findings—and that's why this book tries to rely on neuroscience findings that we can be sure enough are robust. And findings that, like prediction error, also relate to the real world.

In war, and in everyday life, prediction error matters. Surprise is an example of prediction error: something occurred and it was not anticipated ("Learn! Something unanticipated happened!"). Predictability is the flip side, where fewer prediction errors give fewer signals to learn ("Yeah, as expected . . ."). More prediction error *and* less prediction error matter.

Prediction error can explain a wide variety of psychological effects in war. The bombing of cities is an example.[22] First, let's consider an event that occurs but was not expected. Such an event has a large associated prediction error, and so causes a large psychological impact. In the First World War, German air raids on London using zeppelins were actually fairly small-scale. But the raids were unexpected—like a shocking terrorist attack—so they had a massive impact to cause panic among the public on the ground. The public reaction ranged from demands that factories close, to ordinary members of the public assaulting officers of the Royal Flying Corps in the street for alleged dereliction of duty. In the interwar period, leading airpower theorists extrapolated from this to suggest that more powerful and recurrent bombing—again and again and again—would have an even bigger, paralyzing psychological effect, making adversaries collapse.

But what actually happened? In the Second World War, the Germans did bomb London again and again and again. The bombing exerted vastly more destructive power: in a single air raid the Germans dropped more bombs on London than the 225 tons they had dropped in all of World War I. But this time the public had been warned of the horrific raids and then the raids came as expected night after night after night—and because they were expected, these raids had much less psychological impact than forecast. Certainly not the psychological paralysis that interwar airpower gurus had written about. To be sure not everyone acted perfectly, but on the whole morale really did hold up with the famous "Blitz spirit."[23]

And finally, consider events that are expected but don't occur. When war had broken out in September 1939—a year before the Blitz—terrifying newspaper predictions of hundreds of thousands of air raid casualties had primed the British public to expect terrible bombing, likely with poison gas.[24] In only three days, 1.5 million people were evacuated from cities. And then . . . nothing. Something nasty was expected, and then in a pleasant surprise it *didn't* happen. After that positive prediction error, a puzzled optimism formed among much of the public. Eventually even this pleasant surprise wore off after months of Phoney War, but it shows the power of a positive prediction error. Later in the war, Hitler's propagandist Joseph Goebbels would harness the effect of positive prediction errors after Allied air raids: Goebbels initially spread rumors magnifying the number of casualties, so that he could later issue "official" positive corrections to make ordinary Germans feel better.[25]

Still today, managing prediction errors is a powerful tool for propagandists, as we see on social media. They can harness surprise, use predictability, and sculpt expectations.

To discuss this challenge, I once gave a keynote address at a nondescript building in Ballston, Virginia, six metro stops from the Pentagon near Washington, D.C., at the headquarters of an organization founded because of prediction error.

In the early years of the Cold War, the United States felt confident in its technology. Then, on October 4, 1957, the Soviet Union launched the first ever satellite: Sputnik. U.S. President Lyndon B. Johnson would later recall "the profound shock of realizing that it might be possible for another nation to achieve technological superiority over this great country of ours."[26]

The U.S. response was to found a new organization, the Advanced Research Projects Agency (ARPA). It's now called DARPA, with a "D" for defense added to the beginning. Since that 1957 "Sputnik Surprise" its aim has been that the United States "would be the initiator and not the victim of strategic technological surprises." DARPA helped invent things from the internet to stealth technology. As a visitor, I already had high expectations, and DARPA exceeded them (a pleasant prediction error).

DARPA invited me to speak about how populations can be influenced by the prediction error framework. I began by discussing an MIT study on fake news. This examined some 126,000 stories tweeted by about 3 million people over 4.5 million times—showing that novelty and surprise were key for ideas to spread on social media.[27] Then I discussed the flip side of surprise, predictability, and cited the work of David Kilcullen—who as it happened was the other keynote speaker at DARPA that day. A former Australian Army officer, Kilcullen is a leading thinker on counterinsurgency. The central idea in much of Kilcullen's work on counterinsurgency stresses that success relies on producing predictability and managing expectations to give people a predictable, ordered life without too many unpleasant surprises.[28]

Not long after that event at DARPA, one of the world's most successful recent information operations was carried out by the United States and Britain—and it centered on managing prediction error. In early 2022 they went public with detailed intelligence about Russian preparations to invade Ukraine *before* it happened.[29] Reducing surprise reduced the invasion's propaganda impact internationally. Moreover, many outside Ukraine expected swift Russian victory, so that when Russia's shambolic campaign failed to meet expectations, the failure caused a positive prediction error for observers in the western democracies.

* * *

It was very different in 1940. During eight months of "Phoney War," French troops mostly waited around. The philosopher Jean-Paul Sartre in his army station completed a volume of writings. Some 15 percent of France's front-line troops were on leave.[30] A world of calm predictability.

Unexpectedly, early in the morning of May 10, Germany then unleashed its *Blitzkrieg*: "lightning war." At 04:30 hours, *General der Panzertruppe* Heinz Guderian, commander of XIX Corps, crossed the Luxembourg border. Guderian was a tough-looking man with a wry smile, often pictured in his long military coat. "*Panzer*" means "tank," and his *Panzer* spearhead was central to the German advance.

Why did *Blitzkrieg* cause such surprise? It really shouldn't have. Guderian had planned to harness surprise for years; it was even a major recommendation in his bestselling 1937 book. "Since time immemorial," Guderian wrote, "there have been lively, self-confident commanders who have exploited the principle of surprise—the means whereby inferior forces may snatch victory, and turn downright impossible conditions to their own advantage."[31] The book's title was *Achtung Panzer!* Or in English, *Beware the Tank!*

But the French Army was considered the strongest, and few heeded Guderian's book.

To ensure surprise in practice, the Germans kept the *Blitzkrieg* so secret that some officers were away from their regiments as it began. Additional surprise was achieved by the sheer speed of the German *Panzer* advance. "Time and again," recalled a *Panzer* commander,[32] "the rapid movements and flexible handling of our Panzers bewildered the enemy." They used the novelty of airborne troops and special forces to infiltrate Allied front lines and strike deep in the rear.[33]

They struck through the Ardennes forest, hitherto believed impassable for large forces. German commanders correctly anticipated that the best Allied forces would rush upward into Belgium. That allowed the German *Panzer* troops from the Ardennes to get behind those Allied forces—and drive all the way to the Channel coast to cut those Allied forces off from France. It would become the famous "sickle cut."

All this surprise had a catastrophic impact on the Allies and especially the French.

The *Panzers* reached the French town of Sedan on the River Meuse, a natural defensive barrier, in just three days. On May 13, Guderian prepared river crossings either side of Sedan and sent assault pioneers paddling furiously across to attack the concrete bunkers with flamethrowers and satchel charges.[34] As dusk fell, rumors spread among terrorized French reservists that tanks were already across. The French artillery began to retreat, abandoning stockpiles of ammunition, and the divisional commander himself fell back.

In the early hours of the next day, Captain André Beaufre entered the headquarters of the French field commander, General Georges.[35] "The atmosphere was that of a family in which there had been a death," Beaufre recalled. "Our front has broken at Sedan!" Georges told him. "There has been a collapse." Georges flung himself into a chair and burst into tears.

Such collapse in the High Command of the French Army—so recently thought the world's strongest—was itself a demoralizing prediction error. Beaufre wrote that "It made a terrible effect on me."

Many French troops were so stunned to meet Guderian's forces that they immediately surrendered.[36]

At 07:30 on May 15, French Prime Minister Paul Reynaud phoned his British counterpart, Winston Churchill. "We are beaten; we have lost the battle," he said. "The front is broken near Sedan; they are pouring through . . . The road to Paris is open."

Next day, the military governor of Paris advised that the whole administration leave the city. Civil servants threw armfuls of papers out of windows, and panic seized the population.[37]

In Belgium, General Gaston Billotte, commander of the French First Army Group, was given the task of coordinating British, French, and Belgian operations—and he reportedly burst into tears at news of the role.[38] By May 15, his headquarters were in a state of psychological collapse, with many officers in tears.

On May 20, Guderian's forces reached the Channel coast, completing the "sickle cut" to isolate Allied forces in Belgium.

The British planned a counterattack, and a British general visited Billotte's headquarters.[39] He found Billotte

> in a state of complete depression. No plan, no thought of a plan. Ready to be slaughtered. Defeated at the head without casualties . . . I lost my temper and shook Billotte by the button of his tunic.

We must remember that the Allies had been *materially* superior. No single factor can explain anything as complicated as French collapse—but if anything the French were defeated by prediction error.

"The scale and suddenness of Germany's victory," concluded the eminent Harvard historian Ernest May in his book on France's fall, "has to be explained primarily, I believe, as a result of the surprise achieved."[40]

FIGHT? FIGHT!

Serotonin is a small molecule, broadcast (like dopamine) from cells in the brainstem up throughout much of the brain. In depression and anxiety, negative events cause outsized bad impacts on sufferers' thoughts and behavior—and both conditions are linked to serotonin.[41] Researchers can also temporarily lower serotonin levels in healthy people, and have shown that this worsens the impact of losing money or of receiving negative social reactions. When people participate in lab experiments for money, lowering their serotonin reduces cooperation and makes participants more likely to punish others.[42] In contrast, enhancing serotonin using tryptophan supplements or MDMA (aka "ecstasy" or "Molly") made people more generous and cooperative.

To be useful, the brain's Models must include systems for looking at life's *darker* sides, and here serotonin plays a key role. But these systems are far from perfect.

We often struggle to look squarely at unpleasant options. As in a chess game, life often involves branching sequences of decisions stretching into the future—and if there's an unpleasant option early along one of the branches, we tend to dislike thinking much beyond it to consider what might follow.[43] That is, we tend to "prune" the decision tree behind an unpleasant initial option, even if the branches we've pruned away turn out *better* overall. Chapter 9 describes this type of decision-making in more depth. Many of us experience this in everyday life: we may not want to think through what will happen if we make a difficult phone call to a superior or spouse, but behind that initially unpleasant option we may find the best overall outcomes.

Obviously, we can't consider everything, and such pruning has a place—but sometimes we must force ourselves to think what opportunities lie behind unpleasant options. Otherwise, we will make choices that are initially more comfortable but ultimately catastrophic.

* * *

The Phoney War that preceded Nazi Germany's *Blitzkrieg* was replete with failures by British and French leaders to think through unpleasant possibilities. A prime example: while crucial German forces—including Guderian's *Panzers*—were away invading Poland, many Anglo-French leaders avoided seriously contemplating an offensive in the west. They had at least four weeks to overcome weak German forces and capture the key Ruhr industrial basin, which would likely force Germany into a losing war of attrition. But the option of serious, immediate war horrified them compared to sitting comfortably.[44] In another example during the Phoney War, although it sounds almost bizarre to us now, many British and French leaders avoided facing the possibility that Hitler actually wanted war in the west.[45]

To their credit, though, British and French leaders and publics did at least go to war for Poland, supported by the Commonwealth and the French equivalent. Every other country looked on: Denmark, Norway, Sweden, Ireland, the Netherlands, Belgium, the United States. America was big enough and far enough away to feel secure, but for the rest this proved to be an absurd inability to look unpleasant facts in the face. Belgium and the Netherlands stayed neutral right up until the moment Germany attacked them on May 10, 1940. Dutch forces surrendered after five days. Belgian forces surrendered before the month ended.

After three short weeks, the French were almost certainly defeated. Now they faced a new sequence of big decisions: how to act in defeat. Once again, sadly, many failed to consider the longer-term benefits of immediately unpalatable options.

One question was whether to defend Paris: to give the city up, or make the Germans fight for it. On June 11, Prime Minister Churchill met the French government and urged them to turn Paris into a fortress, to fight in every street.[46] "It is possible that the Nazis may dominate Europe," Churchill told the French, "but it will be a Europe in revolt" so that in the long run the Nazis would lose.

At this, a British eyewitness noted, "the French perceptibly froze."[47] Everyone knew what had happened when the Poles fought for Warsaw in 1939: the *Luftwaffe* pummeled the once beautiful Baroque city, killing some 6,000 soldiers and 25,000 civilians.[48]

French leaders made their choice: Paris was declared an open city, did not fight, and it remained (architecturally) glorious.

Some French troops chose to fight on bravely, but counterattacks and defenses were rare. They caused few German losses—only 27,074 killed—in the whole campaign. One and a half million French troops surrendered, probably half of them doing so before France sought an armistice.[49] They also chose to hand over huge amounts of vehicles and supplies intact, which would prove invaluable when Germany invaded Russia a year later.

Collaboration was broader, too. France could initially be held down by as few as 30,000 German troops in 1941.[50] In the first eighteen months of the Occupation, *not one* German was deliberately killed by the French in Paris.[51] By 1942 fewer than 3,000 German police were needed to handle all of occupied France.[52] And more French bore arms for the Axis than for the Allies during World War II.[53]

This in no way diminishes the many brave French who did resist, nor the tough choices they all faced, nor the failures of other nations that put France in this position. But we must acknowledge that democracies can collapse and collaborate. Can lose, and choose badly.

Those who avoid choosing initially more unpleasant options have to live with the consequences. "If Great Britain is not forced to its knees in three months," the French general who signed his country's surrender is supposed to have said, "then we are the greatest criminals in history."[54]

After the fall of France, only Britain and the Commonwealth opposed Germany. Fascist Italy entered the war on June 10. Even friendly observers, such as the U.S. Army chief of staff in Washington, George C. Marshall, assumed Britain must surrender.[55]

Why didn't it turn out that way?

* * *

Aggression isn't an aberration. Sometimes survival requires humans and other animals to fight, and fight aggressively, to get basics like food, water, or sexual partners.[56] But aggression risks injury, so our Models must also regulate aggression.

Serotonin is fundamental to how we do that.[57] Lower levels of serotonin correlate with aggression, while raising serotonin levels with drugs like Prozac reduces the harm individuals say they would do to others.

Noradrenaline, another key chemical surging up from the brainstem, is also implicated in aggression. Drugs that target specific types of noradrenaline receptors in the brain can increase and decrease measures of aggression in humans and animals alike. Our brainstem cells that produce noradrenaline also arouse us, which is essential for any clash.[58] In studies involving mice we can actually stop the production of noradrenaline. This reduces aggression despite leaving other things like anxiety unaffected.[59] But the most remarkable recent work has involved a very different species.

Earlier in the chapter, David Attenborough sped up time to witness plants in combat. In your house today you might witness another fascinating world if, instead, you slowed down time to observe the fruit fly.[60] *Drosophila* is excellent for studying the effects of brain chemicals because these fruit flies breed fast, and because specific neurons among the 140,000 in their brain can be switched on and off.

In slo-mo, we can witness *Drosophila*'s remarkable aggressive strategies, which they regulate according to context. In the early stages of male fights, they first orientate themselves and approach each other. During these preliminaries, they "fence" by touching forelegs to swap chemical information. They also make visual displays like the "wing threat"—a rapid charge with wings thrust forward and then raised at 45-degree angles.

Fights often escalate. In "boxing," two males strike each other with front legs. In "tussling," they grapple each other. And in the "lunge," one rears on its hind legs and slams its body down onto its rival. (Female aggression often takes the form of a "head butt.")

Drosophila use a brain chemical closely related to noradrenaline. Selectively removing it in lab studies makes aggression almost entirely disappear. Restoring it restores much of the aggression. Fruit flies have far simpler brains than us, but we, too, have neural machinery to dial aggression down, and *up*.

The chemicals surging up from the brainstem that we have met in this chapter have powerful effects. But as we've seen, they're only a part of the brain's wider orchestra. To mention them is not to suggest that, say, the French would have fought to defend Paris if the whole nation had been given a noradrenaline boost. Humans are more complicated than that. But as we move farther up the brain, it's important to remember, however sophisticated our thinking may be, that these brainstem chemicals continue to affect our overall behavior. Compelling and arousing.

* * *

French collapse heaped new dangers on Britain at sea. The French fleet was the world's fourth largest. With that fleet the Axis powers could win the Mediterranean, crucial for British oil supplies. It could help strangle Britain's Atlantic supplies: German attacks on merchant ships had only worsened since they sank the liner *Athenia* the day war broke out, killing more than a hundred people, including twenty-eight Americans.[61] Worse, that French fleet would be invaluable to launch an invasion of Britain.

British leaders chose to neutralize the threat.

The Royal Navy gave the French warships a choice: join the British to continue the war; sail to a British port; sail to a French port in the West Indies or to the United States; or scuttle their ships within six hours. If they refused, the British commander was given orders "to use whatever force may be necessary to prevent [their] ships falling into German or Italian hands."[62]

The French refused, and between July 3 and July 6 the Royal Navy carried out what it regarded as the most shameful duty it had ever been asked to perform: sinking French ships at Mers-el-Kébir and other North African ports. More than 1,250 died. This had certainly been an unappealing branch on Britain's decision tree.

But around the world, this dramatic "dialing up" of aggression had a remarkable effect. Six months later, Churchill was told by an American emissary that this action against the French Navy had convinced U.S. President Roosevelt that Britain had the will to continue the fight, even alone.[63]

Churchill himself became unassailable as prime minister, and the Royal Navy remained a significant obstacle to German invasion at sea.

But what about the air?

How could the British conceivably withstand the German Air Force? The *Luftwaffe*. The storm of men and steel that had smashed all who stood in its way? If the Royal Air Force (RAF) pilots were to have any chance, they would need to ramp up aggression in the fight, and dial it down during rest periods on the ground. Brain chemicals like serotonin and noradrenaline would be key to that.

They also needed *skill*.

The *Luftwaffe* had 656 Messerschmitt 109 (Me109) fighters; 168 Me110 twin-engine fighters; 769 Dornier, Heinkel, and Junkers 88 bombers; and 316 Ju 87 Stuka dive-bombers.[64] And that was just in France. It could draw on many more planes across occupied Europe.

By contrast, RAF Fighter Command's commander-in-chief, Hugh Dowding, had 504 Hurricanes and Spitfires.

THE RAF

Roald Dahl, later famous as a children's author, went as a young British fighter pilot to fly Hurricanes in Greece, shortly after the Battle of Britain. Sitting in his tent with a Battle of Britain veteran, Dahl admitted how little he knew. "I can do take offs and landings, but I've never exactly tried throwing it around in the air."[65]

His companion, David Coke, told Dahl what to do if he met a Messerschmitt 109 fighter.

> "You try to get on his tail," Coke said. "You try to turn in a tighter circle than him. If you let him get on your tail, you've had it."
>
> I tried to digest what he was saying.
>
> "One other thing," he said, "never, absolutely never, take your eyes off your rear-view mirror for more than a few seconds. They come up behind you and they come very fast."

Dahl asked what to do if he met a bomber.

> "The bombers you will meet will be mostly Ju 88s," he said. "The Ju 88 is a very good aircraft. It is just about as fast as you are and it's got a rear-gunner and a front-gunner. The gunners on a Ju 88 use incendiary tracer bullets and they aim their guns like they are aiming a hosepipe. They can see where their bullets are going all the time and that makes them pretty deadly. So if you are attacking a Ju 88 from astern, make quite sure you get well below him so the rear-gunner can't hit you. But you won't shoot him down that way. You have to go for one of his engines. And when you are doing that, remember to allow plenty of deflection. Aim well in front of him. Get the nose of his engine on the outer ring of your reflector sight."
>
> I hardly knew what he was talking about, but I nodded and said, "Right. I'll try to do that."

How is it possible for human beings to coordinate their actions, with split-second timing, under threat, to fly a fighter plane like this? Or indeed for a captive warrior fighting Aztec champions, twisting and flashing his sword, to constantly adjust his stance and grip when fractions of a second could kill?

Direct feedback from our body's senses is too slow. It can take 50 to 150 milliseconds for a motor command to be generated in the cerebral cortex—an area much higher in the brain that we'll see in a later chapter—and then for that action's sensory consequences to return to the cerebral cortex.[66] That's an impossibly long delay for fine coordination in a life-or-death fight, or indeed in many everyday actions.

This is where the cerebellum comes in. The cerebellum, or "little brain," looks like an extra little brain stuck on the back of the brainstem. It does not initiate movements but enhances coordination by using a Model and prediction errors.[67]

When we generate an action, the cerebellum receives a copy of the motor signals being sent from higher up in the brain down to the muscles, and—incredibly—the cerebellum's Model can use this to predict the sensory consequences of the action. To give an example: if I make an action to use a finger on my left hand to tickle my right forearm, then the Model predicts the sensory consequences for the skin on my fingertips and on my right forearm. It then receives inputs from the body's sensory receptors and compares what was predicted with what was actually sensed.

If this reveals a mismatch—a "prediction error"—we're alerted that the movement may no longer be smoothly on track.

I have treated many patients with a damaged cerebellum. They can still function, but all smoothness is gone. Eyes move jerkily from side to side. Speech muscles are uncoordinated, so they sound slurred and are sometimes thought to be drunk. Walking is unsteady. Asked to touch a nose with their finger, they overshoot. They certainly can't fly planes in battle.

As well as saving precious milliseconds, the cerebellum also helps us focus, by tuning out the sensory consequences of our own actions. This explains why you aren't constantly, accidentally tickling yourself—for instance, when you put your finger on your forearm. When your motor system issues commands for movement (such as tickling), your Model generates predictions of the sensory consequences—and so the sensation generates no prediction error because you knew exactly what would happen. We've also learned a lot from the way these Models go wrong: some individuals with schizophrenia have difficulty telling apart the actions they produce themselves from actions produced externally—and they *can* tickle themselves.[68]

When you pilot a Spitfire—or indeed a Messerschmitt 109—you need to know what your body is doing, so that you can focus on the enemy, coming up behind you very fast.

* * *

Britain was fortunate that, years before, just as Germany's Heinz Guderian had anticipated how to use *Panzers*, Air Chief Marshal Hugh Dowding had anticipated this aerial warfare. Dowding had spent years leading the construction of RAF Fighter Command. He had championed Robert Watson-Watt's pioneering radar technology and built sophisticated ground-to-air communications to support the world's first integrated air defense system.[69]

On "Eagle Day," August 13, 1940, when the full German onslaught began, British radar picked out some three hundred aircraft heading toward the city of Southampton, against which the RAF scrambled eighty fighters. All told, 1,485 German aircraft crossed the Channel that day.[70] The RAF lost thirteen aircraft and three pilots were killed—but shot down forty-seven German aircraft and killed or captured eighty-nine *Luftwaffe* aircrew.

The next day, five hundred aircraft attacked.

The day after saw an even bigger onslaught: 520 German bombers and 1,270 fighters crossed the Channel between 11:30 and 18:30. The *Luftwaffe* lost seventy-five aircraft that day—they called it "Black Thursday"—but the thirty-four British losses had not been light. And the RAF couldn't long sustain such losses.

As Dowding knew well, the heart of his air defense system were the pilots themselves. He cared deeply about his "dear fighter boys" and earned devotion in return. Pilot losses were his biggest anxiety. Altogether, 2,940 aircrew served in the Battle of Britain. Some 600 came from across the world, including 145 Poles, 126 New Zealanders, 98 Canadians, and 88 Czechs.[71] Most British fighter pilots were aged under twenty-two. Many were so tired they fell asleep at meals.

Hitler threw everything he had at Britain's defenders. The fight continued ferociously, reaching its zenith on September 15, 1940, which started with a raid on London by one hundred German bombers and four hundred fighters.[72]

"How many reserves have we?" Churchill asked the RAF commander.

"There are none," came the reply.

And yet the Germans lost twice as many planes as the British.

For a long time, the *Luftwaffe* continued to believe it would win, an expectation fed by overoptimistic intelligence about British losses. But as British resistance violated that expectation—a prediction error—*Luftwaffe* morale plummeted.[73] And eventually Hitler postponed the invasion.[74]

Hitler's first major defeat.

* * *

At the start of this chapter, we met the idea of a Model and saw how Models help simple organisms stay alive. We saw how more sophisticated lifeforms, facing more complicated threats, use more sophisticated Models to keep themselves alive. And to illustrate this bedrock knowledge about ourselves, we met a captive warrior atop his stone platform in the Aztec capital—an archetypal warrior reminiscent of Michelangelo's statue of the warrior David atop his stone platform—but a human made of flesh and blood, fighting to save their life.

The brainstem's Models protect our airways, breath, and circulation. They are crucial for the tissue-damage alert system we know as pain. The brainstem broadcasts powerful chemicals—dopamine, serotonin, and noradrenaline—upward to help the rest of the brain change its Models, look at life's darker sides, and dial aggression up or down. Our Models help us *anticipate* more about *reality*, and if the predictions are wrong, then collision with reality causes *prediction errors* that help us *flexibly* change our Models.

And the cerebellum, tucked behind the brainstem, adds an extra loop of processing to coordinate actions initiated elsewhere in the brain. That extra loop of processing isn't burdensome brain bureaucracy, burning up expensive resources. It earns its keep, as do all the other loops we'll meet in future chapters. Each additional loop enhances our capacities, all the way up to those loops that enable us to think about our own thinking—as your brain may be doing now. From a fruit fly to the jolly robin in my garden, to a monkey, to an RAF pilot, every additional loop turns us into an ever-smarter living organism.

The lowest parts of the brain have given us a living human. In the next chapter, we move up in the brain to explore the inner workings of our vital drives: hunger, thirst, sleep, warmth, and sex.

2

VITAL DRIVES

THE ROLES OF HYPOTHALAMUS AND THALAMUS

Here is another archetypal fighter.

This soldier marches through Belgian mud all day—again—carrying 50 pounds.[1] Four hours marching; collapse on the roadside to rest a few minutes; then up again to march. Over and over. His boots and clothes are soaking. He's eaten nothing since that morning. And now night is drawing in.

His eyes glaze as he stares through the gloom at the pack of the man marching in front. He remembers sitting a few weeks before in a comfortable, warm tavern, trying to catch the eye of a nice local girl. Just before they got the news that Bonaparte was on the move again. At least today he had water; yesterday they'd gone thirsty.

At last, he slumps down to sleep in a field, while it streams with rain. Despite some false alarm in the middle of the night, he snatches precious sleep.

He wakes to a gray and breakfastless morning, on June 18, 1815: an infantryman somewhere near the middle of the British army, exhausted and hungry. Waiting was physically tiresome and emotionally frustrating. Would there be a battle? Like most veterans he would rather fight today than tomorrow if it were unavoidable.

After 11:00 he hears battle begin. Then a long day. Fatigue, hunger, thirst, smoke, noise. Smells of mud, blood, shit, and gunpowder. His battalion forms lines while artillery balls smash into their ranks. Then a square that French cavalry can't penetrate. Finally the French infantry march toward them to fire from 50 yards away. The back of the French column starts to turn, and flees.

After nearly twelve hours under arms, ten under fire, and eight hotly engaged in some shape or other—he sags down to rest, indifferent to the wounded around him. He knows little of what happened beyond his immediate fight, or if this was the first of many battles.

He couldn't know that this Battle of Waterloo ended Emperor Napoleon Bonaparte's spectacular career. Ended twenty-five years of war that had killed millions. And ended the last general war between Europe's great powers—until the First World War ninety-nine years later.

The physical experience of battle is revealed by many remarkable personal records from the Battle of Waterloo. Those records put us in the soaking wet boots of our second archetypal fighter, and help answer the question:

What is it like to be in battle?

Much of the physical experience would have been similar at battles fought nearby over many centuries: Agincourt in 1415; the Somme in 1916; or when Guderian's *Panzer* forces made their victorious "sickle cut" in May 1940.

We often want to protect ourselves from such discomfort—like in the French Maginot Line that Guderian bypassed, which had kitchens, medical facilities, and air-conditioning. "I asked you to go without sleep for forty-eight hours," Guderian told his XIXth *Panzer* Corps that month. "You have gone for seventeen days. I compelled you to take risks. . . . You never faltered."[2] Today's U.S. Navy SEAL selection course simulates brutal discomfort. Today's soldiers—and many civilians—face it in Ukraine and Israel-Palestine.

Thirst, hunger, warmth, sleep, and sexual reproduction. These five *vital drives* are vital in the true sense of the word, which comes from the Latin word *vita,* meaning life. They are necessary to continue life.

The hypothalamus is an almond-sized structure that sits immediately above the brainstem, containing specific groups of cells crucial to manage each of these five vital drives. We will study each vital drive in turn, though as we will see all five are intimately interconnected. And once again, Models are key.

In our comfortable lives now, without even noticing thirst, we turn on a tap expecting water to pour out, and we drink a glass of water. The Model for this vital drive *anticipates* our needs. We may not even have realized we did it if we were thinking about something else. It seems effortless to fend off problems before they even happen.

So please: stop and think about it. We can die if Models like this one fail. In the last chapter we saw the *reality* that death can arrive in minutes for choked breath or lost blood—and here we see that these vital drives stave off certain death that would otherwise arrive in hours, days, or weeks. These Models are powerful, survival-grade neural machinery. The vital drives together form a protective iron cage inside which we experience our lives. We may barely notice that cage's constant guidance, but if we try to break free of the cage—as many people do who try to lose weight through dieting—then we see its force.

Better self-knowledge of these Models can help us sculpt this cage. And to do that we can apply three aspects of our Models that we met with the single-celled organisms, and the jolly robin, in the last chapter. The acronym RAF can help us remember these three aspects, which matter for every Model throughout the brain: *reality*, *anticipation*, and *flexibility*.

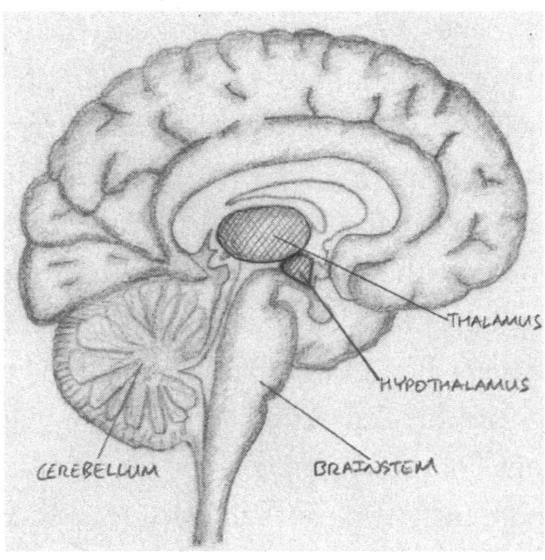

FIGURE 3: The hypothalamus sits immediately on top of the brainstem. Again it is buried within the brain, so we show the brain cut down the middle. The thalamus sits atop the hypothalamus ("hypo" means "below"), and we'll meet the thalamus later in the chapter.

REALITY

Many ideas about war and life, no matter how "realistic" they seem, are matters of opinion. But here I want to consider brute facts that are unavoidable, life-threatening rendezvous with reality. You survive only minutes without air, and the previous chapter described the brainstem that protects your air supply. You survive only hours or days without water, and immediately above the brainstem sits the almond-sized hypothalamic region that is crucial for thirst. For our Model of thirst to save lives, it must be anchored to reality.

But anchoring to reality doesn't mean we get a direct readout of reality. Our Models for the vital drives like thirst illustrate something profound about how our Models relate to reality—which tells us about our capacity for self-knowledge as humans, and how neuroscience can enhance that self-knowledge. Intuitively, these Models *seem* to us like straightforward readouts of reality, and indeed they *seem* that way to me now as I reach for a cup of tea. But they are not. Self-knowledge of how our Models work from neuroscience, rather than how they just *seem* to work, helps us better harness their power and avoid the problems they cause. Consider thirst.[3]

Intuitively, you may think that the body senses that it contains too little water (for example, because your blood gets more concentrated), which then causes you to feel thirsty, so you drink water—and this water corrects the deficiency in your blood, which then turns off thirst. There's some truth to this. But while the blood's saltiness and blood pressure are crucial for survival, these indicators *lag*, so that after drinking it still takes tens of minutes to affect them. If we relied on these indicators alone we would carry on drinking long after we should stop—not only wasting time drinking and worrying about thirst, but also drinking too much, which risks dangerously over-diluting our blood.

In fact, our Model for thirst is *more useful* than a direct readout of reality now in our blood. Instead, to quench thirst we rely on hypothalamus-related neurons (neurons are brain cells) that respond to the physical act of swallowing liquids. Our brain's Model can then compare how much water we need with the amount of water we seem to be drinking. The Model can tell us when we've had enough and leave us feeling instantly hydrated.

In other words, our Model *anticipates* the effect of what we drink, before the effect happens in our blood. This is a more useful Model of reality. No longer thirsty, we can get on with other things.

Of course, everything has drawbacks, and this Model can be fooled. Some laboratory methods are direct. Pioneering research in the 1950s infused concentrated salty water into the hypothalamus of goats, causing them to drink intensely and retain water.[4] More recently, scientists have identified specific brain cells just adjacent that can be switched on and off—and this switches thirst on and off, regardless of actual need for water.[5] *Your* Model has experienced this sort of fooling outside the lab. After you stand outside in the hot sun, for example, if you drink either (a) water or (b) a sugary beverage, in both cases you'll feel instantly refreshed. But with a sugary beverage the refreshing feeling is illusory, and you soon become thirsty again. Sugary beverages fool our thirst Model, much as optical illusions fool our vision.

Thirst also illustrates another way in which our Models relate to reality, in this case the reality of how thirst affects the rest of our thinking. That is, when we are thirsty it may *seem* to us like we get worse at problem-solving, but that's often not the case. In fact, many studies have shown that thirst changes mood (how we feel) more than cognition (our ability to think).[6] So if we do get thirsty—like in a battle in the desert, as we'll see later—we maintain our desire for water but can still solve problems to get it.

Retaining our ability to think is critical because humans evolved to depend more on external water sources than other primates.[7] About 2.5 million years ago we changed from the short, stocky *Australopithicus* to the taller, slimmer genus *Homo*—the first apelike human. We lost body hair and gained more cooling sweat glands, which allowed us to be more active: traveling on two legs in open environments with tools in our hands to hunt over long periods. But sweating can cause dehydration, so we compensated by using our clever brains: mapping watery locations, identifying alternatives like low-alcohol fermented drinks, and securing supplies with our allies and against our competitors.

As with many human evolutionary advances, our clever new abilities brought new vulnerabilities, and these have featured in conflict since the Earth's first states emerged 6,000 years ago. Those first states came to blows over water rights, and cutting off others' access to water helped secure victory. Making thirsty enemies desperate for life-giving water has been a weapon ever since. The Greek historian and general Thucydides lived some 2,500 years ago. Thucydides described a turning point in the Peloponnesian War, when desperately thirsty Athenian soldiers needed water so badly that they waded into a river to drink—even though that rendered them defenseless against the Spartans on the opposite bank. More recently, during the German *Blitzkrieg* in May 1940, French troops who were surprised near Sedan remember being crazed by thirst as they zigzagged for hours through woods. More recently still, in 2014 Islamic State poisoned wells.[8]

Mastery of logistics to protect your own force can also be a weapon. Winston Churchill's ancestor the Duke of Marlborough was a master of logistics: his men appeared in places it seemed impossible they could reach, well fed and watered at the end of each day's march, and able repeatedly to defeat the larger armies of Europe's then superpower, France.[9]

Since World War II the U.S. military's mastery of logistics—the getting, storing, and delivering of supplies—meant it hasn't needed to "fight its way to the fight." But that can change. Adversaries' long-range precision weapons—missiles, drones, cyber—can disrupt logistic supply chains. Ukrainian forces demonstrated this in 2022 by cutting the supply lines to Russian soldiers and so forcing them into retreats. The Russians reciprocated. DARPA recently began a program to generate water for isolated troops, because they know you don't always choose where you must fight.[10]

* * *

In June 1940, Italy's dictator Benito Mussolini followed the French collapse by declaring war on Britain. This threatened vital British oil supplies from the Mediterranean and Middle East. All at once, 36,000 British and Commonwealth troops in Egypt had to defend against Italy's 215,000 troops in nearby Libya.[11] The outnumbered British had to learn to live and fight in the world's thirstiest battleground: the desert.

This unusual arena was largely empty of people except at the coast, and proved good going for tanks. The great limit to free movement was supply: fuel, food, and water.

In early December, with only four days of supplies, the British convoys rolled into no-man's-land toward supplies they'd cleverly positioned there in advance. Outnumbered around four to one,[12] they won a stunning victory. "Then using captured vehicles and captured dumps of water and fuel," as a British officer recalled, they could "maintain this four-day battle into what became an offensive lasting weeks."[13]

Over two months, the British swept forward 500 miles along the coast, capturing 130,000 Italian prisoners, 380 tanks, and 1,290 guns along with vital supplies[14]—not least water.

To be clear, the Italians did not lack courage, as William "Strafer" Gott told the British Foreign Secretary. They were simply unprepared for the realities of desert warfare.[15] Midday temperatures reached 122°F (50°C), causing soldiers wearing steel helmets to suffer splitting headaches, largely from dehydration. Diseases spread through lack of good water.

But on February 12, 1941, the dynamic German *Panzer* commander Erwin Rommel landed in North Africa. With twenty-five thousand German troops to strengthen the Italians, he now launched an offensive. Epic campaigns seesawed to and fro over hundreds of miles, as both sides struggled for advantage. Rommel, who became famous as the "Desert Fox," had the edge in tactics, but the British the edge in logistics.[16]

We leave this desert battleground with the British and Commonwealth forces besieged by the Nazi Germans at Tobruk, on the evening of December 6, 1941. This is a date to which we will return at the end of the next three chapters, because it marks the eve of a great turning point in World War II, and in world history.

The rest of this chapter's story of World War II turns to history's biggest ever land war, which Nazi Germany launched that summer. A war in which a second vital drive would be central: hunger.

ANTICIPATION

You've seen that without water you die in hours or days. And you can anticipate with certainty that without food you will die in weeks. Your Model for hunger is set up to anticipate life and death in emergencies like war, not only what happens in everyday life. To avoid the end point of death—which we know from prison hunger strikers can happen after around sixty days—the vital drive of hunger can from long beforehand dominate our consciousness.

Berta Zlotnikova was a teenager trapped in Leningrad under Nazi siege, starving. "I am becoming an animal," she confided to her diary. "There is no worse feeling than when all your thoughts are on food."[17]

Leningrad (now St. Petersburg) was cut off from the rest of Russia on September 8, 1941, by the Germans. During November alone eleven thousand starved to death in Leningrad, almost three times the rate of deaths from shells and bombs. As December approached, Leningrad's frontline troops got 18 ounces (500 grams) of bread per day. Factory workers received half as much. Everyone else got just a quarter—roughly two slices. Some ate twigs. Ivan Pavlov's dogs—famous from experiments in which they learned to salivate over a bell that predicted food—were themselves eaten. Some two thousand people would be arrested for eating human flesh.[18]

Leningrad's siege lasted 872 days and killed more than a million people—more than all the British and American military and civilian deaths during the entire war.

Starvation was not incidental but central to German plans for Soviet Russia. A month before invading, German planners announced internally what came to be called the "Hunger Plan."[19] Nobody raised objections.

Germany invaded the Soviet Union in the early hours of June 22, 1941. Operation Barbarossa, as it was code-named, achieved almost complete surprise along a 1,100-mile (1,800-kilometer) front from the Baltic up north to the Black Sea down south. A shocked Stalin was woken at 03:30 to be told of the attacks. His face was white when the Politburo met at 04:30. A week into the invasion he seemed to suffer a breakdown during which he wandered around his dacha near Moscow, unable to undress or sleep. "Lenin founded our state," a shocked Stalin was heard to say, "and we've fucked it up."[20]

In the shock of *Blitzkrieg*, the *Luftwaffe* lost just 35 aircraft compared to some 1,800 Russian fighter planes and bombers. By June 28, two large *Panzer* formations, one under Guderian, achieved their first encirclement of Soviet forces to trap 417,000 men. Despite some superior Russian tanks,

Russian crews were less skillful. The Germans had lost 213,000 casualties by July 31, 1941, but by September 30 the Soviets' irrecoverable losses were almost *ten times* as many.[21]

As part of the Hunger Plan, the Germans deliberately starved many captured Russians to death. The German quartermaster general declared that prisoners unfit for work "were to be starved." At one camp near Minsk, some 109,500 prisoners died. Prisoners at another camp submitted written petitions—they asked to be shot rather than anticipate slow deaths from hunger.[22]

How does hunger drive us so?

* * *

Starvation stalked our ancestors through most of human history. The brain's Model for hunger—like for thirst—is built to *anticipate* our needs.

The hypothalamus turns hunger on and off. Hunger drives us because it is unpleasant. In mice, researchers can directly turn on and off the hypothalamus cells that control hunger. Switching on these cells can drive mice—even when well fed—to try to relieve hunger pangs by poking their nose at targets that release food. In essence, the hypothalamus causes a bad feeling—hunger—and we eat to get rid of that bad feeling.[23] How does our Model decide if we should feel hunger?

Similar to thirst, there are time lags between swallowing food and getting useful nutrients in our blood, so our Model for hunger anticipates changes in the body's energy balance.[24] It uses multiple sources of information to anticipate these changes. This can help us avoid overeating. When we've eaten food but not yet had time to digest it, for example, the gut releases hormones to inform the hypothalamus that undigested food is onboard and will be digested soon—so we can stop feeling hungry. Other sources of information might lead us to anticipate reduced energy balance, such as noticing lunchtime is approaching, and so make us hungrier. Our Model can also go on to compare these predictions against nutritional changes that actually occur, so that it can respond if there are discrepancies. That is, if there are prediction errors.

Humans also anticipate challenges like starvation on a longer timescale.[25] Body fat produces hormones that call out to the brain when fat reserves are low. Our bodies store calories as insurance against future food shortages, and those fat stores are important because—as with thirst—we humans have evolved to depend on flexibility from our clever brains to secure food. Technologies like weapon making, animal herding, and cooking enable us to hunt, gather, and process otherwise inaccessible foods. As a result, our bowels got smaller, our brains bigger.

Starvation and underfeeding matter long before military operations begin. Before World War II, malnutrition associated with the Great Depression took a physical toll on American men. The U.S. Army accepted almost anyone sane, over 5 feet tall, 105 pounds in weight, with 12 or more of their own teeth, and free of flat feet, venereal disease, and hernias—yet 40 percent of citizens failed to meet these criteria.[26]

Starvation matters during military operations, too. In 1944, the psychologist Ancel Keys led the landmark Minnesota Starvation Experiment.[27] Thirty-six conscientious objectors agreed to six months of semi-starvation. They became gaunt, receiving only 1,570 calories a day instead of the 2,500 recommended for men. Strength, stamina, and heart rate decreased. Body temperature and sex drive declined. The starving men became obsessed: dreaming, fantasizing, reading, and talking about food. They reported low mood: fatigue, irritability, depression, and apathy. They also reported reduced mental ability, although their actual test scores didn't decrease. As with thirst, recent studies confirm that hunger affects mood more than cognition.[28]

But for most of us in today's nutritionally opulent western reality, starving is no longer the major risk to life. That's obesity. Obesity contributes to the American population's poorer health compared with all other rich countries.[29] In 2016 data, even the relatively poorer Chinese population overtook America's in healthy life expectancy.[30] Long-term population health relates to long-term national security. The relationship is complicated, but strikingly at the end of the Cold War, despite Soviet Russia's strong outward appearance, its poor population health reflected internal decay and preceded its collapse.[31] America today has many strengths, but this parallel shouldn't be completely ignored—and obesity is a major factor.

Alas, our brain's Models aren't set up to correctly anticipate the preposterously calorific environment in which many rich-world populations now live—unprecedented in all human prehistory and history. One problem is that we consume high-calorie modern foods much faster than our Models are built to *anticipate*, so our Models don't stop us from overeating. Compare how many slices of soft white bread you can scarf down in the time taken to chew old-fashioned crusty bread. A U.S. National Institutes of Health study compared two groups of people for twenty-eight days:[32] one group eating "ultra-processed foods" (containing ingredients not found in a home kitchen, like high-fructose corn syrup), the other group eating a less processed diet. Both diets were matched for calories and were rated as equally tasty—but the group eating ultra-processed food ate faster and ended up about four pounds heavier than the other group. Put simply, helping people eat fewer ultra-processed foods can help their Model better anticipate their reality.

To improve population health, such prevention of obesity is better than a cure. But cures have a place, too: low-calorie dieting is moderately effective in some people, and new drugs like semaglutide (which likely acts on the hypothalamus to reduce hunger) also help.[33] Moreover, of course, diet is not only about too few calories or too many, which brings us to a new dietary opportunity: optimizing variety in our food.

For centuries, lack of variety caused terrible suffering to sailors. Our bodies hadn't evolved for extended periods at sea and millions of sailors died of scurvy. This is how U.S. Navy surgeon Usher Parsons described scurvy's effects:

> "The gums become soft, livid and swollen, are apt to bleed from the slightest cause, and separate from the teeth, leaving them loose." He describes ever worsening disintegration until "All the evacuations from the body become intolerably fetid. Death closes the scene."[34]

We now know the problem was a lack of vitamin C, a mystery resolved by the eighteenth-century Royal Navy surgeon James Lind. To remedy this, the British stored citrus fruits on ships, earning the nickname of "Limeys."

Vitamin C is one of many vitamins and minerals we need. Recent work suggests getting five servings of fruit or vegetables a day improves health, and that a good rule of thumb is to eat a varied diet with some fifteen to thirty types of minimally processed foods per week like nuts, seeds, fruits, and vegetables.[35] Militaries are considering how personalized, targeted nutrition can improve performance.[36] I've eaten on enough U.S. and British military bases to know that our militaries are nowhere near this—but better nutrition could be a small, practical improvement to help build advantage.

In the summer of 1941, though, it was not varied diet but the brute reality of starvation that Germany used. Hoping to starve Britain into surrender using U-boats, and to starve millions of Soviet citizens.

But the Russian summer was ending. Temperatures dropped, and for the German armed forces another basic reality came into play. For which, once again, the hypothalamus is central.

FLEXIBILITY

The Germans knew well what had happened when Napoleon invaded Russia. Hitler's library contained many books about it, his own handwriting scribbled in the margins.[37]

He knew that Napoleon had set off in midsummer, on June 23, 1812, with the largest army Europe had ever seen: some half a million men. Napoleon's army captured Moscow and won a battle. But disease, desertion, battle, and the Russian winter's infernal cold meant that only some twenty thousand escaped alive.

Hitler's invasion started one calendar day earlier than Napoleon's, on June 22. And Operation Barbarossa made rapid progress across a thousand-mile-wide expanse: from Leningrad in the north, to Ukraine in the south. Victory after victory. By the end of November, the Germans reached the outskirts of Moscow.

But then the thermometers fell.

German plans assumed the invasion would be accomplished by now. They'd failed to prepare for the cold.

The Italian journalist Curzio Malaparte described sitting in a café in Warsaw when troops came past, returning from the Eastern Front:

> I was struck with horror. They had no eyelids . . . Thousands and thousands of soldiers had lost their limbs; thousands and thousands had their ears, their noses, their fingers and their sexual organs ripped off by the frost. Many had lost their hair . . . Many had lost their eyelids. Singed by the cold, the eyelid drops off like a piece of dead skin.[38]

* * *

Ordinarily, the temperature in our "deep" body tissues like brain and heart is around 98.6°F (37°C). Fatal damage occurs if this core temperature rises above 107.6°F (42°C), or below 80.6°F (27°C).[39]

And yet . . . humans can run the 156-mile Marathon des Sables in the Sahara Desert at 122°F (50°C), and we can dive into water little warmer than freezing. This illustrates another crucial aspect of our brains' Models: *flexibility.*

We can achieve these feats because the hypothalamus receives inputs from peripheral and central temperature sensors, and our Model drives a number of responses.

If core temperature rises, our abundant sweat glands perspire. In excess heat we reduce activity, stretch out our body, and eat less because metabolizing food produces heat. Behaviors change, too. In higher temperatures, car drivers honk more often, especially without air-conditioning—and, more seriously, higher temperatures may relate to increased crime and violence.[40]

In mild cold, we conserve heat by constricting peripheral blood vessels and raising our body hair. If necessary, we shiver. Behavioral responses include increased activity, huddled body position, and increased appetite.

But severe cold is entirely more serious.

Hitler boasted of his own hardiness. "Even with a temperature of 10 below zero," he said in 1942, "I used to go about in lederhosen."[41] But no amount of willpower could overcome the objective reality of cold in a Russian winter. Hitler deluded himself, at a terrible price.

Only *technologies* created by our large brains give *any* human the flexibility to survive such crazily inhospitable climates. One such revolutionary human technology is . . . clothing. In August 2012, an eleven-year-old boy was exploring a frozen bluff overlooking the Arctic Ocean when he found a woolly mammoth's leg bones peeping out of frozen sediment.[42] Investigations showed that humans killed the mammoth. Its eye sockets, ribs, and jaw had been battered, apparently by spears, and one spear had dented its cheekbone. This happened 45,000 years ago, so we know humans had invented clothing so they could survive in such extreme cold at least that long ago.

Another potential technology that could be equally transformative—if we can make it work in humans—is hibernation. The hypothalamus plays a key role in hibernation, and focusing on fundamental brain regions like the hypothalamus could yield huge prizes for humanity. Hibernation could help us survive much worse than the Earth's least hospitable environment. Astronauts traveling to Mars anytime soon must survive months on a tiny spaceship with minimal food, endure microgravity where bones and muscles waste away, and suffer cosmic radiation bombardment. Hibernation reduces metabolism; torpor preserves bone structure in bears and squirrels; and hibernating squirrels resist high levels of radiation.[43]

Genetic studies suggest our common mammal ancestor may have hibernated. Studies indicate hibernation's mechanisms may aid weight loss, help diabetes, and help clear harmful protein tangles in Alzheimer's disease. Hibernators also live longer than non-hibernators of the same size, and new research in bats and marmots shows that hibernation slows aging.[44]

But not only new moon-shot technologies can enhance our flexibility. So too can better self-knowledge of how our Models work.

* * *

A sleeping human body is defenseless, and yet we render ourselves so vulnerable because without sleep we die. Sleep-deprived lab rats die within a month. Humans with the rare hereditary disease fatal familial insomnia can meet the same fate within three months. Nobody knows why we sleep, but we do know a lot about how this vital drive works.[45]

Two distinct processes make us want sleep. Together these give our Model the flexibility to cope when events—shift work, a new baby, oncoming tank divisions—conspire to disturb our sleep.

The first process is the ongoing twenty-four-hour circadian rhythm, driven by a specific group of cells in the hypothalamus called the suprachiasmatic nucleus (SCN).[46] This causes the rise and fall of bodily functions, such as urine production, temperature (just above 98.6°F [37°C] in the afternoon and just below 98.6°F after midnight), and wakefulness. At dusk, the SCN sends out melatonin to tell the rest of the body it's nighttime. Once sleep is underway, it decreases melatonin levels. And when light enters the brain through the eyes (even through closed lids), melatonin shuts off entirely, causing us to wake.

The SCN helps explain jet lag: after we fly across time zones the SCN's circadian rhythm is wrong. Sunlight readjusts the SCN, but only by about one hour a day: another example of how our evolved Models haven't kept up with technology.

The second process, sleep pressure, involves a steady accumulation of the chemical adenosine while we're awake.[47] Adenosine peaks after we're awake for twelve to sixteen hours, causing the urge for sleep to take hold. Watch online videos[48] of sleep-deprived people in sleep labs, and you can almost feel the sleep pressure weighing them down. If you get insufficient sleep, adenosine can build up over days to create a sleep "debt" that causes tiredness.

Insufficient sleep carries costs. Over the long-term that includes things like increased risks of Alzheimer's. And in the day-to-day it degrades our performance.

The hit to our performance is made worse because we lack self-knowledge about *how* sleep deficiency affects us: we consistently *under*estimate how much it degrades our cognitive performance.[49] Sleep deficiency differs from thirst and hunger, which made us feel bad but in reality often spared our cognitive performance. Sleep deficiency does degrade our problem-solving. And although a common assumption is that tiredness makes us slow, in fact it's worse than that: sleepiness makes us entirely *miss* responses when we are carrying out tasks.[50] These "micro sleeps" cause road traffic or industrial accidents—and combat catastrophes when seconds count.[51]

Sleep deprivation damages learning, because memories are often consolidated during sleep, and it damages creativity, too. While sleeping we go through 90- to 110-minute cycles that each begin with a longer period of non-rapid eye movement (NREM) sleep, followed by a period of rapid eye movement (REM) sleep in which the eyes dart around. Although both help refresh you, REM sleep also includes dreaming, during which the brain gets creative with memories to explore new combinations of ideas.

Self-knowledge about how sleep (and sleep deficiency) works can give us four important lessons about how to manage sleep more flexibly.

The first lesson: we can *choose* what type of performance to damage. Heinz Guderian's *Panzer* troops fought day after day with little sleep to win the Battle of France in May 1940. If they'd stopped for a good eight hours of sleep every night, they couldn't have won. In a more everyday example, a student might "pull an all-nighter" to finish a long essay due the following morning—but an all-nighter would be counterproductive before an exam when a good night's sleep will help you perform better. West Point cadets need both: sometimes to push through sleep deprivation *and* other times to enhance learning through better sleep. Like doing cardio and weights for all-round fitness.

Second, good sleep routines help your hypothalamus know it's nighttime. Many books list the "dos and don'ts."[52] A cool room helps, and so on. And taken together such marginal gains do help.

Third, medications help some people, sometimes, but should be used sparingly.[53] Research on sleep-deprived Navy SEAL trainees during "Hell Week" showed that 200 and 300 milligrams of caffeine (roughly two to three cups of coffee) made them shoot more accurately and get their weapon sights onto targets faster. But taking caffeine late in the day can disturb sleep. Modafinil (trade-named Provigil) can help sleep-deprived people stay awake, but overuse may shift sleep patterns in unhelpful ways: the hypothalamic circadian rhythm moves only so fast; and we can't outrun sleep deficits forever.

Fourth, digital technologies can monitor sleep patterns to provide personalized "sleep credit" or "sleep debt" information. And digital platforms can deliver cheap, convenient, effective treatments like cognitive behavioral therapy for insomnia.[54]

Better ways to manage sleep are always crucial, because operating effectively when humans are built to be asleep can provide an edge. For the hunters in a war zone—and for hunted humans attempting to avoid annihilation.

* * *

In 1941, Russian troops needed every tool to fight back. One was to use the night.[55]

The German *Blitzkrieg* repeatedly encircled Soviet forces, but time and again the Soviets broke out using surprise attacks at night. At Smolensk on the night of July 23, for example, fierce Soviet night counterattacks extricated five divisions. The chief of staff of Germany's 4th Army in front of Moscow characterized the Russians as "night-happy."

But such escapes couldn't halt the advancing Germans. By December 1 the German heavy artillery was in range of Moscow, and any further Russian retreat would surrender the capital.

Georgy Zhukov was the Russian general who had just successfully led Leningrad's defense—and now he was charged with defending Moscow. Zhukov, a brilliant battlefield commander and squat fireball of energy, was perhaps World War II's key military figure.

Zhukov launched his counterattack to defend Moscow on December 5, and night attacks were crucial. Such night attacks devastated the Germans, as described in this German account of a raid on Guderian's Second *Panzer* Group south of Moscow:

> About twenty tanks led the Siberian attack. The mere appearance by night of tanks in front of the lines of the 112th Division produced a severe shock. No means of defense were at hand. Complete panic broke out.[56]

Against the German juggernaut, would Zhukov's counterattack be enough to preserve the millions of humans fighting so desperately to save their lives?

LIFE'S SECOND DEFINING FEATURE

Life. Everything you've read so far in these two chapters has been about maintaining order within the body to sustain life. But life has a second, equally necessary, defining feature: reproduction. Life reproduces in a way that means an organism's key features can be inherited by its offspring.[57] Since the first cells appeared on Earth 3.8 billion years ago, life has reproduced in an *unbroken* chain until the present day.

To you.

For two billion years, that meant asexual reproduction, in which an organism divides to make offspring. That's still with us, in organisms such as bacteria. And in your body: every day a human can lose over one million skin cells and replace them this way.

Sex is the second way to reproduce. An organism's genome is its complete set of genetic information. Sex is when an organism tears their genome in half and combines it with half of a mate's genome, to create a new genome. Most animals, including humans, do that by having two sexes perform sexual intercourse.

What does this fifth vital drive—sexual reproduction—have to do with the brain and war?

The aim of reproducing is to successfully raise offspring who can themselves successfully reproduce. Human offspring can't survive without a lot of help, which is why families matter so much. Consider the strong bonds of maternal and paternal love that help motivate all the hard work of raising offspring. The hypothalamus releases hormones such as oxytocin to help build these parental bonds—and although in many situations oxytocin decreases aggression, when it comes to defending offspring, oxytocin can make animals such as female rodents *more* aggressive.[58] Having children changes the brains of human parents. Mothers scanned before and after giving birth show rewiring of many brain systems. Those brain changes were still present two years later, and the most strongly bonded mothers showed the greatest changes. Brain scans of first-time human fathers before and after birth also show changes, albeit smaller and more variable.[59]

Humans tend to care deeply about their families, and this drives parents, children, and siblings to act if they perceive threats or conflict involving family members. Parents often bend social systems to help their children, and throughout history some went on to murder and war. Families have fought innumerable wars to create and maintain dynasties since Earth's first civilizations emerged six thousand years ago in Sumer (roughly modern Iraq). Napoleon Bonaparte put his family on thrones across Europe. Three of the Group of Seven (G7) rich countries are still monarchies; and U.S. politics is dominated by families like the Kennedys, Gores, Cheneys, and Bushes. Kim Jong Un is the third in his dynasty to rule North Korea. In China the offspring of senior Communist Party members are known as "Princelings"—including current paramount leader Xi Jinping. Xi's father and family upbringing, as we will see, profoundly shaped Xi.

Stalin leveraged family bonds to keep soldiers in the fight against Germany. A month after Operation Barbarossa began, Stalin ordered that anyone who retreated without specific orders, or who surrendered, was a "traitor to the Motherland." And that put their family at risk of imprisonment.[60]

But before we humans can raise offspring, we must *create* them.

Humans are primates, as are other apes and monkeys. Primates' sexual relationships vary between two basic forms:[61]

- In *pair-bonding* species, like marmosets, males and females are similar in size and appearance. Males do a lot of parenting and remain pair-bonded long-term.
- In *tournament* species, like chimps, males are a lot bigger than females and look more flamboyant. Only a few males win aggressive competitions for high-dominance rank, and they impregnate a lot of females, with whom they don't stick around.

Humans are *in between*. Men are 10 percent taller and 20 percent heavier than women and have shorter lifespans and slightly longer canines. This makes the variety of human relationships more understandable: some strongly bond with a partner; and others may go around trying to have lots of sex. All such types of relationships are associated with war.

Romantic love is a deep bond of attachment, a complex, goal-oriented emotion associated with many brain regions, including reward, motivational, and cognitive systems.[62] Homer's ancient Greek epic the *Iliad* centers on a war caused when a wife is snatched from her husband by another man. Homer's *Odyssey* tells of another husband's dangerous journey back to his wife, who has remained faithful to him.

Sex is a powerful drive in itself. In humans, just thinking about sex can release dopamine. Most human males find it rewarding to see pictures of attractive females. (And not just humans: thirsty male rhesus monkeys don't ordinarily allow mere pictures to keep them from water—unless the pictures are saucy shots of female rhesus monkeys.)[63]

In war, sexual relationships are often freely given in casual encounters and as commercial transactions. In the trenches of World War I, "trench foot" came to stand for the unhealthy conditions men faced, but in reality they were five times as likely to end up in hospital with syphilis or gonorrhea.[64]

Sometimes, sex becomes the horrific sexual violence we know as rape. Rape is often opportunistic, but throughout history it has also been organized. Serbian men raped tens of thousands of Bosnian women in 1990s rape camps, a "tool of war" whose children are now thinking and feeling adults.[65] Victorious Soviet troops raped some two million German women in 1945. Stalin told a fellow Communist:

> Imagine a man who has fought from Stalingrad to Belgrade—over a thousand kilometers of his own devastated land, across the dead bodies of his comrades and dearest ones. How can such a man react normally? And what is so awful in having fun with a woman, after such horrors?[66]

Sexual violence in war also happens to men. A *Journal of the American Medical Association* study surveyed adult male fighters in the Liberian war, of whom some one-in-three had suffered sexual violence.[67] Castration is common in some conflicts.[68] In 2022 Russia was widely condemned after video footage appeared to show a Russian soldier castrating a Ukrainian prisoner.[69]

But whether against women or men, the perpetrators of sexual violence are usually men. And that is true of serious violence more broadly.

In almost all societies, serious physical violence is mostly carried out by men: male and female bodies, brains, and behaviors are not identical.

Most warriors in organized states, almost everywhere, have been men. That doesn't mean women haven't fought aggressively and skillfully in the past. The famous female warrior Boudicca led a revolt in Roman Britain. But even outside the state, a large study of twenty-one nomadic hunter-gatherer societies recently found at least 135 lethal events—and females were the killers or co-perpetrators in only 4 percent.[70]

Where differences between men and women exist, it helps to consider that (a) the average differs; *and* (b) there is significant variation within each group; so that (c) the groups can also overlap. Men are 10 percent taller on average, for example, but there are many tall women and short men.

Male and female brains are largely the same, *and* differences exist. An important cause of differences originates in the hypothalamus, which controls how testes (in men) and ovaries (in women) produce the sex hormones testosterone and estrogen. From moment to moment, and over a lifetime, these hormones affect humans from head to toe.

My own research has examined testosterone, which affects behaviors in men and women. Learning is one area that I tested with colleagues at Queen Square, in London. Giving women a short boost of testosterone, compared to placebo, improved how fast they learned to identify certain difficult visual stimuli.[71] We further examined social interactions in another study. We gave pairs of women a boost of testosterone during a task that required them to collaborate.[72] Testosterone damaged collaboration because it made people use their partner's opinion less: testosterone made them more egocentric.

In males, testosterone affects competition for status. Levels rise among various primates when their dominance hierarchies are forming or changing; and among humans competing for status, testosterone often increases aggression.[73]

Testosterone changes men lifelong, too, starting when a fetus's gonads start secreting hormones at around eight weeks to help masculinize its brain. Average human male and female brains differ in specific regions—by about 1 to 3 percent once correcting for differing overall brain size—such as the amygdala that processes emotions like fear.[74]

Nurture also matters, as shown across the twentieth century. Women's social status changed, and this combined with the demand for ever more workers to fight "total war," so that women increasingly undertook wartime roles more similar to those of men.

Germany expanded female workforce participation in World War I, which meant it entered World War II with high levels of women in work. Even so, until 1943 when the war began turning against Germany, Hitler remained reluctant to use women in many war industries. "No, the women must be preserved," Hitler's chief bureaucrat recalled Hitler saying. "They have other tasks. They are for the family."[75]

Britain began conscripting women in December 1941. Women served in Britain's Special Operations Executive (SOE) that fostered resistance overseas. SOE's F section sent more than four hundred agents into France, of whom thirty-nine were women.[76]

Russia went furthest in using its women's strength. They dug defenses around Leningrad. As the Germans advanced on Moscow, 250,000 mostly female civilians built new defense lines, under attack from German aircraft. During the war, some 27,000 Soviet women fought the Germans as guerrillas.[77]

The Red Army called up 1 million to 1.5 million women,[78] some in all-female combat units. The most famous was the 588th Night Bomber Regiment. All members were women, from pilots to commanders and mechanics. The *whooshing* sound of their silenced planes led German soldiers to call them the "Night Witches." Thirty pilots died fighting, and twenty-three received the Hero of the Soviet Union medal. Nadezhda Popova, who flew 852 missions, remembered her comrades as "clever, educated, very talented girls."[79]

Families, love, sex, men, and women all arise from the vital drive for sexual reproduction, which has always been a reality for the continuation of human life that's as hard as diamond. For which humans fight, kill, and die—as they do for hunger and thirst. If it weren't, there would be no unbroken chain of reproduction stretching back from you through uncountable past generations. How these realities manifest in a given time and place is wonderfully flexible across human societies, as we see in the changing roles of families, men, and women in war. Self-knowledge about humanity recognizes both the realities and the flexibility. The Night Witches, for example, were daughters who dropped real bombs—and their great-grandchildren remain alive to this day.

LOW ROADS

In this chapter we've seen that the almond-sized hypothalamus, atop the brainstem, governs five distinct vital drives: thirst, hunger, warmth, sleep, and sexual reproduction. All are distinct, specialized systems—but all are also *integrated* so that the vital drives connect intimately. Body temperature rises and falls with circadian rhythms, and with a woman's ovarian cycle. Starvation can override sleep. Closer to the battlefield, sex often loses importance as people get more busy, frightened, or tired.

After World War II a new term was applied to our overall, generalized response to such demands: *stress*.

The hypothalamus is central to our stress response. It controls release of the stress hormone cortisol that gives us a short-term surge to overcome a crisis, and postpones longer-term projects like building strong bones. Until the crisis ends, cortisol mobilizes energy stores, heart rate, blood pressure, and glucose. And cortisol keeps the brain focused and alert.

Stress can be lifesaving, but overwhelming stress causes problems. Surprise and lack of control—essentially increased prediction error—increases stress. Norwegian soldiers studied through parachute training, for example, showed dramatic stress responses within minutes of their first jump, but in later training jumps that stress changed to thrill.[80] That's why training is crucial to avoid the kind of collapse that occurred among French soldiers around Sedan in May 1940, to help people cope with the unexpected. And coping better with extreme stress also matters because extreme or extended periods of stress can contribute to problems like post-traumatic stress disorder (PTSD). Everyone needs time to recover. In war, even veterans can crack.

And even someone born some 5,300 years ago, in prehistoric times, shows the physiological response to stress.[81]

Ötzi was wiry, short (5 feet 2 inches or 158 centimeters), left-handed, and about forty-six years old when he died. We know that, and more, because he was found perfectly preserved in the icy mountains of Italy's South Tyrol. Ötzi probably had brown eyes and dark brown hair. He wore clothes of fur and hides, and he carried weapons including a flint dagger, bow, unfinished arrows, and a copper axe. His sixty-one tattoos map onto the places where his bones and joints show wear and tear. During his lifetime he'd fractured several ribs and broken his nose.

We know that Ötzi lived with stress because he had fingernail markings called Beau's lines, which I learned about at medical school. These suggest he endured three periods of intense stress during the last months of his life, occurring two, three, and four months before he died. The final episode was the most serious, and lasted at least two weeks.

But something else actually *killed* Ötzi.

On Ötzi's right hand, a gash between the thumb and first finger reveal that he was stabbed a few days before he died. It was an active defensive wound, meaning Ötzi likely tried to grab the blade. The wound was still healing when he was attacked again. This time, an arrow struck him in the back and tore an artery in his left shoulder. Stress weakened him, but what *killed* him was combat.

* * *

Specters loom out of darkness. A flash of metal or claw. Sometimes we have only fractions of a second to respond. How do we react so fast?

On top of the hypothalamus is the 2-inch-long egg-shaped thalamus. The thalamus is a gateway that relays every type of sensation from the eye, ear, skin, and so on (except some smells) before they go up to the cortex. *But* it can take 300 milliseconds to send sensory data up via this "high road" to the cortex for more meticulous analysis[82]—perhaps a deadly delay to identify the gist of a threat, process it, and respond.

That's why the thalamus *also* identifies threats from rapid, early analysis of sensory information, and urgently sends this via a "low road" directly to lifesaving systems that initiate responses like fear or fight.

But what are those lifesaving systems?

3

STAND AND FIGHT?

ACTIVITIES OF AMYGDALA AND INSULA

Not all warriors begin as professionals. Many are swept up from everyday life by war's turmoil. On December 6, 1941, one among the millions in combat with Nazi Germany had been, until war broke out, a businessman. Twenty-two when the war started, he had grown up comfortably enough in North London. He soon became a lieutenant in the Royal Tank Regiment.

He commanded tanks through many years of bitter fighting in North Africa and then Italy. During a battle for two rivers, he commanded flame-throwing tanks called "Crocodiles," and he was awarded the Military Cross. As the recommendation for that high award for bravery described:

> In every action in which his [unit] was employed this Officer carried out reconnaissances on foot often under heavy fire and in dangerously mined areas in order to determine the best positions for flaming. His courage and disregard for his personal safety and his devotion to duty were at all times an inspiration to his [unit] and greatly contributed to the success of the actions in which they were employed.

This man was, as it happens, my great-uncle Sydney.[1]

His sister, my grandmother, was very fond of her brother. Years after the war she was at a dinner in Croydon, South London. It turned out that another guest that evening had fought alongside Sydney for years. He said that her brother had been a brave man.

But although I told you my great-uncle Sydney's story, I *could* have told such a story about one of the many other brave men and women among the millions of humans that war swept up across the globe.

That includes in China, where war drew hundreds of millions of people, as soldiers or civilians, into the epic tale of *China's* World War II—a tale we hear in this chapter. Although the story is barely known in the west, it's impossible to understand modern China without knowing it. And we must remember that these Chinese people, too, were great-uncles, fathers, mothers, daughters, sons, and brothers.

For each of them, as for Sydney, a question arises: How many times can a living human run the risks of combat, bravely, for years, without death or serious injury?

I don't pretend to know what happened in Sydney's head, when he did the things for which he was commended. It is very likely he felt fear. But when asked to move forward, he did attack. He risked his life, fulfilling the unlimited liability clause that makes a soldier's life different from a nine-to-five job. It's worth noting that his willingness to risk death differed from only a willingness to kill, in the way that separates the soldier from the mercenary. And he would not have survived so many years if he were reckless: he took only the risks he felt he must take. Among Sydney's officer training class, almost no one survived death or serious injury. Yet with his comrades in arms, he fought on.

Why do humans fight on, instead of running away?

Fear is so powerful because almost no human wants to die: self-preservation is a basic feature of all life on Earth. In humans, the amygdala—an almond-shaped area just next to the thalamus—is the heart of the brain systems that manage *fear.* But simply running away is often not the best way to succeed or even survive. And so humans, along with all mammals (and even fish and birds), also evaluate and manage *risks.*

Risk processing involves the *insula*, a long area that lies inside the brain next to the amygdala. The insula also helps explain another reason soldiers remain in the fight: the powerful social bonds with members of their unit, bonds that they don't want to break and so let down their comrades. To be sure, ideology, culture, and higher motivations can be further influences to stand and fight—as we see later—but they just add to this basic mix.

That's why surviving combat, and fighting bravely, often rests on the Models that give us the *visceral instincts* that seem to well up from somewhere deep inside—to help us face uncertain, dangerous environments. Not too neat and precise, they're often good enough. And, of course, these visceral instincts guide much of our everyday lives, too.

This chapter is about how three sets of visceral instincts—emotions, risks, and social motivations—help us feel our way through the chaos of danger. So we can respond, despite uncertainty, at great speed. That is, without time, perhaps, for our higher cognitive abilities to think things through, or when no matter how much time we have, uncertainty is irreducible.

Let's look at a first visceral instinct that helps us survive and thrive: fear.

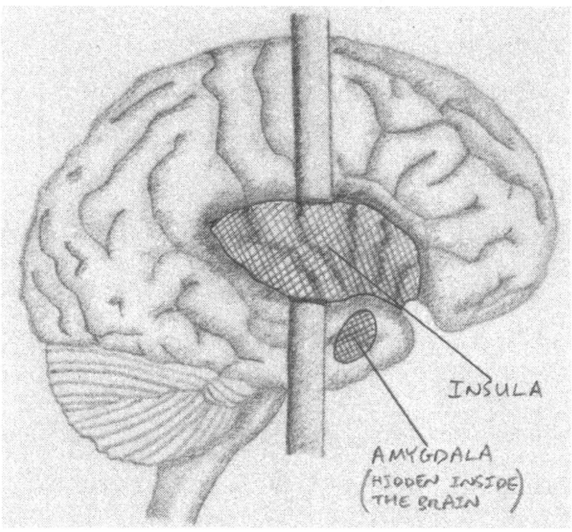

FIGURE 4: The amygdala is an almond-shaped structure buried deep in the brain just to the side of the thalamus. The insula is a long brain region, which is shown here with the parts of cortex that normally cover it pulled back by surgical instruments. There is one amygdala and one insula on each side of the brain.

FEAR

Fear is useful. I once spent a few days with two middle-aged German ladies, identical twins, who came to my brain imaging lab in London for tests. Standard tests of intelligence and perception were unremarkable, as were those for emotions like anger or happiness. Yet the twins did not feel—and could not detect—the emotion of fear. Their families said this got them into tricky situations. But they were luckier than another woman, known as "SM," studied by a colleague of mine. SM had the same condition as the twins, Urbach-Wiethe syndrome, but she lived in a more dangerous place.

SM came from a rough part of Los Angeles. She had been held at gun- and knifepoint, and almost killed in a domestic violence attack. In many situations SM's life was in danger—corroborated by police reports—yet her behavior lacked any sense of desperation or urgency. She struggled to detect looming threats in her environment, or to learn how to avoid dangerous situations. You might think SM's lack of fear would make her a violent criminal, but it's the opposite. She has never been convicted of any crime. Instead, she is often a victim.[2]

The two Germans who came to my lab for testing and SM all had one thing in common. They had all lost their amygdalas, the brain structures next to the thalamus that are crucial for fear.

Fear is often associated with a present and identifiable threat, but it also relates to broader anxieties about threats even years into the future. The amygdala achieves this remarkable range by drawing on multiple distinct networks across the brain.[3] If you only have *milliseconds* to react, then inbuilt defensive reflexes could save you from injury or death. You've likely experienced examples like the startle reflex, or reflexively withdrawing your bare foot if it steps on a nail. Given *seconds* to react, inbuilt defensive responses can include facial expressions and vocalizations (like a look and scream of terror)—or your whole body can freeze, flee, or fight defensively. You can also use responses learned through experience and training, like a soldier in trenches ducking after a loud noise. Longer term, you can anticipate and strategize about threats that are *days, months, or years* ahead—and that can draw in your most sophisticated human cognitive machinery for forward planning. You can ruminate on complex, abstract worries such as climate change, or your security slowly eroding months or years in the future.

This range of fear responses helps us survive the range of threats in war—and of course fear is common in war and combat. Interviews among U.S. combat divisions in World War II found that only 7 percent said they never felt afraid. Three-quarters reported trembling hands, 85 percent were troubled by sweating palms, and 89 percent tossed sleeplessly at night.[4] In societies threatened by looming warfare, people at every level—from the public to national leaders—are shaped by fears and anxieties that feel pressingly concrete. Fears of invasion, occupation, or even annihilation often *have* been valid, and can keep us focused on preparing for potential dangers years ahead of time.

But fears also cause problems. Anxiety disorders—essentially fear run amok—are curiously common in today's largely peaceful western societies. In 2021, some 6 to 8 percent of people in countries like France, Germany, and the United States had an anxiety disorder in the past year alone. These rates didn't radically alter over the previous thirty years and may be higher than in poorer countries that suffered conflict.[5] The problem arises because our survival-grade fear machinery is built for life-threatening environments where missing threats is costly, so it would rather issue a few false alarms than miss too many real threats.

Even when fear is reasonable—like when civil war looms—fear can still cause problems by spiraling out of control. In what's known as a "security dilemma," people fear for their own security and so take actions to enhance it; but these actions lead other people to fear more for their own security and so they, too, take defensive actions; and on it spirals. In combat, excessive fear can turn into panic that becomes contagious, spreading in combat units to turn an army into a mere crowd—as seen among some French units in May 1940. Excessive or prolonged fear can also lead to PTSD, which is a type of anxiety disorder. PTSD affects ex-service personnel overall at rates of about 8 percent over their lifetime, which is comparable to, or slightly above, rates for civilian populations—but specific deployments involving greater combat exposure, fear of death, and seeing others die can lead to lifetime rates perhaps as high as one in three.[6]

So what factors *aggravate* these problems from fear?

Greater unpredictability, surprising threats, and lack of control—that is, prediction errors—worsen fear, which is why training and experience are crucial.[7] Sustained stress from other factors can worsen fear and fear contributes to stress[8]—a nasty feedback loop, which makes time to recuperate crucial. Modern treatments can use talking therapies and medicines to help us actively *un*learn fears and so shorten illnesses like PTSD, whereas a lack of access can worsen outcomes.[9] Loneliness or isolation can aggravate problems from fear, because comrades often provide crucial support.[10]

A final aggravating factor is that fears can provoke a defensive attack when we feel cornered.[11] Russian President Vladimir Putin is an unpleasant former agent of the KGB—the Soviet security services—who's shown he understands fear and how to manipulate others' fears. Including when they're cornered. He often tells a story of growing up in a dilapidated Leningrad apartment building, where he used to chase rats with sticks.

> "Once I spotted a huge rat and pursued it down the hall until I drove it into a corner," he recounted. "It had nowhere to run. Suddenly it lashed around and threw itself at me. I was surprised and frightened. Now the rat was chasing me."[12]

* * *

Valid fears were aggravated by a cauldron of factors among China's leaders, troops, and people after the last Chinese imperial dynasty collapsed in 1911. Millions found themselves cornered, in unpredictably shifting, dangerous environments, with sustained stress and fracturing social networks.[13] The Qing dynasty's collapse engulfed China in decades of civil wars, which blended into China's epic Second World War tale—and the legacy of those civil wars is central to world politics today.

1911 wasn't the first time a Chinese dynasty collapsed into civil war.

For much of the time since China's first unification, in 221 BCE, it has been a state with taxes, administrators, and boundaries. But dynasties waxed and waned. Battlefield success established most new imperial dynasties. Then, as dynasties declined, peasant rebellions occurred, and power struggles emerged between regional warlords.

China's final imperial dynasty, the Qing, was established by a successfully invading steppe nomad people in 1644. The Qing saw success and stability. But internal unrest erupted from the mid-nineteenth century, including the vast Taiping Rebellion (1850 to 1864) that left twenty-five million dead.[14] External threats loomed from western countries and a rapidly modernizing Japan.

After the Qing collapsed in 1911, the new Republic quickly descended into a kaleidoscope of clashing forces. The kaleidoscope's pieces constantly and unpredictably shifted their positions and allegiances. Competing warlords often ruled like kings in areas the size of large European states, and by 1924 about 1.5 million men served in warlord armies.[15] The kaleidoscope also included external players like the European powers and America.

Three pieces of the kaleidoscope became the major protagonists in these civil wars and in China's Second World War: the Nationalists under Chiang Kai-shek; the Communists under Mao Zedong; and the Japanese.

Chiang Kai-shek, the Nationalist leader, was wiry, with a neat military mustache and bald head.[16] Chiang was politically adept and leveraged his position as commandant of the Whampoa Military Academy—China's "West Point"—to reorganize the army under his command and successfully defeat many warlord forces. In 1927 Chiang established a new national government and attacked the Communists.

Mao Zedong, the communist leader, was born in 1893 to a farming family in central China, a few years after Chiang. Mao was a large man, with relentless energy and ruthless self-confidence. He saw at close hand the revolution to overthrow the Qing and served briefly as a private in the local republican army. There he came across socialist pamphlets and embarked on self-directed study.[17] In July 1921 Mao was one of the small group that founded the Chinese Communist Party (CCP). By the end of 1931 their Red Army totaled 150,000 men[18]—and we must remember: each one a real person, an individual who had perhaps been swept up by war like my great-uncle Sydney.

But Chiang Kai-shek's attacks forced the Communists onto the Long March of 1934 to 1935, a ravaging retreat of 6,000 miles that reduced the Red Army to some thirty thousand troops.[19] Even so, Mao's personal fortunes rose. Mao became the CCP leader and rebuilt his forces, in the northern mountain fastness that remained Mao's powerbase throughout World War II.

The epic rivalry of Chiang and Mao reverberates to this day: Chiang died in 1975 as the president in Taiwan; and Mao died in 1976 as China's leader in Beijing.

And what of Japan? It got less than it hoped out of World War I, after which Japan's increasingly militaristic leadership aimed to expand its empire. China was an obvious target.

On September 18, 1931, Japanese soldiers in northeast China blew up a short section of a Japanese-owned railway. Japan's military used this as a pretext to storm the Chinese garrison in the port of Mukden and expand its empire. Japanese troops fanned out and by early 1932 occupied the whole of Manchuria: conquering hundreds of thousands of square miles.[20] Between 1933 and 1935 they seized more land as far south as the Great Wall, and set up a Mongolian puppet state.

To confront the Japanese threat, the rivals Chiang and Mao were forced together. Stalin instructed Mao to work with the Nationalists, while two of Chiang's own generals kidnapped Chiang so that he would do the same.

This backdrop, however, did not *have* to mean war between China and Japan: indeed spring 1937 was a period of calm.[21] A new Japanese prime minister in early 1937 claimed, "I have no faith in a pugnacious foreign policy." Japanese field officers were instructed to avoid further incident.

But in this unpredictable, stressful environment of relentless turmoil—in which leaders, armies, and civilians alike risked being encircled, cornered, and killed—many now feared events might worsen further. And when events are finely balanced, emotions can tip that balance.

EMOTIONS GUIDE US

Anger, fear, sadness, disgust, happiness, and surprise—that's a useful palette of emotions.[22] Emotions help us survive because, despite limited information, we often need Models that help us make broad and sometimes rapid responses. That link senses to actions. Happiness, for example, isn't always a neat, tidy, beautifully calibrated guide, but if we sense an event such as seeing something good happen to someone we like (or something bad happen to someone we dislike), then happiness can *usefully* guide our actions.

Emotions can be life-savingly useful in situations like combat, to guide a broad bunch of brain processes. Consider three.

Emotion guides what we perceive and what we pay attention to. Quite literally, we perceive the world differently when we feel angry, fearful, or sad. Angry people are biased to detect threats: so they are more likely to misidentify neutral objects as guns, and therefore incorrectly identify unarmed people as armed.[23] Fear creates similar effects.[24] Anger biases perception by shaping what people predict they will see in such situations, so that angry participants expect to encounter more armed suspects. Chapter 5 looks more closely at perception, but the short version is that we use Models to cope with the vast amount of incoming data—and emotions guide what our Models expect to perceive.

Emotion guides what we learn, remember, and forget.[25] When we look back on our lives, we remember emotional events like getting into a college, a first kiss, or being told about a death. Emotion guides us to remember some things more vividly. In "flashbulb" memories, for instance, we remember where we were when a public event became known, like the terrorist attacks on September 11, 2001. (I was sitting with other medical students in a seminar room in North London.)

The amygdala plays a role here. Emotion enhances how well rats learn mazes, and removing their amygdala removes this emotional boost to learning. Humans tend to remember arousing events for longer than they remember non-arousing events—and human patients with amygdala damage lose that ability.

Emotions guide our decision-making. My own work with collaborators at Peking University in China (where Mao Zedong once worked) explored one major way this happens. We looked at how our emotions affect our decisions, even when they're completely *unrelated* to those decisions. We used videos to induce disgust in participants—and showed that this made participants more likely to approach nicer things and avoid nastier things while making risky decisions for money in the lab.[26] One idea for why emotions have these effects on decisions is that they provide a common currency between disparate types of inputs and options[27]—a role that helps explain, for example, why low morale, even from seemingly irrelevant grumbles, can corrode teams and organizations.

Emotions guide us in more ways than we have space for here. But the point is that when we must act in high-stakes situations, with only patchy and uncertain information, emotions guide us.

* * *

In early summer 1937, after what seemed a calm spring, Chinese troops went to strengthen shoreline defenses on the river near a bridge called Lugouqiao, ten miles southwest of Beijing.[28] The granite bridge was decorated with the carved heads of nearly five hundred stone lions. It had been admired by the traveler who spawned its western name: the Marco Polo Bridge.

Beside it, a strategically important railway bridge had been built, and—as international agreement allowed—Japanese troops often exercised nearby.[29]

On July 7, 1937, the Japanese made the bridge the base of a night maneuver. The Japanese troops were authorized to simulate combat by firing blank cartridges into the air. Some Chinese troops happened to be there, and it's unclear what they thought was happening. But at 22:30 the Chinese troops fired shells into the Japanese position, which caused no casualties.

It could have ended there, as an uncertain and confused set of misunderstandings. But when, at roll call, one Japanese soldier was missing, what had happened to him was uncertain. The local Japanese commander thought he had been captured by the Chinese and demanded entry to the village to search for his missing soldier. Chinese troops refused, and the Japanese commander ordered an attack.

This attack can be considered World War II's first clash.

As it happens, the missing Japanese soldier had only been lost and eventually made his own way back. But it didn't matter. The following day Chinese troops attacked the Japanese position. Over the next few days, local, regional, and national leaders on both sides made uncoordinated statements.

"Who started the fighting is still not clear," the *North-China Daily News* wrote on July 10, "but it is considered probable that the Chinese, guarding the railway bridge-head, seeing an armed party advancing along the embankment in the dark, challenged them and on receiving no reply opened fire, thinking them to be plain-clothes men or Japanese staging a real attack."[30]

Information was patchy and uncertain for everyone. Would this event die down as others had before? Or escalate?

Chinese Nationalist leader Chiang Kai-shek heard about the incident while he was meeting with his military council. He was uncertain how to respond.

But Chiang came under mounting pressure from emotional outrage among the Chinese public. Compromise would likely mean losing the former capital, Beijing—a place, as one historian writes, "of immense cultural and emotional significance to many Chinese."[31] In the end Chiang compromised no further.

On July 26 the Japanese struck, and Beijing fell.

On August 7, the Chinese government held a confidential Joint National Defense Meeting in China's then capital, Nanjing. Now Chiang had decided—and he used emotion to sway others. He criticized those counseling further appeasement and argued that "the invaders will lose. The Japanese can only see materiel and troops; they don't see the spiritual aspect."[32]

Chiang challenged the meeting: "So, comrades, we need a decision. Do we fight, or shall we be destroyed?"

Those who favored war were asked to stand. All stood.

CONTROLLED EMOTIONS

Sometimes we act on emotions. Other times—strange though it may seem—we act in spite of them. How many Chinese and Japanese mothers smiled at their beloved sons departing for war? Controlling their sadness, to give their boys a happy memory. How many soldiers acted the same for their families? Those soldiers also had to control their emotions on the front line, for their own and their comrades' safety. It's fashionable now to deride the "stiff upper lip." But at times we must all control emotions.

As a neurology doctor in Oxford, I used to cover pediatric neurosurgery wards overnight. Emotionally, I found it hard to smile and look cheerful while putting intravenous drips in small children, their eyes streaming with tears. Children often cannot control their emotions; adults often must.

Ideas about how we control emotions have been around for millennia. Many ideas suggest that decisions arise from multiple competing systems.[33] Plato suggested a charioteer driving a pair of horses, one noble and one beastly. Freud came up with the conscious and unconscious, or ego, superego, and id. Cognitive psychology from the 1970s and '80s developed dual-system models, such as "fast and slow"[34] or deliberative versus automatic.

An analogy that fits better with current neuroscience is that of a concert orchestra. The orchestra's sections—strings, percussion, and so on—work together. The output of any one section alone would not give a Beethoven symphony.

In the brain, more "bottom-up" systems use Models that give the orchestra abilities such as reacting to pain, the vital drives like hunger, and visceral instincts like the emotions of anger or fear (as we've seen so far in the book). In addition, more cognitive, "top-down" systems arise from higher brain areas like the prefrontal cortex, which use Models that give the orchestra abilities like control and the reflection that thinks about our own thinking (as we'll see later in the book). Humans need the Models from both "bottom-up" processes *and* "top-down" processes—and these work together to give us the overarching Model that is the symphony in which we live our conscious life.

The decisions that emerge from this orchestra of Models working together are remarkable: far beyond any current artificial intelligence. In this book we return to this analogy of the orchestra many times. For now, the key point is that emotions guide us *but are not the only inputs to our decisions.* So, how do more "top-down" systems help us better balance the orchestra, to make the most of our emotions?

As a neuroscientist, I think of three strategies to regulate emotions that all have a place:[35] suppression, cognitive reappraisal, and building reserves.

Suppression, such as smiling when upset, aims to inhibit behaviors that express emotion. Suppressing negative emotions, distress, and pain *is* extremely adaptive in stressful environments like combat, because it can increase effectiveness and even survival.[36] And suppressing negative thoughts can be good for our mental health in everyday life, too.[37] If, as a doctor, I have learned not to burst into tears when faced with a heartrending clinical case, I suspect most people prefer it that way.

Because suppression can work short-term, it's endemic to military culture. The downside is that emotional suppression can prevent individuals from seeking help before problems threaten a unit's safety, or those suppressed emotions can manifest in harmful outlets like excess alcohol or drug use. Long-term suppression also requires significant mental exertion, which can affect memory,[38] and even worsen negative emotions like fear or anger. That is: yes, suppress, but sparingly.

Cognitive reappraisal aims to actively reinterpret emotional stimuli to change their impact. In a job interview, for instance, you might reassure yourself that the interviewer may have been coached not to give applicants positive feedback. Studies show this reappraisal can be more effective than suppression in some aspects of everyday life.[39] Militaries often employ related strategies informally, using humor to reappraise situations.

But cognitive reappraisal, too, has drawbacks. Military personnel need realistic Models of the world, and reappraising a situation so it feels nicer for oneself (rather than reappraising to enhance accuracy) could undermine situational awareness. More broadly, is it good to reappraise every hard challenge? Should university students who fail hard courses, for example, simply reappraise failure to decide that hard courses aren't valuable? If at first you don't succeed, reappraise? Additionally, reappraisal draws cognitive resources away from other tasks like getting the mission done. A U.S. military experiment tested cognitive reappraisal and found it didn't work well, suggesting it's just one tool.[40]

In a third set of strategies, we can build reserves. Thinking hard is itself effortful, as we'll see in chapter 9. Giving soldiers leave, support, a good culture, reduced stress, better sleep, and so on all build resilience. For active recovery after periods of high emotional strain, something like mindfulness might help. No single part of building resilience like this is decisive, but together the marginal gains could be significant.[41]

Finally, we must remember that emotional control can be put to good or bad ends.

To me, those Battle of Britain RAF pilots who overcame their fear (and some couldn't) put that emotional control to good ends. But what about this:

> **Most of you will know what it is like when a hundred corpses lie together; when there are five hundred, or when there are a thousand. And to have seen this through, and—apart from exceptional cases of human weakness—to have remained decent, has made us hard and is a page of glory never mentioned and never to be mentioned.**[42]

The speaker was Heinrich Himmler in 1943, talking to SS officers about the emotionally taxing job of exterminating Europe's Jews. The SS controlled their emotions all too effectively but—unlike the RAF pilots—for a bad end.

* * *

The Battle of Shanghai would be the largest engagement of this Sino-Japanese War. Manifestly brave Chinese troops *controlled* their emotions to stand and fight.

On August 14, 1937, to deflect the Japanese from northern China, Chiang Kai-shek's troops attacked Japanese ships in Shanghai. Japan sent fifteen new divisions to China, and both sides fought ferociously from trenches dug in Shanghai's streets. The destruction wore on into October, with heavy bombing and reports of "severe hand-to-hand fighting in the maze of streets."[43]

In late October the Japanese launched a fortnight of formidable attacks, and finally broke Chinese defensive lines. Chinese discipline and morale had held up well, absorbing staggering casualties, but finally collapsed. The battle killed or wounded some 250,000 of Chiang's finest forces, almost 60 percent. Most divisions lost more than half their strength, including 10,000 officers.[44]

The Japanese rolled on toward China's capital, Nanjing, where they would infamously show what it means to *lose* control.

Following the Japanese entry to Nanjing on December 13, 1937, there were mass rapes and killings of Chinese civilians. Precise estimates range from tens of thousands to three hundred thousand casualties.[45]

Why did the Nanjing Massacre happen?

It was not cold calculation. Instead, as historian of the conflict Rana Mitter suggests, Japanese troops acted as they did because they were "deeply angry."[46] They had faced little opposition since 1931 and expected a fast victory in Shanghai. The big prediction error from that fierce battle enraged troops already whipped up by propaganda and hardened by brutal training. Japanese commanders failed to provide adequate food and rest,[47] depleting soldiers' cognitive reserves to keep under control. And often it was resentful conscripts, rather than Japan's finest troops, who lost control.

It is self-knowledge about ourselves as humans that we must sometimes control the visceral instincts in our brain's orchestra. *And* that we need those visceral instincts to survive.

RISKS AND COMRADES

The visceral instincts help us respond effectively to situations at survival speed—and they must include guidance from more than just our emotions. It is often just as important to quickly grasp our environment's risks.

Animals are highly sensitive to risk: sometimes averse, at other times seeming to be thrill seekers. We see this from fish, to birds, to bumblebees.[48] And in primates. A male gorilla who listens to a rival silverback's chest thumps must consider the *risks* of challenging or retreating. These visceral instincts for risk can save lives.

The Prussian scholar of war Carl von Clausewitz described the realities of risk assessment on the battlefield in a famous passage. Clausewitz described "the brigadier, a soldier of acknowledged bravery, but he is careful to take cover behind a rise, a house or a clump of trees."[49] (Or to quote Robert De Niro's character in the 1998 film *Ronin*, when asked if he's worried about saving his own skin: "Yeah, I am. It covers my body.") In other words, caution is compatible with courage.

To identify and manage risk involves a network of regions across the human brain. A key area is the insula, that elongated region tucked deep within the brain, a little to the side of the amygdala, with which it's heavily connected. Among other things, the insula processes risk. Researchers have combined neuroscience, psychology, ecology, and economics to identify distinctive aspects of risk processed in the brain.

You can explore them yourself.

First question: Would you rather choose either $5 for certain, or a risky option in which you could get either $10 or $0 on the toss of a coin? Both options have the same outcome on average, so your choice depends on your preference for risk. Mostly, people are risk averse when considering gains: that is, they choose gaining $5 for certain.

Okay, now consider a second choice: Either you *lose* $5 for certain; or you choose a risky option in which you could *lose* either $10 or $0 on the toss of a coin? Most people tend to be risk seeking for losses, which means they choose the risky option of losing $10 or $0 on a coin toss. Psychologist Daniel Kahneman made the difference between losses and gains famous, and more recent work—including my own brain imaging studies—shows its basis in brain systems for fear, threat, and punishment.[50]

In a third choice, would you rather have either (a) a risky option ($10 or $0 on the toss of a coin); or (b) an option with *ambiguity* in which you could win $10 or $0 but you don't know how likely each outcome is (this time it's not a known coin toss)? Ambiguity gives an extra layer of uncertainty, so that actions or events are open to multiple interpretations before we even consider their risk. People tend to dislike ambiguity. This can be used to advantage in conflict. In 2014, Russia's invasion of Ukraine wasn't clear-cut, as it was later in 2022, but used "little green men"—soldiers who had no military insignia—so that, for populations observing in western countries, the Russian offensive action was more ambiguous.

There are other kinds of risk, too: high-impact-but-unlikely risks (your house burning down, or winning the lottery) differ from average risks (for example, stock market returns are on average more risky than bonds). And as my research has shown, we can distinguish the neural processing in each case.[51]

What's incredible is how quickly we get the gists of all these types of risks and make decisions—and how consistently an individual chooses when they face many such choices over time.

Moreover, the general tendencies described earlier are broadly consistent across many cultures. I've seen this conducting my own science experiments on risk-taking in western countries, China, and Iran.[52] And in a project for the Pentagon where I reviewed many experiments testing risk-taking across cultures.[53]

That said, while most people tend to have pretty typical preferences, there is still important variation *between* people: we humans vary in how much each aspect of risk affects us. Significant minorities even show opposite likes or dislikes to most of the population. Finding appropriate roles for people with usual and unusual preferences—in war and everyday life—could bring great advantages. In the wrong roles they could be deadly: either catastrophically cautious or ruinously reckless. Either way, getting gambles wrong has big consequences.

* * *

The year 1938 would become the most deadly one—for both sides—in this Sino-Japanese War.[54] Japanese victories had given them Beijing to the north and Shanghai to the east. Now Japanese leaders took a risk: they sought to force Chinese collapse or surrender. To do so, they launched a huge pincer movement to capture the Chinese heartland's great commercial capital: Wuhan.

Wuhan lies some 300 miles west of Shanghai along the Yangtze River. By March 1938 the Japanese neared victory in an area imperative for capturing Wuhan.[55]

To stop the Japanese, the local Chinese general also took a calculated risk, confronting the Japanese at the city of Taierzhuang with its traditional stone walls. He gambled that the cramped conditions would nullify the Japanese technological edge. Both sides sent in forces, and for a week from April 1, 1938, the battle blazed.

Frontline troops in the Battle of Taierzhuang managed thousands of risks, like von Clausewitz's brave brigadier described earlier, who used cover where he could. As a Chinese officer recalled of fighting in the streets and houses:

> Neither side was willing to budge. Sometimes we'd capture a house, and dig a hole in the wall to approach the enemy. Sometimes the

> enemy would be digging a hole in the same wall at the same time. Sometimes we faced each other with hand grenades—or we might even bite each other.[56]

The Japanese broke and fled, leaving some eight thousand dead. Across unoccupied China, people rejoiced. Unlike Shanghai, the Battle of Taierzhuang was no valiant defeat. This Chinese gamble paid off with a decisive Chinese victory. But happiness was short-lived: the Japanese rebalanced and moved westward again toward Wuhan.

To slow them, Chiang Kai-shek faced a terrible choice. Option A: break the massive dikes along the Yellow River to release floodwater in the path of the Japanese heading to Wuhan, slowing the Japanese but potentially killing hundreds of thousands—maybe millions—of civilians. Option B: if he did not break the dikes, the Nationalist government in Wuhan might not have enough time to relocate farther west and would be even more likely to surrender.

Chiang chose. On the morning of June 9 the dikes were breached. The Japanese advance was slowed. Some five hundred thousand people died, and three million to five million became refugees.[57] The Nationalists blamed Japanese bombing, but western observers knew the truth.

After ten months of Chinese fighting for Wuhan—including the victory at Taierzhuang—on October 24, 1938, Chiang flew out of the city. The next day, Wuhan fell.

Mutual exhaustion brought a new, slower, and lower stage for the big players in China's kaleidoscope:[58] a stage in the war dominated by *attrition*. Soldiers don't find attritional warfare as glamorous as the maneuvers described earlier, but it can be just as effective. It aims to efficiently manage your own risks, while grinding the other side down by increasing their risks. Like the World War I trenches, or the guerrilla war the United States would face in Vietnam, or much of the Ukraine war following Russia's 2022 invasion.

And what of the great Japanese risk taken, that they could force Chinese collapse or surrender? As 1938 ended, the Japanese had lost that great gamble. They hadn't gained vast natural resources for Japanese industries—instead the Nationalists refused to capitulate, which meant a long war that sucked in hundreds of thousands of Japanese combat troops.

Chiang Kai-shek's Nationalists set up a new capital, even farther west, in Chongqing. And what of the third big piece in China's kaleidoscope: Mao's Communists?

* * *

A few years before World War II, the Communists had suffered a shattering *material* defeat in China's civil wars. In 1934, Chiang Kai-shek's Nationalists had encircled the communist bases in southeast China and then chased them more than 6,000 miles on what became the fabled "Long March." In a year of marching and fighting, the Communists lost nine-tenths of the army that had set out. But the Long March had been a victory of human will. As Mao Zedong wrote in December 1935: "It has proclaimed to the world that the Red Army is an army of heroes."[59]

By the time Wuhan fell in October 1938, the Communists had rebuilt their strength. Not least because—among their own troops and among local populations—they skillfully harnessed powerful social motivations like the rejection of unfairness and injustice.

Some think fairness and justice *ought* to matter for moral or religious reasons. Biology tells us that rejecting unfairness *is* a deep-rooted biological drive, for which humans are prepared to pay large costs. A visceral instinct welling up inside us, as powerful as the emotions and risk.

In a classic example called the ultimatum game, one individual gets an amount of money (for example, $10) and proposes a split with a second player (for example, $9 for herself, $1 for the second person). The other individual then decides whether to accept the offer (in which case both get the split as proposed) or reject the offer (in which case both players get nothing). Despite receiving an offer of free money, the second player rejects offers of less than 25 percent of the money around half the time.[60] Many refuse "low" offers even when stakes are many months' salary.[61] In my lab at Queen Square, I conducted an experiment where I made people uncomfortably thirsty by hooking them up to a saline drip—and participants had to respond to offers about how to split a large glass of water. Despite their thirst, people still rejected low offers of water from other people if they felt they were unfair.[62]

Social rules, such as acting fairly, give us Models of how other people should behave, and violating these social rules brings unwelcome prediction errors. My own brain imaging in humans shows how this brain activity varies along the length of the insula cortex according to different social contexts—findings that then predicted results from experiments that causally stimulated the insula in nonhuman primates.[63]

Perceived social inequities can recruit and inspire people to stand and fight.[64] *Liberté, égalité, fraternité!* cried the French revolutionaries. In the Arab Spring and in post-Saddam Iraq, insurgents and revolutionaries offered people a path to reject injustice.

Mao and his capable military commander, Zhu De, harnessed these motivations for Red Army recruitment—and went further to win the sympathies of local populations. They built the Red Army to behave better among civilians than other Chinese armies. "The soldiers are the fish," went the famous saying, "and the people are the water."[65] Treating the population fairly was central to the "five rules and eight points" instituted for their guerrillas' personal discipline, which included "Do not steal from the people; Be neither selfish nor unjust; Be courteous; and Return what you borrow."[66] Mao redistributed land more fairly and sought to draw local populations into decision-making. The Communists also used social motivations to help maintain order: often using a version of the traditional *baojia* mutual-security system in communities, where social norms and group responsibility kept discipline in five-person "mutual guarantee groups."[67] (China's current leader, Xi Jinping, has been expanding modern versions of such *baojia*.[68]) Winning the peasants' sympathies gave communist forces indispensable intelligence and logistic systems.

In combat, too, social motivations drive us: "I fight for the men around me." We don't want to let them down, and we don't want to be let down. I recently spoke with a former Israeli Defense Force chief psychologist, Reuven Gal, himself a veteran of the 1967 Arab-Israeli War. To Gal, group membership was key for the will to fight: it encouraged soldiers to fight out of reciprocal obligation, to preserve the honor of their unit, and to protect their friends.

Even self-discipline has a social dimension, as influential nineteenth-century French thinker Colonel Charles Ardant du Picq described:

> What makes the soldier capable of obedience and direction in action is the sense of discipline. This includes: respect for and confidence in his chiefs; confidence in his comrades and fear of their reproaches, and retaliation if he abandons them in danger; his desire to go where others do without trembling more than they.[69]

Mao's communist forces needed those visceral social motivations to stand and fight. As Mao described in *On Protracted War*, published in 1938, the guerrilla war of attrition with Japan was the first stage in what would become a conventional offensive—against a tough foe.[70] In August 1940, the communists did launch a major conventional military offensive against the Japanese: the "Hundred Regiments Campaign." They struck Japanese strong points and communication lines. The communists lost about one hundred thousand men in months of fighting.[71] But crucially, communist troops demonstrated their willingness and capability to stand and fight in conventional war.

In our comfortable everyday lives in the rich, peaceful west, it is easy to decry—rightly—the dark sides of what we do for "our group," but they are the flip side of social motivations that can keep us alive. Combat thus provides a fresh lens, helping us see why these social motivations are so powerful.

We rely on our comrades, and they rely on us. Our group. Friendship. Comradeship.

The will to fight must always be a factor in war: as China's story shows, or as the poorly armed Taliban showed against awesome U.S. technology. But the will to fight is not only the will to risk death—victory also requires another kind of will.

WILL

Willingness to risk being killed is not—if you pause and think about it—the same thing as willingness to fight aggressively and kill.

Mercenary forces may contain many who are willing to kill others, but like warlord armies in China's civil war they often crumble against those—like Mao's Red Army—with greater will to risk death. Among soldiers willing to risk death, surprisingly few *also* have the will to kill, if they can avoid it.

U.S. Army Lieutenant Colonel S. L. A. Marshall interviewed World War II soldiers and found that even in close-fought infantry actions only 15 to 25 percent of the men in a company fired their weapons in an average stern day's action.[72] The essence of his findings, despite methodological issues, seem to be corroborated by other research.[73] The U.S. Army Air Force estimated that fewer than 1 percent of its military pilots accounted for 30 to 40 percent of enemy aircraft destroyed in the air during World War II.[74] And U.S. General Wayne Downing, who served from Vietnam to Afghanistan and led Special Operations Command, remarked that a typical infantry platoon's thirty soldiers included only three or four who would effectively kill the enemy.[75] Many of the rest engage in "posturing," such as holding their rifle in a threatening way but actually firing into the air or at an angle that reduces the chances of killing.[76]

To avoid losing wars, we need individuals willing to risk death *and* fight aggressively. Neither alone is sufficient.

From comfortable civilian life one might think such aggressive warriors are mentally ill, or evil. But Dave Grossman, author of *On Killing*, describes many studies that show no greater inclination to violence among combat veterans compared to nonveterans.[77] And of his research among those prepared to fight aggressively, Grossman says that "since returning from combat they have, without fail, proven themselves to be above-average contributors to the prosperity and welfare of our society."

Moreover, having the will to kill doesn't mean killing without restraint, as Vietnam veteran Dave Nelson described:

> I could not tolerate the abuse of civilians—especially not children and women. It was a very personal thing with me . . . That made my decision to be a sniper. Killing clean shows respect for the enemy, but to kill civilians or to lose control of yourself and your concepts in life in combat is wrong . . . that's the concept behind the warrior. Kill cleanly, kill quickly, kill efficiently, without malice or brutality.[78]

So, how can we—ethically, and in ways that build in restraint—increase the will to fight aggressively, and to kill if required?[79]

The powerful brain systems discussed in this chapter provide avenues. Emotion regulation techniques like reframing, described earlier, could potentially reduce aversion to aggressive acts during training for combat. Such techniques could also reduce excessive remorse.

Social motivations are potent. Armies have long used recognition from symbols like medals to reward aggression. Pressures from social groups can be important: S. L. A. Marshall found firing rates of nearly 100 percent on weapons operated by a crew of multiple people in World War II.[80] New technologies will provide new ways to apply social pressures. Troops will be covered in ever more sensors—heart rate, eye gaze, weapon direction, and much more—and these will increasingly detect soldiers who might (if unobserved) avoid killing or avoid restraint. So soldiers can no longer fire into the air or deliberately target civilians, giving troops ever fewer options except to fight aggressively and with restraint.

During immersive training, digital monitoring of where trainees look, the speed of trigger pull, and other measures could all help personalize the feedback trainees receive—to reinforce both their aggression *and* restraint in avoiding harm of noncombatants. Training environments are already being developed that can more closely simulate real combat using Augmented Reality (AR), in which the training environments frequently change to keep them fresh with prediction errors to stimulate learning. Such training can help personnel develop more effective emotion control and risk assessments.

Data collected during training will also provide a valuable resource when trainees later go into the field. With real-world outcomes, analysts can then go back and examine training data, to identify characteristics (such as patterns of eye movements or trigger pulls) that might help predict who in reality goes on to fight bravely, aggressively, and with restraint.

Such technologies can improve the training for aggression that was until recently barely more sophisticated than plunging a bayonet into a straw dummy. At the same time, successful technologies to shape our visceral instincts and habitual responses inevitably take away from something else valuable: an individual's free will.

That's no simple trade-off, because people with the will to fight bravely, aggressively, and with restraint—as Mao's forces did—can overcome seemingly insurmountable odds.

* * *

It seemed improbable back in 1941, but neither Chiang Kai-shek nor the Japanese would win in mainland China.

Decades later, in the capital of the People's Republic of China that Mao founded, I came to Peking University, which westerners often call "China's Harvard." From our pleasant meeting room, I looked out on an attractive, spacious campus. A relative oasis in Beijing's bustle. It was not long before the COVID-19 pandemic, and I sat at the head of a long, polished wooden table. I was co-chairing a day of meetings alongside my neuroscientific collaborator at Peking University. We had brought together leading neuroscientists from China, Britain, the United States, Japan, and France to discuss the brain and free will.

It was a lively, excited discussion very much focused on the brain. But as I sat there I couldn't help question how much free will many people in China—or anywhere—really had amid the turmoil of twentieth-century history.

At the same Peking University, a group had met almost exactly a century before to discuss Russia's Bolshevik Revolution of 1917 and its lessons for China. Peking University's head librarian, Li Dazhao, was one of the organizers. His group included a young man who often attended and also had a job in the library: Mao Zedong.

Li Dazhao told China's youth that the roots of Marxist socialism could be looked for "in three aspects of our psychology:"[81] knowledge, feeling, and will.

Li's group would also have known Karl Marx's most famous thinking on free will:

> Men make their own history, but they do not make it just as they please; they do not make it under circumstances chosen by themselves, but under circumstances directly encountered, given and transmitted from the past.[82]

How much "free will" did the soldiers drafted into the Nationalist, Communist, or Japanese puppet forces have? How much free will does a soldier in a foxhole with a comrade have? How is that different from the instinct of the rat that turned to fight back against a young Vladimir Putin in Leningrad? Does a soldier have the free will to abandon his comrades? How much free will can—and should—a soldier have? How does that change over time? Does a veteran have more free will than a rookie? A soldier less than a civilian?

Free will is often considered from the pleasant calm of an office desk and chair—but my point here is that we cannot view free will only from that single slice of life. War sharply illustrates how much our free will is in reality constrained by the iron cage of our vital drives, and the visceral instincts that guide us and those around us. Choices are often far less simple than they appear from a comfortable perch. Our visceral instincts don't tell us everything about free will, and we'll consider much more in our journey through the brain, but these fundamental brain regions are a part of the story that cannot be ignored.

War can be bleak. And this chapter has touched on unwelcome ideas like fear and injustice. But it's worth pointing out that we can move through these things.

My great-uncle Sydney was just one of millions who fought right up until the last months of the war in 1945. And he survived.

I remember him as a cheerful man, who lived happily by the sea with his wife. When I visited as a child, he pushed me around his garden in a wheelbarrow. On his hundredth birthday he was surrounded by grandchildren and great-grandchildren—and the photo at the start of this book shows him holding my son.

He survived, like his sister, my grandmother. They were Jewish, and survival was easier in Britain than in the occupied countries. Had Britain succumbed, war would have swept her into hiding, into a death camp, or perhaps into exile—by sailing across the oceans.

4

WHERE, WHEN, AND WHAT IF . . .

HOW THE HIPPOCAMPAL-ENTORHINAL REGION MAPS OUR WORLDS

Horatio Nelson was the greatest admiral in the age of sail. In the summer of 1805, Nelson and the British Navy stood in the way of French Emperor Napoleon Bonaparte, who had massed more than 160,000 assault troops ready to invade Britain.[1] Could Bonaparte concentrate his scattered fleets, for the twenty-four hours he believed necessary to cross the English Channel?

In a vast cat and mouse game, the French fleet in the Mediterranean used a storm to evade Nelson's British ships, then sailed more than 4,000 miles to the West Indies as a lure. Nelson gave chase. But the French dashed back for the Channel. British ships intercepted and fought an inconclusive engagement off the Spanish coast. Next, the French hid in the Spanish port of Cadiz, while Nelson sailed for England. By August Napoleon conceded defeat. For the time being.

This wasn't the first time Nelson had thwarted Napoleon. Seven years before, in 1798, Napoleon had sailed an army across the Mediterranean to conquer Egypt and maybe even India. Coastal geography made the anchored French fleet seem impregnable. But Nelson's fleet found a route between the French ships and the coast, attacking at once to take out eleven of the thirteen main French ships.[2]

Remember, Nelson did this without spotter planes, radar, or GPS.

In October 1805, the combined French and Spanish fleet emerged again. At the Battle of Trafalgar, Nelson was outnumbered by 30,000 French and Spanish men with 2,568 cannon against his 17,000 men with 2,148 cannon[3]—but Nelson attacked.

He used mastery of position to cut across the line of French and Spanish ships. Nelson broke with orthodoxy and headed with all sails set toward the enemy, exposing his ships to murderous broadsides during which his fleet couldn't fire back. He didn't use the term "prediction error," but it was implied: "I think it will surprise and confuse the enemy," Nelson had explained to a friend a few weeks before the battle. "They won't know what I am about."[4]

Nelson's ships braved this terrifying advance—and, as Nelson anticipated, the front of the enemy's fleet sailed on, which enabled Nelson's ships to destroy the enemy's center and rear. Nelson's plan worked brilliantly, and the Battle of Trafalgar ushered in two centuries of Anglo-American naval domination of the world's oceans.

Nelson's mastery of position and movement across vast oceanic expanses, or among local winds and conditions, brilliantly illustrates a key challenge that faces our Models: *Where do we live?*

Nelson must have had an impressive hippocampal-entorhinal brain region. This runs backward from the amygdala for about 2 inches (5 centimeters; a long way in the brain), and contains "place cells" and "grid cells" that make maps of the world. *The maps in our brains are not just a metaphor.* These cells model the physical world with precision, enabling many animals, including humans, to search for the best route forward in complex environments.

Humans navigate across many mental geographies. In war, the *seas* are often every bit as vital as the land: neither Napoleon nor Hitler could defeat the Royal Navy, and the seas provided routes to eventual victory. A naval brain looks for options in a landscape of tides, winds, and sea beds. A soldier's brain is afforded options by mountains, roads, and cities.

Brain imaging shows that in humans this region also maps entirely abstract terrains, including timescapes, the social world, and invented spaces described only by symbols.

Future spaces will be created in the brains of those who operate in those spaces, and may need to fight there, too. I have spent time with space forces who operate in the three dimensions and orbits of outer space, and with cyber forces who operate in cyberspace that is partially geographical and partially abstract. These mental geographies may prove as crucial for our survival in future conflicts as the English Channel was to Nelson in 1805.

In the last two chapters we paused the story of World War II on December 6, 1941. Remembering this pause is itself possible only thanks to another function of this remarkable brain region: it helps us create memories of the past, simulate possible alternatives, and imagine potential futures. This neural machinery allows us to ask "what if?"

What can we learn by asking "what if" about our own era? In which, for the first time since Trafalgar, the world's largest navy is neither British nor American, but Chinese?[5]

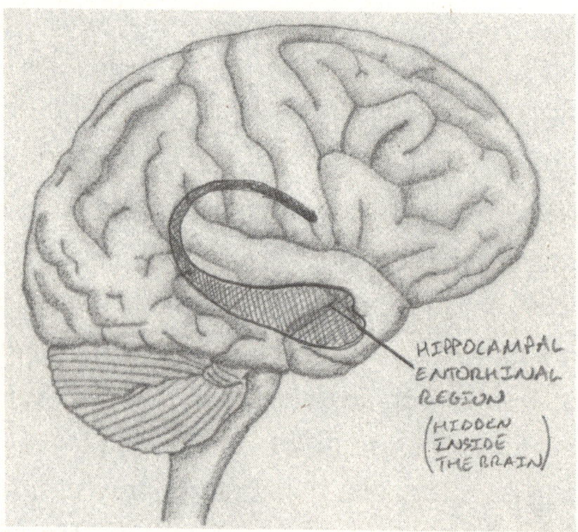

FIGURE 5: The hippocampal-entorhinal region is long and thin, once again buried deep in the brain with one on either side. It curves up and around.

MAPS IN OUR BRAINS

A brain locked away in its dark, bony box receives a lot of pretty raw data from the world around it.

The challenge: How do you know where things are in the world around you? Where *you* are? How do you navigate? Our brains orient and navigate so effortlessly that we can forget how remarkable this is.

An example from my life: a few years ago, on Friday afternoons in my lab building at Queen Square in London I would leave my desk. Demis Hassabis, the founder of Google DeepMind—and now a Nobel Prize–winning AI pioneer—had a desk in the same office as me. I can remember its exact position in my map of the lab. Everyone from the office went out into the hall and climbed three floors up to the seminar room for what we called the Brain Meeting. Celebrities in the world of neuroscience, such as Peter Dayan (of prediction error fame) or brain imaging pioneer Karl Friston, often stood at the back of the room or sometimes sat on the floor.

Today, sitting at my desk a couple of miles away and a few years later, I easily remember the space and can navigate around it in my mind's eye.

Also sitting at the back, sometimes, was a man with a neat white beard. This was John O'Keefe, whose discovery of "place cells" won him a Nobel Prize in 2014. His work allows us to understand how our brains build a Model of space. Let's see how the Model works, step by step.[6]

STEP 1: WHERE ARE YOU NOW?

In 1971, O'Keefe and a colleague were studying electrical activity in rat brains, including the long, thin hippocampus that stretches back from the amygdala, just below the insula.

When the animal visited a specific place in its environment, specific brain cells in the hippocampus increased their electrical firing: a "place cell" for that location. Other place cells were active for other locations. Right now, whether you are reading this book in your bedroom, a local park, or a train carriage, a specific cell is strongly active in your hippocampus. This place cell tells you where you are.

Place cells are incredibly precise. If we record from a hundred place cells at the same time in a rat, we can read that rat's map—and locate the rat in the real world to within 2 inches.

STEP 2: HOW FAR DID YOU GO AND WHERE DID YOU ARRIVE?

A place cell tells you that you are standing in a specific place. But if you walk for a while to another location, how do you know the distance between the two places?

"Speed cells" help solve the problem. Speed cells increase their activity when the animal moves faster. Speed cells are found in a brain area just next to the hippocampus called the entorhinal cortex, which is another long, thin area that runs beside the hippocampus so they're like two sides of a zip. And because the brain keeps track of time, your brain can use the speed to calculate how far you went.

Distance can be combined with direction. "Head direction cells" fire when an animal faces its head in a specific direction in space, like a compass but relative to your private map instead of the magnetic poles. Thus, in one environment a head direction cell might fire when the head points toward magnetic north, but in another environment it fires when the head points to magnetic east.

STEP 3: WHAT ALTERNATIVE WAYS MIGHT WE LOCATE OURSELVES AND NAVIGATE FROM A TO B?

"Grid cells" provide an even richer map. These, too, are found in the entorhinal cortex. A specific grid cell activates when an animal passes through *many* different locations in a given environment. For each grid cell these locations form a grid of places where it is activated. Each grid cell's grid is hexagonal (that is, the grid looks like a honeycomb).

This is different from a place cell, which activates when visiting one place in an environment.

Each grid cell forms a unique grid pattern that is slightly different from the grids of nearby grid cells—and *combining* lots of overlapping grid patterns together fills out the whole environment with an incredibly precise map.

Using only one grid cell, you cannot be sure where a laboratory animal is located. But recording from multiple grid cells in a rat and combining activity in those cells, you can pinpoint current location with great accuracy.

These combined grid patterns serve as a map in the brain—they *are* a map in the brain. And because this map enables us to precisely measure distance between different locations, it helps us navigate.

Grid cells also provide maps at different scales: so that Nelson could switch instantly from contemplating whole oceans to hyper-local shorelines, winds, and tides. You do this yourself when you think of things in your house, your local area, your city, and beyond. Along the entorhinal cortex, grid cells represent an environment at multiple scales.

STEP 4: HOW CAN WE ANCHOR THESE COGNITIVE MAPS TO REALITY?

For brain maps to be useful, the organism needs a mechanism to connect map coordinates to fixed things in the environment that they can perceive. That is, to link the map to the terrain.

Boundaries and landmarks help anchor our maps to reality.[7] Boundaries include things like the location of a room's walls. When signs on the walls of a space are rotated around the center of that space, this causes grid patterns to rotate. If one of the walls moves to make the room larger or smaller, then the grids can also expand or contract.

Landmarks are items that stably relate to specific locations or bearings on the map, such as buildings, statues, or mailboxes. They can also be more distributed things such as the shape of a room or the layout of a landscape. In a naval context they might include stars, coastal landmarks, or other ships.

These maps in our brains are not just metaphors, they're *really* in there. Work over the past half century has identified how these maps work in rodents, monkeys, and humans.[8] And we now have a veritable zoo of interesting cells in the hippocampal-entorhinal region that build this Model of space: "place cells," "grid cells," "head direction cells," "boundary vector cells" (active at a given distance away from a boundary in a particular direction), "goal direction cells" (active when an animal's goal is in a particular direction relative to its current movement direction), and more.

Nobody knew we had such remarkable brain maps at the time, but they were crucial to those defending Britain's supply lines in September 1939.

* * *

Britain would lose everything if it lost at sea. The sea brought supplies of food and fuel. "The only thing that ever really frightened me during the war," recalled Winston Churchill in his memoirs, "was the U-boat peril."[9] Germany's feared *Unterseeboot* or submarine.

Britain entered World War II as probably the most formidable naval power. The United States had a similar array of battleships, aircraft carriers, and naval workhorses like the smaller destroyers. But Britain also controlled key naval choke points that remain important today. It controlled both ends of the Mediterranean, holding Gibraltar in the west, and Suez in the east. Controlling the Strait of Malacca gave it control over passage from the Pacific to the Indian Ocean. That said, Britain's equally vast responsibilities presented a smorgasbord of enticing treats for enemies to attack.

Before World War II, the German Navy's "Plan Z" had been to build a surface fleet big enough by 1944 to destroy the Royal Navy and starve Britain to surrender[10]—but Hitler inconveniently went to war too early. In a change of plan, the German Navy attacked the rich streams of Allied shipping with U-boats. One of these submarines sank the commercial liner *Athenia* on the first day of war, killing twenty-eight Americans among over a hundred dead.[11] But the main threat to Allied commerce was expected to come from surface raiders, like Germany's powerful "pocket battleships."

Before invading Poland in 1939, Germany had pre-positioned a pocket battleship, the *Graf Spee*, in the South Atlantic.[12] The *Graf Spee* was a formidable ship: its six guns with 11-inch-diameter barrels outranged by nearly two miles the 6-inch and 8-inch guns on the British cruisers sent after it. On September 26 Hitler ordered it to attack.

The *Graf Spee* sank five ships in less than four weeks between Brazil and West Africa, sailed into the Indian Ocean to sink another, then reentered the Atlantic.

Those defending against the *Graf Spee* required cognitive maps working at different scales: oceanic and in close battle. To search on oceanic scale, the Allies created half a dozen hunter-killer groups, each with some three cruisers. After two months they got a lead when two of the *Graf Spee*'s victims bravely sent out messages before being sunk.

Commodore Henry Harwood used this new information and tried to put himself in his adversary's mind. Where would they go? Harwood commanded one of the less powerful hunter-killer groups, with the cruisers *Ajax*, *Achilles*, and *Exeter.* He reasoned that the *Graf Spee* would try to vacate the area of its recent captures as soon as possible and head west to where shipping lanes out of South America converged. Harwood doodled his ideas on a piece of message paper, anticipating that the *Graf Spee* would arrive between Montevideo and Rio on the morning of December 12. That's where Harwood took his ships.

At 06:10 on the morning of December 13 (only a day late!), one of Harwood's lookouts spotted a trace of smoke. Switching by now to a smaller-scale map, Harwood ordered his three ships to increase speed and spread out to attack from different quarters, splitting the *Graf Spee*'s capacity to fire back.

The *Graf Spee*'s captain was confident ("We'll smash them," he said[13]), and its 11-inch shells hit the *Exeter* seven times in twenty minutes. Soon the *Exeter* had only one working gun and began taking on water and listing to starboard. Harwood ordered the *Exeter* to retire. Now the *Graf Spee*'s shells smashed into the remaining two cruisers, putting both rear guns on the *Ajax* out of action, and decimated the crew on the bridge of the *Achilles.*

But the outgunned British ships' attacks from multiple directions meant they also landed blows on the *Graf Spee.* The *Graf Spee*'s captain decided that damage to its freshwater and food supply systems meant they must head into the neutral River Plate for repairs.

The *Graf Spee* couldn't stay long in the neutral port. British disinformation tricked the captain into thinking more powerful backup ships had arrived, and on December 17 he scuttled the *Graf Spee.* With one exception, no later German warship convoy raider *ever* got out of the North Atlantic.[14]

LEARNING TREASURE MAPS

In children's treasure maps, a giant X marks the spot of buried pirate loot—and other exciting features loom unfeasibly large, too, such as the sequence of steps needed to reach that treasure. Our brain's maps, while wonderfully accurate, are similarly warped by what we value, and by how the world works. That is, we don't map the world simply as it is, but as it is *useful* for us: and we particularly value places with resources, potential mates, friends, threats, or others' territories.

Our experiences warp the maps that we learn, to try to make our maps more useful. Even the landscapes we experience while growing up shape our maps. Recent research looked at nearly four hundred thousand people from thirty-eight countries who played a game in which they navigated a boat to find checkpoints on a map.[15] People growing up in cities with more grid-like street layouts (for example, Chicago) performed better on regular layouts, whereas people growing up outside cities or in cities with irregular street layouts (for example, Prague) got a boost on more irregular video game scenarios.

Experts can spend years learning maps that are useful to them—Nelson joined the navy at age twelve—and such experience can literally change the hippocampus's size and shape. My late colleague Eleanor Maguire at Queen Square studied London taxi drivers, who must learn the names and layout of more than twenty-six thousand streets in London, along with thousands of points of interest.[16] They begin training with a hippocampus no different from otherwise similar individuals—but learning "the Knowledge" increases the size of the back part of the hippocampus. Candidates who failed the exams did not show a change in hippocampal size.

The locations of things we find rewarding are overly represented in the brain's map[17]—especially if the rewards are large and unexpected (that is, with bigger prediction errors). Rewarding locations create clusters of place cells. Even if animals in an open field approach an unmarked zone where rewards are delivered, this causes increased grid cell activity. Recent work has found specific hippocampal neurons that are active when an animal nears a reward. And dopamine surging up from the brainstem affects this map learning. Drug addicts often find drugs really rewarding, which helps explain why addicts build strong associations that link specific locations to drug use—so a specific house, alley, or bar can set them off.

We also learn where nasty things are. The hippocampus is crucial for learning places to fear: if rats learn a fear response to an electric shock in a specific place, removing their hippocampus can make them lose that fear response.[18] And as well as what's nice and nasty, it can be life and death to map what's *ours*.

The robin redbreast we met in chapter 1 is jolly, yes, and also fiercely territorial: willing to fight and die for the territory to survive and raise its offspring. In many animals, a useful boundary is the extent of *my* or *our* territory (whoever I or we are), to secure resources like food, breeding sites, and safety from predators. Caring about territory evolved independently across numerous animals from ants to birds to apes—and produces diverse behaviors.

The precise ways that territories matter differs even among our ape relatives. Chimps and bonobos only evolved separately about 1.8 million years ago, and contrary to the image of bonobos as the "peace and love" primate, male bonobos can be more violent than male chimps.[19] But they treat meetings across territorial boundaries differently. Adult male bonobos from neighboring communities sometimes enjoy playing a game in which they slowly chase each other around a sapling, each trying to grab the testes of the fellow in front.[20] Adult male chimps sometimes have similar fun playing the "ball game" in their own community—but instant hostility is the only relationship ever seen between neighboring territories.

Gorillas illustrate another aspect of how territories can work among apes. Gorilla groups have a home range, and close to its center may include regions for priority use or exclusive use that they will defend by physical aggression. But at the same time, in other parts of their ranges, groups can overlap and even peacefully coexist.[21] That is, territories can be permeable rather than hard, and still real.

Among human hunter-gatherers, territories often mattered[22]—and to this day, physical territory remains central to the definition of every state. Sure, behaviors across countries' borders differ. And sure, a country's borders may be permeable—China's "Great Wall" regulated rather than stopped all movement. But that doesn't make borders less real, and competing over territory has caused conflict since history began in ancient Sumer. And ever since.

Territorial ambitions—and worries—were central to World War II.[23] In the early 1920s, Hitler decided that Germany's survival required *Lebensraum* ("living space")—and it would be in the east. Japan sought territory in China. The interwar "isolationist" United States cared deeply about territory and wasn't actually isolationist, but rather sought security through control of the Americas. This continued the nineteenth-century Monroe Doctrine. As the "isolationist" aviator Charles A. Lindbergh, a leading voice of the America First Committee, said in a 1941 speech: "We will fight anybody and everybody who attempts to interfere with our hemisphere."[24]

Today's territorial tensions include Russia's claims on Georgia and Ukraine. The People's Republic of China claims Taiwan, as well as land in the South China Sea, East China Sea, and along the China-India border. India fought border conflicts with China and Pakistan. Land matters in Israel-Palestine.

Where one can act on the high seas is often ambiguous but can also lead to war. The seventeenth-century Dutch jurist Hugo Grotius wrote an influential book, *The Free Sea*, which argued that the seas were international territory and should be open to all.[25] For centuries, global powers used this to justify sailing merchant ships where they liked when at peace, except for short distances from another's shore. But they also fought for control of the high seas in battles like Trafalgar. And in blockades, such as Germany's unrestricted U-boat warfare in World War I, which killed U.S. citizens in the Atlantic and helped drive the United States to war.

Today countries still argue over who can do what and where in the sea. Take the example of the South China Sea, through which 20 to 30 percent of world trade travels,[26] and over which many countries lay claim, including the Philippines, Vietnam, Malaysia, Taiwan, and (most expansively) China.[27] In the 2010s China sought to bolster its claims by pumping vast quantities of material from the sea bed onto rocky outcrops, creating large islands—unsinkable aircraft carriers—that now house extensive military facilities.[28] The United States and its allies argue that under international law these manmade islands don't bolster Chinese claims to the seas around them—but China interprets things differently. Who's correct?

Just as we struggle to agree over the management of the seas, so we argue over new kinds of terrain, such as cyberspace. It has a geography—and by the 2010s that alternative geography had given Idaho and Kansas everyday, real-time digital borders with China, Russia, Australia, and elsewhere. Russian and Chinese hackers could easily cross those borders and also increasingly used servers physically based in western countries. How can a country like America defend these borders and pursue adversaries effectively across allies' computer networks while also respecting those allies' territorial integrity?

The U.S. military's official 2018 document entitled *Cyberspace Operations* states that if an adversary like Russian intelligence controls a node in an ally (for example, the Netherlands), then that node may be considered "red" (adversary) cyberspace.[29] But how would the Netherlands feel about that? This point may seem arcane, but U.S. thinking on cyber has been moving ever more toward ideas like "defending forward," "proactive defense," or "persistent engagement" that push these boundaries—and without which it's very hard to compete in this geography.

"Cyberspace" is highly abstract *and* it relies on physical undersea cables, servers, computer code, and satellites.

Those satellites themselves form part of an alternative geography as singular and significant as cyber: outer space.[30] In the geography of outer space, the most valuable real estate for satellites is a geostationary orbit. From this small and valuable area, 22,240 miles (35,790 kilometers) from Earth around the equator, satellites appear stationary from the ground and can cover large parts of the Earth's surface. Other places have their own benefits and vulnerabilities in the maps held by space warriors—a term that would have seemed fantastical to me if I hadn't met many of them on my projects with the Pentagon.

China and Russia use lasers to dazzle satellites, or cyber to hack them.[31] Missiles from Earth can destroy satellites. From 2013 to 2017 Russia conducted a number of "rendezvous and proximity operations" in which space vehicles, sometimes previously hidden as inert satellites, can get close to an adversary's satellites. Chinese military space strategists describe "Space Blockade Operations" that could blockade terrestrial space facilities, orbits, launch windows, or data links.[32] Outer space is the "new strategic high ground," according to China's President Xi Jinping.[33]

Then there is the moon. Who owns the territory on the moon? Will existing laws really answer that question? In 2013 China became the third country to put a rover on the moon. Israel and India are in the race. China plans to send a human, soon, to plant a Chinese flag.[34] For your brain to think through that last sentence you can rely on a map of the moon and its relation to Earth that already exists in your brain—even though you've never been near it. And what if Chinese ideas of "Space Blockade" extend to war on the moon? Your brain can imagine it if I conjecture a war on the moon and the supply lines to it, a war that hinges on ferocious attacks and daring defense of those critical supply lines in space.

Armadas of undersea boats blockading from beneath the waves may have seemed equally fanciful to many in 1906, the year Germany launched its first submarine, the *U-1* (for *Unterseeboot 1*). But from 1914 to 1918 German U-boats sank many millions of tons of shipping and could have won that war.[35]

* * *

Germany's U-boat mastermind in World War II was Karl Dönitz.[36] Pinch-faced, reedy-voiced, and highly effective, Dönitz had been a submariner in World War I. Now he imagined a new way to attack—not as single submarines, but as "wolf packs." He skillfully moved his subsea forces to where they faced the least danger and sank the most value.

He relied on a handful of U-boat "aces" who had remarkable skills to think not only along the two dimensions of the water's surface, but also above and below. They spent years learning their expertise at sea.

Weeks into the war, one of those aces, Günther Prien, captained his submarine into Scapa Flow off Scotland where Britain based many important ships. Scapa Flow was surrounded by islands, had only three access passages, and was well guarded by submarine nets, minefields, and coastal batteries. Prien navigated above and below water to get past them all, sank a battleship with the loss of more than eight hundred lives, then outmaneuvered his British pursuers to return safely home.[37]

Dönitz mainly targeted commerce, though, and in the first six weeks of the war his U-boats sank some ten merchant ships per week. That increased dramatically once Dönitz could use French ports. Between September 2 and December 2, 1940, his wolf packs sank nearly 850,000 tons of shipping. A rate Britain couldn't sustain.[38]

But in March 1941, Dönitz lost three of his U-boat aces, including Prien.[39] The British had rethought *where* U-boats would be most vulnerable during close battle when wolf packs attacked a convoy.

The legendary escort Captain "Johnnie" Walker was as effective as Dönitz—but Walker's specialty was *anti*-submarine warfare. Walker brought a blistering energy to the windswept bridge of the warship from which he commanded his group. He cared deeply about his sailors, losing only three of the many warships under his command during the war, and still sinking more U-boats than any other commander.[40]

Other escort captains struggled with how on earth to counter barely visible (or invisible) U-boats attacking out of nowhere to sink supply ship after supply ship. Walker drew on over two decades of expertise to devise new maneuvers around the convoy during battle: both above and below the water. In three dimensions. He perfected his "creeping attack" to catch a submerged U-boat: only one warship in his group kept its sonar switched on and stayed a good distance from the U-boat, so that other warships could quietly get right overhead without the U-boat knowing.[41] If a U-boat entered and attacked a convoy, the escorts coordinated their movements to attack where the U-boat would likely emerge.[42] Walker eventually lost his own life, but he proved the U-boats could be beaten.

And the British and Commonwealth navies increasingly got new help: from America. On October 31, 1941, a U-boat torpedo sank the U.S. Navy ship the *Reuben James*—the first U.S. blood officially spilled in World War II.[43]

Yet Hitler remained far more restrained in the Atlantic than many of his admirals wanted. He remembered all too clearly how unrestricted U-boat warfare brought the United States into World War I. Memories are powerful, and those, too, are organized in the hippocampal-entorhinal region.

MEMORY IS FOR THE FUTURE

We remember not for the past, but for the future. Our memories don't exist to create a complete, accurate record of past reality (although to be useful our memories must often be anchored to reality). Instead, memories help us create a landscape of possibilities to navigate the present and beyond. Without memories, we're lost.

I saw this on my neurology ward in Oxford's big teaching hospital, when a tall, well-built man in his early sixties wandered out of his room. He was friendly and cooperative but perplexed. He didn't know *why* he was in the hospital. He couldn't remember the events immediately before he came in, and he had trouble making new memories. He met me and his other doctors every day, but for him the meeting was always new. His other faculties were fine. But memory damage left him adrift.

Brain scans showed abnormalities around his hippocampal-entorhinal region. Blood tests showed a rare immune disorder that attacks that part of the brain.[44] Happily, treating that immune response led to a magnificent recovery.

Human hippocampus is involved in truly remarkable types of memory. To be sure, all animals (not just humans) journey through time, aiming to navigate toward futures promoting survival, and away from futures endangering it. And humans also have important types of memory based outside the hippocampus, such as our procedural memory for skills like typing, or our short-term memory for things like remembering a phone number. But injury to the human hippocampus damages our incredible capacity for *explicit memory*: to remember events and facts, both personal and general, that we can consciously access and verbally describe.[45]

Explicit memories give our Models a treasure trove of people, stories, places, and ways the world works, which help us navigate the future. These include memories of episodes in our own lives, in which we were the agent or recipient of some action—and which describe what happened, where, when, and with whom. (For example, cutting my finger, with my new penknife, in my childhood house, on a wintry evening at age nine, and being comforted by my mother.) They also include more factual memories, shorn of the context in which those memories were learned. (For example, I know France's capital is Paris, and concepts like how to tell the time, but I don't recall the contexts in which I learned them.) The hippocampus also helps organize, process, and relate these memories for events and facts so they don't become a jumbled mess. And that even includes hippocampus helping us "map" memories along the passage of time.

"Time cells" in the hippocampus were recently discovered in rat and human brains.[46] They are similar to place cells, but instead of mapping *where* things are in space, time cells map *when* things are in time. Your brain recognizes that an event, such as a movie or dinner party, is a specific chunk of time, and your brain can roughly estimate that event's duration. Then, as that event unfolds, each time cell fires at different time windows; so, for example, one time cell might fire after ten seconds, then another after one minute, then five minutes, and so on. Other types of cells add to these time maps—such as "ramping cells" that fire intensely as an episode starts, which is analogous to an episode's "border" in a map of space rather than time.

Our map of time is also warped to be useful, as we saw earlier with maps of space. Emotions, for example, can make episodes go faster or slower.[47] Moreover, our brain can stitch episodes together along the line of time, order them, and put them within an appropriate time frame—which is why we can watch a "reverse chronology" movie like *Memento* in which scenes shown earlier in the movie actually happen later in the chronological story. That ordering is crucial because we can remember only a fraction of the oceans of experiences in which we swim every minute, hour, day, year, and decade of our lives. We must remember *and* forget.

That's why *forgetting* is an active and useful process: not a bug, but a feature. Indeed, for Models based on our memories to be *flexible*—and so useful in a changing world—we must forget effectively.[48] Memories that are too precise don't predict the future very well, because events rarely happen again identically. In contrast, memories that become less precise over time can be useful despite some things about a situation changing slightly—so these mistier memories help us understand more diverse situations. Moreover, if information becomes outdated, then forgetting it can help us adapt to new circumstances. Indeed, in conditions like PTSD, for example, the point of talking therapies is *un*learning, so that we can change. Memories are not static; memories are dynamic.

Humans are social animals with collective memories, and these, too, are dynamic. Scholars who explore how humans collectively understand ourselves and the world often stress remembering and forgetting: from Ernest Renan's 1882 lecture *What Is a Nation?* through to Benedict Anderson, who wrote the seminal book *Imagined Communities.*[49] Anderson added an entire chapter in 1991 entitled "Memory and Forgetting." The stories we tell about ourselves and events, including war, are shaped by our social interactions. We talk and listen, read books and newspapers, visit war memorials, and watch television or movies like *Band of Brothers, Saving Private Ryan, Darkest Hour,* or *Dunkirk.* And our memories of events are often actively shaped.

In Britain and the United States, World War II is now largely remembered as a victory of freedom over tyranny, leading to a postwar global order that, however imperfectly, promoted freedom and democracy. Other parts we tend to forget. For example: how incredibly effective the Germans were at fighting on land.

We now have a rosy view of the soldiers from democracies, who were inspired by freedom and so outfought inflexible authoritarian henchmen. But many who actually fought or led in the war—from Churchill himself down to young officers like Michael Howard, who later became a great military historian—knew that on land the Germans fought better than the British and Americans until pretty much the end of the war.[50] It's true that the democracies won, but we shouldn't forget that an authoritarian regime's troops did—and can—fight more effectively.

French collective memories altered considerably after World War II for understandable reasons, converting a story of mostly collaboration to a story of resistance. Henry Rousso's classic 1987 book, *The Vichy Syndrome,* described the complex struggles of remembering and active forgetting that reconstructed the story as one of resistance.[51]

Chinese memories of World War II have changed even more—certainly recently—and these changes matter *now,* in the twenty-first century.[52] As the previous chapter described, World War II in China was part of a series of civil wars. Under Mao Zedong's rule, the story was told as one of class struggle and the rise of communist ideas. But more recently, particularly since Xi Jinping assumed power in 2012, Chinese narratives have sought to redefine China's World War II. They increasingly include the Chinese Nationalist (not just Communist) soldiers fighting bravely against the Japanese. This newer narrative places a strong, victorious, and morally righteous China at the creation of the postwar global order. As President Xi Jinping put it:

> **The Chinese people's victory in the War of Resistance against Japan was the first complete [*wanquan*] victory in a recent war where China resisted the invasion of a foreign enemy.**[53]

Our brains enable us to look back at our memories and to imagine something new. As Nelson did at the Battle of Trafalgar, and as Dönitz did with his U-boat wolf packs. In 1940, could Britain do it once more?

SIMULATE AND INNOVATE

A mouse sits, motionless in the maze. But more is going on than meets the eye. Hippocampal neurons encoded the animal's location in the maze when it was moving previously, and now—as it sits—those same cells are spontaneously sweeping through patterns of activity that repeat the animal's recent path through the maze. This "replay" activity often happens when such animals are resting, and it happens at accelerated speed. Remarkably, the procedure can stitch together segments of space previously only experienced separately and can synthesize new sequences.[54]

Still more remarkably, replays can traverse areas of space the animal has *never* physically visited.[55] In one experiment rats were given full view of a maze, but they could only access some parts. When food was dropped into inaccessible parts, brain recordings showed replay sequences for routes into those places the animal had never physically visited. Moreover, resting rodents' brains not only replay their past experiences, but can also "preplay" activity that predicts their subsequent activity in environments never visited before.

In other words, the brain's Model of space can simulate new creative scenarios—scenarios based on the causal structure of how that world works. If you need to get from one side of a mountain (or a city) to the other side but you only know parts of the terrain, then your brain can simulate alternative routes in its Model of the terrain. You can use the Model to plan potential routes from A to B for you to follow, and while en route it can help you keep on track. Your brain can also explore the Model "offline," to find new links, routes, and patterns—really getting to know the map and seeing it from fresh angles.

Think for a second what a time-saver this simulated environment is, allowing us to test potential plans without actually doing them. And it keeps us safe because we can experiment with options that would be dangerous in the real world: like considering different ways to hunt dangerous prey.

We can create and navigate around strikingly abstract Models, too. A brilliant example is a study in which participants learned about an abstract two-dimensional coordinate system.[56] Most of us are familiar with map coordinates, as you might find on the X (horizontal) and Y (vertical) axes of a graph. It's already quite impressive that most of us can quickly identify the point where, say, 10 on the X-axis meets 10 on the Y-axis. But researchers made the space even more abstract. Instead of numbers for the X and Y dimensions, the participants saw a picture of a cartoon bird—and learned that the length of its legs defined one dimension, and the length of its neck defined the second dimension.

Each participant saw lots of different versions of the cartoon bird, with many different leg lengths and neck lengths. Each bird represented a different place within the space. So, for instance, a bird with middle-length legs and a middle-length neck would be in the middle of the space.

Over time, participants learned to navigate and locate symbols within this highly abstract space, based solely on neck and leg lengths. And brain scanning demonstrated that brain regions that were activated when doing this task—including the entorhinal cortex—were correlated with grid cell maps. In other words, participants used the same principles to simulate and explore abstract spaces as they used in physical spaces.

Our brains can go even further to simulate and explore elaborate potential futures—in this case by building on the treasury of memories processed in the hippocampal-entorhinal region. Memories and imagination, it turns out, are intimately linked.[57]

Demis Hassabis, the AI pioneer who founded DeepMind, studied imagination and the hippocampal-entorhinal cortex during his Ph.D. at my old lab in Queen Square. One of his studies examined patients with selective hippocampal damage.[58] Not only did the patients have profound amnesia, they also struggled to imagine many scenes and future events. When asking the patients to imagine "lying on a white sandy beach in a beautiful tropical bay," they struggled.

Intact human brains, however, can use their treasury of memories to simulate myriad "what ifs," giving us a vast repertoire of analogies, metaphors, and imagined events to explore.

And we can go further, simulating still more creative, innovative "what ifs" by integrating our various Models.

If each of our different Models of tasks or situations were isolated from each other, we would have to build a new Model for each one.[59] But many regularities exist in the world—and our brains benefit from these regularities by putting Models *together* to learn general structures. Children who watch many movies soon extract general structures about how stories work in movies. From reading storybooks they extract additional general structures. And they can combine such general structures from movies and books together.

As with story structures, so we can find general structures with social networks.[60] Consider the networks around a singer like Beyoncé in her social world, the British Royal Family, or our own workplaces. Across all these types of networks we see individuals (Beyoncé, the King, a boss) who play a central role influencing the rest of the network. From these specific social networks, we can imagine more general structures.

By combining loosely related experiences, we can imagine the outcomes of novel choices.[61] If animals learn to choose stimulus A over B, and separately to choose B over C, then even on the first presentation many animals will quickly see that they should choose A over C. Similarly, teaching animals that A leads to B, and later that B leads to a reward, they will afterward prefer choosing A rather than an otherwise similar option, because A implies a reward. In both cases the animals have combined experiences, a capability that in many animals requires a hippocampal-entorhinal region.

That's extraordinary—but nothing compared to our human capacity to decipher sequences.[62] We can put in order the labyrinthine plots of movies like *Pulp Fiction*, *Kill Bill*, or *Everything Everywhere All at Once* for which we must infer all sorts of things from chopped up and even time-reversed episodes. And if we see both the movies directed by Quentin Tarantino, we can also formulate general ideas about his movies and about movies more broadly.

This doesn't mean that we must force all our beliefs to be immediately consistent with one another: the world is too complex for that. It's also useful to retain distinct theories—like how to fight on land, at sea, and in the air.

We often then benefit from laying different ideas beside each other, seeing how they fit together and diverge. When considering how giant wars start, for example, it's worth comparing historical analogies like the run-up to World War I and the run-up to World War II—as we do later in this book. If we are thinking about what war may look like in cyberspace, then it's useful to compare analogies like war on land, sea, air, or outer space—and how deterring cyberattacks might be analogous to deterring terrorism, conventional war, economic warfare, espionage, or even nuclear war. Fixing too quickly on a single analogy can bias and narrow our vision. All analogies are wrong, but some analogies are useful.

Real intelligence requires us to understand things in multiple ways: by tackling a problem with a variety of separate metaphors or views, and also sometimes by integrating different Models to imagine something creative.

* * *

After France's fall, Mussolini's navy was the most powerful in the Mediterranean. It had 6 modern battleships, 19 cruisers, 59 destroyers, and the world's largest fleet of 116 submarines.[63]

The British responded creatively by using sea power and air power *integrated* together. Only three navies at this time had aircraft carriers—the British, American, and Japanese—and what the British did next revolutionized naval warfare.

The main Italian battle fleet, with six battleships, lay protected at Taranto inside the heel of the Italian boot.[64] The British carrier HMS *Illustrious* made a high-speed run north from Malta on November 11, 1940.

Her Swordfish planes were fitted with auxiliary fuel tanks for the long flight and the pilots had rehearsed night attacks. In the dark, just after 20:00, the *Illustrious* turned into the wind to launch twenty-one planes. Half the planes were armed with bombs and half with torpedoes, and they arrived over their target at 23:00. One Swordfish became separated and arrived early, alerting the defenders and raising a cloud of antiaircraft fire.

The first planes dropped parachute flares to light up the harbor before bombing the fuel tanks ashore. Then the torpedo planes arrived. The 16-foot-long and 1,548-pound torpedoes could only be launched while flying below 150 feet and slower than 80 miles per hour. At least one pilot claimed his wheels touched the water.

At 23:14 a torpedo ripped a 27-foot hole below the waterline of a battleship and sank her. In a matter of minutes they took out two more Italian battleships.

This revolution at Taranto was about integrating sea power and air power, not using one or the other alone—much as *Blitzkrieg* integrated land and air power.

As the British admiral reported, twenty planes launched from a carrier "inflicted more damage upon the Italian fleet [at Taranto] than was inflicted upon the German High Seas Fleet" at Jutland, World War I's largest naval battle. The battleship was no longer queen of the oceans—the Fleet Air Arm was now central to any navy's striking power.[65]

Soon after, a Japanese delegation to Taranto took special interest in the British raid. They particularly noted how effective torpedoes were in relatively shallow waters.[66] On December 7, 1941, the Japanese would show the world what they had learned.

* * *

But let's pause on December 6, 1941. Britain and the Commonwealth were now the only democracies in the fight. On land, the Germans remained more effective and threatened Moscow's outskirts. China, despite brutal defeats, had not capitulated.

In this chapter we've learned how the human brain equips us to ask "what if" questions.

The most common "what if" in popular books and movies on World War II is time traveling to kill Hitler before war started. But instead of magical thinking, here are some "what ifs" that were within the power of the western democracies.

- What if France and Britain had anticipated events on land and better harnessed human factors like surprise with the technologies of their day?
- What if neutral European democracies had anticipated events and helped stand up to Hitler's Germany alongside France and Britain? It could have prevented French defeat.
- What if Britain and France had acted aggressively on land during the Phoney War, while German troops were away in Poland?
- What if so many in the occupied democracies had not collaborated?
- What if Britain had surrendered in 1940, as many predicted, or collapsed? While Britain continued to fight, Germany could never bring as much as 60 percent of its armaments to bear on the Eastern Front.[67] And, without Britain, it's unclear how U.S. forces could have got at Germany.
- Outside the democracies, what if China's Chiang Kai-shek and Mao Zedong had capitulated? Freeing some half a million Japanese troops to attack elsewhere.[68] Or what if Russia had capitulated?

Every one of these "what ifs" involves human factors like the will to fight, creativity, aggression, shock, daring, and the ability to look imaginatively into the future. The precise incarnations of such human factors always change as societies and technologies change. But human factors have always been central to the *nature* of war between humans, and always will be.

In our time, each of these "what ifs" finds an echo. You only need to change the names. What if democracies don't stand up to authoritarian states? What if they do?

And we face new questions, too: What if authoritarian aggression succeeds and sparks nuclear proliferation among those who feel threatened?

What if the authoritarian powers develop better human-AI teams that prove as decisive as *Blitzkrieg*? What if China's economy tanks and its ordinary people increasingly resent inequalities with opulent elites? What if research on hibernation leads to treatments that massively slow aging? What if we could grow humans in artificial wombs? What if I ate a second donut?

As this last question suggests, we use "what ifs" all the time in our personal lives, too. Who hasn't left a gathering and then suddenly imagined the perfect witty remark—just after the moment to make it has passed? Who hasn't gotten themselves into a tangle during some job interview, or on a date, and afterward replayed the event a dozen times to see all the ways to avoid the mess? We might ask ourselves: What if I resign? What if I decide to put more into my pension (or less)? What if I have just one more drink at this party?

For both war and our personal life: *What if we had better self-knowledge?*

* * *

Self-knowledge is power, and we've learned much about ourselves in our journey through the fundamental and internal brain regions in Part I. We've traveled from a robin redbreast that uses a Model to link sensation and action to stay alive; past the vital drives that use Models to help us eat, drink, and reproduce; through the visceral instincts of the emotions, risks, and social motives that help us thrive in an uncertain world; and onward to explore Models of physical and abstract spaces and imagine new futures.

All these Models describe how senses can be linked to actions that help achieve goals. They contribute wonderful sections to the orchestra of Models by which our brain achieves its basic goals, the defining features of life: to maintain the body's internal order, and to reproduce. We've seen that we need Models that are close enough to *reality* to be useful, *anticipate* potential problems, and help us act *flexibly*. These ideas, which the acronym RAF can help us remember, motivate cutting-edge neuroscience and remain critical for every new Model we see across the brain.

This chapter also added a radically new capability to our Models, which is crucial for almost everything we see from now on: Models can have internal representations of the world, on which we can run simulations. In this chapter, for example, we saw Models that represented physical space, giving us maps to explore in the safety of our own brains. In the rest of our tour, such internal Models will do so much more.

We're moving up and out now, to the fancier real estate on the outside of the large cerebral hemispheres. This cerebral cortex is what most people visualize when they imagine a brain. Part II will introduce the regions of cerebral cortex that process sensory inputs like vision, sound, or touch (chapter 5) and generate outputs to act in the world (chapter 6). Both perception and action use internal Models to represent the outside world—and how this works may turn upside down what you thought you knew about yourself.

Part II
Proper Application of Force

Almost everybody has hammered a nail into a piece of wood. You need to look carefully to avoid bending the nail or hitting your thumb. Perhaps less consciously, you also need a good deal of information from your joints and skin: Where exactly is your left hand? Where is your right hand? What is this specific hammer's weight and balance? Hammering nails is harder than it may seem.

Teaching my own young kids reminded me how tricky it is to properly apply such force. Especially because I'm right-handed and my kids are left-handed, so I had to swap hands to demonstrate. (Try writing, or hammering, with your nondominant hand and you'll see it's a lot tougher.) Keep checking the nail is at the correct angle. Don't hold the hammer too close to its head. Start tapping gently so you feel the nail getting purchase in the wood, then gradually hit harder. My kids ended up with a piece of wood covered in tiny holes (where nails pinged out), many bent nails, and a smaller number of nails inserted properly. As they grow up, they'll learn about many sizes and shapes of nails, hammers, and materials.

My parents taught me to hammer, I'm teaching my kids—and we're all at the end of a long chain of teaching and learning. The first hammers appeared some three million years ago.[1] The human brain evolved more sophisticated tool use as we used more sophisticated tools. Hammers were given handles tens or perhaps hundreds of thousands of years ago.[2] Since then, the process of cumulative improvement continued but used learning and teaching, rather than evolution. Newer types of hammers enabled new ways to use hammers, for which we fashioned newly specialized hammers, and so on. Hammers are now used to apply force in ways far beyond their origins.

As a neurology doctor, I carried a hammer in my briefcase. The reason began in the nineteenth century, when doctors developed special hammers to tap patients' chests—to hear whether the chest sounded resonant and full of air, or dull and full of gunk. Later that century, doctors adapted the use of those hammers to tap patients' reflexes—and that was the use of my "reflex hammer."

Gradually, reflex hammers and their uses developed over the decades. In the 1920s it's thought that Miss Wintle, a nurse at Queen Square, developed the "Queen Square" reflex hammer that I use: a beautiful design with a heavy, circular, rubber-edged head attached to a long, springy stick.[3]

Wielded by the neurology doctors who taught me in Oxford and at Queen Square, this hammer is an incredibly powerful tool. It applies a beautifully regular amount of force to tap a patient's arm or leg—enabling experts to observe the resulting reflex. An expert neurologist has learned the range of normal and abnormal reflexes from thousands of cases, and can compare this against what they perceive in any specific patient.

This is something new in our journey through the brain—our brain's *most* exquisite capacity at perception and action.

In Part II of our journey, we are now up on the outside of the large cerebral hemispheres, where our abilities start to pull away from other animals. A fruit fly has no cortex. It can fly to a banana and land smoothly, yet it cannot learn to pilot a jet plane. Chimpanzees have many of our capabilities, but lack crucial features of how we use tools, teach, and learn. There is no chimp Sherlock Holmes.

The author of Sherlock Holmes, Sir Arthur Conan Doyle, was a doctor. He based Holmes on one of his old medical teachers, whose powers of perception in the outpatient ward were truly as astonishing as Holmes's.[4]

I, too, have had the honor of working with doctors who can perceive the most subtle clues in a patient's appearance.

Perception is crucial for any clinical doctor, as with many specialists in other fields. I used to run a Queen Square neurology teaching course for doctors from around Britain. A crucial lesson is always: before touching a patient, first *observe.* From the end of the bed: What can you see? What can you hear? Often generalists literally cannot see signs that seem obvious to someone more expert. Only when told the answer can they perceive it.

That's tricky enough with a cooperative patient. But it's harder to put it all together at 04:00 in the emergency room, with the patient's arms and legs flailing around. Getting things wrong here can be dangerous for a patient, even deadly.

And in war, the risk to life is even greater.

* * *

Major Carroll C. Smith was the leading U.S. night-fighter ace in the Pacific theater, downing five Japanese planes.[5] To *perceive* those planes at night and direct fire against them effectively, his brain had to manage fire hoses of raw sensory data.

A single human eye sends more than a million nerve fibers streaming backward in its optic nerve.[6] Those fibers have already summarized data from about 125 million light sensors that enable us to see in dim light (called rods), and another 6 million to 7 million sensors that function better in brighter light for color vision and fine detail (called cones). Most of us have two eyes, providing complementary data so we can calculate depth.

On top of that data from the eyes, we have streams of data about every joint's position in our body, every inch of skin, every smell, and every sound.

Even as Major Smith's brain handled this data to perceive the world, he also had to *act*. Long sequences of complicated movements with arms, hands, feet, neck swiveling, and all the rest.

When artificial intelligence (AI) research began in the mid-1950s, many researchers thought that it would be pretty easy to control an arm to pick up a glass of water from a desk, bring it up to the lips, take a sip without dribbling, and set it down on a table—but that playing chess would be hard.

Wrong.

In what became known as Moravec's paradox, exactly the opposite turned out to be true.[7] Motor skills—just like perceptual skills—require enormous computational resources. We humans don't notice their difficulty, because we are just so awesome at making actions.

So how do we do it?

Our most precise capabilities for perception and action rely on Models that are representations of ourselves and of the outside world.

We don't perceive the world by passing sensory data upward from the bottom of our sensory system to some kind of passive television set in the brain. We perceive a Model of our perceptual world that is a best guess of what's out there, and that Model is updated using sensory data. We act using Models of where our body is and where we want it to be.

These highest-quality efforts from the cortex are needed to compete and survive in combat. The previous chapter stopped at December 6, 1941. If we return to that moment, what precisely can a Russian sniper see looming out of the snow outside Moscow? On that same night, as a New Zealander in the North African desert slides his bayonet into the sand feeling for land mines, what exactly is that resistance he feels? If he can't get through the minefield before sunrise, the men behind will fall victim to German fire.

The next day, December 7, 1941, the Japanese joined the Germans in war—no longer fighting only in China but against the democracies, too. The Japanese launched a surprise attack, of which Winston Churchill learned while at his country residence with the U.S. ambassador. In his memoirs, Churchill later reflected on the magnitude of that attack on Pearl Harbor:

[N]ow at this very moment I knew that the United States was in the war, up to the neck and in to the death.

So we had won after all! Yes, after Dunkirk; after the Fall of France; after the horrible episode of Oran [Mers-el-Kébir]; after the threat of invasion, when, apart from the Air and the Navy, we were an almost unarmed people; after the deadly struggle of the U-boat war—the first Battle of the Atlantic, gained by a hand's breadth; after seventeen months of lonely fighting and nineteen months of my responsibility in dire stress. We had won the war . . .

We should not be wiped out. Our history would not come to an end. We might not even have to die as individuals.

Hitler's fate was sealed. Mussolini's fate was sealed. As for the Japanese, they would be ground to powder. All the rest was merely the proper application of overwhelming force.[8]

But the *proper* application of force is no simple task.

5

PERCEIVING REALITY

THE POWERS OF SENSORY CORTEX

The Japanese pilot jumped into his cockpit. In his preflight checks he had inspected the look and feel of every last piece of machinery as if his life depended on it. Because it did. At 06:00 that morning the aircraft carrier turned into the wind, and he took off shortly after.[1] It was December 7. By 06:45 some 183 Japanese aircraft were heading southward toward the American battle fleet in Hawaii, at Pearl Harbor.

He looked out of his cockpit with pride at the sight, and remembered just two weeks before watching the rising sun over the bay on Etorofu Island. That's where, secretly, over several weeks, Japan had assembled the most powerful concentration of naval air power in the world: six aircraft carriers. They moved stealthily almost 4,000 miles, undetected, to the far north, where scarce shipping and frequent rain squalls gave a curtain of concealment.

Having avoided U.S. perception, now they would play havoc with it.

The pilot looked down to see the tip of Hawaii's Oahu Island. He focused on his task: the biggest mission of his life. One that could give his country enough time to consolidate conquests in the Western Pacific—if they could destroy the main American battle fleet.

Swooping in from the north, he saw seven battleships moored in the middle of the anchorage: a clear view for targeting bombs and torpedoes.

The flight leader broke radio silence for the first time since leaving Etorofu Island, to announce complete surprise: "*Tora, Tora, Tora*" ("Tiger, Tiger, Tiger").

Below, on Oahu, it had been a sleepy Sunday morning. A warning had come in on November 27, so the vast U.S. base at Pearl Harbor was on alert for sabotage. But nothing like this was expected.

Indeed, someone on an American ship spotted the feather of a submarine periscope, but the ship's report at 06:53 was met by skepticism.

At 07:02 in a new radar station on Oahu's north shore, inexperienced operators were looking at the radar display and thought they perceived two pulses. After using a few different ways to look—and to check if it was an equipment defect—they finally decided it was some sort of flight. But the duty officer expected a flight from California that morning and told them to "forget about it."

In the harbor almost every American who saw the planes assumed they were friendly aircraft on maneuvers. A few officers, annoyed at hotshot pilots flying low on a Sunday morning, tried to read their plane numbers to report them. People saw, largely, what they expected to see.

One U.S. veteran recalled a Japanese pilot with his canopy back:

> **He flew so low that I still remember him. He had the leather helmet, like World War II had, and the goggles, and the reason I remember, he had a real thick mustache. As he flew over, he kind of smiled and looked at the ship and flew over toward the hangar there, when he starts laying his first bomb.**[2]

U.S. forces manned their weapons, but too late. The Japanese sank or damaged 18 ships, destroyed 188 American planes, and killed 2,403 U.S. personnel.[3]

When seeking to target deadly force—or, indeed, to defend yourself—no question matters more than this: *What do we perceive?*

For a brain, stuck in its dark, bony vault, to work out what's happening in the world outside is a huge challenge. External reality is like a large, darkened room. A thin beam of light shining into that darkened room can illuminate a narrow slice through the darkness—perhaps revealing parts of some furniture, wallpaper patterns, one side of a child's face, or part of some animal that darts through the beam.

If we add another sense—like adding hearing to vision—a second shaft of perception illuminates a second slice of reality, although the rest remains dark. Then we add more slices from taste, smell, and touch. The darkened room of reality is now sliced up by multiple beams of perception that intersect in places and—although most of reality remains dark to us—within the beams we can search for predators and prey, and perceive enough reality to be useful for survival.

To perceive yet more reality, we could add entirely new beams of perception: the senses we humans inherited are far from the only ones we could have. Many fish, such as sharks, perceive electricity to hunt, elude predators, and attract mates. Bats and dolphins use echolocation.[4]

We could also widen each existing beam of perception: we humans, for example, see only a narrow part of the spectrum of light. Strolling through a meadow or park, we are oblivious to ultraviolet (UV) markings on flowers, which shine out to bees like bright landing beacons. UV lies only slightly above the rainbow of light frequencies we see.

Over time, predators and prey evolve new, wider beams of perception—and new ways to conceal, communicate, confuse, and cheat within these beams. Humans are no different except that we also develop technologies to help us, and these have always been applied in war. When Galileo perfected his first telescope in 1609, he first sought to prove its worth to the leader of Venice through its military uses.[5]

Information gathering has gone from the eye to the telescope to the radar, through different layers of thinking in bureaucracies—and now also through AI. But every new means of perception brings new potential for deception and uncertainty. The west's most famous scholar of war, Carl von Clausewitz, wrote that "War is the realm of uncertainty; three quarters of the factors on which action in war is based are wrapped in a fog of greater or lesser uncertainty."[6]

How does our brain, locked away in the skull, perceive enough of reality to be useful?

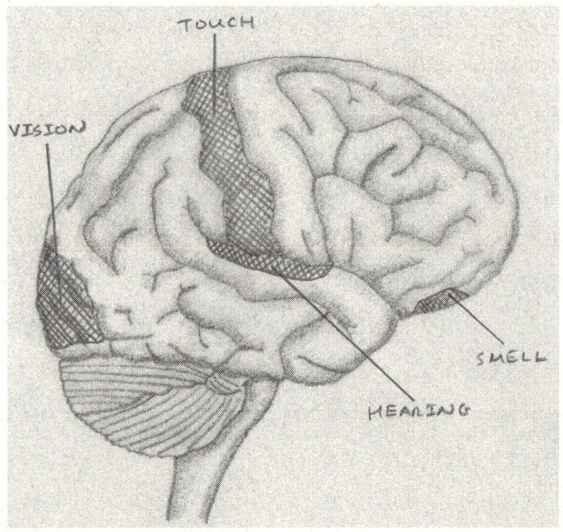

FIGURE 6: Sensory cortex. The cortex has specialized areas for processing sensory data. Visual information is processed at the back of the brain in visual cortex, which receives data from the "high road" up from the thalamus, and as this data moves forward through visual cortex there is processing of more and more aspects like edges and colors. Touch is processed by a strip down the middle of the brain, and sound in an area just below that. Smell and taste are unusual in that they rely on the most ancient parts of cortex, down nearer the bottom of the brain, and do not come via the relay station of the thalamus.

PERCEIVING OUR CONTROLLED MODEL

A typical commonsense idea of perception seems very compelling. Let's take the example of vision. Objects in the real world (whether they're teacups or tigers) give off light waves that hit the retina in our eye. Sensors called rods and cones convert light into electrical signals that pass upward into the brain. Progressively more sophisticated processing identifies features like edges and colors until—like an image on a passive television set—a teacup or a tiger appears in your mind. Finally, by looking at the image on your brain's TV set you can set about dealing with the teacup or tiger (that is, drink or run).

As a notion of how we perceive, this is compelling. Indeed, that's how it intuitively *seems* to me right now as I look at my desk, typing this. But it cannot be right for several reasons. Here are three.

First, we often perceive things that aren't actually there.[7] No "bottom-up" signal exists out there from which they *can* arise, and yet they can look or sound like an entire TV or radio program. About one in ten elderly people with severe hearing or visual loss experience vivid hallucinations, like hearing a choir accompanied by a full orchestra, or seeing people or colored patterns. Hallucinogenic drugs can create the same effect, as the author Aldous Huxley described after taking mescalin, in his 1954 essay *The Doors of Perception*:

> Buildings now made their appearance, and then landscapes. There were Gothic towers of elaborate design with worn statues in the doorways or on stone brackets.[8]

Research also directly links the cortex to perceiving things that aren't actually there. Canadian-American neurosurgeon Wilder Penfield pioneered a technique to map areas of the cortex during neurosurgery. The patient is awake and an electrode is placed on the surface of the brain. (This causes no pain.) A small current passes through the electrode to activate brain cells in that area. This can cause vivid perceptions, as this patient describes:

> A figure, on the left side. Seems like a man or a woman. I think it was a woman. She seemed to have nothing on. She seemed to be pulling or running after a wagon.[9]

Secondly, if we look out of a window, or at the room of a house, it seems that we perceive the whole visual scene in detail and in color—but that cannot be true if the commonsense idea of perception is correct. The human eye has two types of light sensors, called rods and cones. Only the very middle of our retina has the closely packed cones that are good for color vision and fine detail—so only that part *can* see in color and in detail. Only 6 million to 7 million cones cover that small region in the center of our visual field, compared to 120 million rods that cover the rest and sense light and shade. If only "bottom-up" signals coming up from our retinas drove perception, then everything outside the narrow center of our view would be blurry and colorless.[10]

Finally, objects in the world are three-dimensional (3D), and we vividly experience a 3D world of objects—yet our retina can only receive flat two-dimensional (2D) images. Moreover, those 2D images arise from many different lighting conditions and angles. If we look at a white teacup in the garden in bright sunlight, and then see it inside a dimly lit cupboard, the outdoor and indoor light reflecting off it comprise different sets of wavelengths—but still we perceive the same white teacup. How, when we see it from many angles, or in different light, or partly hidden by a teapot, do we still perceive the same cup? This feat of perception is outrageously good: consider that by 1997 computers had conquered the best human chess champion, but it took until 2012 for a computer to attain such abilities to recognize objects even in limited conditions.

The commonsense bottom-up view faces more problems like these—and that's why many in neuroscience have now concluded, essentially, that we perceive a *controlled Model* of the world.[11]

The Model is *controlled* in two ways. One controller is our *expectations* about the world. We expect, when we're outdoors, that light shines from the sun above, so that shadows will be underneath the objects we see. We expect, when sitting at a desk, to see the teacups and books that we left there. And we expect, in London, that tigers are found in the zoo, not in cafés. But our Model must also be anchored to the changing reality outside us (those planes at Pearl Harbor started dropping real bombs). That's why a second controller is the *sensory data* coming up from receptors, such as the retina's rods and cones. This data updates our perceptions and expectations to keep them anchored to reality. This helps us update our Model of the world. If a discrepancy emerges (a prediction error between what was expected and what actually occurred), then something may need explaining: "Look out—tiger! Tiger! Tiger!"

In other words, what we perceive is not a passive TV set in the brain but an actively created Model. And perception isn't a static photograph but a rolling process in which each new version of the Model provides a new set of expectations to compare to the next round of sensory input.

To compete with others—as predators and prey must do—we need both reasonable Models *and* good sources of new data. Both *good expectations* and *good updating*. This applies to all kinds of perception, up to and including patterns in abstract, high-level data. But let's examine a simple example.

If I take my kids to London Zoo, I will see organisms I have never previously seen and behaviors that are new to me. So how can I have good expectations, or even any expectations at all, to make sense of what I perceive?

We approach this kind of situation by using *hierarchies* in our Models. (As you'll see from now on in the book, the idea of hierarchies helps explain a lot of how our brain functions, so it's worth slowing a little.) By hierarchy I mean an ordered set of levels, in which the simpler lower levels serve as building blocks or inputs to the more complicated levels above.[12] In this case, we perceive higher-level things in the world (an animal in the zoo) that are composed of lower-level features (four limbs, a tail, and a face), themselves composed of features that are lower level still (faces have eyes, a nose, and a mouth), and so on.

Hierarchical Models explain much about how the cortex works, and for perception they help organize the cacophonous confusion we face out there: physical features, types of actions, situations, and much more. You are using hierarchical Models right now to understand the words on this page. Tiny lines make up each letter (two lines make T). Letters combine to make words (T, H, and E make THE). You grasp the whole word at a glance, without spelling it out. Words combine to make sentences, sentences to make paragraphs—then chapters, books, and entire libraries.

To generate useful expectations about a specific instance in front of us, however, our Models are not only hierarchical but also *generative*. Generative models are fashionable at the time of writing: helping students do (or cheat on) homework through programs like ChatGPT (Chat *Generative* Pre-trained Transformer) and driving trillions of dollars of tech company stock price changes. But such generative models aren't a new idea.[13] A generative model is a model that can generate new instances of data, such as new pictures of dogs or cats. It does this by learning how the properties of each type of thing varies, so it learns what pictures of dogs can look like and what pictures of cats can look like. From this knowledge it can generate new instances of pictures of dogs or cats. Or even "dog-cats," a picture that mixes the two categories.

With perceptual Models that are hierarchical and generative, we possess a good repertoire of expectations. On my family trip to London Zoo, we're ready to see unusual animals—and if we found a dog-cat we'd soon guess what it might be. But as this trip to the zoo suggests, our controlled Model also needs good updating.

Good updating requires our brain to balance top-down control (by expectations) and bottom-up control (by new data). It does this by taking into account both the strength of our expectation (tigers in the zoo café are very unlikely) and the strength of new sensory evidence (wait!—that *really* looks like a tiger padding between the tables) to help decide what we perceive.[14] If what we perceive differs from our original expectation, that prediction error can update our expectations ("Tiger, run!"). Now we have new expectations to enter into our rolling process of perception (we have a much lower threshold for perceiving tigers in cafés).

Military calamity can ensue without good expectations and updating. Western militaries use the acronym ISR, which stands for "Intelligence, Surveillance, and Reconnaissance." *Intelligence* is crucial for setting good expectations: at Pearl Harbor U.S. leaders at many levels simply did not expect Japanese air attacks, despite the British success in a similar raid at Taranto in Italy the year before. Expectations, as we've seen, led some American onlookers literally to see the Japanese planes as hotshot Americans. Good updating requires actively using *surveillance and reconnaissance*, without which we may not get—or may ignore—useful new data.

At Pearl Harbor, flawed expectations caused a failure to perceive the attack until it was too late. But six months later, improved U.S. intelligence, reconnaissance, and surveillance contributed to the greatest naval victory in a single engagement during all of World War II.

* * *

Aircraft carriers had shown their power at Pearl Harbor, and as the Japanese sought further victories, they outnumbered the Americans in terms of big and capable carriers. But the Americans *also* had an edge—from superior intelligence (including broken Japanese codes) that enabled better expectations, and superior reconnaissance that enabled better updating.

In mid-April 1942, Admiral Chester Nimitz trusted his intelligence and sent two U.S. carriers—*Lexington* and *Yorktown*—against the two large Japanese carriers on the way to attack Port Moresby. In the Battle of the Coral Sea, on May 8, U.S. planes could see one Japanese carrier well enough to damage it, but clouds obscured the second Japanese carrier so it escaped. Japanese pilots sank the *Lexington* and repeatedly hit and damaged the *Yorktown*. Importantly, this fed into a false expectation for the Japanese: following their successes and their exuberant pilots' reports, the Japanese expected the *Yorktown* had sunk and wouldn't trouble them again.[15]

Then a brilliant U.S. intelligence team pieced together scraps of information from scores of Japanese radio transmissions.[16] The team forecast that at the end of May or in early June the Japanese would send four or five carriers to attack an island 1,100 miles northwest of Pearl Harbor, called Midway.

The Japanese sent only four of their six big carriers, because they incorrectly expected that the *Yorktown* had sunk, so that they could rest their two big carriers from the Battle of the Coral Sea. Nimitz sent the *Hornet*, the *Enterprise*, and the repaired *Yorktown*. Adding in the airstrip on the island of Midway for the coming battle, that made it roughly four versus four.

The Japanese sent diversionary forces to distract the Americans. But with strong expectations from his intelligence, Nimitz wasn't fooled. "The striking force," Nimitz told his commanders the day before the battle, "will hit from the northwest at daylight tomorrow."[17]

As he expected, the Japanese attacked Midway Island's airfield at dawn.

Now Japanese reconnaissance failures took center stage: that morning a Japanese reconnaissance plane flew over the U.S. fleet without seeing it, while other reconnaissance planes remained aboard the carriers.[18] Japanese commander Chūichi Nagumo had no reason to worry, because he expected no American strike force within reach. A Japanese pilot eventually reported ten enemy ships north of Midway, but didn't specify what type.

After ten more minutes the pilot reported U.S. ships with no carriers, and only after ten more minutes again did he report: "Enemy force [is] accompanied by what appears to be an aircraft carrier."[19]

At 10:20 Japanese Vice Admiral Nagumo had every reason to believe he was winning and just needed to complete a change of weaponry on the hangar deck. At 10:22 one of the lookouts on the flagship pointed skyward and screamed, *"Kyukoka!"* Dive-bombers![20]

U.S. dive-bombers preferred to dive down out of the sun to conceal themselves from the enemy. One survivor recalled that they looked "like a beautiful silver waterfall."[21]

Those dive-bombers from the *Enterprise* under Lieutenant Commander Clarence Wade McClusky had initially flown too far south, but after a box search, McClusky had spied a lone Japanese destroyer. Its bright white bow wave on the blue sea enabled him to calculate it was speeding to catch up with the main Japanese force.

In five minutes, between 10:22 and 10:27, the Japanese lost the initiative in the Pacific. The Battle of Midway was a stunning success: all four Japanese carriers sank, along with highly trained pilots who were never replaced.

It might not have finished that way. As Nimitz's report described, "Had we lacked early information of the Japanese movement, and had we been caught with Carrier Task Forces dispersed . . . the Battle of Midway would have ended far differently."[22]

Better expectations from intelligence *and* better updating from reconnaissance were crucial.

But, just maybe, those Dauntless dive-bombers coming out of the sun could have been spotted, if the Japanese ships had *extended* their perception, using a new invention being fitted to British and American ships: radar.

PERCEPTUAL ARMS RACES

Survival in the darkened room of reality is competitive. Living organisms have long competed to master—and extend—the narrow beams of perception through which they perceive others, and manage how they themselves are perceived. To grasp how perception works, we must always remember this element of competition.

At London Zoo, my kids love spotting the colorful tigers that stand out so brightly against lush green or dry brown backgrounds. But surely tigers need concealment to get close enough to surprise their prey. Why such bright stripes?

The point to remember is that tigers must be concealed within their *prey's* visual beam of perception. Deer cannot see the colors we can, so the tiger's orange looks the same as green, and it matches the background. And the tiger's stripes help break up its outline to conceal itself and confuse prey.

To compete, the deer can *extend* their beams of perception, for instance by extending their field of view to see more widely (which they do). The deer can also extend the range of colors they "see," for instance by getting help from the warning cries of nearby langur monkeys, who can, like humans, perceive orange as well as green.[23]

Predator and prey can also compete *within* the beams of perception they already have. Faster and more accurate perceptual Models may, for example, help the deer better see the tiger's outline among the trees despite the tiger's stripes.

And as one side extends its perception, or enhances its capabilities within a beam of perception, the other side faces pressure to adapt in the perceptual arms race.

We humans use *technologies* to extend our narrow beams of perception—analogous to how we extended our digestion through technologies like cooking and animal herding.

We can extend beyond the eye's physical limitations in magnification and resolution by employing a microscope, magnifying glass, or optical telescope. As late as the American Civil War in the mid-nineteenth century, only objects visible to the naked eye could be effectively targeted.[24] By World War I, snipers systematically used telescopic sights out to 350 yards—and, by World War II, out to 650 yards. Very useful in some circumstances. But although such extenders may seem to bring pure benefits, there are always trade-offs. A telescope sees farther, for example, but reduces the total field of view so that you see more of less. And as with the deer, sometimes a wide field of vision is better to warn of danger from all sides.

Seeing in the dark has obvious benefits. We humans see the rainbow of colors from red to violet that form a small part of the electromagnetic spectrum—and *below* the red we see, some snakes hunt in the dark using special pits on their forehead, which detect infrared light from their prey's body heat. Machines have existed for some time to extend our sight below and above the electromagnetic spectrum that our eyes can detect, but the usefulness of such extenders depends on whether their benefits outweigh their costs, such as high energy use or being cumbersome. In World War II, reconnaissance aircraft could take infrared photographs that saw through enemy ground camouflage, but it took until the 1960s for real-time thermal imaging to start becoming practical for night vision. Technologies to amplify ambient light provide another way to see at night, and by the Vietnam War the U.S. Starlight scope enabled sharp images out to 400 yards and may have accounted for 15 percent of night kills.[25] But it wasn't until the 1991 Gulf War that improvements to all these night-vision technologies enabled the benefits to greatly outweigh the costs—and so create what U.S. General Barry McCaffrey called the "single greatest mismatch of the war."[26] For at least a couple of decades, these extenders enabled the U.S. military and its allies to "own the night."[27]

Humans can also build sensors for completely *new* beams of perception—at least, new to us humans. A compass senses magnetic fields, so, like the robin redbreast, we can use these to navigate.[28] Bats (in the air) and dolphins (underwater) can perceive reality by sending out waves and sensing how they bounce back. Remarkably, some blind humans have learned echolocation by using clicks from their mouths to detect objects and navigate. The British used sonar in the Battle of the Atlantic and radar in the Battle of Britain. Radar on ships started the war as a novelty, but the British quickly found it useful—and as we've seen, the Japanese might have benefited from it at Midway.

That said, extending our beams of perception only gets us so far. Imagine in the future some super-duper binoculars that can look through walls, or a control panel that displays all the outputs of an array of super-duper quantum radars. Still, for practical reasons (as well as ethical ones), there will be humans somewhere in the loop. Even if it's just a single human commanding a swarm (or swarms) of drones. And enemies can exploit how these humans use Models to perceive what's happening—exploiting expectations, or updating, or both. A human will be perceiving, as was the case in 1941 with the super-duper new technology of radar on Oahu. And someone on the other side will be trying to evade our beams of perception or develop countermeasures. We mustn't fall into the hole of thinking that some elusive technological breakthrough can dispel the fog of war. As a 1943 psychology manual for the U.S. armed forces put it: "Take advantage of another man's brain, use its own rules to deceive it, to make it perceive something that is not real."[29]

Within our beams of perception—however we extend them—as predator and prey, we will always compete to conceal, confuse, communicate, and cheat.

Concealment has long formed part of a warrior's tool kit, from the ancients like Sun Tzu and Homer's Odysseus, to the modern day. Hunters attempt to mask sounds and smells. Camouflage tries to anticipate perception and foil attempts to detect, identify, and pursue.[30] In World War I, as a U.S. colonel noted in 1915, "concealment comes first, and protection is secondary."[31] Every side in that war tried to exploit features of our perceptual system to counter the seeing eye: like using netting to blur edges (our visual system is developed to detect edges) and techniques like painting objects lighter at the bottom to cancel out shadows. Artists were often employed as "camoufleurs" in both World Wars.

One of DARPA's greatest claims to fame is for concealment—their head offices near Washington, D.C., display the stealth technologies they invented to conceal aircraft from radar. But, of course, each new technology will be countered. The Chinese, Americans, British, and others are developing quantum radar that could make current stealth planes look as obvious as a World War II bomber would to a modern radar.[32]

Confusion is a potent perceptual weapon: a zebra's stripes confuse predators' range-finding and edge-detection abilities, particularly while running alongside fellow zebras. Zebras' stripes may also help them avoid parasites like flies by confusing the flies' landing process. Militaries have harnessed this effect, such as in the "dazzle" camouflage that painted big, jagged patterns on World War I warships. Cluttered environments like forests, mountains, and cities may become attractive battle spaces for this reason, compared to the plains on which many great battles of the past were fought. Another way to confuse an adversary's perception is to use decoys, such as deploying flares to misdirect heat-seeking missiles. In World War II, some RAF bombing raids dropped "chaff," tiny metallic strips that confused German radar. And future swarms of drones can introduce a whole extra layer of confusion.

Communication with the enemy can be equally powerful, and its success depends on what the enemy perceives. Sometimes you want to stand out. Brightly colored poisonous frogs blare out "I am danger!"—as do conspicuous military maneuvers made to deter an enemy. Hospitals communicate they are harmless, to avoid air strikes. But, of course, not all communications are true.

Cheating enables harmless butterflies that mimic poisonous species to deter predators—and do so without wasting resources to produce toxins themselves. In some lizards, males mimic the markings of females to sneak past dominant males and reach potential mates.[33] In World War II, some German special forces dressed in Allied uniforms during the Battle of France, and would do so again in 1944 against the Americans in the Battle of the Bulge. During World War II, the Russians honed what has been a hallmark of Russian warfare for centuries: *maskirovka*, which translates as "something masked."[34]

Carl von Clausewitz's "fog of war" doesn't just happen. It is also manufactured and improved.

* * *

On December 6, 1941, we left British and Commonwealth troops fighting in North Africa to hold off the *Panzer* leader Erwin Rommel. By June 1942, Rommel had pushed to the Egyptian border, threatening the Suez Canal—and Middle Eastern oil.

The British launched a deception operation code-named Sentinel that introduced dummy gun emplacements and a whirl of fake activity. Their communication cheated German intelligence into thinking an army camped in the sandhills before them. Facing such a force with his stretched supply lines, Rommel couldn't advance.[35]

But Sentinel only won a delay.

Rommel outnumbered the British tanks and attacked on the night of August 30. Due to the "Ultra" decrypts of German messages, the British expected the attack. Now they had carefully concealed real positions along the long shallow Alam el Halfa ridge, onto which they lured the *Panzers* to repel them again and again. The battle was over by September 4.[36]

Now it was the new British commander's turn to plan his own attack. Bernard Montgomery was vain, egotistical, and talented. And two months after Alam el Halfa, Montgomery planned to surprise the Germans at El Alamein.

The deception plan for the battle was code-named Operation Bertram and comprised seven interlocking subsidiary operations.[37] Cunning methods manipulated enemy perceptions: a supply dump could look like a lorry, a lorry like a tank, and a tank like a supply dump. Ingenious devices included the "Cannibal," which from the air looked like a lorry in a dispersed park of other lorries, but was actually a 25-pound artillery gun. There were four hundred such guns.

One subsidiary operation, "Martello," managed expectations and prediction errors to move tanks toward the front undetected.[38] Initially hundreds of real lorries parked in an area frequently so that enemy reconnaissance got used to them. Then at night the lorries left and were replaced by dummy truck covers, inside which tanks could arrive and hide before sunrise. Those tanks came from farther back, and in turn dummy tanks replaced them so it looked like they hadn't moved.

And so on, with careful camouflage, shadows, and all the rest to confuse, conceal, communicate, and cheat.

And it worked.

The British attack began at El Alamein on October 23, 1942, and ground forward in a brutal battle that lasted the twelve days Montgomery had predicted. The British and Commonwealth forces suffered 13,560 casualties against 20,000 for the Axis. More importantly, the Germans abandoned tanks and guns.[39]

El Alamein was a major, decisive, morale-boosting British and Commonwealth land victory over the Germans, who now retreated fast.

Then far to the west, on November 8, Vichy-held Morocco and Algeria saw the greatest amphibious operation since the Persians crossed the Hellespont in 480 BCE or the Mongols set off to invade Japan. Three-quarters of the troops were American. The Vichy-French collaborators fought back—causing 2,225 Allied casualties—but soon surrendered.

The Germans were caught in a giant nutcracker, with the British under Montgomery advancing from the east, and the largely U.S. forces coming from the west. In six months, 230,000 Axis forces became prisoners of war.

Brilliant perceptual tactics had been key. But in the military it's often said that amateurs talk tactics while professionals talk logistics. Allied victory in North Africa had *only* been possible because, for two tough years after June 1940, superior British logistics with supplies like water and fuel had sustained the fight. Well, what about the logistics of perception?

LOGISTICS OF PERCEPTION

In the darkened room of reality, we can often build more useful Models if we combine our beams of perception. Within the brain each sense gives us singular information: color is a visual event; pitch is absolutely auditory.[40] But instead of a disjointed representation of the surrounding world, we enjoy an integrated multisensory experience.

Combining the senses starts low down in the brain. A rustling sound alone could just be the wind, but combined with a glimpse of animal movement it might be a snake—and the brainstem can make you orient rapidly toward the potential threat. Higher up in sensory cortex, regions that are mainly visual or auditory can be enhanced by perception in the other senses. And the large areas of cortex that lie between sensory and motor cortex—the subject of chapters 7 to 10—often respond to stimuli involving multiple senses.

Again, a note of caution is worthwhile: because our Models use expectations, this means that even multisensory inputs can be led astray.

We tend to think of listening to speech, for example, but what we *see* can influence what speech we *hear*. Listen to a person say "fa" while watching a video of someone saying "ba"—and what you perceive clearly goes with what you see ("ba"). That illusion works because we have strong expectations that speakers' lips normally correspond to the sounds we hear.[41] Our coherent multisensory representations are often more useful than those from one sense alone, but there's never a free pub lunch.

As well as combining beams of perception *within* our own brains, we can also combine beams of perception *between* brains.

Many animals combine perception with other individuals. For a herd of deer threatened by tigers, many eyes help spot predators, and even langur monkeys can contribute. Birds known as babblers live in Africa's Kalahari Desert, and they cooperate in perception: squeaking in alarm so their group can act in response to threats. In larger groups, babblers take turns to perform sentinel duty on a high branch or post. Some of the Kalahari's mammals show similar behaviors, such as the meerkats that also post sentinels.[42]

And humans?

Two hunter-gatherers stalking prey in the Kalahari, crouching next to each other behind long grass, might share information. "I *think*," says one, "I may have seen a movement over there." If the other replies, "I'm *sure* I saw one dead ahead," then their differing levels of confidence can help them combine their perception. So they can decide how best to act. Many experiments show that humans often benefit from such collaboration in perception.

I tested how that works in experiments conducted with colleagues at Queen Square. We tested pairs of participants in the lab.[43] Sitting in a room together, each looked at their own computer screen on which they saw visual stimuli briefly flash on two occasions. Their job was to decide whether the first or second occasion contained a slightly brighter target. After both participants had acted to input their own individual choice, the pair then discussed what they thought the correct answer was—and then one of them would act to input that answer. Collaboration boosted the participants' performance, so that the joint answers were better than even the better participant working alone. Many factors affect that boost from collaboration—as we'll see in Part III—including confidence. And it can be crucial. Logistics is the getting, storing, and delivering of supplies where they're needed, and getting flows of perceptual data or information from sensors like eyes to where they are needed can revolutionize human capabilities.

As humans went from hunter-gatherers to form ever larger preindustrial societies, we developed ever better ways to collaborate perceptually—even changing our very language for colors.[44] Many languages lack terms for color, or only have light and dark, so they may describe a brilliant blue sky as "dark" or like dark dirty water. Languages that develop three terms typically add "red," and numerous languages have five by further adding yellow, and green-blue. The Old Testament and Homer are fuzzy on colors—the sea and sky aren't blue—because their language for describing colors hadn't yet developed as far as in our modern societies. Modern English has eleven basic terms: black, white, red, yellow, green, blue, purple, orange, pink, brown, and gray. The precise terms are largely arbitrary because the color spectrum is continuous, without fixed positions. Korean speakers have fourteen. The broader point is that they ramp up humans' collaborative capabilities.

As societies industrialized, *we industrialized the logistics of perception.* Sensors produced images at industrial scale that were processed, combined, and supplied where needed. By the end of World War I, in 1918, photographs of the trenches from above were taken at a staggering rate of one thousand pictures daily by the British, four thousand by the Germans, and ten thousand by the French. In 1918, the American Expeditionary Force took one hundred thousand pictures in a mere four days before one offensive.[45] A 1918 article in an American scientific review described how images were supplied:

> Cases are on record where only twenty minutes have elapsed from the time a photographer snapped his camera over the German trenches until his batteries were playing on the spot shown. In that time the airman had returned to his lines, the photograph had been developed and printed, the discovery made, and the batteries given the range and ordered to fire.[46]

During the Cold War, America's U-2 spy planes flew over Russian missile sites. These supplied President Dwight Eisenhower with what he needed in order to recognize by the end of the 1950s—despite Russian boasts—how small the Russian nuclear missile arsenal really was.[47] Supplying what he needed to decide how to act.

By the early twenty-first century we'd gone from hunter-gatherer to preindustrial to industrial, and into the *digital* age. We digitized the logistics of perception. Today myriad digital sensors record vast amounts of big data—from computers, smartphones, radars, doorbells, kitchen appliances, cars, satellites, and public surveillance systems—and that data moves at lightning speeds. In this digitized logistics of perception the problem isn't usually lack of data, but how to make this fire hose of data *useful* by turning it into *information.*

Information can be defined as useful data—and turning data into information is where artificial intelligence (AI) comes in today. AI can be defined as computers doing things that would be considered intelligent in humans.[48] A big technical leap in 2012 greatly improved AI for tasks related to perception: of images, speech, or patterns in big data. This technology was then rolled out in digital assistants like Amazon Alexa (auditory perception) or facial recognition (visual perception). Perception was also the point of the biggest U.S. military AI program, known as Project Maven, which harnessed masses of perceptual data from sources like video to perceive objects useful for humans to examine.[49]

These new AI advances are powerful, and perception has been central to their story, so it's a good opportunity to slow slightly and admire these AI advances in more detail. To see how they can reshape the logistics of perception.

This AI revolution built on existing "deep-learning" methods directly inspired by the brain, and key pioneers studied the brain at Queen Square, including the two 2024 Nobel Prize winners for AI: Geoffrey Hinton (who founded a computational neuroscience unit at Queen Square, where my Ph.D. supervisor was based) and Demis Hassabis (with whom I shared an office as he finished his Ph.D. research and I started mine). Their ideas were steeped in neuroscience. The big AI advance in 2012 came from work led by Hinton, which combined three factors: an increase in raw computer power; new datasets for training (a big library of labeled photographs); and some moderate improvements to deep-learning algorithms. Hassabis founded DeepMind, which in 2016 used deep learning to beat the Earth's best human player at the ancient Chinese board game Go. Then around 2020, and building on this work using deep learning, came a big advance in "generative" AI that can *generate* new perceptual information (remember the generative Models from earlier with my kids in London Zoo). Once again this big advance came by combining vast datasets (most of the internet); more computing power; and some technical advances. AI got much better at generating new perceptual information like pictures or sounds (such as "deepfakes," which are media in which people do things they didn't really do), and other types of information like writing (such as ChatGPT).

But while AI now excels at many aspects of perception, or at making decisions in bounded environments like a board game, two big weaknesses currently remain.[50] AI still requires vast amounts of (often previously labeled) data to learn many tasks. And AI remains poor at understanding context, so it lacks common sense: Does that picture show a baby clutching a toothbrush or holding a gun? It's unclear if these weaknesses will be overcome in two years, twenty-five years, or longer. So to harness AI's benefits for the foreseeable future, *human*-machine teams will remain central throughout the logistics of perception. Like any human infant, in this respect, AI needs teachers, supervisors, and helpers.

Chinese military writings suggest these new AI advances are moving us beyond the digital age into an "intelligentized" era.[51] This is probably true, as AI helps us turn fire hoses of digital data into information. But in this new era, regardless of whether AI technologies can overcome current technical limitations, they can *never* remove the "fog of war" against capable adversaries. AI will help as we look into the dark room of reality, *and* AI will add more layers through which we perceive, add more ticker tapes of data or information to interpret, and add more avenues to conceal, confuse, communicate, and cheat. It was the same with the optical telescope, and will be with any other new technology—even hypothetical future "quantum" tech.

As we peer today at reality using quantum physics, particles seem to exist in two places at once, time can stand still, there may be no empty space, cats can simultaneously be alive and dead, and a 2022 Nobel Prize was won for teleporting a tiny particle across the river in the city of Vienna (where Hitler lived before World War I). Chinese quantum scientists are technically capable and even currently lead in some areas of quantum science.[52] And what if future quantum tech lives up to our wildest dreams? In that hypothetical future world with a super-duper quantum logistics of perception: whatever reality looks like to us through quantum perceptual extenders; however brilliantly quantum AI turns data into useful information; and however awesomely quantum communication networks move that information—there would still remain enormous opportunities to manipulate a quantum-infused fog of war.

So too with AI. However solid our perception *seems*, we can only ever perceive part of reality. AI can never *dispel* the fog of war. Instead, already today AI is *changing* the character of perception in war and its associated fog. These colossal changes from AI are the latest in the historical progression as we've gone from hunter-gatherer to preindustrial, to industrial, to digital, and are now entering the intelligentized era. And in any era, however good your logistics of perception—*the other side can always fight back.*

In the Ukraine war of the 2020s, both sides fielded tens of thousands of drones to perceive the battlefield more closely than ever before.[53] That sparked fierce perceptual arms races to use dummy tanks, camouflage, and other creative techniques. It sparked competition to disrupt each other's drones. And it sparked competition to disrupt other parts of the logistics of perception that link sensors to actions. Vital to the logistics of perception are the networked computers in local command posts that link the drones' sensors to "shooters" that deliver firepower—the chain from sensing to acting sometimes called a "kill chain,"[54] which is an updated version of what we saw previously for the World War I trenches. Enemy cyberattacks, for example, can disrupt flow in that chain. A command post's networks can also be physically attacked: they emit electromagnetic fields that the enemy can perceive in order to target them (like sharks detecting their preys' electric fields in the ocean), so today fierce competition rages to perceive, hide, and even mimic those fields.[55] Each side attacks the other's logistics of perception, aiming to prevent the other side properly applying force.

Israel's advanced surveillance apparatus on its Gaza border was outwitted by Hamas on October 7, 2023.[56] Then in the ensuing Gaza campaign, Hamas knew it couldn't successfully compete head to head in the type of warfare at which Israel excels—so instead, Hamas changed the rules of the game by concealing fighters underground and in complicated urban terrain, sidestepping Israel's awesome perceptual logistics for targeting. Forcing the other side to play another kind of game.

You may have amazing abilities to gather data and turn it into information for the board game of chess. But that can become largely wasted perception if your enemy forces you to play an altogether different game of poker.

* * *

This, in effect, is what the Russians did to German forces in 1942. Russia's Georgy Zhukov, that ferocious fireball of energy, had begun his winter counterattack two days before Pearl Harbor and it had saved the Russian capital. But now, months later in the summer of 1942, the Germans had many options for a new onslaught—and they chose to strike farther south, to capture the Caucasus that supplied 90 percent of Russia's oil.[57]

The German plan relied on huge, sweeping maneuvers across hundreds of miles. That *Blitzkrieg* relied on excellent land and air reconnaissance working together on an industrial scale, for which the Germans had prepared for years. In 1938 the German Army's commander-in-chief, Werner von Fritsch, had emphatically stated that the military organization with the best aerial reconnaissance would win the next war.[58] The Germans excelled at producing industrial-scale products to help maneuver troops vast distances across unfamiliar terrain. Over three billion map sheets were produced during the war by the Germans, Russians, British, and Americans—and the Germans accounted for almost half of this output.[59] In 1942, sweeping German maneuvers in the south successfully pushed hundreds of miles farther east than Moscow.

Naturally, the Germans wanted to play to their strengths in the logistics of perception across wide-open vistas.

The Russians wanted to play a different game. To fight in the cluttered confusion of a city of rubble: Stalingrad.

Close-quarters street fighting in Stalingrad nullified many sophisticated German capabilities. Now the crucial field of view might be measured in a few yards, feet, or inches. Russians kept their front lines as close as possible to the Germans to give the *Luftwaffe* little opportunity to target their trenches. Men in patrols fought with submachine guns, knives, or sharpened spades—and they often attacked through cellars and sewers in what the Germans called *Rattenkrieg.* War of rats. They often attacked at night. Frightened German sentries would panic at any sound and start firing. To sidestep the German advantages, each of the multitude of small-scale fights was intimate, personal, and at close quarters—and together across Stalingrad's rubble these fights formed a battle at truly industrial scale.[60] A type of industrialized warfare that, in 1942, better suited the Russians.

Russia's version of industrialized perception included mass-produced scopes for sniper rifles—so they had more snipers, with more scoped rifles, than Germany could match early on. By 1942 they were producing 53,000 annually of the famous "PU" sniper rifle variant alone.[61] Industrial numbers of perceptual extenders enabled industrial numbers of snipers that became seeing eyes scouring Stalingrad for targets.[62] Such snipers became the stuff of Soviet legend. Graduates of the Central Women's School of Sniper Training alone were credited with killing twelve thousand Germans in the whole war.[63]

The Russians held Stalingrad against months of ferocious German attacks, from late August to the winter.

And then the Russians were ready to counterattack.

Zhukov reconnoitered in person. Soviet troops were well camouflaged and brought up at night to be concealed in evacuated villages. At 07:30 Moscow time on November 19, a Soviet bombardment began that feet felt on the ground 50 kilometers away.[64] British and American bombing of the German homeland had called away reconnaissance aircraft,[65] without which the German Sixth Army headquarters missed the Soviet plan that encircled 330,000 Axis troops.

On February 2, 1943, the remnants surrendered. Never before had Germany's army suffered such a big defeat.

Russia and Germany were powerful *industrialized* countries in World War II. The Russians held on in Stalingrad using a type of industrialized warfare that better suited *their* strengths—at a time when they struggled head-on against the Germans' preferred type of industrialized warfare. What lessons can we learn from this as AI moves us into the *intelligentized* age? Already, Chinese military writings argue for sidestepping the type of warfare in which the west currently excels.[66]

Many technologies of war today would be unrecognizable to Britain's desert victor Montgomery, *Panzer* leader Guderian, or Russia's whirlwind Zhukov. When we hear what's possible, it can make the heart sink. Flocks of AI-enabled land mines roosting in trees that can hear the specific language spoken by people below? Underwater drones loitering outside our ports, listening for exactly the right acoustic signature of that aircraft carrier? Enemy soldiers seeing, hearing, and attacking us using packs of robot dogs or swarms of flying drones?

But each of these rely on perception and can, at least in theory, be countered or even made irrelevant. Vital ingredient of that are better understanding how perception works and how perception fits into the bigger picture.

PERCEIVE ⟷ ACT

So far we have thought about the brain in a straight line that goes: *Perceive → Model → Act*. That helps me, writing this book, to explain how the brain works bit by bit. The cortex has large regions specialized mainly for sensory perception, described in this chapter, and other regions mainly for action, as the next chapter describes. But it's truer to say that perception and action are inseparable.

After all, our actions alter perception by changing incoming sensory data. So, if we are going to make good perceptual predictions, then we must take account of our actions. We've already seen that a healthy brain takes account of the sensory consequences of our own actions, such as when our Models prevent us constantly tickling ourselves, so that we can focus on other things.

The eye does the same. The image of the world hitting our retina is constantly jumping around because we move our eyes. How does our brain know that it's our eyes moving, rather than something in the world moving? The nineteenth-century German scientist Hermann von Helmholtz realized that *before* our eye moves our brain already has information about the movement, because the brain sent signals to move the eye's muscles—and this can help predict changes in visual input when the eye moves. Such predictions help us perceive the world as stable. This stability matters for survival, because sudden sensory changes are often caused by things like prey we want to catch, or predators we want to avoid.[67]

In the context of surviving in war, the rolling process of controlled perceptual Models, with expectations constantly updated by incoming data, can seem an exhausting, never-ending struggle. But it's also key to the many ways we enjoy ordinary life, and how as individuals, and as a species, we cumulatively enrich our lives over time. Doctors in training learn to better see and hear their patients. As individuals, when we learn more about new cuisines, we begin to appreciate subtle differences in taste lost to us when we first tried those foods. The same with wines, or fruits, or many other things.

Artists learn to present the world to us in new ways—and that process is often cumulative. The Renaissance saw a flowering of new techniques. The Impressionists gave us new ways to perceive something as familiar as a lily pond. In the later twentieth century Mark Rothko painted abstract blocks of color to create emotional effects, and Bridget Riley put colors, shapes, and patterns together to create optical illusions. During their lifetimes, and from artists before them, these artists learned how to make actions with brush, chisel, or other tools to create their intended perceptual effects. Actions, perceptions, and Models develop together.

Each of these artistic innovations might have military applications, but that's not why I mention them. (Anyway, the traffic runs both ways: war artists have changed the perception and political thinking of civilians.) More fundamentally, artists and warriors alike are trying to form a good Model of the perceptual world. As are we all.

In fact, *everyone's* brain is trying to form a good Model of the perceptual world, which means making fewer errors—and how the brain achieves this goal brings action and perception together in unity.[68]

We've already seen that one way to minimize prediction errors is to update our Model so it is more consistent with the sensory data entering from the world. But another way to reduce future perceptual prediction errors is to make actions—so that the new sensory data will be more consistent with our Model. That is, we change the world to make it more like our expectations.

This point can sound quite mysterious, or even mystical, so let's walk through a couple of everyday examples you might meet in a cozy London pub.

You repeatedly throw darts at a dartboard, each time trying to hit the same number. Each time you throw, you have an expectation of getting the specific number you want. If you get it, that's great, and you've fulfilled the perceptual expectation. But if you don't hit the number, then that is a perceptual prediction error that tells you something useful—and you can make changes to how you act to try to reduce future prediction errors. You might try changing your foot position or keeping your entire body steady so only your arm moves when you throw, or try improving your follow-through, or how you grip the dart, and so on. That is, changing how you perform the action (throwing the dart) helps you actively reduce future perceptual prediction errors (darts missing their predicted number). And you might try changing other aspects of the world to reduce prediction errors, too, such as using darts with different shaft lengths or fin shapes.

To get more advice, you might look at your smartphone, which leads on to a second example. If you are an Apple iPhone user, making actions on the phone to open up screens or navigate between web pages causes few prediction errors, because what occurs after each action fits its expected sensory consequences. But if your battery runs out late at night in the pub, you may borrow a friend's phone. Then if you use an Android smartphone (or vice versa for Android users) and some of the actions no longer lead to the predicted sensory data—this can seem quite jarring. Actions no longer fulfill their anticipated sensory consequences, giving you prediction errors. What then? Well, we can then actively probe, change, and explore different variants of actions to find out which actions reliably give us the sensory consequences we expect. Honing how we swipe, tap, pinch, drag, scroll, flick, shake, and rotate to reduce future uncertainty about what the actions achieve. And again, we can change other aspects of the world to reduce future uncertainty: for example, by changing software defaults to those we are more used to or downloading a familiar maps app.

In both these examples, we hope to minimize perceptual prediction errors by making actions that are more likely to fulfill our predictions. We *actively* sample actions and shape our world.

Equally, our sensory organs actively perceive the world around us: it doesn't seem true, but the gaze of our eyes constantly flicks around to explore visual scenes. My Queen Square colleague Karl Friston pioneered such ideas and describes another example:[69] place your fingertips gently on your leg, keep them motionless for a couple of seconds, and then ask—does your leg feel rough or smooth? It's hard to say, because most of us actively *move* our fingertips over objects to feel roughness or smoothness.

To understand the brain, we *can* begin by considering action or *can* begin by considering perception, but actually they are inseparable.

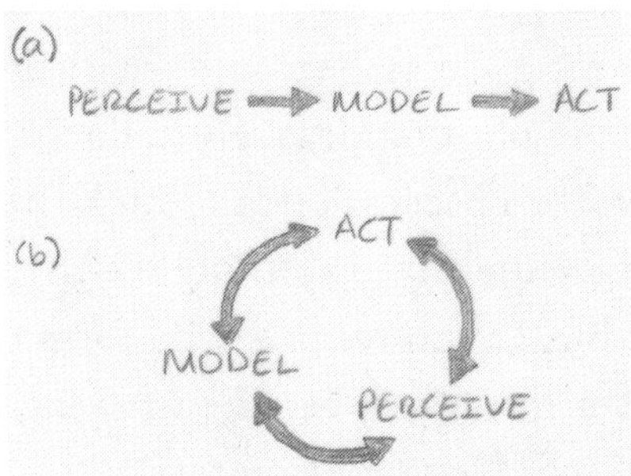

FIGURE 7: Both these perspectives help us understand the brain.

The unity of action and perception can seem enigmatic, like a chicken-and-egg problem where we cannot say definitively which came first or last. Or like paradoxical stories from ancient Greece of an uncatchable fox being chased by an inescapable hound. Ancient Chinese thought contains similar concepts, such as yin and yang in which each contains the seed of the other. Paradoxical ideas have the capacity to chase around and around in our minds. I can find such ideas perplexing and uncomfortable. Should I start with the fox, or hound, or both, or neither?

We should try to become comfortable with such paradox: to learn about the parts, and about the whole, too. We will need such ideas to understand the brain and human societies.

* * *

Karl Marx's tombstone in Highgate Cemetery, not far from me now in London, states: "The philosophers have only interpreted the world in various ways; the point is, to change it." This means that we can't solve philosophy's problems by passively perceiving and interpreting the world as it is, but only by shaping the world to resolve its inherent philosophical contradictions.[20] Marx's tombstone engraving is taken from his *Theses on Feuerbach*, which are the main source of the Marxist doctrine of "the unity of theory and practice," which for Marx meant resolving theoretical problems through practical activity.

Mao Zedong was, as we've seen, part of a Marxist study group at Peking University just after World War I. As Mao became the communist leader over the following decades, he would—with others' help—develop an enormously influential set of ideas. He believed strongly in his earlier years in the power of observation, and took time in 1927 and 1930 to produce reports meticulously examining the rhythms and structures of everyday peasant life.[71] Communists who formulate and implement policy must be forever flexible rather than relying on abstract theory, because as a historian of Mao's China put it: "[I]n Mao's terms, the only correct theory and practice are theory and practice that interact constantly in the concrete here and now of specific conditions."[72]

Mao's 1937 work *On Practice* described the centrality of learning from errors.

> If a man wants to succeed in his work, that is, to achieve the anticipated results, he must bring his ideas into correspondence with the laws of the objective external world; if they do not correspond,

> he will fail in his practice. After he fails, he draws his lessons, corrects his ideas to make them correspond to the laws of the external world, and can thus turn failure into success.

Mao went on to describe the rolling process of observation, theory, and action:

> The perceptual and the rational are qualitatively different, but are not divorced from each other; they are unified on the basis of practice.[73]

Marxism and Maoism are powerful belief systems not only because they tap into visceral instincts like rejecting social injustice. They also get at profound ideas like the unity of perception, theory, and action. These belief systems are not as outdated as many western readers may suppose. After all, China's powerful leader Xi Jinping looks back ever more to the ideas of Mao.

* * *

Our neural machinery perceives the world as it is *useful* for us to perceive it—to be linked to actions that help us survive and thrive. To be useful our Models must usually be anchored to reality—so we aren't run over by a bus, or so we can perceive an attacking tiger—but they are not set up to discern pure objective reality (even though that's how it *seems*). Self-knowledge of how our Models actually work is more interesting than that, and on a practical level, knowing how our Models are warped to be useful helps us anticipate the likely direction of future tech.

The last chapter recalled the warped nature of a child's treasure map, in which an oversized X marks the spot of buried treasure—and our perception, too, will always be warped as our brains attempt to identify what likely matters most to help us act. Good things and bad things. Our perceptual systems cannot simply process their vast amounts of incoming data like a passive TV set; and our gaze doesn't cover every part of the world equally, like an old-fashioned scanner copying every square inch of a piece of paper. Instead, the eye moves around a visual scene looking for what is likely to be most important—things like faces, and within faces things like eyes that often impart the most valuable information. We have the remarkable ability to focus our attention, so that at a cocktail party, for example, we can listen to the conversation we are engaged in and still hear someone nearby mention our name. Put simply, human perception of reality—warped to be useful—is no passive TV set, but already *is* augmented reality.

Silicon Valley companies are spending tens of billions of dollars researching technologies for *augmented reality*, such as special glasses that overlay information onto a view of the world. These technologies differ from extenders like binoculars (that magnify) or spectacles (that correct refractive errors in our eyes' lenses), because they add information that might be useful for us to act—like the name of a plant that might be edible. Or the customer ratings of coffee shops as you peruse an unfamiliar city street. Or as you look in your fridge and see that the milk is low, do you want to order more? Or at a party, where did she buy that dress, and do you want to order it? Or what's his name? Or which people at a cocktail party might be rich, or famous, or dangerous?

Coercive or useful? It's a matter of opinion, but the link to action is unmistakable.

Many people are currently skeptical that augmented reality will become widespread. But we should remember that new augmented reality tech simply supplements how human perception works anyway—which is why augmented reality technologies *are* likely to become ever more part of our future.

Once, of course, augmented reality technologies become practical and affordable enough. In militaries, where cost is less of a barrier, they have been useful every day for decades.[74] In the mid-1980s, Apache helicopter pilots got the first widely deployed head-mounted display that combined head tracking with an image display, which was linked to a thermal imaging sensor—and to weapons. Usefully linking perception to action.

The U.S. F-35 stealth fighter takes this further. Its pilots' helmets cost around $400,000 each and are tailor fitted to each individual pilot's head. Pilots get data from cameras and infrared sensors distributed across the plane, giving them a 360-degree view through the aircraft's frame in any direction using real-time video, thermal imagery, or night vision. The helmet can overlay information from myriad sources about what is valuable and dangerous—the limit is the pilot's brain—to help consider possible actions. And the pilot's gaze can steer a missile.[75]

Such military augmented reality seamlessly extends perception, overlays information useful for acting, and directly links perception to actions. And where military technologies lead, civilian technologies often follow.

Quite a few civilian cars today already have heads-up displays. Big tech companies like Apple and Meta are releasing new head-mounted displays. It seems likely that once devices become unobtrusive and affordable enough they will replace many of our existing screens—just like in fighter planes. Enabling us to perform once unthinkable actions.

6

LEARNING TO ACT

HOW MOTOR CORTEX CONTROLS MOVEMENT

The samurai warrior could draw his sword to parry or strike in any direction from the saddle of his horse. The sword had been in his family for generations, and since childhood he had spent years practicing what was taught to him. Teaching that imparted the cumulative knowledge passed down over generations.

His tool, his weapon, felt like an extension of his arm.

His descendants lived as samurai until the nineteenth century, and dedication to military expertise lasted into the twentieth century even as the tools changed. Japanese pilots flew the fearsome Zero fighter plane in World War II. "I felt that a Zero fighter was to me what a sword was to the samurai," a fighter pilot recalled, "and I felt that I must manipulate the plane just as if it were my own body."[1]

But total war requires more than specialists: millions needed training to fight. In 1940 the U.S. military started with 458,365 soldiers, sailors, and marines. By the war's end 12,055,884 men and women served in all U.S. military branches.[2] Civilians like my great-uncle Sydney Spiers learned to be citizen-soldiers.

So, *how do we learn to act?*

The motor cortex is a large region just in front of the middle of our brain. It initiates the movements we make, from sword thrusts to tool use. As we learn, motor cortex can change its structure and how it functions. Such change is seen in many parts of the brain, like when humans learn to drive a taxi, or when monkeys learn to use a rake as a tool to get food. Neuroscience helps us understand how that learning works. What really, for example, does ten thousand hours of practice achieve?

The brain also rewires itself around the implanted electrodes used in direct brain-computer interfaces, for which research advances are announced every year from Chinese labs and Elon Musk's Neuralink. How could such plasticity enable the control of hands, or octopus tentacles, or abstract cyber defenses in battle spaces beyond our current comprehension?

Humans are better at learning to do a wide range of actions than any other known organism. And that involves our brain's relationships with three things: teaching, learning, and tools. Most of us learn skills, teach others, and use tools in our everyday lives at work or with our families—and self-knowledge of how this actually works, not just how it seems, can help us do this better.

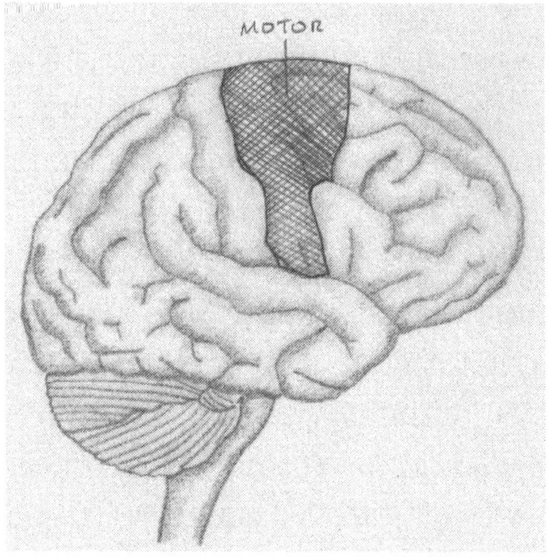

FIGURE 8: The motor cortex.

PLASTIC MODELS

Everything our brain does is to help us act more successfully, to achieve our objectives. Apart from secreting things like sweat, we act entirely by controlling our muscles. Muscles give us our voice, our writing, our nonverbal communication through gestures, our eye movements. The author Jean-Dominique Bauby was almost totally paralyzed, but he could move the muscle that blinked his eye to dictate *The Diving Bell and the Butterfly*.

Learning to act is hard, but we take it for granted. For half a century after AI research took off in the mid-1950s, it failed to get close to the motor skills of a human toddler.

Why is it so difficult? Take a moment to consider the sheer complexity of movement when we play tennis.[3] We have uncertainty about where the ball will strike the racket, and which type of shot we want to make (lob, passing shot, and so on). Our body's sensors aren't perfect, which adds variability about where they tell us our arm and body are. Muscles aren't perfect either, so if we try to play exactly the same forehand many times we always find a spread in where the balls land. We have about two hundred joints and six hundred muscles, giving us many different ways these dimensions can combine. This leads to complex dynamics: if you are standing up and you raise your arm, for example, then the first muscles that contract are in your legs, to keep you from falling over. Time delays make control hard: what you see of the world is delayed by about a fifth of a second. How your muscle systems work also changes over time: within a single match, fatigue changes the dynamics of how your arm works; and over longer periods you may lose fitness, regain it, and eventually get old.

To cope with these complexities, we have a large region of cortex for motor control that sits just in front of the middle of the brain (Figure 8). This motor cortex is crucial for us to learn, plan, control, and execute movements. Nerve fibers go directly down from motor cortex to the spinal cord, where they connect to fibers that directly stimulate muscles. As a student at Queen Square, I volunteered to have my motor cortex stimulated by having a magnetic pulse directed onto it through my skull (a safe technique called transcranial magnetic stimulation, or TMS). It's strange to see your hand move without you doing anything.

A fly can land without a cortex, but as we noted earlier a fly can't pilot an aircraft—because cortex gives the flexibility to learn amazingly sophisticated actions and to generalize between actions. The motor cortex adds an additional loop of neural machinery, above more primitive control systems lower down in the brain that it controls and shapes.[4] It can translate abstract intentions into movement patterns, and can flexibly generate many different movements in response to the same sensory signal. That's why a tennis player can learn in the abstract about crosscourt forehands, drop shots, and defensive lobs; can generalize between similar types of shots or between contexts like singles and doubles tennis; and can choose flexibly—in an instant—which shot to use. Cortex also enables us to generate actions that barely depend on outside prompts, like physically sitting down to write poetry.

Central to how our motor system learns and makes actions are Models that help us turn a more abstract representation into a practical set of movements, such as learning to use a new tool in the kitchen or garden. To illustrate how we start with an abstract representation of a new action, consider the revolutionary "Fosbury flop."

In high school, Dick Fosbury was a good high jumper, but to win the engineering scholarship he wanted, he needed to improve.[5] Like other high jumpers he had learned to scissor his legs over the bar, to avoid injury by landing on his feet. But after his school replaced the wood-chip landing pad with soft foam rubber, he realized that instead he could turn his body, sail backward over the jump, and land on his back. Once he turned this idea into action, he won gold at the 1968 Olympics in Mexico. Every competitor afterward copied his invention (and he got his scholarship.)

To be clear: Fosbury settled on an idea and learned through practice to do it again and again so it became easy. He started more abstractly, and then learned over time to build basic patterns and link them together.

Some aspects of motor learning are always abstract and independent of which muscles turn them into concrete actions: as you can try right now with a pen and paper.[6] First, sign your name with your dominant hand. Then use your nondominant hand. Then hold your pen between your teeth. Then between your toes. The signatures get less smooth, but remain startlingly similar.

Models also help us execute our actions. In the last chapter we saw how our Models give us a colorful, three-dimensional view of the world even though our retinas actually receive mostly black-and-white, two-dimensional images. Similarly useful Models of ourselves and the world facilitate actions.[7]

If we want to hit a return shot in tennis, then our perceptual Model will estimate the ball's velocity and position, to simulate the ball's expected trajectory and account for delays in sensory processing. Our motor-planning Model simulates the ball's current trajectory and our potential body movements (such as a forehand or backhand) to generate an action plan. Once the action plan has been specified, motor commands can be kept on track by Models that combine sensory feedback and predictions—as with the Model that stops us tickling ourselves—to cancel out irrelevant sensory effects.

So we have wonderful Models to develop abstract representations of plans and execute them. But like Fosbury practicing his flop, our Models must also be learned, practiced, and *changed*.

Something is "plastic" when it is easily shaped or molded. Neural plasticity is a general term that refers to our brain's functional and structural changes as we develop, interact with our environment, age, and respond to trauma.[8] In chapter 4, we saw that when London taxi drivers learn an enormously detailed London map, they physically change the structure of their hippocampus.

Learning actions changes the physical structure of the brain regions that control those actions, including motor cortex. We can detect these structural changes using magnetic resonance imaging (MRI). A number of studies have looked at how brain structure varies with expertise for specific actions. In professional typists, areas including the motor cortex correlate with the individual's typing experience. In golf, greater expertise correlates with significant change in areas including motor cortex. Professional musicians have increases in the auditory and motor areas compared to nonmusicians, and the amount of practice usually correlates with structural change in these areas. Other studies show causal links, for example scanning brains before and after training.[9]

Recent work also shows how our models can flexibly generalize our learning between skills[10]—something that even today's most advanced AI can't yet do well. That is, we can learn remarkable Models for tennis, and if we play with a new racket or switch from tennis to squash, we can generalize from one experience to the others. For a single tennis shot, the brain can draw on multiple memories, each in proportion to how much the brain believes that memory is currently relevant. If the context seems new—like the first time playing squash after years of tennis—then the brain can generate a new memory for that context. Over a lifetime, humans learn to skillfully handle an astonishing number of objects, from shoelaces to chef's knives. This creates a wealth of partially overlapping Models for skills, and we can apply relevant ones to give us a head start in new situations.

Of course, such plasticity takes time. But how much time? Or, to put the question differently, what enables some humans to develop high expertise?

It's not only innate ability, or only many hours of practice, or only learning effectively. All three are necessary and none alone is sufficient. Innate abilities vary between people, but although talent is crucial it isn't very rare for many skills. Spending a lot of time acquiring expertise in fields like music, tennis, or surgery is extremely valuable because it gives the feedback from which our Models can improve (for example, learning in detail about sources of variability in ourselves and the world). Spending a lot of time also gives us the wide range of contexts that helps us build good Models (like unusual tennis shots or types of opponent, or unusual medical cases for surgeons). Something like ten years or ten thousand hours of practice—figures largely based on research by K. Anders Ericsson—isn't a bad rule of thumb to excel at fields like professional golf, music performance, or chess. We do need innate ability and time, Ericsson argues, and in addition, we also need the third factor: to learn effectively through higher-quality practice that can be called "deliberate practice."[11]

Such deliberate practice helps develop extreme expertise, and it is also key to learn skills well enough to be useful at many levels—whether in twenty hours, fifty hours, or a thousand hours. During World War II, the United States military expanded from half a million to twelve million personnel so rapidly that there wasn't time to train everyone to ten thousand hours of expertise. The aim was getting *good enough* to carry out their roles. Good enough skills, as well as extreme expertise, matters today, too.

This is illustrated by a recent report from my think tank in Washington, D.C., the Center for Strategic and International Studies, hypothesizing about a near-term U.S.-China war over Taiwan.[12] That report suggests that support personnel on U.S. bases now are too specialized, and that given the number of casualties predicted on U.S. bases, surviving personnel will need broader skills to cover multiple roles.

So, what is deliberate practice? Deliberate practice is goal-oriented. By knowing what you are trying to achieve (like Fosbury developing his flop, or an adult learning to touch-type) you can work backward to practice the various components. That also helps eliminate irrelevant training. Breaking the plan into smaller steps with deadlines can help, to provide feedback on progress.

It also helps to get feedback from someone experienced, or by making a record of yourself at the task. To become a good public speaker, you might record yourself and compare it to other videos of speakers. Teachers or role models can help us see errors and omissions, as we'll see later in the chapter. Getting worse before you get better is a real possibility, because stretching yourself often provides the most informative feedback for your Models. And don't worry if you didn't start learning a skill as early as Tiger Woods started learning golf, because it often helps to sample different activities so your Models can generalize between them—something that particularly helps in "wicked" environments. In such environments the rules are often incomplete or unclear, patterns may not repeat themselves, and feedback can be delayed or inaccurate.[13] Like in war.

Better self-knowledge of how we humans actually learn—and what improves learning—is crucial for every military, because training has been central to military supremacy since ancient times. A crucial foundation of Roman military success was the disciplined training of new soldiers by their legions. These long-standing institutions had strong identities and experienced centurions to induct new soldiers.[14] "Their exercises are unbloody battles," wrote Flavius Josephus of the Romans in 75 CE, "and their battles bloody exercises."[15] In the late 1500s the rediscovery of "Roman" ideas of discipline and training revolutionized European militaries, and hugely amplified European states' strategic power.[16] From ancient

China, we have only one story that purports to come from the warrior-philosopher Sun Tzu's life—about how he trained the emperor's once-giggling concubines to perform disciplined military maneuvers.[17]

Military training has many functions. It helps soldiers assimilate new tactical thinking well enough to apply fluidly, like Fosbury's flop once he'd practiced. It enables soldiers to come to grips with—and master—innovative technologies. It standardizes the behaviors of troops, so they can better coordinate with each other and be commanded more easily. Inculcating battle drills and set procedures also means that when exhaustion or fear makes rational thought all but impossible—as we saw in chapters 2 and 3—individuals can still react and, in the words of a military scholar, "in the process they regain themselves, pushing fear aside."[18]

Training will be crucial in any China-U.S. war over Taiwan. China has fought no wars since its 1979 border conflict with Vietnam, so good training is China's only route to military effectiveness. U.S. troops have learned from recent high-tempo life-and-death conflicts. But only some of that U.S. learning will generalize, because nobody since the British in the 1982 Falklands War has done anything like the combined naval and air operations that could decide a China-U.S. war. For that, both sides can only train.

And how well do Taiwan's soldiers train today? In Ukraine in 2022, training by British and U.S. forces *before* the Russian invasion was pivotal for Ukraine's surprising success.[19] In contrast, Taiwan's conscripts often liken their time training to "summer camp," and joke about sweeping floors, not learning to fire weapons.[20] To stand a chance, Taiwan must train effectively.

* * *

German troops were more effective on land than their opponents in World War II—and training played a large part. Before World War I, the Germans spent more on training grounds than the French.[21] During that war they devoted more thought and resources to training "storm troops," which would provide core ideas for training in the interwar period. And interwar thinkers like the *Panzer* pioneer Heinz Guderian placed high value on training at all. As Guderian wrote in the 1930s: "Fire control and a high standard of [tank] gunnery training are the factors that will contribute most toward victory."[22]

Before World War II, and in its early phase, the Germans crammed in as much training as possible, which was crucial because during 1939 their army grew fourfold: from 1.1 million to 4.5 million men. Five divisions created shortly before war began had received a mere eight weeks' training. That's why the Phoney War of 1939–1940 was a lucky opportunity for the Germans to train intensively, learning from the lessons of the Polish campaign. Well-trained troops made the German *Blitzkrieg* possible, in highly trained infantry units as much as in specialist *Panzer* and aircraft crews.[23]

By 1943, many German troops had also learned from years of hard fighting, adding to their advantages from training. Something almost no Allied land forces could match.

And by 1943, the shock of the previous year's defeats on land in North Africa and Stalingrad had spurred the Third Reich to throw off any complacency.[24] Armament production had more than doubled. That put better German tanks, aircraft, and submarines in the hands of skilled operators, who inflicted terrible losses on the Allies.

On the Eastern Front, on July 5, 1943, the Germans attacked again. They had more than 750,000 soldiers, 2,450 tanks, and 1,830 aircraft in place. Learning from the Stalingrad debacle, they chose more open ground around a bulge in the Russian front line near Kursk. Victory would trap 75 percent of Russian armor.[25]

How could the Russians withstand them?

A conventional view is that the Red Army overwhelmed the Germans with sheer numbers and buried them with corpses. That is not right.[26] By 1943 Red Army units were short of manpower, too. The Red Army had tried continuously from 1942 onward to learn from mistakes, improve training, and modify tactics to reduce losses. Specifically, in defense of Kursk, an intensive program of training was undertaken for Russian antitank and artillery forces.[27]

Commanded once more by Georgy Zhukov, the Russians held, and eventually unleashed a massive counterattack. The Russians had raised their game.

And as the war progressed, a new weakness in the German and

Japanese training, particularly of pilots, became evident: they did not send their best pilots back as teachers.[28] Slowly but surely that began to tell, because nothing matters more for human success than teaching.

TEACH ⟷ LEARN

Send most individual humans naked into the African savanna without any equipment and we would die. Nineteenth-century European or U.S. explorers, tough and resourceful as they might be, could starve to death surrounded by unfamiliar foods that local hunter-gatherers knew to prepare the right way. Mind you, if you were to send a hunter-gatherer into outer space to conduct a spacewalk in an astronaut's suit—well, *they* would struggle to survive. Indeed, they might struggle if dropped into downtown modern-day Minneapolis. How we act often *seems* so straightforward that this obscures from our self-knowledge the outrageous reliance we have on those who came before us.

Our human ability to develop *cumulative* knowledge between us through teaching *and* learning—often over many generations—gives us the repertoire of actions we need to survive. Teaching and learning are mutually reinforcing: being a better teacher pays more dividends when you have better learners; and being a better learner pays more dividends when you have better teachers. A little improvement in teaching enables a little improvement in learning, and so on. In a continuous spiral of improvement that accumulates in a way you wouldn't get from either teaching or learning alone.[29]

And we can get better at both sides of this teaching-learning spiral.

Teaching is so central to humans that it helps explain why our lives go through such distinctive stages: from fat and uncoordinated babies who are learning machines, through to the elderly who can no longer reproduce or hunt but have a reservoir of skills to teach.

Teaching is fundamental to the evolution of human societies, and it's surprisingly rare in nature. As late as 2006 teaching was thought to be uniquely human,[30] and there remain no convincing examples of teaching in many species where we might expect it, like the nonhuman primates. Chimps are good at learning by watching and doing. Young chimps are adept at learning new skills from their mothers, such as how to use a stone tool to crack a nut. But no concrete evidence shows that chimp mothers actively teach. Why?

Teaching is a special form of helping behavior in which a teacher goes out of their way to help others learn, and like with all types of helping, there is a cost to the teacher. Species teach when the benefits outweigh the costs—for instance when getting actions wrong is dangerous and costly. It costs a young chimp little if they go wrong cracking nuts or fishing for termites because those activities aren't dangerous, and anyway nuts and termites are niche items in a chimp's diet.

The cost-benefit balance is different for meerkats, who live in extended family groups in the Kalahari Desert. Adult meerkats teach pups how to handle dangerous prey like scorpions, which are nutritious but can kill. To learn well, pups need teaching.

Very young pups are given freshly killed food. A little older, they get a scorpion with the tail nipped off. Eventually pups get live, intact prey. This procedure is a bit of a fuss for the adults, but the benefits outweigh the costs.[31]

Our own ancestors would have got a good return on investment for teaching increasingly sophisticated ways to hunt, make tools, forage, and cook—all things that take time to learn and are necessary for survival. Gradually, the teaching-learning spiral's cumulative knowledge took us ever further from our evolutionary origins as more typical apes, and we came to depend ever more on these skills and on teaching itself.

We humans also became particularly good at *social learning*—that is, learning from other humans who might have something to teach us. Far better than our ape kin.

Researchers compared 106 chimpanzees, 32 orangutans, and 105 German children across thirty-eight different cognitive tests.[32] The two-and-a-half-year-old humans had bigger brains than the chimps, but differed little on tests of space (for example, rotating objects), quantities (relative amounts, adding or subtracting), and causality (select the right tool to solve a problem).

Both proved a touch smarter than orangutans. Instead, the human toddlers trounced chimps and orangutans alike at social learning, where the participants observed a demonstrator use a tricky technique to get something valuable (like getting food from a narrow tube). Moreover, humans keep getting better at social learning for a couple more decades, whereas chimps and orangutans reach their peak in these tasks by three years old.

Other studies have shown that our tendency for social learning is so strong it can even get in the way. Although a random action might be advantageous in games like rock-paper-scissors, we tend to copy each other automatically when one person reveals their choice slightly before the other.[33]

We also "over-imitate" what we've learned socially. Research compared human children, adults, and chimps who watched someone perform a series of steps to get a reward out of a large, opaque, sealed box.[34] Unlike the chimps, human kids and adults tend to copy irrelevant steps, even when we're alone or have been told explicitly not to copy them. Such findings occur in industrial societies and also in Kalahari Desert populations who lived until recently as foragers.

A variant of that task used a clear version of the box to show that some steps were pointless—and chimps outperformed Scottish children aged three to four years. The kids carried on copying all the irrelevant actions, but the chimps immediately dropped the irrelevant steps. We can't help ourselves; we are avid social learners.

But what might seem pointless isn't actually always pointless. When I was a medical student, I often learned long, detailed procedures—such as the neurology examination in which you use a Queen Square tendon hammer—and back then, many steps seemed pedantic or pointless. Or perhaps just hidebound tradition. But months or years later, when I understood more, I realized many actually did have a good rationale. It's easy to cut corners and skip steps during practice, but in the real world they can save a life. And I'm sure that once I was a bit older and became a teacher, others went through the same process as they learned from me.

Our roles in the teaching-learning spiral change over a lifespan, which helps explain changes in brain and behavior over our lives. And perhaps why we live so long.

Human infants are weak, fat, and uncoordinated[35]—but their brains are in many ways developmentally advanced at birth compared to other mammals'. Before infants can walk, they selectively learn from others based on signs of the others' competence. These advanced brains are highly plastic, because unlike those of other primates, much of the human brain's wiring remains uncoated with myelin for many years. And the brains continue to expand fast. Infants and toddlers are social learning machines.

Children become sophisticated judges of other humans' mental states by about age four or five, as we will see in the next chapter. This helps the children infer others' goals, strategies, and preferences in order to aid or trick those others—*and* it helps the children copy and learn.[36]

Adolescence is a distinct biological period of development, beginning with puberty, which typically occurs at eleven or twelve years old in the developed world. Adolescence isn't a purely western phenomenon, with a recent study of more than five thousand people aged ten to thirty, for example, showing remarkably consistent developmental trajectories across eleven countries, including Jordan, Kenya, the Philippines, the United States, China, India, and Columbia.[37] And adolescence goes on later than most people think, with significant changes in connections between brain regions continuing up to around twenty-five years of age. Adolescence is associated across many cultures with changes in risk-taking, self-consciousness, and peer influence. In 2018, 70 percent of enlisted troops (that is, not officers) in the U.S. Marines were under twenty-five[38]—big, strong, and prepared to take risks for comrades, but with more to learn.

The strength and speed of human hunters in hunter-gatherer populations peak in their twenties, but because hunting success relies more on skill, that hunting success actually peaks around age forty.[39] Chimpanzees also hunt and gather, but humans in hunter-gatherer societies take much longer than chimps to be capable of attaining enough calories to sustain themselves (roughly eighteen years in humans compared to only five years in chimps), and humans keep on learning for many years after reaching that break-even point.

In modern armies like the American and British, more senior enlisted troops such as drill sergeants or sergeant majors are often around thirty years old or more—older than most troops and junior officers—and their experience provides a vital backbone. This follows in the footsteps of what military historian John Keegan described as the Roman army's ultimate strength: "The Roman centurions, long-service unit-leaders drawn from the best of the enlisted ranks." Keegan describes how these centurions "imbued the legions with backbone and transmitted from generation to generation the code of discipline and accumulated store of tactical expertise by which Roman arms were carried successfully against a hundred enemies over five centuries of almost continuous war making."[40]

Rome's teaching-learning spiral changed world history.

What about elderly humans? Human hunter-gatherers live decades longer than other primates[41] and often act as a crucial store of cumulative knowledge. It helps explain why human females in particular live so long after menopause, which happens at around fifty years old in hunter-gatherers or modern society—and this is in stark contrast to all our primate kin who, as in most species, keep trying to breed until death. It seems likely that as well as providing another pair of hands, grandmothers acted as repositories of knowledge about topics from breastfeeding to childhood illnesses.[42] And cumulative knowledge may also help explain the elderly's prestige in most traditional societies.[43] In many accounts of such societies, the elderly were revered and received special treatment due to knowledge of important domains like lore, magic, hunting, rituals, decision-making, and medicine. In the modern military, they might be invaluable mentors. And then, when their mental faculties decline, they tend to rapidly lose status. When they are no longer useful to teach.

* * *

The German military had a long tradition of teaching land warfare seriously. Not least following reforms by Carl von Clausewitz and others in the early nineteenth century. Their systems went from schools teaching children all the way up to military colleges. Guderian himself taught military history and tactics during the mid-1920s.[44]

The first serious U.S. encounter with German troops, during 1942 in North Africa, was a rude awakening: inexperienced U.S. troops were soundly beaten at the Kasserine Pass.

In 1943, U.S. forces would have to do better, because success required them to conduct complicated amphibious landings in Italy—followed by fighting off an inevitable German counterattack. It is a testament to American military education that it rose so rapidly to this challenge. And to a remarkable U.S. soldier who anticipated this challenge many years ahead of time: George C. Marshall.

Marshall was sworn in as the Army chief of staff on September 1, 1939, the day Germany invaded Poland. For six years, Marshall would direct the training, equipping, and leading of U.S. forces that swelled from some half a million personnel to twelve million. Winston Churchill called this remarkable man the "organizer of victory."[45] And Marshall had anticipated, *more than a decade* before even being sworn in, that this would require industrial-scale teaching.

Back in 1927, Marshall had begun revolutionizing the methods and content of teaching at the U.S. Army's top training institution, the Infantry School at Fort Benning, Georgia.[46] He was directly responsible for its curriculum. He anticipated then that most troops would arrive as civilians in a future mobilization. "We must develop a technique and methods so simple and so brief," Marshall maintained in 1929, "that the citizen officer of good common sense can readily grasp the idea."[47]

To help students apply key ideas, Marshall moved the tactics course mostly into the field, and staged the tactical problems to become increasingly challenging.

He threw unexpected scenarios at officers in every exercise—so they could learn from and cope with prediction errors. Instead of instructors conducting field exercises in the same old training areas, he asserted that good tactical teaching "demands a wide variety of terrain and frequent contact with unfamiliar ground."[48] He made students lead real units across real terrain in the field, and taught coping with adversity and learning from errors—not how to do things perfectly. He also reduced the class size so that although fewer officers were educated, each spent more time learning—and these better educated officers were then expected to go back to their units to teach others. The teaching-learning spiral.

Marshall's reforms changed U.S. Army teaching for years afterward, and passing through as students or instructors during his time were some *two hundred* future generals.[49]

In our time, AI is moving us far beyond the industrial era into what the Chinese military call the "intelligentized" era. Would a modern-day Marshall try to move us from industrial to intelligentized teaching and learning? Probably. Generalizing learning across contexts is crucial for our Models to learn. Clever new training ranges can change daily using moving walls and augmented reality, to provide multiple prediction errors and contexts. So far no military has begun to systematically develop such revolutionary AI-enhanced teaching—but if (when) they do, then success will depend as much on self-knowledge about how our plastic Models actually learn as on any technology. So we can effectively teach and learn the myriad military Fosbury flops. And a lot of that will involve learning how to use weapons, and other tools.

TOOLS ↔ BRAINS

Human evolution cannot be understood without tools. Violence, hands, weapons, and other tools all play parts in how our human ancestors evolved over the past 6 million to 8 million years, as we turned from the common ancestor we share with chimps, into modern *Homo sapiens*. Around 4.2 million to 6 million years ago we developed the ability to walk on two legs, which gave us the chance to develop our exceptional hands. About 2.6 million years ago, early humans in East Africa started holding hammerstones in those hands to smack stones to create sharp flakes. Such tools helped us butcher large animals.[50]

Around 400,000 years ago, early humans began fashioning a powerful new tool that our hands could throw: wooden spears that could kill large animals, and kill from a somewhat safer distance. Three long wooden spears from that time were found at Schöningen, Germany, with stone tools and more than ten horses that had been butchered.[51]

Our use of these tools, and related technologies like domesticating animals, literally reshaped our bodies. Compared to chimpanzees, we are wimps.[52] A juvenile chimp can easily overpower strong adult human males in a wrestling match, even without its ferocious canines. Tools that changed our eating habits and diet withered our bowels compared to other primates: our mouths and lips are small, our chewing muscles puny, our stomachs have only 60 percent of the typical surface area, and our short colons only weigh 60 percent of what they should.

We depend so much on tools that this couldn't have happened overnight. Once again, in this process our bodies and brains co-developed with our tool use. We became ever smarter in our use of tools and ever more dependent on using tools: a *brain-tool spiral* in which one facilitates improvement in the other, which further facilitates improvement in the first, and so on, resulting in a continuous spiral of improvement. Each step may be small, but the *cumulative* effects are profound.

It's hard to imagine teaching the nuances of a Queen Square tendon hammer to an early human, who was unacquainted with even the first hammers (which, you recall, had no handles). But then nor would it be easy to teach even an intelligent ancient Greek citizen some fairly elementary computer skills.

Tools also change our brains *within* our lifetimes. This helps explain why tools can feel like a direct extension of our bodies. Classic research with monkeys shows this change taking place and—full disclosure—my wife did some of this research during her Ph.D. in London and Tokyo. Her professor in Japan, Atsushi Iriki, recorded from brain cells in macaques, which are active when the macaque sees something near its hand.[53] He then taught the monkeys to use a rake to retrieve things (a bit like a croupier at a casino), and soon afterward those same neurons responded if the monkey saw things near the rake's end—as if it was an extension of the hand. MRI scanning of macaques before, during, and after they learned to use the rakes also showed changes in brain structure related to this tool use.

Exploring these effects in humans has huge potential to restore the movements of people who are paralyzed, and to extend our bodies by giving us an extra thumb, or perhaps even a tentacle. Researchers from Queen Square[54] recently showed that people can learn to use a "third thumb"—a robotic digit strapped to a user's hand and controlled by their big toes. Brain imaging showed that this altered the brain's Model of the hand. To examine how the brain represents such prostheses in the real world, the researchers studied London litter pickers who use a grasping tool to pick up objects with very different shapes and weights, such as cups containing fluid or cigarette butts. Once again, the brain's internal representation of the tool changed.

New tools will still require learning and teaching—giving someone a tentacle doesn't make them a tentacle expert overnight. It may take weeks of deliberate practice for basic competence, and years to become a true tentacle samurai. To reshape our plastic Models as we do when mastering other skills.

That training could save lives, as could the tool's design. The B-17 Flying Fortress dropped more bombs than any other American aircraft in World War II, and many were lost during combat. But many also crashed while landing back at base—and nobody could work out why. Eventually someone found that the "safe landing" switch (for the landing gear) and the "crash" switch (for the flaps) were very close and looked identical.[55] Between a tool and the user's brain there should have been a better interface.

The character of the brain-tool spiral is likely to change dramatically in the near future, because of two new technologies. One is a new type of "tool." The other a new type of interface.

As a child, I watched the BBC TV program *One Man and His Dog*. Shepherds would guide their sheepdogs to gather a herd of sheep, keep the sheep together, and navigate the sheep around obstacles into a pen. The shepherd's incredible range of whistles and calls subtly controlled (or tried to!) exactly how the dog crept, ran, lay down, and so on. And humans don't only work this closely with dogs: horses and their riders can seemingly meld to form cavalry, or like the samurai who began this chapter.

We humans work with a spectrum of aids, which can be distinguished by their capacity to think freely. At one end of the spectrum are inert tools like hammers. At the other end are fellow humans: like a colleague or a partner in doubles tennis. In between lie animals such as horses or domesticated dogs (to herd sheep, guide the blind, or pull a sled).

New AI technologies can now enhance tools that lie in the middle of that tool-colleague spectrum. We are already seeing early versions of such *AI-enabled tools*, like the widely used AI assistants that help computer programmers write code or students write pieces of work.

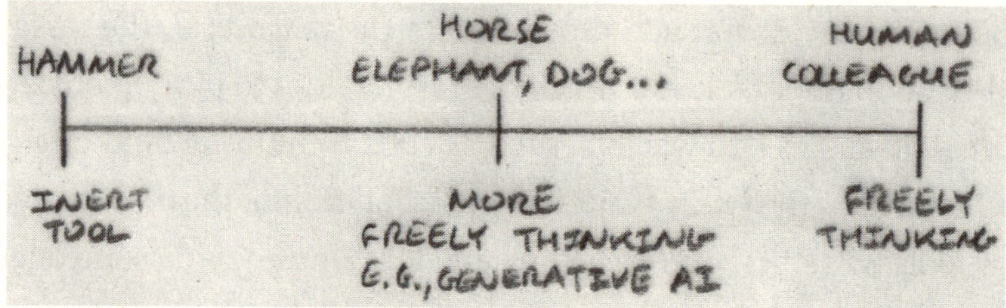

FIGURE 9: How freely thinking is our “teammate”? The spectrum going from an inert tool like a hammer through to the freely thinking agent that is a human colleague.

AI-enabled tools will keep moving further along the middle of this spectrum. A key question will be how to communicate so we get the best from these enhanced tools. We have typically “communicated” with machines like cars, tanks, or aircraft using interfaces like steering wheels, levers, or buttons. Or switches like on the B-17 interface discussed previously. We communicate very differently with domesticated animals.

Communication is wide and deep in the middle of the spectrum, with dogs or horses, to become part of a relationship. We move toward the mix of verbal and subtle nonverbal communication that we have with other humans (discussed in chapters 7 and 8). Increasingly, AI-enabled tools will interpret our facial expressions, tone of voice, and other cues to gauge and anticipate our confidence, emotions, and intentions. Will there be a hammer that “reads” my children, to help them bang nails more efficiently?

Indeed, the interface could go even further—using a second set of new technologies that give us another route to communicate with our tools.

Brain-computer interfaces are machines that directly read from, or write to, the brain.[56] It has already been done many times, both using so-called “invasive” methods like implanted electrodes, as well as “noninvasively” through methods like brain scanning. At the time of writing, however, practical blockages limit these approaches. Invasive methods struggle as the brain’s scar tissue (gliosis) often impairs electrodes. Noninvasive methods struggle out in the real world because interference affects the reading of electrical (EEG) or magnetic (MEG) fields, and MRI scanners are very bulky. But organizations like DARPA and the billionaire Elon Musk’s Neuralink in the U.S., and the Chinese government, are pouring resources into overcoming these obstacles—so these blockages could dissolve overnight to unleash a wave of new innovation.

If the practical blockages to brain-computer interfaces dissolve, what's possible? These new communication routes will increase the bandwidth of human-tool teams to allow humans to control tools (such as a swarm of drones or a cyber defense network) with a subtlety, speed, and coherence currently beyond human-tool interfaces that go through our muscle-enacted actions (such as moving our hands, feet, or eyes, or dilating blood vessels to flush our skin). It may take years to work well even after a breakthrough, to find the best ways to work on both the brain and the tool sides of the brain-tool spiral, and we will still need learning, teaching, and expertise. Over time, we may go beyond even the bandwidth of human-human communication, at least in the direction from the brain to the machine.

AI and brain-computer interfaces will also develop together. Unless governments restrict this research, over the next few decades it seems more than an even chance that humans will develop extremely powerful AI that directly communicates with the human brain at high bandwidths. For *Blitzkrieg*, Guderian combined the technologies of his day—internal combustion engines, amphetamines, and radio—with human factors to act faster than his opponents. Militaries with the fastest and best interfaces to control swarms of robots in physical space, or programs in cyberspace, could similarly overwhelm opponents who lack them.

Will these new technologies be developed, if they can be? Almost certainly yes. AI has huge economic advantages, and brain computer interfaces have wondrous medical uses. AI and brain computer interfaces may not be developed for military uses, but the technologies are dual use. Steam engines and internal combustion engines had huge civilian uses. Yet once tools exist, they afford military applications.

AFFORDANCES

In 2009, a five-year-old African American boy named Jacob Philadelphia stood in the Oval Office and patted the hair of President Barack Obama, to see if it felt just like his. It did. An iconic photograph of that moment captures the power of role models. Of seeing what is possible.

The brain constructs possibilities for action based on what we perceive in our environment. Neuroscience calls these options *affordances*.[57] And affordances govern much of what humans do, before we even make decisions.

Tools can change the affordances we perceive. E-readers have different affordances from tablets, because they facilitate different actions through the different types of computer programs they run. And, if you perceive it, both afford use as a table mat or Frisbee. When I taught my kids to hammer nails into pieces of wood, they brought to life the old saying that "To a man with a hammer everything looks like a nail." This new affordance channeled their perception and action—suddenly, all over the place they saw things that could be bashed or nailed.

As Part II ends, affordances also give us a chance to look again at four key ways that the Models in cortex work. This will help us in Part III, which will examine how our cortex does "thinking." Our Models in cortex are *cumulative, hierarchical, integrative*, and require *processing efficiently.* Adding these CHIP factors to the RAF of reality, anticipation, and flexibility examined in Part I, they stand us in good stead to understand everything up to the most sophisticated human thinking. So let's take the four CHIP factors for a spin, by looking at the possibilities for action known as affordances.

Cumulative knowledge from the learning-teaching spiral gives us humans vast numbers of affordances. My parents taught me to hammer, now my kids have learned it from me, and they see possibilities for hammering. The world we grow up in today teems with wheels, springs, screws, projectiles, elastically stored energy (for example, for bows or spring traps), and fire.[58] A brain full of affordances in which to act.

And pause to remember: although such cumulative knowledge *seems* obvious, that isn't reality. The wheel was never invented and maintained in the Americas or Australia. The Aztecs we saw in chapter 1 built colossal cities and a complicated culture—and did so without the wheel. No tools using elastically stored energy or compressed air were invented and maintained in Australia, as far as we can tell: so no bows, blow guns, flutes, or horns.[59]

If we do have these affordances, however, they become building blocks for more, because our brains can combine concepts. Projectiles *plus* elastically stored energy *gives us* bows. We speak using muscles to control airflow through our mouths—and our communication ability *plus* hand movements *can invent* writing. We can write numbers using cumbersome ancient Greek or Roman numerals, but most of us prefer the more versatile Arabic numbers, as well as the Indian zero that affords more sophisticated mathematical options. Or we can write maps, books, or scientific papers. Or computer programs written on punch cards, as the scientist Alan Turing pioneered at Bletchley Park during World War II. Or use computer programming languages like MATLAB or Python, with which I wrote learning agents and analyzed brain imaging data. Simple and complex components can be combined.

As we saw in the previous chapter, many of our most important Models are *hierarchical*—by which I mean they work at multiple levels of abstraction. We perceive higher-level things (like an animal in the zoo) composed of lower-level features (like four limbs, a tail, and a face), themselves composed of lower-level features (like faces have eyes, a nose, and a mouth).

We organize actions into hierarchies, too, as we saw with the components building up Fosbury's flop. And Fosbury developed his flop itself as part of a higher-level plan to study at university, which was itself part of . . . and so on. In your own life you might trace up the hierarchy from a single finger muscle's contraction, which contributes to typing the letter "t" on a computer keyboard, up to typing the word "the," then a whole sentence, up to an application form to study for a university degree, then actually doing the degree, then launching a career, and so on.

The teaching-learning spiral hands down actions at dozens of levels of abstraction, affording us libraries of possible actions at each level: from "grip a piece of wood" to "make a bow and arrow" to "learn to be a samurai."

It would be hopeless to plan high-level activities, such as "start a career as a samurai," in rigid terms such as "contract the quadriceps muscle to begin rising from a kneeling position." Because who knows how the environment might change, or from which direction a threat might come? Hierarchies enable us to plan activities across seconds, minutes, hours, days, years, and lifetimes.

Integration is the bringing together of separate elements, as we saw at the end of the last chapter for the unity of perception and action. Integration is crucial for affordances because affordances are possibilities for action that we perceive in the environment—that is, affordances are another way that our brains integrate perception and action.

And a final challenge is that this must all be *processed efficiently.* Our brain only has finite processing power (it runs on around 20 watts, enough for a dim incandescent light bulb). For perception, we saw how our controlled perceptual Model helps the brain cope with the fire hoses of data coming from our senses. For action, our brain faces the challenge that at any point we could make an almost infinite number of possible actions—and here affordances help us, by turning those infinite possibilities into a manageable menu of options. If a Spitfire pilot is struck by an enemy bullet in a dogfight, he can choose from among the menu of actions that his capabilities and situation afford (which probably won't include immediately getting out pen and paper to write poetry).

Learning can expand our toolbox to change the options on our menu—and context can radically change which affordances present themselves. In normal times, in most modern societies, you don't simply smash a shop window and take what's inside. That isn't one of your affordances while strolling down the street on Sunday afternoon. But when society breaks down, as happens throughout history, what wasn't an option becomes an option.

So, too, in every sphere of life. In politics, many observers claimed President Donald Trump's 2016 election moved the range of what is seen as possible in U.S. politics—for good or ill. It made the "unthinkable" thinkable.[60] Many in society try to deliberately create affordances, such as marketers trying to create new options for desire. Academics and writers can do the same: "Madmen in authority, who hear voices in the air," observed economist John Maynard Keynes, "are distilling their frenzy from some academic scribbler of a few years back."[61] Events also change which affordances we see—and this often channels the course of war.

* * *

Changing affordances help us see why the Allies bombed enemy cities in World War II. As war began, RAF commanders were informed that "the intentional bombardment of civil populations as such is illegal."[62] So initially they mostly bombed Germany with leaflets. What changed?

The *Luftwaffe* bombed London on August 24, 1940, and then began the full-scale Blitz on London. Those events, as the RAF's head put it, allowed the RAF to "take the gloves off."[63] In November 1940, a terrible German raid destroyed much of the British city of Coventry—and a month later, on December 16, the RAF launched its first deliberate "area raid" on Mannheim.

With hindsight, it is easy to criticize the humans who chose to bomb cities, but militarily this bombing was Britain's *only* affordance for striking back directly at Germany. A military saying, which derives from affordances, captures this: "Capabilities create intentions." In civilian life we see this if we must prepare dinner but, lacking ideal ingredients, must cook with what's in the kitchen cabinets. And the bombing did also afford ways to survive, and to help defeat Nazi Germany.

Diplomatically, the bombing afforded a powerful way to impress the Americans and Russians—vital for British survival. Churchill was dining with the U.S. ambassador when the RAF's first "thousand-bomber raid" took place on May 30, 1942, and Churchill's announcement led the ambassador to cable President Roosevelt that "England is the place to win the war." When Churchill met Stalin in August 1942, British bombing was the only activity that impressed Stalin.[64]

And strategic bombing *did* significantly help Russia. A March 12, 1943, raid damaged German *Panzer* production, buying time for crucial Russian anti-tank training before Kursk.[65] Most importantly, in the spring of 1943, 70 percent of all German fighters were stationed in the west.[66]

The power of affordances is even more sharply drawn by the radically new destructive force that appeared at World War II's end: nuclear weapons.

In today's world, the knowledge for building nuclear weapons is widespread. Many people wish this affordance could be eliminated. But it cannot be "uninvented." Nuclear weapons can be made using many methods, even by countries as small and poor as North Korea. And somewhere like North Korea may find willing buyers for such know-how, because when countries fear they cannot withstand a conventional war against potential aggressors, nuclear weapons afford options to level the playing field. We discuss nuclear weapons later, but a simple fact is that exploding one today in lower Manhattan will kill a lot of people.

That said, nuclear weapons have neither been used in war since 1945 nor proliferated beyond a handful of countries—and that illustrates that even though we can't always abolish affordances for nasty things, we can successfully manage those affordances. To make the world better.

And we can manage affordances for more positive things, too.

Mentors or role models can be so valuable at home or work because they help us see possibilities, to which we might otherwise be blind. I've benefited hugely from mentors (whose names appear in the Acknowledgments) who at critical points helped me see new affordances and narrow down the sometimes bewildering array of affordances I faced. Many of my mentors, I am sure, received similar help from others, as mentoring is often cumulative and passed down almost as an apostolic succession.

Mentoring helped many of America's World War II military leaders. General John Pershing led the U.S. armies in World War I, and he took a young officer called George C. Marshall under his wing. Pershing helped Marshall see the unwritten rules of how to command at that level, and even supported Marshall when the young man's wife died unexpectedly.[67] Marshall carried on this legacy, mentoring many officers who would lead U.S. forces to victories across the globe.

Marshall did not constrain his subordinates but afforded them opportunities amid challenging duties to realize their full potential. Dwight D. Eisenhower, who would go on to lead the Allied invasion on D-Day, became Marshall's assistant. Eisenhower recalled that in his first interview Marshall said:

> "Eisenhower, the department is filled with able men who analyze their problems well but feel compelled always to bring them to me for final solution. I must have assistants who will solve their own problems and tell me later what they have done." "I resolved then and there," Eisenhower said later, "to do my work to the best of my ability and report to the General only situations of obvious necessity or when he personally sent for me."[68]

Marshall opened the horizons of protégés like Omar Bradley, who alongside Eisenhower became one of those rare five-star generals. Bradley recalled how Marshall advised them and afforded them an example to follow, an example they then tried to impart to those they mentored.[69]

The proper application of force, in Churchill's memorable phrase, requires difficult choices taken by humans who live history forwards, not with hindsight. Who build cumulatively on what generations of teachers and mentors afford, to perceive and act better.

* * *

In our journey through the brain, Part I gave us a living warrior with vital drives, visceral instincts, and a map. In Part II we climbed up onto the outside of the giant cerebral hemispheres and considered the loop of sensory and motor cortex that makes our brain's most meticulous efforts at perception and action. Perceiving and acting both *seem* so straightforward. But now we know better how we humans really perceive the world: not passively but through our controlled perceptual Models, forged in a perceptual arms race, and warped to be useful. And we have better self-knowledge of how we really act, using our wonderfully plastic motor Models that rest on teaching, learning, and tools. Astonishing, and to be sure, these brain regions matter for any sophisticated animal.

But what goes on *between* perception and action adds much more of what makes us distinctively human. That processing is the domain of the rest of the cerebral cortex, and can colloquially be called *thinking*.

Part III

End and Start Again

Many people would think of the year 1943 as a turning point in a world war that would soon end. And that war's ending, like every ending, would also mark a new beginning.

That year was just as much a turning point in our understanding of the brain. Over preceding decades neuroscientists had discovered much about brain and behavior that remains foundational. Nineteenth- and early twentieth-century researchers, for instance, created maps of the cerebral cortex based on the types of cells seen in different areas, and began to uncover what such areas might do. This helped divide the cortex into areas of sensory cortex and motor cortex—as well as the "association cortex" that sits between sensation and action, on which Part III will focus. But 1943 was a time of exciting *new* ideas about what such brain regions do, including one idea you've been reading about.

That year, a young British scientist at Cambridge University, Kenneth Craik, published a slim book. In it he wrote:

> If the organism carries a "small-scale model" of external reality and of its own possible actions within its head, it is able to try out various alternatives, conclude which is the best of them, react to future situations before they arise, use the knowledge of past events in dealing with the present and future, and in every way to react in a much fuller, safer, and more competent manner to the emergencies that face it.[1]

Craik's book remains a cult classic among neuroscientists. It is probably the first to suggest that organisms have such internal Models of the external world and to suggest why.[2]

Also in 1943, another young British scientist, Alan Turing, was visiting Bell Labs in New York to work on secure encryption between London and Washington. Back in 1936 Turing had described an artificial device that could compute anything computable: what became known as a "Turing machine." Now in 1943 Turing was chatting about building an electronic brain over coffee and lunch with Claude Shannon, the American who invented much of information theory.[3] Each of these two scientists was, within their *own* brain, constructing new Models about how brains work—and communicating with each other, to check and improve their Models.

And . . . in that same year, the American Norbert Wiener and colleagues had just published a seminal paper on feedback in the brain, while his compatriots Warren McCulloch and Walter Pitts published a paper describing algorithms operating in networks of brain cells.[4] It was quite a turning point.

Craik died tragically young when a car hit his bicycle in Cambridge in 1945, but his idea remains at the heart of an approach to the brain that combined these scientists' insights. In essence: the brain manipulates representations of the world to make predictions and generate behaviors. This new approach had consolidated by the early 1950s and launched a flourishing in the human understanding of the brain.[5] One that has underpinned neuroscience's huge success ever since, to vastly expand our cumulative understanding of our brains.

That humans could do this relies on the Models from our "association cortex." These large tracts of cortex sit between sensory and motor areas to give us our most distinctively human abilities: reading others' intentions (chapter 7), communicating through language (chapter 8), reasoning (chapter 9), and reflecting on such functions (chapter 10).

In part III, we will see ourselves proceeding up the hierarchy to ever more abstract levels of planning and reflection on that planning. We'll think about the very highest goals for our life, and ultimate causes. We've come a long way from the brainstem merely keeping us alive.

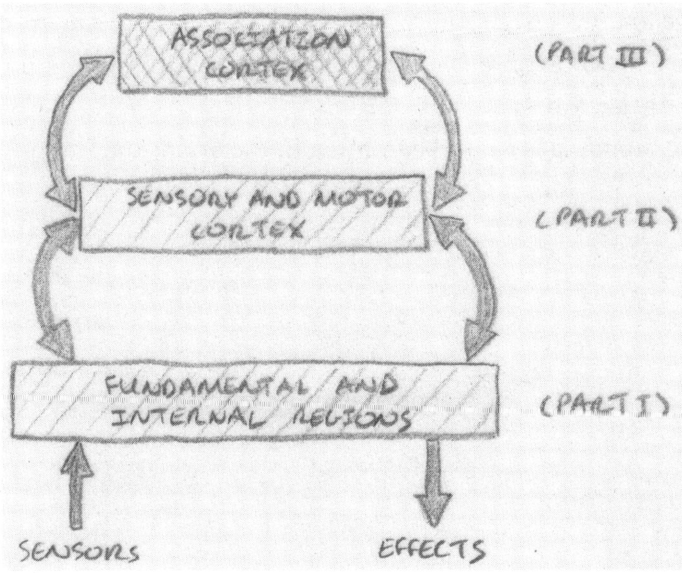

FIGURE 10: The loops in our brain. Where the more instinctual and reflexive loops in Part I ended, above them started new loops of processing for exquisite perception and action in Part II, and then, as they ended, the additional loops of processing in association cortex start again to add new capabilities for thinking in Part III.

Our brains have remarkable range: we can juggle abstractions such as infinity or zero, while eating breakfast. Up in the association cortex, the power of our thought can build castles in the sky that can be scientific, ideological, artistic, practical, or a thousand other types (including trivial, amusing nonsense). But in war and peace alike, these castles can be as real as steel. A U.S. dollar bill counts for little in itself as a piece of paper, but a U.S. dollar is a powerful social fact. Other social facts are the leaders who shape our lives and the identities that drive us. In our twenty-first-century era, we can hope to be as wise as leaders like Winston Churchill, George C. Marshall, and Martin Luther King Jr.

Alas, no castle in the sky can ever be perfected to represent a definitive end, because each new generation arises to create their own Models of themselves in the world. The process is cumulative—we can learn from the best and avoid the worst—but there will always be change and new beginnings. There will always be a Kenneth Craik, with a slim book of revolutionary ideas, a new MLK—and probably a new Hitler, too.

Every ending is a new beginning. In the brain, and in war.

7

OTHERS' INTENTIONS

PARIETAL CORTEX TO UNDERSTAND ALLIES, ENEMIES, AND PEACE

David was savagely beaten and left for dead. An alliance of two of his enemies proved too powerful for him. But David came back. He needed to bluff his adversaries into thinking that he wasn't as badly injured as, in reality, he was. And then having allies gave him the power to retain his leadership.

David was a strong and skilled fighter. But it was his skill at building alliances that enabled him to rule for twice as long as any other known group leader.[1]

David almost certainly had only a fraction of *your* ability to build such Models of the social world: he was a chimpanzee. Living in a troop of chimpanzees, in the forests of Senegal, West Africa.

But like ancient China's Sun Tzu and the twentieth century's Winston Churchill, he knew that attacking others' alliances, and building your own, can win battles and wars. There's an advantage for those who most skillfully navigate the social world, where attack and defense rest on trust, allies, and deception.

How can we understand others' intentions so that we can trust allies, wrong-foot enemies, and forge peace?

Humans possess extraordinary machinery for Modeling others' intentions—and key parts are contained in our parietal cortex. Parietal cortex is a large region stretching between the sensory cortex for vision at the back of the brain and the motor cortex farther forward (Figure 11). It contains a big chunk of the "association cortex," which sits between sensory and motor cortex to help us think. To be sure, the machinery for Modeling others' intentions involves other parts of the association cortex, too, and parietal cortex executes more than just this one function. But it's key.

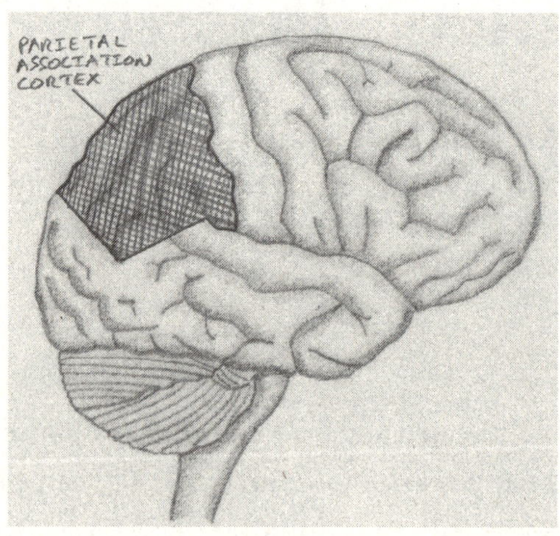

FIGURE 11: Association cortex sits between sensation and action. There is a large area in the parietal lobe.

This neural machinery works to understand others, whether they're individual humans, abstract shapes, machines, groups, or conspiracies. It helps us see how to build the trust that's crucial for collaboration. The British and Americans brilliantly collaborated planning D-Day. If the Germans and Japanese had worked together even a fraction as well, then they could have won the war: Heinz Guderian's *Panzers* were beaten back from Moscow's outskirts by Soviet troops no longer needed to face Japan.

Equally, this machinery helps us see how to deceive, without which it's impossible to conduct strategy: whether as a tennis player choosing to play across court or down the line; an employee deciding to work or shirk; or the Allied commanders choosing to locate the D-Day landings in Normandy or Calais. "In wartime," as Churchill said, "truth is so precious that she should always be attended by a bodyguard of lies."[2]

Knowing how we humans understand others' intentions also gives fresh perspectives on profound moral questions: Where, for example, does responsibility lie between the commander and the people (or AI-powered machines) trying to carry out the intent? And this self-knowledge helps explain why many common views on creating and maintaining peace are dangerously incomplete.

ALLIES

How do we understand other peoples' intentions? To see how, let's go back to tennis.

We've already seen how the brain uses a Model of the tennis ball's movement and prediction errors to update the Model. It does much the same to Model the intentions, beliefs, and feelings of an opponent. Or a doubles partner, because to play doubles well we must Model our partner's *intentions*—hidden deep in their brain—to cooperate and coordinate with them. A partner's cheeky smile between points may suggest how they intend to serve next. But how does our brain work that out?

It's trickier than Modeling a teacup, because we don't need a Model of what the teacup intends. Or how the world looks from the teacup's perspective. Or what the teacup thinks of us.

But the basic ideas are the same. To perceive a teacup, my brain actively creates a *Model*, which is *controlled* by what my brain expects to see and by prediction errors from sensory data to update my Model. To perceive another's intention, there are essentially just more stages in between their intention (in their brain) and my Model of their intention (in my brain).

If my doubles partner smiles at me, the intention hidden in their brain is expressed through intermediate stages, like commands to the many muscles that move their face. I might see the resulting expressions from various angles or in various lighting conditions. Light waves eventually get to my retina. And from those 2D images, I must reconstruct what's going on inside their brain.

For that, my brain uses *hierarchical* Models. Lower-level features like the movements of mouths and eyes explain higher-level features like facial expressions. In turn facial expressions—along with gestures and sounds—fit into even higher-level representations I have of the other. Such as their reputation for fair play, being a sore loser, or how they bear up under the stress of big points.

Moreover, to play tennis well together, my Model of them can also include their Model of me. And, indeed, their Model of me thinking of them thinking of me . . . And so on.

Putting this all together, the brain simulates others as agents with intentions that cause things to happen. This ability is called *mentalizing*.[3] And we humans mentalize all over the place. Not just about other individuals but also about groups of people, fictional characters like the robot WALL-E in movies or books, and even animated triangles in a short cartoon.

Most of us mentalize so effortlessly that we barely even notice how remarkable it is—unless this machinery goes wrong. In schizophrenia, paranoia about others' intentions can become totally disabling. In autism, reading others can be a struggle. In both cases the impact on social lives can be enormous.

One sophisticated feature of successful mentalizing is that we can decouple *reality* as *we* understand it from reality as the *other* understands it. That is, we can *anticipate* what the other will believe, regardless of whether the other's belief is actually true or false: and that can help both of us in shared tasks like hunting together (or playing doubles tennis).

A study from the early 1980s showed that these capabilities develop over our lifetimes. A child is told that

> **Maxi is given a bar of chocolate. Before he goes out to play, he puts his chocolate in a safe place; the blue cupboard. While Maxi is out, Maxi's mother moves the chocolate to the red cupboard. When Maxi comes back, where will he look for his chocolate?[4]**

Children younger than four to six years old say the red cupboard—but older children can take Maxi's perspective and find this task incredibly easy. Trickier tasks show that humans' mentalizing improves into young adulthood, and that changes in brain activation accompany these improvements.[5]

A brain imaging study I conducted with colleagues at Queen Square helps illustrate where and how this happens in the brain.[6] Participants played a fairness game, and in their brains the insula cortex tracked unfairness (as chapter 3 described). How much the participants cared about what others received affected activity in two different parts of the brain. Those two parts of parietal cortex are both associated with mentalizing: the temporoparietal junction (TPJ) and the precuneus.

Putting evidence together from many mentalizing studies helps us see what these regions do.[7] The TPJ and neighboring regions seem concerned with prediction errors; so that for instance it shows greater activity when a partner makes unexpected choices.[8] Disrupting the TPJ's functioning using a technique called transcranial magnetic stimulation (TMS) also seems to disrupt predictions.[9] The precuneus, meanwhile, is often involved in taking perspectives in physical space—and in mentalizing, the precuneus seems to help us take others' perspectives that differ from one's own.[10] Adding to these brain regions, a third crucial area for mentalizing lies farther forward, in the prefrontal cortex that Chapter 9 will explore.

This network of brain regions for mentalizing has been shown with remarkable consistency during twenty-five years of studies by numerous researchers, using brain imaging and many other techniques.[11]

Other animals, however, can cooperate without such sophisticated neural machinery to "mentalize." Chimps like David can still manage alliances, and orangutans can perceive others' intentions.[12] Even ants rescue nestmates injured in battle.[13]

Why then do humans expend so much energy on this fancy mentalizing machinery?

In a word: *flexibility.*

Evolution has equipped us to cooperate more flexibly across situations. Ants may cooperate with close relatives, and some animals can even trust strangers in some situations: but our expensive mentalizing abilities help us flexibly calibrate our trust when we cooperate with distant relatives, nonrelatives, or even strangers. It helps us collaborate more flexibly across varied situations, with varied types of people, in varied ways—so we can cooperate more often and more deeply, and bring together specialized individuals.

We learn complicated ideas about others' reputations, high up in the hierarchy of our Model about them. We may not need this much when two individuals repeat the same tasks many times for relatively low stakes (like co-workers in a supermarket). In that case, simple reciprocity can enable cooperation. "You scratch my back and I'll scratch yours." But such machinery can be lifesaving if the task is high stakes or infrequent, or involves many people—as is often the case in fighting or war.

The Turkana are semi-nomadic, pastoral people from a dry region of northern Kenya[14] who face such a challenge. They rely on their livestock. In extreme scarcity they might raid neighboring territories to steal cattle—a dangerous business that kills one in a hundred men in the fight. Some men succumb to fear instead of cooperating in the raid and flee home to safety. Such cowardice is scorned, in particular by unmarried women—and those men gain reputations not just as cowards but as generally undesirable marriage partners. Moreover, after a raid, a meeting discusses how to handle deserters. If they warrant punishment, their same-age peers tie them to a bush and beat them.

Managing our own reputation involves mentalizing to take another's perspective and estimate how various scenarios might alter their beliefs about us. We can imagine scenarios and "what ifs"—as described in Chapter 4 on the hippocampus—to see what others would think about us if we were brave. Or if we were cowards. Such mentalizing makes us better at creating and nurturing alliances, as well as at anticipating and detecting social threats.

Our Models also help us cooperate better than other animals by bringing together varied individuals. We can use teamwork between individuals who take on specialized roles, such as among the three people it takes to operate a machine gun. And we can bring together people with complementary talents and gain benefits from heterogeneity in our teams, so that groups become more than the sum of the parts.[15]

Chimps, in contrast, don't really do specialized teamwork for hunting—and in fact dogs outperform chimps on team communication tasks with humans, such as when humans point to signal where something valuable is located. Interestingly, wolves don't have the same ability as dogs, a difference that suggests the human domestication of dogs—which took tens of thousands of years—helped dogs evolve abilities for perceiving human signals as cooperative.[16]

In our lifetimes, with remarkable speed, AI is moving along the spectrum from inert tool (like a hammer), past an electronic calculator's entirely predictable outputs, toward something more freethinking like a dog. As with dogs, we can expect to build sophisticated *relationships* in these new human-machine teams, and improving these relationships requires better understanding of the humans and of the machines.

Understanding human intentions will be central, because humans will increasingly tell the computer what we intend will happen but not how to achieve that intent.[17] The need for other agents to understand and follow our intent isn't new—and indeed it's central to military command at every level. Like leading a squad of soldiers through a jungle. Or like Horatio Nelson's intentions for the Battle of Trafalgar. But finding new methods for commanders to communicate their intent faster and more flexibly can provide a serious military edge.

In May 1940 German commanders used systems to communicate that gave them big advantages over their French counterparts. The Germans gave orders more as a broad commander's intent that their followers could decide how to implement, while instead the French orders were far more sclerotic and prescriptive.[18] Guderian famously called on his *Panzers* to get a "ticket to the last station," intending them to make their sickle cut to the Channel coast.[19]

The British and Americans essentially copied the German idea of *Auftragstaktik*—decentralizing authority and autonomy to achieve objectives—and follow it to this day under the name of "Mission Command." Their commanders issue the "Commander's Intent:"[20] a description of what a successful mission will look like, from which to work out the "who, what, when, where, and why" of how to achieve it.

Soon, however, humans throughout modern militaries will increasingly need to communicate their intentions to AI, whether they're a frontline soldier operating a small reconnaissance drone or an admiral on a flagship. They will have to learn how to effectively communicate their intentions to the AI, in a high-stakes version of how today many school children and office workers are learning to communicate with generative AI bots. To fight effectively, it will become essential to manage human-AI relationships. And one day that might even give us something like the enormous power we humans have gained throughout history—power gained from skillfully managing our *human-human* relationships.

* * *

In World War II, the difference between victory and defeat required mentalizing in relationships between large abstract groups and key individuals.

The D-Day landings in June 1944 required exceptional collaboration. The Allies faced formidable German coastal defenses, including four million land mines and *Panzer* forces that could fling the Allies back into the sea. British and American collaboration on D-Day was deeply integrated from Supreme Commander Dwight Eisenhower with his British deputy, far down through the chain of command: as Figure 12 shows. Eisenhower went out of his way to build collaboration between the British and Americans. He once punished an American officer for careless talk—not for calling a colleague a son of a bitch, but for calling him a *British* son of a bitch.[21]

This deep trust and collaboration was long in the making, driven by Churchill, Roosevelt, and their top military advisers. Immediately after Pearl Harbor the British and Americans formed the Combined Chiefs of Staff in Washington. Their teamwork—including all the arguments and rivalries that have been chronicled in so many histories of the war—made for better strategy.[22] Long before Eisenhower's involvement in D-Day, an Anglo-American planning staff was set up in London—and their thinking was crystallized in a "Rattle Conference" enthusiastically chaired by British Admiral Louis Mountbatten. That conference was almost an old-world gentlemen's party, with serious meetings alongside a whirl of social occasions and outings.[23]

We now take for granted such collaboration between allies—but this World War II collaboration was pathbreaking and far beyond anything the French, British, and Americans achieved in World War I. It seems so ordinary now to collaborate deeply in the North Atlantic Treaty Organization (NATO) or in the "Five Eyes" intelligence production apparatus (between America, Britain, Canada, Australia, and New Zealand),[24] but that is itself a result of cumulative learning. Building on success.

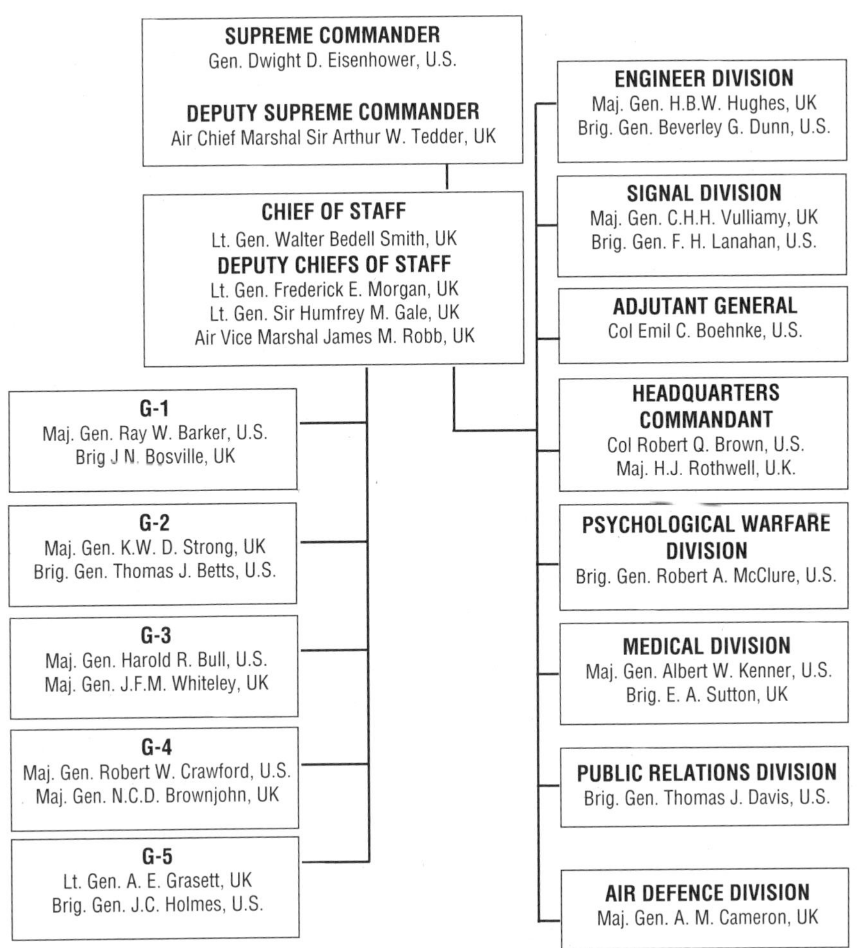

FIGURE 12: A chart that depicts the remarkable collaboration between the British and American militaries. This is the Supreme Headquarters Allied Expeditionary Force (SHAEF) chain of command. Source: Dr. Samuel J. Newland and Dr. Clayton K. S. Chun, *The European Campaign: Its Origins and Conduct* (U.S. Army War College Press, 2011).

Germany would likely have won if it had collaborated even remotely as well after 1940 with Japan, Italy, and fascist Spain.

Earlier in the war Hitler *had* collaborated successfully with Stalin in the 1939 Nazi-Soviet pact, which carved up Poland and removed a threat to Hitler's east while he attacked France. That collaboration was a means to an end for Hitler, as he'd written beforehand in *Mein Kampf*:

> Let no one argue that in concluding an alliance with Russia we need not immediately think of war, or, if we did, that we could thoroughly prepare for it. An alliance whose aim does not embrace a plan for war is senseless and worthless. Alliances are concluded only for struggle.[25]

But as the war progressed, Hitler lost the benefits of collaboration with other powers: Moscow was saved in 1941 by Siberian divisions no longer needed to defend against Japan; and the next year Japanese forces in the Indian Ocean failed to coordinate with Rommel in North Africa.

Collaboration mattered not only between states, but within states, too. Inside Germany, as the war went on, Hitler largely stopped collaborating with advisers like Guderian, who had helped father the victory over France.[26] In contrast, the three Allied great powers—Britain, America, and Russia—all fought their wars substantially by committee.[27] British Prime Minister Churchill headed a Cabinet, and he didn't overrule his military chiefs once during the war.[28] That British system fiercely challenged ideas and (usually) improved them. U.S. President Roosevelt's team was similarly greater than the sum of its parts.

Even Stalin, who had purged much of the Soviet military leadership shortly before World War II, ran the war through the Stavka (Soviet State Committee of Defense) that was set up shortly after Germany's invasion. Stalin needed to collaborate with skilled commanders like Zhukov. Commanders who could also harness another use of mentalizing that is equally central to survival and victory: deception.

DECEPTION

Why would anyone pay to watch a magic show? Who *wants* to be deceived? Because it is fun. We learn to deceive as children in play, too, so that we can get better at deception when the stakes are high.

Even when playing tennis entirely for fun in the park, deception is both necessary and part of the fun itself. If before any shot you truthfully shouted out your intention—"I'll hit this one down the line!"—the game wouldn't be so enjoyable for anyone. The element of deception—or possible deception—helps make the game worth playing.

Physical skill helps us hit the ball hard and fast. Mentalizing helps us cooperate well with our doubles partner. And then there is mentalizing for the strategic interaction against the opponents. Do you hit the ball crosscourt or down the line? Down the line travels a shorter distance to the net, giving the other player less time to react—but playing that shot every time enables the other to always prepare for it. Thus, to improve your success when playing down the line, you should play crosscourt often enough to keep them guessing. Mentalizing helps anticipate others: to outfox them, and avoid them outfoxing you.

Deception is intentionally causing someone to have false beliefs. For better or worse, it occurs naturally in all kinds of strategic situations more hazardous than tennis.

Many animals deceive to conceive, from lizards to primates. Humans are neither totally monogamous, as Chapter 2 described, nor a totally winner-takes-all tournament species. For a nontrivial number of humans, their father is not who they think it is. The last archbishop of Canterbury discovered at the age of sixty that his father wasn't who he'd thought beforehand.[29]

Many animals, including humans, face a tension between "working" and "shirking." That is, either fulfilling their collaborative responsibilities, or slacking off. In the workplace, polling suggests two-thirds of employees globally are "quiet quitters," who only minimally engage at work.[30] Humans who underwent brain scanning while playing a "work-shirk" game for money in the lab showed activity in the mentalizing network.[31]

World War II soldiers often avoided firing their weapons during even serious fighting, as we saw in Chapter 3. Shirking wasn't possible on crewed weapons, and it largely disappeared. As previously unsupervised soldiers are increasingly monitored on battlefields, will they remain able to avoid killing? More broadly, as we've gone from the industrial age to the digital age, and are now entering the "intelligentized" age, we see ever greater digital and AI-enabled monitoring of workplaces. And monitoring of society more generally: in the west by big tech for advertising; and in China by government for social control.[32] Deception has always been a big deal for us humans.

Studies of humans seeking to deceive others show that children develop the ability at a similar pace to mentalizing in general—most can lie by four years old—although it takes longer to learn to lie effectively.[33] Studying lies in the lab is hard, because it's tricky to know precisely when people have lied or not, while keeping other factors constant. But researchers who scoured the academic journals found twenty-three human brain imaging studies that did a reasonable job of comparing lying to telling the truth—and analyzing all the studies together revealed that the mentalizing network, including parietal cortex, was involved in deceit.[34] Further research since then implicates amygdala in other aspects of deceit.[35] Indeed, deceit draws on diverse brain systems because humans deceive in diverse ways.

Our deceptive methods fall into three broad groups. One is to deceive within the beams of perception we humans use, as Chapter 5 described.

Second, and almost exclusively human, we use language to deceive in words. That is, to lie. Language, as we see in the next chapter, enables humans to build and export Models of the world into the brains of others. Including deliberately false Models.

And a third group of methods, for which parietal cortex is crucial, has been used by magicians (and warriors) for millennia: manipulating attention.

We are consciously aware of only a small portion of the information that might occupy our attention. Attention is our ability to focus awareness on one stimulus, thought, or action while ignoring alternatives.[36] And attention crucially involves parietal cortex.

In humans, the spotlight of our attention can be directed by our "top-down" goals (like paying attention while reading this book) or be grabbed from the "bottom up" (like when hearing a loud bang nearby). Both are shown in the "cocktail party effect," where despite being bombarded by a cacophony of conversations we can focus on one conversation—and yet someone nearby mentioning our name can still grab our attention.[37]

Attention can blind us. Magicians use attention to misdirect audiences.[38] To misdirect *top-down* attention, a magician might *ask* the audience to carefully watch an object manipulated in one hand—while simultaneously conducting a secret action with the other hand. In a famous psychology experiment, participants watched a video of people passing a basketball, and were asked to count how many passes one team made while ignoring passes by another team.[39] In a scarcely believable result, many participants were so busy paying attention to their task that they failed to notice someone in a gorilla suit striding through the video and beating their chest. Many participants must be shown the video again, because they're so disbelieving when told about the gorilla.

Magicians also harness *bottom-up* attention. New, unusual, high-contrast, or moving objects draw the audience's attention. Suddenly releasing a flying dove drives the audience to focus on its flight, so the magician has a few unattended moments for secret maneuvers. If more than one movement is visible, spectators tend to follow the larger motion—hence the magician's saying that "A big move covers a small move." And if two actions start almost simultaneously, the action that starts first usually attracts more attention.[40]

Skillful magicians control our attention by giving every motion a convincing intention, because—as in everyday life—our Models classify others' actions by inferring their intentions. If somebody pushes their glasses higher up on their nose, we assume their glasses needed adjusting and we interpret the action no more. Such innocent actions can hide ulterior motions, like discreetly hiding a small object in their mouth. Whereas just putting your hand over your mouth without a purpose attracts unwanted attention.[41]

Skillful militaries have always used methods like these to misdirect enemies, as when the Germans attacked France in May 1940. Their "matador's cloak" used noisy moves toward Belgium and the Netherlands to attract British and French forces up into Belgium—while the *Panzers'* real blow struck instead through the Ardennes.

How do we defend against deception? It can be deeply corrosive if deceit pervades everyday social life. As most children learn, humans should be cautious with deception.

Sadly, humans are bad at detecting a specific instance of deception. In tests we perform little better than guessing.[42] Methods to increase accuracy like using facial "microexpressions" or tone of voice have modest success at best.[43]

Machines aren't currently much better. The polygraph that measures heart rate, respiration, and perspiration can just about detect lies concerning specific events, but isn't usefully accurate in the field beyond making good theater.[44] Brain imaging can detect the process of lying, but that doesn't tell us what the lie is.

One defensive weapon is gossip and reputation: a person may get away with fifty lies, but being caught out once can destroy a reputation. As with perception, our prior beliefs about another—that is, their reputation—helps us judge if they are deceiving us.

Of course, lies aren't all the same. Little deceits to spare another's feelings differ from lying for personal gain. And deception that's unacceptable in some contexts is allowed in others such as war, intelligence, or politics.

During war, and in many hostile situations, fooling the enemy is necessary.[45]

Intelligence requires deception to reveal others' secrets and protect one's own. In 2015 a cyber-espionage hack into the U.S. Office of Personnel Management stole twenty-two million records for U.S. federal security clearances—a big blow against U.S. intelligence. The hackers were likely Chinese intelligence. They gained access to the servers by using a fake website ("opmsecurity.org") and a seemingly harmless file called "mcutil.dll" to hide the program. That is the game. James Clapper, then U.S. director of national intelligence, noted in a public interview, "You have to kind of salute the Chinese for what they did." A few weeks later, appearing before Congress, Clapper reminded them of "the old saw about people in glass houses shouldn't throw rocks." He went on, "I'm just saying both nations engage in this."[46]

Historically, getting ahead in politics has often required turning a blind eye to deception and dishonesty. Current Chinese President Xi Jinping climbed to power in Fujian province, and must have known about corruption as flamboyant as the multistory Red Mansion, where a businessman lavishly entertained officials. The resulting scandal would have felled most politicians, but Xi's trustworthy reputation among the Communist Party's top brass saved him.[47]

Some politicians blatantly lie for personal benefit—as we'll see in the next chapter with 1950s U.S. Senator Joseph McCarthy—but politics more broadly is a realm of ambiguity. That ambiguity (which seems like lying to many) may even be the only way to ensure peace. Ending decades of Northern Ireland's troubles required ambiguity about bringing killers—on all sides—to justice. Politicians must often speak to multiple audiences at the same time, including domestic and international audiences, which can require them to be, in the old phrase, "economical with the truth."

The intentions behind lies (and behind cooperation) often make all the difference.

Hitler used alliances and cooperation to achieve his dark ends in France after its fall in 1940. A primary task for the SS was finding France's Jews.[48] Censuses in France had not collected data on individuals' religions for privacy reasons, so if the Nazis wanted the police to register people it would require a time-consuming manual process on paper and index cards. Fortunately for the Nazis, the comptroller general of the French Army, René Carmille, owned sophisticated tabulating machines and volunteered to collaborate.

To find the Jews, Carmille developed a national personal identity number. Carmille also prepared the 1941 French census, which covered everyone aged fourteen to sixty-five. Question 11 in that census sought Jews through their grandparents and declared religion. Handy, for the SS.

But months went by, and despite Nazi impatience, the lists did not appear. It turned out that the Allies, too, were using alliances and cooperation: Carmille was one of the highest placed French Resistance operatives. Answers to Question 11 were never tabulated, and the data was forever lost. He saved hundreds of thousands of lives before the Nazis discovered his deception.

In 1944, the SS detained Carmille. He was tortured. He died in 1945, in the Dachau death camp.

Dutch authorities, in contrast, cooperated diligently with the Nazis to identify Jews, and the Dutch had the highest death rate of Jews in occupied Europe: 73 percent. In France the rate was only 25 percent.

René Carmille was a liar. And a hero.

* * *

Deception tricked Hitler into Germany's worst defeat of the war, in June 1944, while German attention was focused on the D-Day landings. On the Eastern Front, Operation Bagration saw 589,425 German military dead in three months.[49]

Brilliant deception meant that, despite needing huge troop buildups, the Russians delivered crushing surprise.

The Russians faked increased threats to the north and south, to distract attention from German Army Group Center.[50] To make their fake forces of dummy tanks and artillery more convincing, the Russians defended them with real antiaircraft guns and air patrols. The Russians also made tread marks, broadcast engine noises, and imitated the tank army's radio networks. Meanwhile, in sectors that would attack their real target—the German center—the Russians instead constructed defensive fortifications like fake minefields.

Like magicians, the Russians combined display and concealment. They systematically targeted what had become, by later in the war, Germany's three main sources of intelligence: radio intercept, aerial photography, and agents in formerly occupied territory.

Deceived, Hitler transferred away the *Panzer* Corps that was Army Group Center's only mobile reserve—handing victory to the Russians.

PEACE

Once D-Day and Bagration were successful, Nazi Germany had essentially no hope of winning the war. But still the Germans fought ferociously—*for longer than France lasted in the whole war*. In December 1944 they even launched a fresh offensive in the West, the Battle of the Bulge.

The Japanese, too, fought tenaciously on all fronts, despite no realistic hope of avoiding defeat. Japan's April 1944 Ichi-Go offensives alone inflicted some three hundred thousand casualties on Chiang Kai-shek's Nationalist forces.[51] Millions upon millions of skilled and dedicated Germans and Japanese fought on, to the bitter end.

On April 30, 1945, at about 15:30, with Russian troops a short walk from Hitler's bunker, he shot himself. Victory against Germany came on

May 8. America dropped atomic bombs on Hiroshima and Nagasaki on August 6 and 9. Russia declared war on Japan on August 8. Victory came on August 15.

Sixty million had died. After almost six years in Europe, and over eight in China, World War II ended. Peace.

It's crucial self-knowledge for us, as humanity, to face how we achieved peace after our last general war: millions of Germans did not change their intentions and stop fighting by force of argument—Germany was invaded and occupied so that German armies *could not* fight. Whatever people's intentions.

Among German military officers, even the handful who tried to assassinate Hitler after D-Day weren't persuaded by the better angels of their nature—they were mostly extreme nationalists, intending to remove an incompetent corporal.[52] Colonel Claus von Stauffenberg, who planted their bomb, despised "the lie that all men are created equal." Neither did ordinary Germans beyond the elites stop fighting because they suddenly realized how nice democracy is. In the years after Germany surrendered, a consistent majority from 1945 to 1949 stated that National Socialism was a good idea badly applied.[53]

The Allies did not want to repeat the mistake they made after World War I. In 1918, despite decisively winning on the battlefield, the Allies *chose* not to occupy Germany and remake its regime. The massive Allied offensive that began in August 1918 broke German military power, capturing 363,000 prisoners (a quarter of the German Army in the field) and 6,400 artillery guns (half of all its guns), so that when the armistice came into effect German war-making power even to defend its borders was within a few days of collapse.[54] But the armistice afforded many Germans the myth that Jews and others stabbed an undefeated German Army in the back. To avoid any repeat of this idea, in 1945 Germany was totally and categorically and demonstrably beaten militarily and occupied.

Yet the democracies *also* chose not to treat defeated Germans as having irredeemably bad intentions. The democracies cooperated, too. Winston Churchill stressed magnanimity in victory.[55] British food rationing worsened at home after the war ended, yet Britain gave Germany humanitarian assistance.[56] The United States launched the Marshall Plan. Germans did not change overnight, but decades of occupation and cooperation from the democracies enabled—and forced—Germans to change. Japan, too, was occupied to enforce change. *And* Japan also received aid.

It's crucial self-knowledge for us, as humanity, to remember that for Germany and Japan, lasting peace rested on both hard-won military victory *and* reconciliation.

Reconciliation is, like conflict, a natural part of us. Sure, humans often seek revenge. An eye for an eye. And humans often fight back to reject unfairness. But we don't *only* leave it at that. We also actively reach out to rebuild breakdowns in cooperation. We even reach out to make peace with enemies who are threatening, or literally trying, to kill us.

In animals, reconciliation is often defined as the first friendly contact between the former opponents within a few minutes after a conflict.[57] Such reconciliation is seen in social species ranging from parrots to red-necked wallabies (marsupials resembling small kangaroos) to nonhuman primates.

Pigs go further, acting as peacemakers.[58] Researchers in Italy recently studied a group of 104 domestic pigs. In six months, they saw 216 fights, in which pig aggressors bit, kicked, bumped, or lifted the victim. After the fights, which lasted from seconds to a couple of minutes, sometimes combatants touched noses to make up on their own. Remarkably, a third pig often stepped in. Bystanders acted as peacemakers. Some engaged with the aggressor to reduce the number of subsequent attacks. Others engaged with the victim, calming them down to reduce anxiety-related behaviors like shaking.

Humans go further still, to rebuild trust and cooperation after it fails. An example in the lab is behavior in the "trust game."[59] In this game, the first player is given an amount of money in each round (for example, $20) and can invest any portion of it (for example, $10) with the second player. Then the investment triples, and the second player decides how much of the money to repay (such as returning $13 and keeping $17). Cooperation, in which higher amounts are invested and then paid back, benefits both sides but carries the risk of exploitation.

When pairs play several rounds of the trust game, we see how humans maintain and repair breakdowns in cooperation. When collaboration falters and investments are low, individuals often build cooperation by making unilateral conciliatory gestures in the form of high repayments—despite the risk that these generous overtures will be pocketed and not reciprocated. Playing the trust game involves both the insula, a brain region we met in Chapter 3 that processes social motivations, and parietal regions involved in mentalizing.[60]

Making positive or conciliatory gestures—appeasement—will always be one tool for success in international politics and everyday life. And we can make conciliation more effective by using prediction error.

In 1977, Egypt had lost two wars to Israel in 1967 and 1973. The Egyptian leader, Anwar Sadat, had made conciliatory efforts that barely changed the attitudes of Israel's decision-makers or public.[61] But in 1977 Sadat made the highly unexpected, novel offer to go and speak in the Israeli Knesset, its parliament. This had a big psychological impact on Israeli decision-makers and the public alike, and opened the path to peace.

* * *

But conciliation is not the answer in every situation, and it certainly wouldn't have stopped Hitler in the 1930s. Given Hitler's intentions, and his millions of resolute followers, few now argue that being "nicer" to Nazi Germany after Hitler assumed power in 1933 would have prevented German aggression leading to World War II. When the democracies did make concessions—like British Prime Minister Chamberlain's concessions in the Munich Agreement—Hitler saw them as weakness.

Knowing others' intentions is a challenge that can only ever be managed and never completely solved. It is illustrated by a simple question: *Is the situation we are in today more like the run-up to World War I, or more like the run-up to World War II?*

The challenge involves both (a) preventing tough policies from provoking spirals of *unintended* escalation that cause war (more like World War I); *and* (b) deterring and defeating those who *intend* escalation to war (more like World War II).

If you know the other's intentions, the answer is straightforward: be nicer in the run-up to World War I; be tougher in the run-up to World

War II. The problem is that we live history forward, with uncertainty about others' intentions. Moreover, we can't permanently put our heads in the sand either, because action (or inaction) helpful in one situation can be catastrophic in the other.

It is easy for us to say now that Chamberlain and others who supported appeasement were naive, weak, foolish, or even cowardly—but that is unfair to those who sincerely tried to divine others' intentions.

The British ambassador to Germany, Nevile Henderson, cabled to London seven months before Germany invaded Poland in 1939:

> My instinctive feeling is that this year will be the decisive one, as to whether Hitler comes down on the side of peaceful development and closer cooperation with the West or decides in favour of further adventures eastward . . . If we handle him right, my belief is that he will become gradually more pacific. But if we treat him as a pariah or a mad dog we shall turn him firmly and irrevocably into one.[62]

Remember that conciliation was popular among the public, too. In 1934 to 1935, some 11.5 million Britons, nearly 40 percent of the adult population, voted in a peace ballot—after Hitler rose to power—in which huge majorities supported the League of Nations and disarmament.[63] People tried. But conciliation failed because Hitler *intended* to rearm and conquer his neighbors. He had detailed it plainly in *Mein Kampf*.

What could the democracies have done differently during the crises of the 1930s? Strong and credible British and French military threats, during Germany's rearmament, could have prevented some of Hitler's easy gains. The democracies could have deterred some of his actions, delayed his advances, and bought themselves time to vigorously rearm.

And yet the run-up to World War I shows that we can't simply always take a hard-line stance and shun conciliation. No country's leadership *intended* to start a general war in Europe. Certainly, some leaders deserve more blame: Austria-Hungary's desire to smash Serbia, Germany's blank check backing them, and Russia's rush to mobilize all attract more blame than France and Britain (although they, too, could have done more).[64] Also, every power got involved in arms races, often for self-defense, that made everyone else less secure. But, in general, more effective conciliation and limiting arms buildups would likely have helped prevent World War I—the *opposite* for the run-up to World War II.

Toughness or conciliation? Both are necessary and neither is sufficient to create and maintain peace. Any argument that the answer is to be always nice, or always tough, is dangerously incomplete.

* * *

In our time, the democracies face uncertainty about others' intentions.

In late 2021 and early 2022 many simply couldn't believe that Russian President Putin really intended to invade Ukraine. That included members of the public like my friend Rick, whom we met in a North London pub at the start of this book, as well as the intelligence agencies and leaders in France and Germany.[65] But that's exactly what Putin intended.

And what about the possibility of war between America and China over somewhere like Taiwan?

For decades, such a war in East Asia was seen as possible but very unlikely. Neither side intended war. If war happened, it would arise from unintended escalation, perhaps after an accidental collision between military aircraft leading to misunderstandings, actions, and reactions that escalated to war. For most analysts in western governments and leading universities, the main analogy was the run-up to World War I,[66] not World War II.

But around mid-2022, something changed radically among even middle-of-the-road analysts in the American and British governments. The probability of war over somewhere like Taiwan was no longer seen as small. And the reason was a radical change in the assessment of Chinese leader Xi Jinping's intentions.

That didn't mean that war was seen as more likely than not. But rather, they now saw a far from zero probability that Xi Jinping might press the metaphorical button.

Threats are often assessed as a combination of intentions and capability. Xi's intentions wouldn't matter if China was incapable, but that isn't the case. In a conventional war in East Asia, the United States could *lose*.

In late 2021, the past eighteen war games by U.S. military planners had shown American forces losing over Taiwan.[67] The think tank I work with in Washington, D.C., the Center for Strategic and International Studies (CSIS), recently made public the results of war games that tested various scenarios for a Chinese amphibious invasion of Taiwan—and they were more optimistic for America.[68] In most—but not all—scenarios the Chinese lost. But even that CSIS study requires Taiwan to resist strongly like Ukraine (which may not happen) and often predicts large U.S. losses (likely dozens of ships, hundreds of aircraft, and many thousands of service personnel). Moreover, while America is powerful in any one theater, it has only limited numbers of some key weapon systems—and could spread itself too thinly if such a war were coupled with conflict in Europe, and war against Iran in the Middle East. Or other serious complications, like some form of (very likely) North Korean involvement, which could create a two-front war in east Asia alone.[69]

The main point is that America *could easily lose a conventional war in East Asia.*

That loss matters in itself. Losing a big conventional war is the first of three ways by which the democracies can lose in our time, which we'll meet over the coming chapters.

But also, before a war, that possibility makes it harder to deter China.

And after the early blows, for example although America retains a reasonable chance of preventing an initial Chinese amphibious invasion occupying all of Taiwan—*if* Taiwanese troops have the will to fight—that is just the first fight. Bigger questions then arise, even if America won that opener: How would thousands of American deaths affect American domestic politics? How would America rebuild given American shipyards' capacity of less than 100,000 gross tons (a measure of ship volume) compared to China's 21 million, even if allies close the gap somewhat?[70] Could this, as great power wars often do, turn into a longer, larger war? If Europe and the Middle East were involved, would this be World War III fought across the globe? After Napoleon's final defeat in 1815, it took ninety-nine years until World War I erupted—and we've had about eight decades since 1945.

We are living history forward, without hindsight. We cannot know what Xi Jinping will decide: real uncertainty exists about his intentions. In his brain. A single brain that matters, because Xi is the most powerful leader in China since Mao Zedong, and he has the power to make this decision.

If Xi decides to attack, it will be up to those in countries like Taiwan, the United States, and U.S. allies to decide how they *ought* to respond.

MORALITY

Every human, every society, is flawed.

Like it or not, every society that fought in World War II believed their war was morally justified.[71] Clement Attlee, a political opponent of Churchill who beat him in the 1945 General Election, recalled that before the war Churchill had cried while telling him about the fate of Germany's Jews.[72] But across the North Sea, Germany's SS Chief Heinrich Himmler, like millions of Germans, thought his work ethically justified, too.

Every neutral society thought that avoiding the fight was justified. Sweden profited nicely selling Germany vital war supplies until late in the war. Ireland's neutrality allowed many Allied sailors to die. Even after the Holocaust was well known,[73] Ireland's prime minister and president gave official condolences on Hitler's suicide.

The belief that war is unjustifiable—pacifism—was widespread in the democracies during the 1920s and '30s.[74] After the terrible losses of World War I, international idealism led to the creation of the League of Nations. In 1928 the American and French foreign ministers persuaded fifty-nine countries to sign the Kellogg-Briand Pact to outlaw war. In 1934 and 1935 some 11.5 million Britons voted in a peace ballot, overwhelmingly supporting disarmament. In 1936 French socialist Prime Minister Léon Blum led a million-strong demonstration through Paris in favor of peace.

Pacifists' political successes intentionally helped to slow the democracies' preparations for war against Nazi Germany. But in Germany, the Nazis sent prominent pacifists to exile, prison, or the concentration camp. Stalin's Russia treated them similarly.[75]

Pacifists in the democracies had no *means* to stop Hitler or Stalin launching wars, and support for pacificism evaporated—something today's pacificists in the democracies might usefully remember when reflecting on how they might *really* react to events. During the war, the British Commonwealth and United States also allowed "conscientious objection" to fighting (again, unlike Germany or Russia). But only a minuscule number took that option: fewer than sixty thousand in Britain out of some five million who served, and only forty-three thousand in the United States out of over twelve million.[76]

At the time of writing, pacifists aren't exactly prominent inside Putin's Russia, Xi's China, Ali Khamenei's Iran, or Kim Jong Un's North Korea. Pacificists don't have much power in any part of Israel-Palestine either, or the dozens of other places with armed conflict today.[77]

Peace is a good *end*, but pacifism seems far from having any *means* of getting there.

So if sometimes morally we *ought* to fight, how can we better morally judge what ends to fight for and what means to use? And how does our brain's orchestra make such judgments?

Thinking about justified wars typically revolves around ethical judgments about going to war, and how to fight in war. Justly going to war requires that a war intends to avert the right kind of problem, and that combatants intend to use proportionate means. Justice within war typically requires that belligerents intentionally attack only military objectives, and that foreseen but unintended harms must be proportionate to the military advantage achieved.[78]

Put another way, intentions and consequences matter. That's also true in much domestic law, where murder is deemed morally worse than manslaughter because it's intentional, and worse than serious assault because the consequence is death.

Neuroscience's biggest finding for morality is that we have no single specialized brain module for moral decisions—instead we assess moral decisions using *the same basic neural machinery as for other decisions.*[79] In our brain's orchestra, our mentalizing machinery helps assess intentions. Other brain systems assess risks, rewards, and punishments to help judge consequences. Hunger can affect the emotions guiding our assessments. And so on. That's why better self-knowledge about our orchestra of brain systems—with all its strengths, weaknesses, and personal preferences—can help us think through ethical challenges.

We can combine this with millennia of cumulative thinking, over which philosophers have invented and refined moral systems. These give us a tremendous collection of lenses. Western philosophy has three main sets of moral ideas, and analogous ideas appear in other traditions like China's.[80] Deontology emphasizes the rightness or wrongness of acts (for example, "It is wrong to kill"). Utilitarianism emphasizes outcomes ("Would more people die if you chose war or peace?"). Virtue ethics asks what a virtuous person would do in the same circumstances ("Would a virtuous person stand and fight against seemingly invincible Nazi Germany?").

All three capture some of what emerges from our brain's orchestra: human brains will care about the intentions of actions (as seen in this chapter) *and* consequences (as we'll see in Chapter 9), *and* how actions relate to identity as a virtuous person (which the next chapter explores). We must consider the whole orchestra, because focusing too exclusively on any single philosophical concept won't accurately predict the messy, ambiguous Models by which humans actually make moral decisions. Focusing purely on consequences and totally ignoring the rightness of acts, for example, won't resonate with many people: Should you intentionally shoot one child in the face to save two children from death? That's a decision on which good people can differ.

Understanding the brain machinery that makes moral decisions also helps us better anticipate how other people will react to events like terror attacks or war. Our own judgments often *feel* right so viscerally, so deep down inside ourselves, that we *feel* like others simply must share them. But that's not correct. Chapter 3 described the visceral instincts that drive people to reject unfairness and their responses to risk—and in both cases people can have very different preferences: some people care a lot about unfairness and others less so; some people like risks of various types, and others dislike those same risks. For each of these varied people their preferences feel right *to them*. And because the same neural machinery used for nonmoral decisions assesses unfairness and risks in moral decisions, those very varied preferences make individuals feel very differently about moral decisions.

A recent brain imaging study showed that an individual's preferences for risk in decisions about money, for example, strongly predicted their preferences in hypothetical moral decisions about life and death.[81] That study revealed brain activity during moral decisions in brain regions related to risk assessment—and this was integrated into the broader decision-making network, which included a key mentalizing region (the temporoparietal junction we met earlier) that predicted how much people cared about the worst outcomes in these moral decisions. Put simply, we should try to remember a useful piece of self-knowledge about us humans: when other people hold different opinions from us and say they feel very strongly about a moral decision, they really might.

Realizing that our machinery for morality is the same as our basic machinery for other decisions also brings another benefit: when considering moral decisions, we can apply the extensive research that's already looked at those more basic decisions. For example, across our globe that's so rich in cultural diversity, factors like risk-taking and rejection of unfairness show greater cultural commonalities than cultural differences (although, yes, some differences exist)[82]—and this is a cause for optimism that cultural divides in morality between societies are not as unbridgeable as they may seem. Large studies of moral decisions across more technologically sophisticated countries revealed the same pattern.[83] As did recent anthropology.[84]

Considering moral decisions in these terms brings yet another benefit: we can apply tools like the extensive mathematical ideas developed to quantify risk or unfairness in fields like economics. That may sound very academic, but we increasingly need clear mathematical rules for morality that we can code into AI. As machines take on more responsibility, and their AI moves toward something more freethinking, what decisions *ought* they to make?

Humans driving cars don't currently specify their moral intentions. But for driving we soon will—as individuals, societies, or both—need to specify our morality in computer code. In the civilian world, driverless vehicles must often make split-second choices between two *bad* options. For instance: (a) run over pedestrians; or (b) sacrifice themselves and their passenger to save the pedestrians. One big recent study asked people what they wanted: and participants typically wanted other people to buy a car that sacrificed its passengers for the greater good; but themselves preferred riding in a vehicle that protected its passengers at all costs.[85]

Soldiers in Afghanistan and Iraq faced millions of decisions that are highly analogous: trading off their personal protection against civilian safety. How should soldiers program their AI systems to make such trade-offs? It will be life and death. As we saw in Chapter 3, soldiers must balance risking their lives, fighting aggressively, and showing restraint. Better AI consciences could make soldiers' autonomous systems more effective—in the same way that Mao Zedong's "five rules and eight points" (such as being courteous and not stealing) helped his soldiers win over local populations.

Applying inspiration from humans to morality for AI also helps us set appropriate expectations for how good AI morality can *ever* become. AI research often takes human performance—for example, in perception—as a benchmark. Human moral judgment is inherently mixed and slippery because it emerges from our brain's orchestra. Can we humans expect better of AI, or even, given our diverging preferences, ever agree on what *better* moral judgment would be? How do we also set an upper limit on the machine's moral horizons? We humans have hierarchical Models, as we've seen, with overarching goals (for example, go to university) under which sit sub-goals (write cover letter), and so on. At what levels in our hierarchies of actions do we justify our means and ends? René Carmille, the French Resistance hero, lied, to achieve a higher end.

Even in a conflict like World War II against Nazi Germany, moral decisions about justified means and ends were easier in theory—and with hindsight—than for people living history forward. And the competition that followed would be even more morally ambiguous.

* * *

Before World War II ended, the Cold War's roots started taking hold, dividing the Anglo-Americans from the Russians. When Stalin met Churchill and U.S. President Franklin Roosevelt at the Yalta Conference in February 1945, Stalin won his desired sphere of influence in eastern Europe. He also consented to free elections there, including in the Baltic States and Poland.

But Stalin had no intention of honoring that promise, and when he imposed a pro-Russian government in Poland, the British and Americans increasingly lost trust in him. Roosevelt died of a brain bleed on April 12, 1945. As Roosevelt had said, just two weeks before, "[Stalin] has broken every one of the promises made at Yalta."[86]

With confidence from the successful July 16 atomic bomb test, President Harry Truman's new administration decided to occupy Japan alone. The atomic bomb itself intensified Russian-American distrust. Stalin, not without reason, saw the U.S. bomb as a means to extract postwar concessions: "A-bomb blackmail is American policy."[87]

Differing intentions were the fundamental reason the Cold War emerged so soon from World War II. The postwar settlement intended by Churchill and Roosevelt would balance power and also embrace principles. Stalin aimed to ensure his security and his country's security, and to foster rivalries between capitalists that would lead to new war—with eventual communist domination of Europe.[88]

The Cold War was a period of what has become called "gray zone" conflict—competition that is neither fully war, nor fully peace. Gray zone conflict has occurred throughout history, such as in the decade of gray zone conflict before World War I, or in the years before World War II. Like those previous episodes, the Cold War wasn't "war" between the west and Russia in the traditional sense, which scholars generally define as serious, politically motivated organized violence between human groups. Yet nor was it peace in the fuller sense, which implies a social and political order generally accepted as just.[89]

But although it was not war, the Cold War was a very big divide.

Only very fleetingly, as the fighting in Europe finished, did human beings from the different sides have a chance to recognize each other's humanity.

On April 25, 1945, the American and Russian armies met at Torgau, on the River Elbe in eastern Germany. As fellow humans the two sides danced and shook hands; men and women kissed; they drank; and they had hope.

Liubova Kozinchenka was a young woman in the 58th Guards Division of the Red Army. As Liubova recalled:

> We waited for them to come ashore. We could see their faces. They looked like ordinary people. We had imagined something different. Well, they were Americans!

From the other side, Al Aronson was a young man from the 69th Infantry Division of the U.S. Army. Al recalled:

> I guess we didn't know what to expect from the Russians, but when you looked at them and examined them, you couldn't tell whether, you know? If you put an American uniform on them, they could have been American![90]

It's almost a cliché, but many travelers who journey far from their own society are astonished to find that the people over *there* turn out to be familiar. It happened to me as a young medical student having grown up in suburban London. I went to work on an aid project in rural Kenya, miles from the single tarmac road that passed through a tiny nearby town. The local community lived in mud huts and practiced female circumcision; some were polygamous (if they could afford it); nobody wore shoes except the local chief; and thousands had died in conflict with a neighboring tribe not long before. After a couple of weeks, once I came to know the people as individuals, I remember being struck by how similar the people were to those in the village in rural Leicestershire where my mother had grown up. It *is* a cliché, but it changed forever how I see myself and see others from very different societies.

How much more intense must the joyous emotions have been, after so much fighting, for those Americans and Russians who embraced at the River Elbe? Considering how joyous this is, it seems regrettable that human beings insist on forcing themselves into separate groups. But as the next chapter will show, the human capacity to form distinctive, coherent societies is one of the leaps that made us the thinking beings that we are.

8

LEADERS AND SOCIAL ALCHEMY

CONTRIBUTIONS FROM TEMPORAL CORTEX

What is a leader? Why, out of the millions of Americans, British, and Russians, were these nations represented at a meeting in July 1945 by Truman, Churchill, and Stalin? What made those three individuals representative of their nations, and also unique, outstanding, and different? To help answer those questions, we'll turn to one of their contemporaries.

In 1934, Mao Zedong went into the Long March as one among many. After the Long March ended in 1935, he was *the* leader. For over a decade more, Mao led forces weaker than his enemies—Chinese Nationalists or Japanese—so that his forces could survive and grow. By 1949 he led the Communists to victory in China's civil war. A year later, Mao chose to send his troops into the Korean War. His soldiers surprised and pushed back the vastly better-equipped U.S. forces, and then sustained a brutal stalemate at the 38th parallel until 1953.

Mao influenced individuals, groups, committees, bureaucracies, and eventually societies far beyond China's borders as a leader of global communism. He led China into the Great Leap Forward that killed some forty million, and into the tumultuous Cultural Revolution.

A leader is not just a guide who points out a direction, nor just a manager who gets things done through people, although Mao could do both. Inspiring, terrifying, and persuasive—he wrote poetry about the Long

March—thousands, millions, and eventually hundreds of millions followed him.

How can one person lead 15, or 150, or 15,000, or 1,350,000,000 others?

Our societies are full of leaders in so many ways. The street party on my suburban road in North London needed someone to take the lead and coordinate the rest of us: decide on a date, apply to the local authority to close the road, arrange the bouncy castle, food, drinks, music, games, bunting . . . Everyone pitched in, but the party only happened because Hannah from number nineteen took the lead.

The temporal cortex lies just below the parietal cortex—and it contains association cortex that shapes both leading and following. Leaders must take responsibility for others, something that many humans don't like doing when they face uncertainty. Many people happily let others take on that burden. But why do they follow one person rather than somebody else—or choose to follow anybody at all? Successful leaders have used the principles of influence to bring others along with them, from Hannah at number nineteen to ancient Greek orators, Winston Churchill, Mao, and Nelson Mandela.

But before we consider how one person leads others, there must be coherent groups to lead: So, how do humans create vastly larger groups than any other primate species? Comparing primate species, the overall size of the cortex roughly relates to the size of social groups.[1] Humans have the biggest such cortex, but even that only predicts groups of 150, or perhaps a few hundred—that's nothing like the thousands or millions in human societies. Something special happened: social alchemy.

Medieval alchemists sought to turn base metals into gold. Social alchemy is far more extraordinary: creating many individuals whose Models of themselves are compatible enough with each other to turn those individuals into coherent groups that can act together. The individuals create the groups *and* the groups create the individuals. Individuals have Models that answer the question "Who am I?"; *and* groups form cultures that are the Models created between individuals to reflect "how things are done around here." Identities help create cultures *and* cultures help create identities. They cycle upward together in an identity-culture spiral.

What truly turbocharged this spiral was a uniquely sophisticated human capability: language. Our language can efficiently capture ideas, communicate ideas, and accumulate ideas. That's a major reason humans (not chimps) built spaceships to the moon. And nuclear weapons.

This chapter examines both parts of the identity-culture spiral: the Model of "Who am I?" and the Model of "How do we do things around here?" We ask how and why leaders can steer our groups. How others—in fact *all* of us in society—influence our groups. And how even the most powerful can lose control.

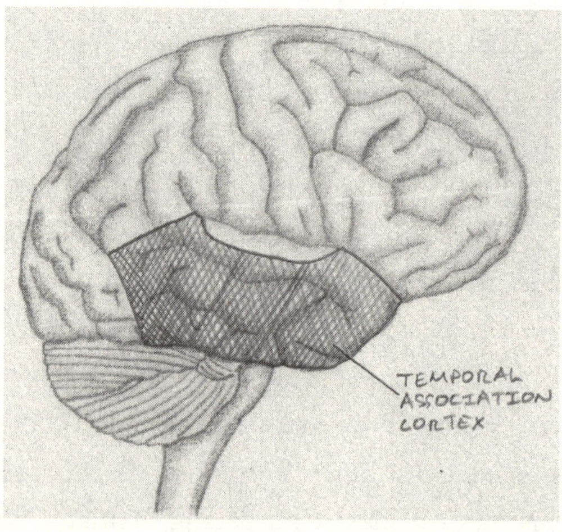

FIGURE 13: The temporal lobe contains a large area of association cortex.

WHO AM I?

Who am I? Who am I *not*? Who was I, and who could I be? The experience of being me *seems* a genuine property of how things are. My identity seems real. As philosopher René Descartes put it: *cogito ergo sum*. I think, therefore I am. But who is "I"?

For a "split brain" patient whose main connection between left and right cortex is cut, one "self" can split into two. In craniopagus twins who share some brain structures, one twin can feel when the other drinks orange juice.[2]

What it means to *be* you arises from your brain. Distinctive brain systems, which crucially include your temporal cortex, combine to build your

Model of who you are. And as described in turn below, this combines your embodied self, your narrative self, and your social self.[3]

The embodied self means your sense that your body is yours, including all its parts, and that you are in the same place as your body at the same time.[4] You have that sense of ownership, a feeling of being alive, and a first-person perspective somewhere in your head behind the eyes. But your embodied self can be disrupted—for example, by directly stimulating the temporal cortex. As a patient exclaimed when neurosurgeon Wilder Penfield applied electrical current to their temporal cortex, "I have a queer sensation that I am not here . . . as though I were half here and half not here."

And your embodied self also illustrates a central feature across all aspects of your self—it *changes*. Those changes happen within limits, but far more than it often seems. Your embodied self changes as you grow up, when your body grows many times in size and capability. It changes if accidents cause loss or disability. And as we saw in Chapter 6, even learning to use tools can change where we perceive our body's boundaries, like monkeys who learn to use rakes, or the samurai warrior with his sword.

The narrative self weaves together different parts of your past life to situate you in the world today and project you into the future. Like every story, your narrative self has characters, a plot, and themes. Many areas of temporal cortex are involved in memory—and, as we saw in Chapter 4, memory is for the future, so that damage to our memory systems casts us adrift in our lives. My patients with dementia, for example, could gradually lose the idea of what makes them who they are.

Your narrative self changes over time. Partly this arises from changing capabilities: because words help us file memories for future retrieval, for instance, young children may only remember events after learning the words to describe them.[5] And partly our narratives are actively shaped. The ability to create a narrative about your life typically comes online in teenage years, so a typical ten-year-old won't see their parents' divorce as a turning point in their life, but a fifteen-year-old likely will.[6] Recent research suggests we can learn to tell better stories about ourselves[7]—and militaries have long used stories to create a sense of belonging to the unit, regiment, country, or religion. Change is central to the identity-culture spiral, and our narrative self draws on themes we encounter in social life.[8] From marketers to militaries and mullahs, all wield narratives. The first DARPA project for which they asked my advice was called "Narrative Networks," which examined how to influence narratives in the brain. A core finding was that our narratives combine with our social self.

The social self is about how you perceive others perceiving you. If you're chatting with someone, for example, and they smile and nod (or scowl), this lets you know that their Model of you is approving (or disapproving). Much of this happens without conscious effort as you go about your life, although occasionally you may stop to reflect, look higher up in your hierarchy of processing about others, and explicitly ask yourself what they think about you. These social skills are crucial because humans spontaneously form groups that can be critical for us to survive and thrive—and our social self reflects the social groups of which we're part.[9]

Family is a fundamental first group. We must recognize family so that we know who we can ask for help; and we learn to act like our kin so that they will recognize us. We soon extend beyond family to those who speak similarly to us. Already by nine to twelve months old, infants prefer familiar songs that signal group membership.[10]

As we get older, we join many groups. By definition, where a group exists of which we are part, an "in-group," there is also an "out-group." Studies show that simply providing differently colored T-shirts to random selections of participants can create in-groups and out-groups.[11] In daily life we shift constantly between political, ethnic, religious, sporting, professional, and myriad other affiliations, which can rouse powerful feelings—joy when our group is winning (in sports or politics, for example, but not only those) and misery in defeat. Militaries institutionalize such basic mechanisms through uniforms, badges, marching, and songs to sculpt the social self.

Militaries also harness the fact that our identities hinge on whom we feel we belong with—and that we cannot separate these identities from how we value ourselves and wish to be valued by others.[12] "I fight for the men around me." "I am a member of the SAS." "I am a Navy SEAL." "I am a Communist." How our social group values us couldn't matter more than when our lives literally depend on our social group.

Militaries who retain recruits for longer can often also benefit from how our social self changes over time, because we prefer to learn from the in-group rather than the out-group, and this tends to strengthen the group's influence on our identity.[13] A brain imaging study in adults, for instance, shows that the prediction errors by which we learn are larger when learning from an in-group.[14] Infants aged only eleven months already mimic members of their in-group more than they mimic other people.[15]

Such learning from our in-group brings benefits. As the Roman legions showed, greater similarity helps group members coordinate, which helps units function smoothly and helps the coordination of units at ever larger scales. For an individual, becoming more like others can help them get accepted—which can be crucial if your life depends on your group in combat. And learning from the in-group makes sense because they're typically less likely to be trying to deceive us than the out-group.

And if an in-group member does deceive us? Then we'll often punish that betrayal (a prediction error) more than for out-group members, from whom we already expect bad behavior. Three-year-old children in one study, for example, only enforced social rules for in-group members in games, but not for out-group members.[16] Like the Turkana raiders we met in the last chapter, if you're caught deviating from your in-group's norms you should expect punishment—in that case a beating, but brain imaging studies suggest even the simple fact of social exclusion can be distressing.[17]

Your embodied, narrative, and social selves combine in the experience of being you. *You* exist with a body that can perceive and act; *you* have a narrative timeline from past to future; and *you* have a social self based on the groups to which you do and don't belong. Each part of your identity can change—and sometimes they must.

* * *

What were German people to make of themselves, among the rubble of 1945, in a country occupied to prevent resurgent Nazism and militarism?

Change came slowly: as we've seen, beliefs about Nazism weren't that unfavorable for quite a while after 1945. Historian Tony Judt's book *Postwar* describes U.S. opinion surveys in the American zone of occupied Germany. Those surveys found that a consistent majority in the years 1945 to 1949 stated National Socialism to have been a good idea badly applied. In 1950, one in three said the Nuremberg trials had been unfair. In 1952, 37 percent said Germany was better off without the Jews on its territory. And still by 1952, 25 percent had a good opinion of Hitler.[18]

A recent study looked at people who had been active participants in Nazi Germany, who then recast their past experience so that they could move on to successful careers—and lives—in postwar West Germany.[19] Because many did.

These past Nazis resculpted their narrative self: not running from memories of their pasts but embracing selective parts of their narratives during the Third Reich.

They also reoriented their social self. Massive occupying armies from the Soviet Russia, the United States, and Britain closed off old affordances. That's why these once-Nazis made the selective parts of their past fit into the social groups that postwar western Germany now afforded to them: the conservative character of a new West Germany, and their side in the ideological contest of the Cold War. The western powers actively supported these new affordances: supporting democracy; providing security from external threats; and most importantly, helping spur the economic growth that afforded German people—and German young people—a new identity that could represent pride in economic success.

But Germany wasn't Europe's only challenge. As Winston Churchill famously described in a March 5, 1946, speech, an "iron curtain" divided the continent.[20]

Stalin's coup in Czechoslovakia persuaded the U.S. Congress to approve the Marshall Plan: offering a vast aid package to all Europe. But as Stalin tried to squeeze the west in the Berlin blockade, how could western Europe keep him out?

At the British Foreign Secretary's urging, secret discussions took place in Washington, and by April 1949 these had led to the North Atlantic

Treaty Organization (NATO) formed by America, Canada, and ten European states.[21] As NATO's first secretary-general, Lord Ismay, described, NATO was created to "keep the Soviet Union out, the Americans in, and the Germans down."[22]

It did a remarkable job. The western allies remained outnumbered on the ground twelve to one, and only two of the fourteen divisions in western Europe were American.[23] But the *identity* of those American soldiers was crucial: any dead Americans killed by invading Soviets would matter profoundly to Americans back home. Part of their in-group.

Western and eastern groupings increasingly formed around the United States and Soviet Russia, as both sides offered very different answers to the question of what it meant to *be* a modern human. People on both sides saw themselves as standard-bearers of progress. Both sides pushed ideas they thought applicable to everyone, everywhere, who must answer the question "Who am I?"

Cold War conflict hardened the differences between these two groupings, and this conflict's core was a clash between sets of ideas. The United States felt it was founded not on myths of blood or common heritage, but on ideas.[24] A country of immigrants in which shared ideas—such as democracy, individualism, and voluntarism—bound its people together. Russia's Soviet regime was also built on ideas—in that case, ideas based on class conflict and the transformation of individuals and societies toward communism—that bound its people together. Their sets of ideas enabled each of the two superpowers to function as a coherent society.

TALKING CULTURES

We might often regret the "them and us" quality of human life, but it's worth stepping back to see how amazing and unique it is that more than hundreds of humans *can* form a society or a group at all. No other primate can.

Over millennia, we unique humans have soared over two hurdles to create our societies' sheer size. No other primate can even hobble over the first.

- Hurdle 1 is getting from hundreds to the scale of *tribes*. Tribes can include many thousands of individuals, and virtually all human societies organized themselves tribally at one point. Nobody knows for certain how we jumped this hurdle, but it probably involved groups developing shared religious beliefs around the worship of dead ancestors, with an individual's role defined by the society surrounding them before birth.[25] Tribal societies are militarily stronger than smaller groups, so as tribes emerged this may have spurred other groups to imitate tribes in order to compete.
- Hurdle 2 is getting to the scale of a *state*.[26] States began around six thousand years ago in the Middle East. States involve a centralized authority with a hierarchy of subordinates and a monopoly of legitimate force within a territory. To create and maintain such complicated structures required religious beliefs, customs, shared ideas, and institutions.

Leaping over both hurdles required shared Models that are created *between* individuals and contain the ideas, customs, and social behaviors that reflect "how things are done around here." That is, culture.[27] And culture requires communication.

Other animals can communicate well, such as dolphins, chimps, dogs, or orcas.[28] But human language gives us communication abilities that far exceed any other animal's.

Language enables us to take the Models we have in our brains *and put them into someone else's brain*. We can have a Model in our head about how to make a flint axe, or how to ford the big river, or what gods look like—and we can communicate that Model's various parts to someone else. During a conversation, I can check that the Model another person is building in their brain is close enough to what I was trying to get across—and if not, I can change how I communicate.

Language enables me to enter a shared mental world. That means I can learn from others' experiences and adopt their Models if they seem better than mine. Sharing our Models also opens up an entirely new way of influencing others' behavior—by giving them new Models of how the world works: gods, new techniques for hunting, or gossip about another tribe member's reputation.

FIGURE 14: A Model in one person's brain can be sent—using language—so that Model exists in someone else's brain, too. The Model can be discussed and changed. The two people (or more) can share the Model.

Language is words used in a structured way to communicate. Language was originally mainly spoken, and spoken language relies on a network of brain regions across association cortex. Regions in the temporal cortex, and adjacent areas of the parietal cortex, are particularly important to comprehend what others are saying. Areas of frontal cortex farther forward in the brain help us produce speech.[29] Much current evidence suggests that humans use Models to understand speech, and use mechanisms involving prediction errors to learn and improve their Models of languages.[30]

Language neatly packages big chunks of knowledge into concepts.[31] It gives us a vocabulary of words like "hammer," "dog," or "discipline" so that we can communicate far more efficiently and so that cultures can create *cumulative* knowledge. We can neatly describe colors as "light" or "dark," and then add more to get the eleven basic colors in English. A new learner need not reinvent "the wheel," "zero," or "submarine," and these rich concepts enable a new learner to better Model and anticipate their universe. The temporal lobe is key for such concepts—as shown by a specific type of dementia that attacks the temporal lobe, which can leave patients speaking fluently but losing knowledge of naming things.[32] Those patients can point to trees in the hospital courtyard, but say, "I don't know what those green things are anymore."

The ability to communicate Models can create and wield power. The neatly packaged concepts in words can transfer complicated, abstracted, and standardized Models of the world—exactly what's needed to shape the compatible enough individuals who can form tribes or states. We shape laws entirely with words, from the Magna Carta to the American Constitution, and on to more recent state building. And the power of language was hugely boosted when, as well as speaking, we began to *write*.

Written language uses the same brain regions used for spoken language, except with different inputs and outputs. Instead of hearing, for instance, it uses inputs from other regions of temporal cortex closer to where we process visual information like words.[33]

Writing first appeared roughly when the first states emerged.[34] As groups of priests and local chiefs scaled up and institutionalized power structures, they used writing to help turn thousands of cultivators, artisans, and laborers into subjects to be counted, taxed, and conscripted. Writing may have led a millennium later to the written *Epic of Gilgamesh*, but writing began for purposes of state.

The U.S. military has a special relationship with writing. Speaking on Veterans Day a few days after the 2020 U.S. presidential election, the chairman of the Joint Chiefs, General Mark Milley, said:

> We are unique among armies, we are unique among militaries. We do not take an oath to a king or queen, or tyrant or dictator, we do not take an oath to an individual. No, we do not take an oath to a country, a tribe or a religion. We take an oath to the Constitution, and . . . each of us protects and defends that document.[35]

Language has enabled our cultures—such as the modern U.S. military's culture—to become enormously powerful. Cultures are one side of the identity-culture spiral, which makes individuals whose Models are compatible enough to form coherent groups that will fight and die together.

But powerful as shared Models can be, no beliefs are *all*-powerful. Hitler's brain dreamed, as we saw earlier, of German supermen who could withstand the freezing cold in lederhosen. But his troops discovered outside Moscow that human ideas can't wish away physical reality.

Similarly, many people hope that culture can abolish nuclear weapons.

Shortly after I moved to Washington, D.C., a few years ago, I went to a talk about nuclear weapons. Partway through, the speaker held up a U.S. dollar banknote and said the bill had value only because we all agreed it had value—and if we all agreed it had no value, then that would be true, too. He then passionately asserted that, in a similar way, if the world community could all agree that nuclear weapons had no value, then—*voilà!*—they would all become obsolete.

Was he right? Only if we could be pretty much certain that everyone, everywhere, who could potentially build nuclear weapons agreed to this shared belief—pretty much indefinitely. Against that we must weigh the physical reality (like Russian winter cold) that a hydrogen bomb let off in Manhattan today would almost certainly kill hundreds of thousands.

Many people even hope culture can abolish war.[36]

But it's unclear how culture could anytime soon—and enduringly—resolve the fears and clashing interests in all places like Taiwan, the India-Pakistan border, the Korean Peninsula, Sudan, Congo, the Middle East . . .

Even if we could, culture will retain the seeds of future war. Classics like Homer, Shakespeare, the Bible, the Koran, and China's classics—all afford war. As does any summary of world history.

Those seeds matter because, for both good and bad, cultures always change. All societies are intergenerational—victories must be won again in the brains of each new generation. Ibn Khaldūn, the fourteenth-century Muslim scholar, believed that empires were created and collapsed over three generations.[37] The first generation are driven founders. The second generation can preserve what they saw their parents create. The third generation's rulers are palace-suckled princelings without the tenacity to sustain the founders' creation.

Khaldūn's hypothesis reflects the process by which our neural machinery comes to understand the world. Each new brain starts as a baby's brain for whom much of the world is, to quote William James, the father of

American psychology, a "blooming, buzzing confusion."[38] Our new brains don't just download our worldviews fully formed and identical to those of our parents, version 2.0. Each child grows up seeing the world through its own eyes and builds its own Models of the world in its brain.

Consequently, our forebears' hard-fought victories are often to us an uninspiring status quo. Millennials in advanced democracies are less satisfied with democracy than the preceding generations and less likely to believe it "essential" to live in a democracy.[39]

This continual generational churn of new Models can never stop. Each generation is destined to learn from their own mistakes. "Most human beings have an almost infinite capacity for taking things for granted," said Aldous Huxley, author of the acclaimed dystopian novel *Brave New World* (and brother of a Nobel Prize–winning neuroscientist). "That men do not learn very much from the lessons of history is the most important of all the lessons that history has to teach."[40]

* * *

In China, unlike Europe, World War II's end marked no clear new beginning. Instead, it allowed the decades-old Chinese civil war to resume. When war once again erupted, Chiang Kai-shek's Nationalists had the crushing numbers and machines to win—but by 1949 Mao's Communists instead won. Why?

Differing cultures were one key factor, which weakened the Nationalists and strengthened the Communists.

The Nationalist armies, as military historians have described, were "handicapped by a Byzantine bureaucratic culture" full of petty tyrants.[41] Instead of well-established common ideas, customs, and behaviors to help them coordinate, the Nationalist forces used an amalgam of German, Japanese, and American methods. And whereas Chiang Kai-shek's Whampoa Academy in the 1920s had imbued his forces with the much vaunted "Whampoa spirit," eight years of hard fighting against the Japanese killed many whose identity embodied that military culture. When Chiang later reflected on the Nationalists' total defeat on the mainland, for him the basic reason was failure to maintain Party offices and political officers throughout the army.[42] That's why after fleeing with the rump of his army to Taiwan in 1949, he reformed political work among his troops. And there, with American support, Chiang remained until his death in 1975, the president on Taiwan.

But the civil war was a communist success, not just a Nationalist failure. Mao and his military organizer Zhu De were a formidable team.[43] Mao brilliantly communicated his political ideas—and Zhu De brilliantly organized the more practical customs, rules, regulations, and behaviors that created a disciplined military culture. That discipline helped to win over populations, and then in January 1949 to win the decisive Battle of Huai Hai. On October 1, a victorious Mao Zedong proclaimed the formation of the People's Republic of China (PRC).

Mao wielded culture throughout his rule over the PRC, to actively shape the identity-culture spiral. He used culture to shape the narrative and social selves, which in turn constructed the culture. Narratives were carefully crafted by Mao for how China's entire history had led toward communist victory,[44] to help people tell the stories of their lives. The social self was shaped by ferocious pressures on how people dressed, spoke, and lived their everyday lives.

And we must remember that although this all sounds imposed (because it was) there were also millions of willing followers. After victory in 1949, large numbers of Chinese people really did flock to the new regime's banner. After decades of war, the communist revolution gave some the opportunity to immerse themselves in something bigger than the individual, something meaningful, to set China right.[45]

The Cultural Revolution best illustrates how ruthlessly Mao shaped the identity-culture spiral, and how millions fervently followed. Mao began the Cultural Revolution in 1966, and it dominated his reign's last decade. He aimed squarely at *both* halves of the identity-culture spiral. "There are two aspects of socialist transformation," Mao once observed. "One is the transformation of institutions, and the other is the transformation of people."[46] It aimed at identity: "The Cultural Revolution was a revolution to touch people's souls," averred a former official.[47] And it aimed at culture, seeking to replace what were slightingly called the "Four Olds": old ideas, old culture, old customs, and old thinking.[48] Violent factions formed, split, and maneuvered as hundreds of millions of lives were uprooted.

The Cultural Revolution profoundly affected every survivor of its chaotic crucible, including those who rose decades later to influential positions. Like a top Chinese nuclear weapons scientist whom I've met many times. Or like a leading thinker on China's role in the world who today argues for a strong, benevolent order—and who recalls from the Cultural Revolution his profound fear, desperation for survival, and a hope that massive war would break out to somehow, someway change his life.[49] Or like a then teenager, forced to wear an iron dunce's cap while a crowd shouted for his punishment, who was desperately hungry but whose own mother turned him away out of political fear, and who was exiled from Beijing to a peasant's life: current Chinese leader Xi Jinping.[50]

Mao was an extremely effective leader, a social alchemist who shaped the identity-culture spiral as *the* leader of China's Communists from 1935, and then as *the* leader of China for decades after 1949. Whether you think the directions in which Mao steered other humans were good or ill, he masterfully used language to lead, to communicate his Model to guide millions of humans. Millions of human followers.

LEADING AND FOLLOWING

Leadership is a relationship through which one person influences others to work together so they can achieve a goal—and leaders do that by communicating a Model that can guide others to accomplish what those others couldn't do working individually.

Leaders don't determine every historical event, and few observers today agree with a "great man theory of history." But it's implausible to suggest that the revolutionary and Napoleonic wars from 1789 to 1815 would have turned out the same without Napoleon Bonaparte. Or to explain World War II without Adolf Hitler, under whose name or signature were issued 578 of the 650 major German legislative orders during that war.[51] Or explain the Cold War without Joseph Stalin and Mikhail Gorbachev. Or the movements led by Gandhi or Martin Luther King Jr. Or the lives of the men in the British World War II tanks led for years by my great-uncle Sydney Spiers. Or the party on our street in London without Hannah at number nineteen. Leaders are only one factor, and leaders matter.

But why do we even have leaders?

Most social species self-organize into social hierarchies because it can help decrease aggression and so conserve energy in the group.[52] The brains of many animals, from rodents to primates, carefully track social status and are changed by social status.[53] The temporal cortex is involved—scanning the brains of macaques, for example, showed that social rank correlated with size and activity in parts of the temporal cortex.[54]

In humans, brain imaging shows we, too, learn models of social hierarchies. Indeed, our brains can create maps to navigate through more complicated social hierarchies, where status varies in multiple ways.[55] Social hierarchies were central, and became increasingly institutionalized, as human societies leaped over the hurdles in group size from hunter-gatherer groups, to tribes, to states.[56]

But hierarchy isn't the same as leading. And "leadership" in animal groups like fish shoals or bird flocks actually arises from simple coordination principles.[57]

Human leadership gets other people to *follow*, and it arises from two separate sources of status: dominance and prestige.[58] Dominance rests more on coercion and threat, while prestige rests more on true persuasion and deferential agreement. We must consider both to understand human leadership.

Dominance is what we typically think of when someone is big and powerful.[59] Dominant people are more likely to "look large" by standing tall and spreading their limbs apart—after winning Olympic judo matches, even congenitally blind humans make the same body postures as sighted judo players. By ten months old, human infants expect size to matter in conflicts between rectangular shapes. In adult brains, temporal cortex activity tracks when people are seeing dominant facial features and postures, and also tracks when people use those features to judge the relative dominance between two individuals.[60] We track such features because they predict success in our social worlds: taller executives earn more money, and people with more dominant-looking faces are more likely to win elections.[61] For children and adults alike—across many divergent types of societies—dominance affects social influence, collective decision-making, and reproductive success.[62]

Another source of status, prestige, involves a respect for admirable qualities. Our remarkable human language abilities are central, as they enable our sophisticated teaching, learning, tool use, and social organization. Research among communities outside the modern state—such as on the Andaman Islands in the Indian Ocean from 1906 to 1908—suggested that such admirable qualities were "skill in hunting and warfare, generosity and kindness, and freedom from bad temper."[63] Prestige is even found in very small, highly egalitarian societies that don't possess formal leadership roles or hierarchy. In such small settings and our modern lives, prestige can give us important clues about potential teachers from whom we might learn: if we are new learners, it's often tricky to know *which* teachers are good, and so a teacher's prestige among more experienced learners can help us decide who to follow. Adults and children are more likely to pay attention, imitate, learn from, and defer to people with higher prestige.[64] And I've certainly used such clues when I've sought teachers, mentors, and examples to follow.

So we have leaders partly because we form social hierarchies, *and* partly because people with dominance or prestige (or both) get other people to follow them. Over millennia this leading and following became institutionalized as we moved from groups to tribes to states. Many compelling experiments have now examined how people follow, including the famous Stanford prison experiments (in which ordinary research participants became unpleasant "prison guards") or the equally famous Milgram experiments (in which participants obeyed instructions to administer apparently dangerous electric shocks). These experiments have shown that many humans—although not all, including some who resist—often do obediently conform to and follow others.[65]

Moreover, we also have leaders because strong leadership brings effectiveness and order in many situations. If a doctor in a hospital is working as part of a large group on a serious emergency trauma patient—they will need someone to lead and organize the team, because a free-for-all is simply less effective, and things get missed. Hierarchy is also needed more broadly in the hospital: as a doctor, if I ask a nurse to administer a medication that I have authority to prescribe—and will be held responsible for having prescribed—unless there is a good reason, the request should be carried out. During China's Cultural Revolution they abolished conventional tokens of military hierarchy in uniforms, but that caused such confusion that they ended up using the number of pockets to indicate rank (officers had two more than enlisted men).[66]

Human groups with leadership are usually far more militarily powerful than atomized, divided groups lacking leadership. Once that is understood, leadership becomes an affordance, a possibility, that cannot be "undiscovered." Napoleon thought of himself as a new Alexander the Great, but the prototypes emerged long before either was born. Tribes have leaders and were often more militarily powerful than smaller groups without such leaders. States have hierarchies and leaders—and are so powerful that almost every human alive now lives in a state.

But while all these reasons tell us why we have leading and following—social hierarchy, dominance, prestige, group effectiveness—they aren't enough to explain: What makes some leaders more or less effective?

Effective leaders require the *self-confidence* to shoulder responsibility for others; a clear Model of what the leader wants to achieve that provides *purpose* for others; and the ability to *communicate* their Model—to place the Model in the brains of other people so it can guide them to accomplish what they couldn't do individually. To be sure, more general factors like courage, energy, and intelligence matter. Context also matters so that no particular leader is effective in every situation: military leaders, for instance, often need a different balance of skills in peacetime versus wartime, and leadership differs across the myriad types of groups in communities, businesses, and organizations. Yet across these situations the core of effective leadership itself remains the same, and we can tackle each aspect in turn: self-confidence, purpose, and communication.

A leader first needs the *self-confidence* to make decisions on behalf of others. Leaders must be willing to make decisions *and* shoulder responsibility for taking risks.

Many people aren't willing to do that, as shown in a brain imaging study by my former colleague Micah Edelson.[67] In Edelson's study, participants first decided whether to accept or reject a series of risky lotteries for money, so he could estimate their preferences. Next, participants faced the same lotteries as part of a four-person group, who they knew from playing team-building games together. In this group phase, they made two types of choices: Half those choices only affected their own earnings, while half also affected the other group members' earnings. Participants could defer their decision to the other group members or take the responsibility on themselves. Edelson found that when the decisions affected others' earnings, then people deferred more often.

Edelson could also measure the participants' leadership using a questionnaire, and in some participants by the actual military rank they attained during their compulsory military service in Switzerland, where Edelson conducted the study. These measures of leadership were not predicted by how much an individual liked risk, nor their overall tendency to prefer taking control. Instead, the best predictor was how much people didn't avoid taking responsibility for others—and those with the highest leadership scores shouldered more responsibility for others. Leaders like Churchill, Roosevelt, Nimitz, Zhukov, Mao, and Zhu De showed this willingness to shoulder responsibility. Even relish it. Brain scanning during the experiment revealed a network underlying these leadership decisions in which temporal cortex regions changed the connections between insula cortex (involved in risk and emotion) and prefrontal cortex (involved in planning).

Few of us want to follow leaders who lack confidence. On the other hand, neither do we want to follow leaders with inappropriately high confidence. Such overconfidence is a danger, because dominant individuals frequently display confidence that can lead to more prestigious reputations than their true skill deserves.[68] A major focus in Chapter 10 is how we can, as individuals and societies, create better systems to calibrate our self-confidence.

The second ingredient an effective leader needs is a clear Model of what they want to achieve, to give their followers clear *purpose*. Modern U.S. and British military leaders issue a "Commander's Intent," a vision of what success looks like around which followers can coordinate their own goals. Such plans are needed at many levels: for the leader of a small group taking an enemy position, a general planning a battle, or a supreme leader planning an entire global war. At the highest levels of war in particular, doing this well requires leaders to believe deeply in their own cause, in their own group[69]—because a clear overall goal enables a leader like Mao, MLK, or Churchill to face and overcome continuous setbacks on the path to bigger eventual victories. Better plans are a big focus of the next chapter.

Third, effective leaders must be able to *communicate* their Models effectively—because no plan, however brilliant, matters if it stays in the leader's brain. Skilled empathy, mentalizing, and communication enabled leaders like Churchill and Roosevelt to lead their top military teams effectively. Mao worked closely with his military leader Zhu De. And effective senior military and civilian leaders in war must also communicate their Models to thousands or millions of people who must carry them out, to embed their Models in their followers' brains. What the followers need to do, why they need to do it, and why they should care—a script for the followers' parts in the action.[70]

Such communication can seem like acting. In a way it is, and that's vital: Heinz Guderian the *Panzer* leader who helped pioneer *Blitzkrieg*, issued his pithy sayings, and British General Montgomery, who won at El Alamein, covered his cap with badges. A retired British general told me that he mentored new generals in "Generalship," and that they went to Britain's top drama school to learn such skills. Leadership skills aren't inherently good or bad: Hitler's earlier military successes came when he worked well with generals like Guderian; and Hitler skillfully communicated his terrible Model to millions of followers. Fortunately, the democracies found effective leaders to counter him.

We need effective leaders with appropriate self-confidence, clear purpose, and good communication—because their task in great matters like war is fiendishly hard. Against the enemy, they may have to compete against leaders like Hitler. On their *own side*, they must steer an identity-culture spiral that is constantly changing, twisting, and threatening to spin out of control. And they must often compete with other leaders in their own societies.

Every leader above the very lowest rungs must rely on other leaders beneath them. Leaders often vie for control with alternative leaders who draw on different power bases or different sources of prestige and dominance. In early modern Europe, power struggles within the state could take the form of religious power versus military and political power:

Henry VIII created the Church of England to remove himself from the Pope's authority. In the modern world, tensions often emerge between *civilian* versus *military* leaders—and this poses challenges for any political system: democratic or authoritarian.

"Political power grows out of the barrel of a gun," Mao Zedong famously noted, and "the party commands the gun and the gun shall never be allowed to command the party."[71] To this day China's military is called the People's Liberation Army and answers to the Chinese Communist Party, not to the state. The top priority of the Chinese regime is regime security, remaining in power. Today's paramount leader, Xi Jinping, has enhanced his political control over the military by using compulsory smartphone apps for political education, and removing top military leaders he deems unreliable.[72]

Xi would never have tolerated the situation in Putin's Russia when the Wagner mercenary group gained so much military power that, in 2023, the Wagner leader launched a military march on Moscow.[73]

Military leaders can enjoy enormous prestige in societies, and when that prestige mixes with the dominance that can accompany guns, it can quickly generate political power. Sometimes too much power for a republic to handle—as with a Julius Caesar, a Napoleon, or whoever's next.

* * *

The most important clash between civilian and military leaders in twentieth-century U.S. history erupted during the Korean War—a conflict in which some thirty-seven thousand U.S. soldiers died,[74] and which began in June 1950 when communist North Korea invaded South Korea.

President Truman had to stand up to the insubordinate General Douglas MacArthur, a popular Second World War hero. As one of the U.S. Joint Chiefs said of the insubordinate general: "He wouldn't obey the orders."[75]

It was only after military failures dimmed the general's prestige—once Mao's Chinese forces successfully intervened to support North Korea—that Truman felt able to sack him. But even after his sacking, MacArthur questioned if he owed "loyalty to those who temporarily exercise the authority of the Executive Branch of the Government, rather than to the country, and its Constitution."[76]

That general's argument—of obedience to something higher than a specific human leader—isn't a million miles from General Mark Milley's words, quoted earlier after the November 2020 U.S. presidential election. True, Truman was acting in his constitutionally approved role—but often in history, when competing leaders clash, such niceties aren't always decisive.

Should a concerned citizen in a democracy, then, simply be suspicious of all leaders? Mutiny and skepticism can seem attractive, and that itself is a source of power.

Joseph McCarthy was a barely known young Wisconsin senator before he whipped up and led a popular anti-communist fervor against senior civilian officials and military leaders—including George C. Marshall. McCarthy began in February 1950, lying that he had evidence of 205 Communists in the U.S. State Department. He also attacked artists. And McCarthy *was* popular. As 1953 ended, polls showed at least half of Americans looked favorably on McCarthy and his tactics.[77]

Even the D-Day hero General Dwight Eisenhower, when running for president in 1952, dared not condemn McCarthy's lies against George C. Marshall.

McCarthy was self-confident and a skilled communicator—but his effectiveness as a leader was limited once it became clear that he had no vision or purpose to offer followers. He was no Eisenhower.

Eisenhower was a highly effective leader. As a general and as a president from 1953 to 1961, Eisenhower had self-confidence without arrogance, a constructive vision, and the ability to communicate purpose to others. Eisenhower's self-confidence was well calibrated so that he both willingly shouldered a vast responsibility like commanding D-Day, and listened as part of a team.[78] As president he had a positive Model that provided purpose: preparing the United States to thrive over the "long haul" against Russia. That required getting the U.S. domestic house in order, keeping the "military-industrial complex" in check, and building strong, financially sustainable defenses abroad.[79] Eisenhower was a simple and effective communicator whose presidential TV ads ran with "I like Ike."[80]

In 1954 McCarthy lost public support during lengthy television exposure of his verbally brutal interrogations. Moreover, Eisenhower, once elected president, conducted a stealth campaign against the senator, pressuring other Republican senators to censure McCarthy.[81] Some senators even used the power of social exclusion: shunning McCarthy and leaving when he rose to speak or approached groups in the cloakroom.

When he was denied the attention he craved, which had become part of his identity, McCarthy's heavy drinking worsened, and he died of alcoholism on May 2, 1957, in Bethesda Naval Hospital.

DOMESTIC POWER—A SECOND WAY TO LOSE IN OUR TIME

These forgotten senators who shunned McCarthy teach us a valuable lesson: *all* of us contribute to the identity-culture spiral in our societies. Deciding who to support; what information to pass on to our friends, family, or colleagues; leading at myriad levels at work, in our communities, or in the military. Contributing on social media. We influence others. Even apathy contributes, because withdrawing support affects how society functions—or falls apart.

Because societies do fall apart. The democracies could lose a conventional war to China in East Asia, as we saw in the last chapter. And there's a second way the democracies could *lose* in our era: domestically.

Titanic external challenges always strain democracy—and in the longer run nothing matters more for democracy than the relationship of society and soldiers. But beyond generalities, what would losing domestically actually look like? The most violent way the United States or China loses domestically in our era is through civil war.

In China, civil war seems unlikely anytime soon. The regime is well entrenched. It has made people richer. Control over the armed forces is strong: both over the rank and file and through sackings of very senior generals. Xi Jinping is haunted by the collapse of Russia's Soviet regime, whose leaders, he believes, were not "man enough" to use force to quell their domestic adversaries.[82]

And America? On January 6, 2021, armed demonstrators forced their way into the U.S. Capitol. Around this event's first anniversary, *The New York Times* and *The New Yorker* saw discussions about the possibility of U.S. civil war.[83] CNN asked, "Is America heading to civil war or secession?"[84] Books asked the same.[85] One in five Americans, according to a national survey published in July 2022, believed that "in general" political violence was at least sometimes justified.[86] I'd been surprised, too—the Capitol buildings were a fifteen-minute walk from the apartment where I'd lived with my young family in D.C. What had been essentially unthinkable became thinkable.

But a real civil war is not just a protest, an armed insurgency, or domestic terrorism—it would require seriously capable parts of the U.S. military to split away and fight. I've met very many military officers and enlisted troops who really believe in the United States, its Constitution, and its military, so that seems utterly implausible to me—unless some significant change to the U.S. regime happened first.

More likely than civil war is the possibility that the U.S. loses domestically through regime change. It need not happen overnight, as regimes often corrode over time. A strong leader gradually becomes overmighty. Elections might continue—as in Putin's Russia—but the regime has changed, because now political opponents can't remove that leader except by using or threatening force in a coup or civil war.

Regime change is common in modern history. Russia's Soviet regime lasted only seventy-four years, and the People's Republic of China only recently passed that milestone. After independence in the late 1940s, India's democracy broadly flourished (despite an interlude in the 1970s), while Pakistan had periods of civil war and military rule. U.S. occupation reestablished Japanese democracy, although a single party has ruled Japan almost continuously since 1955.[87] In the past fifty or so years, many European Union countries underwent regime change, such as Spain and Portugal from fascism, Greece from military junta, or Poland and Hungary from Communism. Hungary has changed regime once again and is now a "hybrid regime" between democracy and authoritarianism. France since 1848 has seen a French monarchy, four republics, and a French emperor, too. Since Germany's founding in 1871, there have been at least five Germanies.

Regime change seems rare from the perspective of America or Britain: but their regimes' durability actually makes them the outliers. The United States has lasted over two centuries, despite a civil war in its first nine decades. And after regime change in 1688, the British regime has flexibly and gradually adapted. Reassuring as that is, any regime can crack—and there will be plenty of sources of strain.

Strains will come from waging "gray zone" conflicts, or from wars like one over Taiwan whether they're won or lost.

Strains can arise from rapid technological change.[88] Authoritarian states like China are becoming "digital authoritarian" states, in which digital surveillance and AI enable more powerful influence over society than ever before. The "social credit system" keeps scores on China's people, and systems monitor time spent on apps learning the thoughts of Xi Jinping.[89] The United States is becoming a digital democracy. In 2012 Barack Obama's campaign harnessed big data to target audiences.[90] By 2016 social media had changed how media and political actors interact: Donald Trump without Twitter would have lacked the platform to influence enough voters to win the Republican primaries and become president. In 2024, he more successfully harnessed podcasts than his opponent—and although podcasts weren't decisive, they helped.[91] The promise of technology was central to the first hundred days of the second Trump presidency. Tech brings disruptive change.

Strains will also be directly aggravated by competitors. During the Cold War, both superpowers set up huge bureaucracies to influence others and defend against others' influence.[92] The Central Intelligence Agency (CIA), set up in 1947, pioneered industrial-scale influence. The CIA's first big covert operation was to defeat Soviet-funded communists in Italy's 1948 election. The campaign tapped into identity with Vatican support, conducted dirty tricks against communist leaders, and used mass letter writing by Italian-Americans to their relatives.[93] During the Cold War, America became more restrained, but the Russians built even bigger bureaucracies for influence. The Russians also pushed the boundaries with their "active measures"—intelligence operations to shape political decisions—such as by spreading false rumors that HIV was a western plot, and by manipulating western peace movements.[94]

China today spends billions on external propaganda and the "three warfares": media warfare, psychological warfare, and legal warfare.[95] Russia's large-scale "active measures" are in full swing again today—including directly within America, which has effects although these remain relatively limited.[96] But such activities may effectively corrode the will to resist among populations today in places like eastern Europe or Taiwan,[97] and they're hardly helpful in America.

And of course this is a two-way street. During President Eisenhower's time, the United States had a strategy of "peaceful evolution" to change China's regime—and Chinese leaders believe America followed that strategy for much of the post–Cold War period, too.[98] All the big players are trying to work out how to use and defend against technologies like AI "deepfakes" (media in which people say or do things they didn't say or do) and mass personalization (tailoring influence to individuals) that are trying to target our brains.

But the main domestic dangers—in every country—arise not from outside but from within. "If destruction be our lot," warned a twenty-eight-year-old Abraham Lincoln, "we must ourselves be its author and finisher. As a nation of freemen, we must live through all time, or die by suicide."[99]

Both sides need to think how they can thrive domestically during a gray zone contest that may last decades. As Eisenhower put it, America needs to prepare for the "long haul." Eisenhower took over a country that had been through a great depression and a world war; he faced a true superpower competitor, many of whose people genuinely believed Communism was the future; he faced corrosive domestic forces like McCarthy—and despite all that he helped put America on an even keel for the long haul. Perfect? No. But domestically strong enough for the voyage ahead.

For Eisenhower there was always a central human dimension to leadership: as U.S. Army chief of staff in 1946, he wrote to the head of West Point that "a feature I should very much like to see included in the curriculum is a course in practical or applied psychology."[100] And for Eisenhower there was always a plan. What's our plan today?

The last two chapters show how humans navigate and construct our social world, which can make the difference between life or death in war, and success or failure in everyday life. But leaders like Mao and Eisenhower knew that although a coherent enough society and military is necessary to win, it isn't enough. A coherent group running straight toward a machine gun nest could get mowed down. Sometimes, you need a clever alternative. We also need our ability to do something else: to plan.

9

CLEVER

PLANNING IN PREFRONTAL CORTEX

What does a doctor do to make sense of a patient's case? My basic approach is this: I read background information. I listen carefully to what the patient tells me, and ask questions to get further information about their medical and social situation. If they struggle to communicate, I get information from someone else. I then examine the patient, perceiving with my eyes and ears, and feeling for masses with my hands. I apply tools like my reflex hammer and stethoscope. I review available results from investigations, such as blood tests, chest X-rays, or head scans.

I use this information within the context of my knowledge of medicine, which is my systematically ordered set of beliefs about various disorders. I think through what is going on, so I can *plan* what comes next.

I write down a list of possible diagnoses, including likely ones, and those unlikely but important to consider (such as a rare but serious disease). I specify my plan for what comes next: treatments to start (penicillin, immediately!) or to stop (their blood pressure is too low for that . . .), further investigations to conduct, what nurses should look out for, which relatives to speak with, and so on.

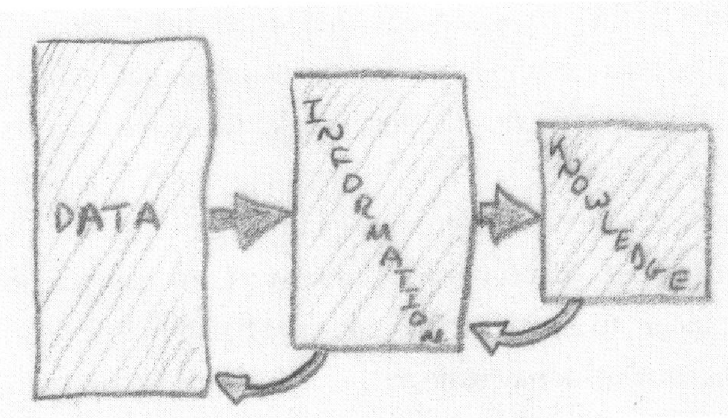

FIGURE 15: Data, information, and knowledge. Consider the chain from data as a "raw material" processed into information (meaningful data); and then knowledge (ordered sets of justified enough beliefs). Chapter 5 on perception described how we go from data to information. The "backward" arrows are shown because the higher levels of the hierarchy can help guide us to collect more useful data and information at the lower levels.

Parts of the plan often involve taking an action, such as a test for a blood clot on the lung. And I specify: *if* that test comes back positive, then we should go down one treatment pathway, or *if* that is negative, then we go down another. In terms we encountered earlier, I look forward through a *decision tree* with different branches stretching out into the future, depending on whether one thing happens or another. (I often advise friends attending an important doctor's appointment to ask "if-then" questions, such as, "What's the plan if the scan is positive, and what if the scan is negative?")

A clearly articulated plan helps—for me, when I come back to review the patient (I could have seen them at 03:00 as one among many patients), as well as for other doctors, nurses, social workers, and others who need to know the plan.

Planning well in medicine saves lives, and it requires specialized medical knowledge—but in fact everyone reading this book plans, all the time. We plan how to shop and cook dinner for a Tuesday evening, at Christmas, or Thanksgiving. An electrician plans how to get their day's tasks done at work. A schoolchild plans how to study for a test.

Part of the planning, for a doctor, is how to communicate information with the patient. After a patient receives a huge piece of information—being told, for instance, they have cancer—they often forget much else that was said. Or forget what questions they wanted to ask. (That's why I often advise friends attending such a consultation to take someone with them to write notes.)

I began this chapter by discussing planning in medicine because that can be easier to read than the topic I raise next: nuclear weapons.

If I say "cancer" to a patient, they may not listen to fine details. If I write "nuclear weapons," you may tune out. They're hard to comprehend. So let's try an experiment: How many of these facts can you remember?[1]

Russia and the United States each have more than 5,000 nuclear warheads. China has about 410, and most observers believe that number is rapidly rising. France has 290 and Britain 225. India, Pakistan, Israel, and North Korea have fewer. The bombs vary in size. The bomb dropped on Hiroshima was about 15 kilotons (equivalent to 15,000 tons of TNT). A single 1-megaton bomb is equivalent to 1 million tons of TNT, and will promptly kill the equivalent of everyone within an 8.8-mile diameter—that's most of Manhattan plus big chunks of the land on either side. The United States has 650 of its largest current bombs in "active service," which are each 1.2 megatons. Russia is more opaque than the United States on its current arsenal, and during the Cold War exploded a 50-megaton bomb.

Nuclear weapons are the only things that could kill over half the American population tomorrow morning. And adding to those prompt deaths, soon after all-out nuclear war the death toll would likely rise far higher—from the results of burns and lethal fallout covering most of America. Moreover, volcanoes have in recent centuries kicked dust up into the atmosphere to cause mini ice ages and crop failures, which suggests that a big nuclear war's atmospheric debris could drop temperatures more than in the last ice age.

No war between the west and Russia or China can be understood without considering the shadow of nuclear weapons. How can we make sense of them, like a doctor facing a patient?

For over a decade, I've discussed nuclear planning with U.S., British, and other officials. While writing this book, I met most weeks with analysts from U.S. Strategic Command (USSTRATCOM), which runs U.S. nuclear planning. They are based in places like USSTRATCOM's headquarters in Omaha, Nebraska, or a short walk from the Pentagon in Crystal City. They are thoughtful, intelligent people who spend their days planning how the United States can deter other countries from using nuclear weapons. And how nuclear weapons might feature in escalation scenarios over places like Korea, Ukraine, or Taiwan.

No western country can destroy all of Russia's or China's nuclear weapons. Both countries have a "secure second strike" so that—whatever the United States does to them—they can hit back and kill millions in the United States or wherever else they choose.

What USSTRATCOM officials tell me they often find most useful and interesting are cognitive insights, about how humans think. They want to influence how others think, not only, or even mainly, at the level of societies but to influence key individuals, too. Their job is to understand the Models that key individuals—like Xi Jinping, Vladimir Putin, or Korea's Kim Jong Un—use to make decisions, in order to influence those Models.

The human brain is central as USSTRATCOM seeks to think through and plan for many potential futures, across a decision tree branching out into those futures. They face the highest stakes and most fiendish complications. But we can all benefit from asking:

How can we make cleverer choices?

The prefrontal cortex does much of our planning, strategy, and thinking ahead. A huge region of association cortex that sits in front of the motor cortex (Figure 16), it integrates inputs from across the brain, to reason ahead and plan clever ways to achieve goals. Those goals may emerge from other sections of the brain's orchestra, such as the vital drives of hunger or thirst, or the visceral instincts of emotions, risks, and social motivations. No robin redbreast or single-celled organism can plan anywhere near as cleverly as this massive neural machinery for how senses can link to actions. Prefrontal cortex is much bigger in humans than other primates.[2] In fact, human prefrontal cortex is so gigantic that this chapter will cover most but not all of it—leaving the very front, the "frontal pole," for our final chapter.

Faster and cleverer decision-making will always give advantages in war. It was central to *Blitzkrieg*. In our time, China, America, and others are building AI aids for human decision-making and even to replace human decision-making. China is a world leader in AI. At the time of writing,

China is only slightly behind the United States in cutting-edge AI science, and is innovating furiously in many practical applications like driverless cars.[3] AI can already create clever shortcuts and brilliant strategies: like those on display when the AI AlphaGo beat the world's human champion at the strategy game Go. The other day in a café the latest ChatGPT thought through a genuinely clever response to my daughter's question: "What if the atmosphere was all turned into peanut butter?" But for most real-world planning even the best AI currently lags far behind our clever prefrontal cortex. How on Earth is our brain so clever?

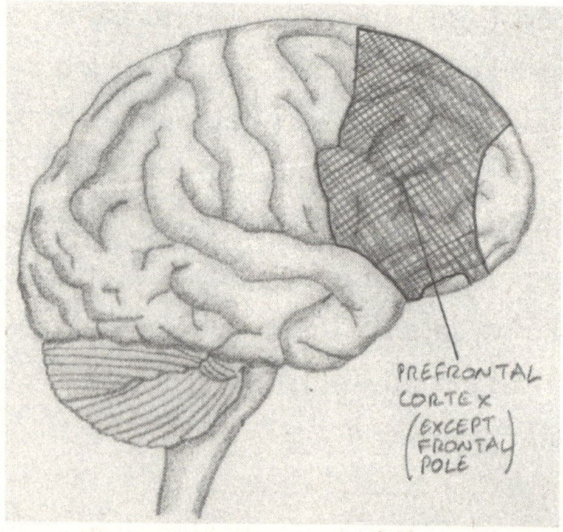

FIGURE 16: Prefrontal cortex is a gigantic area of association cortex. This chapter covers all of the prefrontal cortex except the frontal pole, which we'll explore in the next chapter.

PLANNING

Whether you play Go, chess, or checkers, you know it is impossible to win only by using habits, reflexes, or emotional responses. In life, planning makes the difference between running straight forward into a barrier, or anticipating that barrier and taking a detour instead.

We must often *look ahead* through a decision tree—and as Chapter 1 described, the 1930s illustrate the terrible consequences if we flinch from looking ahead.

An experiment I conducted with colleagues at Queen Square illustrates the difference between planning and more basic responses like habits.[4] Moreover, it shows the crucial role of prefrontal cortex in planning.

People came to our lab in Queen Square and sat in a testing room down in the basement, playing a game on a computer for money. In each trial of the game, participants made a sequence of two choices, after which they either received a reward or got nothing. Choosing whichever option had previously given them a reward wasn't a terrible method—such habits are simple, efficient, and do sometimes win money. But here's the crucial point about this task: participants could also *learn the structure* of how the sequence of choices in each trial related to each other—and use that *Model* of the task to *plan ahead* for which choices could reward them with more money.

This meant we neuroscientists could measure whether the participants' actions resulted more from habit or from planning.

Crucially, before the task we had temporarily turned off part of their brain, by applying a magnetic coil to a specific part of their head. Over the three different days that they came to the lab we did this to three different parts of the brain. And our research showed that inactivating a specific region of the prefrontal cortex reduced their ability to plan ahead.

Humans apply our clever reasoning to plan ahead in many aspects of our lives—and research like ours has shown that prefrontal cortex is crucial for such planning. Our human abilities to plan are remarkable—and even more remarkable than they at first seem, once you realize how difficult it is to think ahead through a decision tree to pick the best option.

Board games are simpler than much of real life, but they illustrate a challenge for anyone trying to look ahead: *combinatorial explosion.*[5]

Take a relatively simple game called Go. Two players take turns to place a stone on a nineteen-by-nineteen board, each aiming to surround as much territory as possible. Yet looking ahead to find a guaranteed win is unrealistic because there are over ten^{170} possible positions (that's 1 followed by 170 zeros). I can make one of many moves, you can respond in one of many ways, then me, then you, and so on. The number of potential combinations explodes. So, how can the human brain—or any other intelligent system—plan efficiently enough to function?

Recent advances on this question suggest the brain uses a treelike

Model of potential futures, and it uses efficient ways to search through them. Figure 17 shows such a decision tree. The current position is the root. Which action to take can be determined either by searching the tree forward from the root to the leaves (the terminal points) or searching backward from the leaves to the root.[6] To be sure, affordances help channel our thinking into such menus of possible options, so that, for example, when planning to cook chicken for dinner we don't normally consider options like serving it raw with a drizzle of engine oil. But even with that help, we still face the problem of combinatorial explosion.

Moreover, the real world is more complicated than a board game. Discussing how to plan nuclear weapons strategy with USSTRATCOM and the British Ministry of Defense, it's clear that no analytical "brute force" can cope with the sheer variety of possible futures.

Consider a simple decision tree about Russia in Ukraine, which is a real question I've recently been asked to discuss by government officials. Suppose that Russia uses a "tactical" nuclear weapon, which is a relatively small bomb similar in size to that used on Hiroshima. This could be: (a) in a demonstration far from Ukraine; (b) in Ukraine for land battlefield effects; (c) in the Black Sea; or (d) on NATO territory. The United States and NATO could respond with: (a) massive conventional precision munitions within Ukraine's pre-2014 international borders; (b) a conventional response against targets within the Russian Federation; (c) a tactical nuclear response; (d) a largely diplomatic response . . . and so on. Other actors such as China complicate matters (for example, how much do they support Russia?), and so does the range of possible outcomes (for example, how much does it affect the battlefield in Ukraine?).

That simple decision tree considers only one level in our brains' hierarchies for understanding the world. The U.S. president, U.S. National Security Council, and Pentagon, for example, consider U.S. policy globally because for them Ukraine is only one subcomponent of strategy. At the same time as considering the Ukraine situation, they must also ask what that simple decision tree's potential outcomes might mean for Taiwan or the Middle East. Complications increase further when you remember that any decision tree is just a fleeting snapshot in time of a single episode with a beginning and an end. Napoleon and Hitler scored victory after victory in stunning battles, but both lost their wars because even decisive battles are often not that decisive, or can even leave you overstretched. America lost the Vietnam War in the 1960s and '70s, but, seen from the perspective of winning the Cold War, was it worth fighting or not? The lives of individuals also have many layers that contribute to any decision tree's complexity. Consider the situation of a woman living in Ukraine. What does that simple decision tree mean for her home city or family? No living human being contemplates a scenario at only one level, and certainly not those at the top of politics or the military.

Finally, one must consider the rules of the game being played. Even in a board game like chess, a famous player can now change the rules of online chess by using a chess computer to cheat. In Stalingrad, as we saw in Chapter 5, the Russians defeated Hitler's war machine by changing the rules of the game.

Once again, these complications could become overwhelming, even incapacitating.

But despite the infinite possibilities, we somehow manage to get on with things. Our brains shape the decision tree by truncating, chunking, and pruning it into a manageable size—a bonsai rather than a sprawling 130-foot oak.

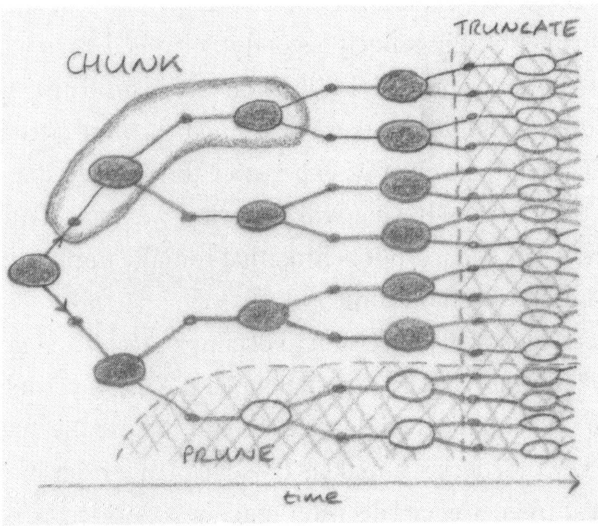

FIGURE 17: Making the decision tree a manageable bonsai. Three key methods are shown and described in the following text: truncating, pruning, and chunking.[7]

Truncating the tree means only expanding it up to a maximum depth.[8] That is, to a maximum number of actions in a sequence. Looking ahead, the brain can work out the value of each possible action by adding up the rewards (or costs) to the end points where the tree gets cut off, and these end points stand in for what might happen afterward.

Humans typically truncate after a depth of approximately three to six steps, which has been shown in multiple studies.[9] AI algorithms also truncate decision trees. To evaluate a potential action in a board game like chess, for instance, an AI algorithm might predict how the game would look after a few moves and add up the remaining pieces' value.

Humans also manage trade-offs when truncating the decision tree. Back in Chapter 5 we saw how a telescope helps us perceive more in a smaller part of the visual field. With decision trees, humans can trade off depth of looking ahead against speed—because deeper looks ahead tend to be better but slower.[10] Essentially, the brain seems to have some type of computational budget, which it can reallocate based on task demands. Thinking hard for several hours can make us mentally exhausted.[11]

A second way to make the decision tree more manageable is *pruning* poor decision sub-trees from consideration, to preserve limited cognitive resources. If there's an unpleasant option early in the sequence of choices, we tend to dislike thinking much beyond it to consider what follows from it.[12] That is, we tend to "prune" the decision tree behind an unpleasant initial option, even if the branches we've pruned turn out better overall. As we saw in Chapter 1, many of us experience this in everyday life: we may not want to think through what will happen if we make a difficult phone call to a superior or spouse, but behind that initially unpleasant option we may find the best overall outcomes.

In the disastrous British decision to occupy the Suez Canal in 1956, key decision-makers ignored what would happen if America didn't back them. And yet that's what happened.[13] More recently, before the 2003 U.S. invasion of Iraq, key U.S. decision-makers failed to plan for significant Iraqi unrest. Once again, experienced decision-makers, supported by plentiful time and planning resources, failed to look beyond a large negative outcome to plan for entirely foreseeable potential outcomes.[14] It's uncomfortable, but when we plan we should remember—failure *is* an option, and we should ask what happens if we fail.

A third way our brain gets to grips with our decision tree is *chunking*, which clusters multiple actions together into an "option" that can be evaluated as if it were a single action. Similar to how an athlete learns all the steps of the Fosbury flop for the high jump. To begin with, each component requires conscious thought to go through each of many steps containing thousands of muscle movements. But with chunking, over time, each part becomes routine second nature. It's the same learning to drive a car.

In the brains of military planners, as well as in organizational processes, chunking is useful. But again, there's a trade-off. Routines can make actors more predictable and thus vulnerable to adversaries. The eminent historian Ernest May wrote a book on why the democracies catastrophically lost the Battle of France in May 1940, in which a key conclusion was that

> Hitler and his generals perceived that the weakness of their otherwise powerful enemies resided in habits and routines that made their reaction times slow. They developed a plan that capitalized on this weakness.[15]

Truncating, pruning, and chunking all involve trade-offs, but they do give us a manageable bonsai tree of possible futures.

Prefrontal cortex doesn't build this bonsai tree alone: it also *integrates* inputs from other sections of the brain's orchestra. It can, for instance, integrate the outputs of our neural machinery for Modeling others, which we saw in Chapters 7 and 8. That's great if you need decision trees in which to think about me responding to you, you responding to me, and so on. People typically apply about one to three levels of such reasoning in strategic games.[16]

Prefrontal cortex can also integrate the maps, memories, and "what ifs" from the hippocampal-entorhinal region, which we met in Chapter 4. Memories of past episodes or facts allow us to imagine possible futures. The hippocampal-entorhinal region can sew together different cognitive maps of the world, including very abstract ones. And it can lay different analogies next to each other, to give us new insights into the structure of decision trees. Are we in the run-up to World War I, World War II, or a mixture?

Experts can learn bodies of knowledge about how different actions are likely to lead on to particular consequences—to integrate cumulative knowledge derived from scientific experiments, statistics, or history.

Our prefrontal cortex helps integrate inputs from across the brain in the decision tree, so we can calculate how valuable (or costly) each sequence of actions might end up being. And we can use the results of such clever planning immediately to help us choose our next action.

But we don't *have* to use the fruits of our planning process right away. We can also work on plans in advance, for later use. This enables us to build vast edifices about the world in our brains. A doctor can have a huge store of knowledge about how different possible actions and events relate to each other—informed by scientific evidence, anecdote, practical experience, and all the rest. So can an artist, gardener, electrician, sailor, or soldier.

No other animal on Earth can build such vast "castles in the sky."

A writer like Karl Marx can spend decades building a towering castle in the sky within his brain and writings. Marx's highly detailed Model described how he thought the world worked: a scientific discovery of the "law of development of human history," in the words of his closest collaborator.[17] Other brains, from Lenin's to Mao's, added to his ideas over decades and communicated them to millions more brains. Ideas about the historical inevitability of communism over capitalism were part of the Models with which millions of clever, diligent communists understood how the world worked.

"Whether you like it or not," the Soviet leader Nikita Khrushchev boasted before western diplomats, "history is on our side."[18]

* * *

In October 1962, Soviet Russia's unpredictable leader, Nikita Khrushchev, hoped to make advances against the young, newly elected U.S. President John F. Kennedy. It caused the most dangerous episode in nuclear history: the thirteen days of the Cuban Missile Crisis.

Looking from the Russian side, recently declassified Soviet documents show that Khrushchev's idea to send nuclear-tipped missiles to defend communist Cuba was a gamble. That's not in itself a problem, but he had poorly thought through the decision tree for that gamble. Its success depended on improbably good luck.[19] Soviet leaders themselves lacked expertise on Cuba, ignored the warnings of experts, and pruned the risks of detection from U.S. aerial reconnaissance, along with everything that followed if they couldn't hide the operation.

Moreover, poor planning for on-the-ground conditions in Cuba also plagued the Russian operation. Commanders did, for example, try to camouflage their equipment with nets—a process they had "chunked" to expertly execute. But the newly released documents show that the nets' color blended with Russia's green leaves and contrasted against Cuba's dry terrain.[20]

In contrast, on the U.S. side, Kennedy and his team carefully thought through their plans and emerged on top.

On October 14, an American U-2 spy plane flew over some construction sites, photographs of which landed on Kennedy's desk two days later.[21] The Executive Committee (ExComm) led by Kennedy met to go through a range of potential actions including: do nothing; diplomacy; secretly approach the Cubans; invasion (the option favored by the U.S. Joint Chiefs); air strike; and naval blockade of Cuba to prevent further Soviet ships arriving.[22]

They looked ahead through the actions and reactions: a decision tree branching into the future in which Kennedy forecast that "doing nothing" would affect credibility with allies; and that "air strikes" or "invasion" could lead the Soviets to take West Berlin by force. Kennedy chose "naval blockade."[23]

His administration and the U.S. Navy carefully thought through the plan and its subcomponents. What, precisely, should happen when new Soviet ships neared Cuba? Then what? And so on.[24] As the historian Lawrence Freedman noted, the civilians were determined "to assess the political sensitivity of every possible move."[25]

Superior U.S. planning paid off. Khrushchev lost because he didn't plan the operation well enough, and those under him didn't plan its subcomponents well enough—and together those planning failures gave him a perilously weak hand in this strategic game over Cuba.

Happily for humanity, when Khrushchev stared down the barrel of nuclear war during the crisis itself, he did at least look ahead to rationally evaluate consequences. On October 28, he announced that the missiles on Cuba would be dismantled. As he had explained two days earlier to an Indian visitor about stopping a conflict: "What's important is not to cry for the dead or to avenge them, but to save those who might die if the conflict continues."[26]

ON TRACK

"Everyone has a plan," said the boxer Mike Tyson, "'till they get punched in the mouth."[27] I've no idea if Mike Tyson read about the most famous chief of the Prussian General Staff, Helmuth von Moltke. But both knew that events always blow plans off track. "No plan of operations," said von Moltke, "reaches with any certainty beyond the first encounter with the enemy's main force."[28] Von Moltke's tenure from 1857 to 1888 saw a string of victories that turned the state of Prussia into the much larger unified Germany. He was part of an exceptional cumulative military tradition, inherited all the way down to Germans like the *Panzer* leader Guderian in World War II.

The General Staff's creators included Carl von Clausewitz (who later literally marked the young von Moltke's course work). These Prussians sought to compete with the military genius of Napoleon Bonaparte, who had defeated Prussia in 1806. Napoleon's capacious brain could look ahead to plan complicated maneuvers for each of the various parts of his army—which could be separated far apart—and then suddenly bring all those sub-plans together when and where he chose.[29]

Lacking Napoleon's genius, the Prussians built a new system to turn the talented non-genius into a better decision-maker. A system that made war a matter of professional expertise, scientific calculation, and administrative planning.[30]

Planning is hierarchical, and part of Napoleon's genius was to fit all his sub-plans together to keep his bigger plan on track. Von Clausewitz learned by fighting against Napoleon, and he described how genius rests on making many good smaller decisions that together comprise the big strategies.[31]

And although we may not realize it, in everyday life, all of us with healthy brains use sophisticated hierarchical planning to keep on track.

We even need this powerful planning machinery for something that *seems* as simple as shopping. In pioneering experiments using the "shopping task," the neuropsychologist Tim Shallice demonstrated the crucial role of prefrontal cortex for keeping plans on track.[32] Working at Queen Square, Shallice took patients with prefrontal cortex damage out into the real world—into a nearby shopping center with a shopping list to buy a set of items within a set amount of time. Healthy participants did this with little bother.

But although the prefrontal patients could work out how to achieve many of the subcomponents considered in isolation, they struggled to put the overarching plan together and keep it on track. One patient wandered out of the shopping center to pursue an item easily found inside. Another failed to buy soap because she visited a shop that didn't have her favorite brand. One got a newspaper but failed to pay. Others failed to group items together that could likely be obtained from the same shop, such as stationery. They all got easily distracted, failed to plan over longer time periods, and failed to prioritize when facing two or more competing tasks. Healthy brains keep hierarchical plans on track so effortlessly that we barely notice the brilliance.

To give an analogy from when I was a doctor treating patients at Queen Square: it's as if I could still do all the subcomponents to perform a spinal tap, or to check a chest X-ray for abnormalities, or to put a drip into someone's arm. But within each task I would struggle to put the various subcomponents together. And on a typical afternoon when I would have to do *all* these tasks on various patients and deal with new challenges that emerged ("Dr. Wright, can you check on Mrs. Smith in bed ten because she has chest pain . . ."), it would all turn into a jumbled cacophony of subcomponents.

So how does prefrontal cortex *guide and monitor behavior* so that plans stay in line with current goals?

One crucial requirement to keep plans on track is detecting when the plan is going wrong. These are prediction errors that signal deviations from the expected course of the plan, and they involve prefrontal cortex. They include large electrical signals measurable from outside the brain using electrodes and thought to arise from prefrontal cortex—called by many psychologists the "Oh shit!" response.[33] Such prediction errors happen at many different timescales, from moment to moment, or at the end of a day, a week, a year, and so on. These prediction errors tell us we might need to "hold back a bit," which is why after an error our responses can slow.

It also helps to know how far through a plan we think we are. An exciting new study, yet to be replicated, found "goal-progress cells" in the mouse equivalent of prefrontal cortex.[34] The mice learned multiple tasks from which they had to string together plans for new sequences of actions—and in these new plans the cells indicated how much progress had been made to achieve sub-goals (for example, 70 percent completed) and the overarching goal (for example, 50 percent completed), acting like the "progress bar" on your computer that fills up as it works through tasks.

Prefrontal cortex also keeps us on track by helping us concentrate on a task. That can be crucial when the plan must compete with strong habits or routines—like when you must concentrate to pick up a pint of milk, despite being on autopilot during a long commute home from work. Concentration is crucial in difficult or dangerous situations, like combat.[35]

Another way we can stay on track is to change our mindset. A "mindset" is a broad constellation of activated brain processes and beliefs.[36] Our mindsets shift in predictable ways, such as the shift from a more "deliberative mindset" that weighs up potential goals, to a more "implemental mindset" that focuses more on achieving those goals.[37] Deliberative mindsets enable less biased assessments to help us choose goals—so that, for instance, people show less confirmation bias, which is a tendency to look for and interpret information consistent with their existing beliefs. But when we need to keep on track, we can shift to more implemental mindsets—triggering a set of biases to help us strive harder, ignore distractions, and persist despite adversity.[38] In the weeks before World War I, for example, that shift helps explain why confidence spiked on all sides once war became imminent, among decision-makers and populations.[39]

We need the grit to keep on track, because so much blows us off track. Not least two disruptors within us: boredom and procrastination.

Boredom can hurt us when we lose concentration in a task, particularly when the task demands sustained attention but is repetitive.[40] Commercial airline pilots may fly their plane for only a few minutes an hour, and my anesthesiologist friends report hours of boredom punctuated by minutes of intense stress. Boredom can corrode military morale, as seen during World War II's "Phoney War" when bored French soldiers found everything a fatigue.[41]

Procrastination affects about 70 percent of students and up to 20 percent of adults.[42] People procrastinate despite knowing the costs of putting off healthy behaviors, filing tax returns, saving for retirement, or studying for exams. Putting off routine maintenance of equipment or exercise can also corrode military effectiveness.

But we're stuck with boredom and procrastination because—strange as it sounds—they arise from systems that also help us survive and thrive. We can easily get *too* engaged in a task, and boredom may usefully signal that we should consider changing. At West Point, for example, some candidates might quit not because they lack grit but because they correctly believe that the course isn't right for them.[43] Always quitting is bad; and never quitting is bad, too.

Procrastination may arise from systems that discount the future value of things like water, food, or money, which may be worth less in the future than they are now. That's why people typically prefer some money today rather than a bit more money in a year's time. Animals from birds to primates seem to discount, and human twin studies even suggest a significant genetic component.[44] We humans may procrastinate because our brain's machinery for discounting isn't perfect. A recent study,[45] not yet replicated, suggests that we discount the future effort of work faster than we discount the future rewards from work—so procrastination arises because an hour's work next month seems much less effortful but not much less rewarding. Brain imaging in that study showed that these future values of effort and reward were integrated in the prefrontal cortex.

The realities we face also blow us off track—and every complicated or long-range plan requires updating in light of reality. Russian failures in the Cuban Missile Crisis were compounded by poor feedback mechanisms that linked realities on the ground back to leaders like Khrushchev.[46]

Reality often forces us to multitask as well, which can hinder performance.[47] We rarely have the luxury of ignoring competing demands—and in war, capable adversaries try to force us to multitask. Multitasking partly causes problems because we have limited bandwidth for paying attention to multiple tasks simultaneously—and partly because, when carrying out multiple tasks, the tasks often use partially overlapping brain networks in prefrontal and other regions, so that information relevant in one task interferes with the other task.[48] Switching between tasks also slows people in each task, producing little hindrances that can add up to reduce productivity. Students who multitask with social media and messaging, for example, learn less and are less accurate on homework.[49] Multitasking also reduces how quickly people react to events: one study found that drivers chatting on cell phones were nearly as dangerous as drivers just above the acceptable blood alcohol limit for driving.[50]

Self-knowledge can help here, because an illusion compounds the problems from multitasking: even when multitasking is objectively harming performance, it can *seem* more productive. Our brain falls prey to many such illusions when thinking about its own processes—like our vision falls prey to visual illusions—which are a big focus of our next chapter. And multitasking, like boredom, can bring upsides, too, if we know ourselves well enough to deploy multitasking at the right time, like when we're struggling to solve a problem. Recent research suggests multitasking may help us fixate less on a problem, so that we solve it more creatively.[51]

Keeping our plans on track is a process and, as von Moltke understood, that *process* is as crucial for success as the plan itself. The cleverest plans are impotent if bogged down by events and blown off track, like Tim Shallice's patients in the "shopping task." As Eisenhower noted: "Plans are worthless, but planning is everything."[52]

If we fail to keep our plans on track, even seemingly overwhelming forces can get blown off track and lose.

* * *

For the Vietnamese communists after 1945, their overarching plans to win wars against foreign forces were always as much political as military—and they kept their plans on track by never losing sight of how military means contributed to their overall political goals. An integrated military and political strategy based on the concept of struggle or *dau tranh*.[53]

They fought consistently and cleverly to keep their plans on track and defeat the French, who left in 1954. After 1965 they did the same fighting directly against the Americans in South Vietnam. The communists' Tet Offensive of 1968, for example, was an attack by eighty thousand communist troops against South Vietnamese towns and cities—and although it was a military failure, it was a successful subcomponent of their overarching political plans. (Like Mao's Long March, in Chapter 3, it was a military failure and a political success.) That Tet Offensive punctured American complacency and brought down Lyndon Johnson's presidency. They relentlessly kept their coherent military-political campaign on track, to eventually reunify Vietnam in 1975.[54]

The United States began in Vietnam with a much fuzzier overall plan. And that was doomed by failure to keep a grip over the plan's various subcomponents—military, political, economic—that all got blown far off track.

This danger of failing to keep on track was foreseeable, *before* President Lyndon Johnson's 1965 decision to engage direct U.S. combat troops. Undersecretary of State George Ball, for example, exactly foresaw this problem in a June 18 memo titled *Keeping the Power of Decision in the South Vietnam Crisis*. Ball argued against escalation, writing that

> **[The President's] most difficult continuing problem in South Viet-Nam is to prevent 'things' from getting into the saddle—or, in other words, to keep control of policy and prevent the momentum of events from taking command.[55]**

Once they were involved, U.S. commanders in Vietnam understood that the goal of pacifying the South Vietnamese population was vital.[56] But they totally failed to integrate sub-goals pursued by a cacophony of agencies like USAID, CIA, and others following their own agendas. Boredom corroded conscripts' morale, and many put off sorting out routine disciplines for jungle fighting that brought longer-term effectiveness to allies like the Australians—it took years after Vietnam to recover lost discipline in parts of the U.S. Army.[57]

Feedback systems could have provided the prediction errors—"Oh shit!" responses—from reality to keep U.S. plans on track, but they were broken because the chosen indicators failed to capture reality on the ground.[58] In fact, the indicators were often counterproductive. Stuff needed to be done, so stuff was done: in 1966 only 15 percent of artillery shells were fired in support of troops, while the rest simply blasted parts of Vietnam.[59] One prominent measure was the "body count," but as a U.S. officer recalled: "If body count is your measure of success, then there's a tendency to count every body as an enemy soldier."[60]

"Things" had got into the saddle for the United States in Vietnam. Clark Clifford became secretary of defense after the 1968 Tet Offensive, and he recalled asking:

> What is our plan to win the war in Vietnam? Turned out there wasn't any. The plan was just to stay with it, and ultimately, hoping that the enemy would finally give up.[61]

President Richard Nixon assumed office in 1969 and gave the South Vietnamese more responsibility, training, and weapons—but their operations failed to stay on track, too. As a historian described of one major offensive, they "drifted along, blown about by the winds of [South Vietnam President] Thieu's political needs."[62]

* * *

The U.S. debacle in Vietnam illustrates the importance of having a plan *and* keeping that plan on track.

But keeping on track is not the same as simply grinding on in the same old way to achieve a goal. Especially in competitive arenas like war or business, where clever competitors adapt to avoid your strengths and exploit your weaknesses.

Grit *and* creativity are both required—as the yin and yang of keeping plans on track. Yin and yang are the ancient Chinese ideas of light and dark, which are interconnected, mutually perpetuating forces that each contain the seed of the other.

In the western tradition, something like this is personified in the *Top Gun* movies. Iceman, and those like him who play by the rules, is needed every bit as much as Maverick, who breaks the rules. Without people like Iceman who play by the rules and keep things going, there wouldn't be a functioning aircraft carrier—nobody wants loads of crazy mavericks free-styling how to wave the stop-go signals on the deck, or in air-traffic control. A whole team of Mavericks would be cacophonous, and in the 2022 *Top Gun*, even Maverick himself relies on the solid, dependable character Hondo.

But equally, without Mavericks pushing the boundaries, creating clever new moves, coming up with crazy plans and sub-plans, being pioneers, we would still be in the cave.

CREATIVITY

Keeping on track requires creativity; and creativity requires method, process, and planning.

Creativity experts (which, to be sure, sounds a bit of a contradiction in terms) generally agree that creative ideas must contain two central elements: they are unusual or *novel* in some way; and they are *useful* for the challenge in question.[63] That's why people can be creative in any sphere, be it cultural, economic, political, social, or military.

Militaries have long needed creativity—and it was another reason the Germans fought better on land than the democracies in World War II. To give one example: for both offense and defense the Germans assembled *Kampfgruppe* or "Battle Groups" that combined miscellaneous, often diverse, military units to tackle a specific operation.[64] *Kampfgruppe* were all about flexibility and creativity.

The *Kampfgruppe* ranged in size from bicycle-riding SS tank-busters who in 1945 fought Russian armor at close quarters, to the big *Kampfgruppe* flung up after D-Day to stop the Allied advance through Holland. They often gave a quite low-ranked commander a striking degree of autonomy to creatively achieve a job. *Kampfgruppe* were often "shock troops" to punch a hole through the enemy's lines or to seal off an enemy's penetration.[65] It reflected the essence of *Blitzkrieg*.

In contrast, the interwar French military actively stifled creativity. The French Army of the 1930s more rigidly applied the rules of its doctrine regardless of circumstances.[66] And it hindered new ideas. In 1935, General Maurice Gamelin, who led the French Army, required preapproval of all military writings, so that only official views were aired. In 1934, Lieutenant Colonel Charles de Gaulle was refused permission to publish an article in the *Revue militaire française*. And after de Gaulle publicly campaigned for armored offensive tactics, he was taken off the promotion list.[67]

The Spanish Civil War in the 1930s saw a host of novel technologies and ideas (like Ukraine today)—and German and Soviet military journals devoted enormous attention to learning from the conflict. But the *Revue militaire française* analyzed it little.[68]

The German advantage arose partly because of interwar France's fierce political polarization—so that the French military high command created poorly integrated bureaucratic silos to try to isolate itself from political interference.[69]

But equally vital was the culture of the Prussian and German General Staff that traditionally encouraged creative problem-solving through thinking, writing, and war games. By one estimate, in 1859 about 50 percent of Europe's military literature was produced in Germany. They pioneered war gaming and the "staff rides" that discussed key battles. They kept refining and using these methods cumulatively, for example developing the "planning game" in interwar years to educate commanders at all levels. Admiral Karl Dönitz's U-boat wolf packs were tested in war games, then in exercises, and then were unleashed in reality. War games were crucial to develop the "sickle cut" that won the Battle of France.[70]

Put simply, the Germans had superior systems, methods, and processes to nurture and develop military creativity.

In today's world, I've spent time in Silicon Valley and China's equivalent in Beijing called Zhongguancun, and have spoken with people from the hubbub of biotech startups around MIT's Kendall Square. As the Prussian military discovered, the systems that support creativity there today benefit from a piece of (perhaps counterintuitive) self-knowledge about us humans—creativity requires method, process, and planning to be efficient and effective. In fact, all of us, in our everyday lives, too, can improve the *process* of creativity.

The process of creativity isn't a simple straight line but does have two broad phases: generating ideas, and then focusing on useful ideas to pursue.

Both parts of the process matter, and they draw on distinctive brain systems. Researchers searched the literature and found thirty-four brain imaging studies of creative thinking.[71] Combining the results, they found that brain activity along prefrontal cortex reflected this process: parts farther back were more involved in freely generating novel ideas, while parts farther forward figured more for integrating ideas.

Once again prefrontal cortex draws on the orchestra of brain regions. The hippocampus is crucial for imagination, "what ifs," and comparing diverse analogies to create new options. We saw that in Chapter 4, when the creative British aircraft carrier raid on the Italians at Taranto changed the rules of naval warfare. Hippocampus is also involved in memory and imagination during studies that directly examine creativity.[72] A brain imaging study of visual artists, for example, gave the artists short written descriptions from which to generate and evaluate ideas for a book cover.[73] Generating ideas the involved the hippocampus. Evaluating their drawings involved increased activity in the hippocampus plus the prefrontal cortex—and greater communication between those areas. Along with work on poets and others, these findings also suggest that creativity involves enhanced communication between brain networks.[74]

Research also suggests ways we can improve the creative process. During idea generation, it can help to first spend time (sometimes a lot) asking the right questions. Effortfully using your clever *conscious* brain to identify the pieces of the puzzle, brings them together, and create Models of the problem, even if solutions stay out of reach. But then we must often let our *unconscious* brain work away on problems. In practical terms, this means first think carefully and deeply about something—then go off and load the dishwasher, have a night's sleep, get on a train, go for a run, and then hopefully *voilà!* Ideas that occur during mind wandering, compared with ideas generated while actively working on the task, are more likely to help overcome an impasse on a problem. That is, to be experienced as "aha" moments.[75]

Idea generation also illustrates that creativity is *cumulative*. The teaching-learning spiral and language give us new building blocks—like the wheel or heavier-than-air flight—that afford creative inventions unavailable to the most brilliant ancient thinker. Over our lifetimes, building cumulative knowledge and *integrating* between fields has fueled creative thinkers. Like Apple's Steve Jobs, whose design aesthetics drew on a calligraphy class. Or like Claude Shannon, who invented information theory and chatted about electronic brains over lunch with Alan Turing in 1943. Shannon was exposed during a university philosophy class to the work of a long-dead, self-taught English thinker who coded true and false statements as "ones" or "zeroes"—and that was vital for today's computing.[76] A study of eighteen million scientific papers found that adding an injection of unusual knowledge combinations into a paper—measured by looking at its list of references—made the paper more likely to become a "hit" paper, which many other scientists went on to cite in the future.[77]

Disassembling the chunked parts of our hierarchical Models can help generate ideas, by looking afresh at our assumptions. Experts possess beautifully chunked knowledge, for example, but can be dogmatic.[78] That's why bringing in somebody from a different field can help, because they don't have the expert knowledge neatly chunked.

A host of other tricks also help generate clever ideas. More heterogeneous groups can spark ideas. Jokes can help us out of ruts in our thought. Avoiding sleep deprivation helps us link concepts. As you drift off to sleep, being briefly woken can let you access creative ideas from the halfway state between awareness and slumber.[79] But which clever ideas are most useful?

Our selection of useful ideas can be equally enhanced. Cumulative learning develops the taste to assess what's plausible—which is why Guderian's expertise in *Blitzkrieg* meant he could be more militarily creative than Hitler. In idea selection, chunking can help because we must think through the plan and its subcomponents. It's great, for example, to think "creatively" about abolishing nuclear weapons on Earth—but as two of my former colleagues showed, unless you are just generating hot air, that requires focusing on the necessary preconditions and steps along the way.[80]

To select ideas more effectively, we can ask others to reflect on our plan. We can also enhance our own abilities for self-reflection, to think about our own thinking, which is the focus of this book's next chapter.

And finally, when selecting ideas we must remember that creative ideas are both novel and useful for the challenge in question. It's a cliché for anyone who attends meetings in large organizations, but it does sometimes help to say, "Let's take a step back, everyone, and ask: What does success look like?" What are we *really* trying to achieve?

* * *

In 1969, Chinese leaders feared a decapitating Russian strike. Russia massed over a million troops on its border with China and dozens of troops died in border clashes.[81] What was Mao to do?

He used creative diplomacy.

Mao generated creative ideas. He recalled four PLA marshals who had been purged during the Cultural Revolution and banished to manual labor.[82] Mao didn't have all the ideas himself, so he allowed others to speak; and in this case the marshals were reassured this was no trick to indict themselves. The marshals built on cumulative knowledge, drawing on tales of ancient China to suggest allying with one competitor to oppose a second competitor.

Specifically, among the marshals' wide-ranging analyses and recommendations was the idea of reconciling with America to face Russia. Startling, because their armies had fought ferociously in Korea less than two decades before, and America still recognized Chiang Kai-shek's Nationalists on Taiwan as China's legitimate government.

Going even further, one of the marshals submitted an addendum, proposing what he called "wild ideas," including that China drop the precondition that they must first settle Taiwan's return.

Mao now selected the creative idea of reconciling with America. Bear in mind, Mao was not abandoning Chinese communism: that remained the goal he was *really* trying to achieve. Mao was pursuing a creative sub-goal to ensure his communist regime's survival. Adding a dose of Maverick.

The question became: How to achieve that creative sub-goal? That itself required creativity at further levels down the hierarchy, to gain such an agreement in practice.

President Nixon had subtly signaled his openness to reconciliation before entering office in 1969, and as Mao sent out feelers, both sides needed creativity. Their creative interactions included Yugoslav fashion shows and "ping-pong" diplomacy in which U.S. table tennis players visited Beijing. Partly they were secret. As Nixon's then–National Security Adviser Henry Kissinger recalled, had Nixon followed professional advice it probably wouldn't have happened.[83]

Even once Kissinger met in China with senior Chinese leaders to hammer out the details, they needed creativity. In their October 1971 meeting they needed a creative way to present a communiqué, and the clever Chinese idea took Kissinger aback: a strong statement of China's position; then a blank to be filled with a strong statement of the U.S. position; then a section where their positions converged. Unorthodox, but it worked because both could express themselves firmly for domestic audiences and also come to an accord. In that accord, most significantly it stated that

> Neither [side] should seek hegemony in the Asia-Pacific region and each is opposed to efforts by any other country or group of countries to establish such hegemony.[84]

Stunning. The enemies of a few months earlier announced their opposition to Soviet expansion. China could now focus on the Russian threat, and in turn agreed not to attempt reunification with Taiwan by force in the foreseeable future.

On February 21, 1972, Nixon landed in Beijing. A diplomatic revolution that shook the world. Mao's last big act on the global stage.

Mao's grit and creativity helped ensure his regime's survival. But what would happen to China after—in 1976—Mao's life ended?

A new start—and one that helps explain a central fact in world history over the past half century, which at the time of Mao's death almost no expert predicted: Why would China's communist regime, unlike Russia's communist regime, survive and grow its economy massively? Many factors contributed, but central was that China (unlike Russia) harnessed creativity *productively.*

After Mao's death, Deng Xiaoping navigated a few years of complicated politics to emerge as China's new leader—and Deng's new era of "Reform and Opening" in the 1980s helped unleash the creative potential of China's vast population. Within China, localities could experiment and innovate. People with entrepreneurial ideas could devise creative solutions to make more money. Including for themselves.[85] As Deng announced at a key Party conference in 1978:

> **The more Party members and other people there are who use their heads and think things through, the more our cause will benefit . . . we need large numbers of pathbreakers who dare to think, explore new ways and generate new ideas.[86]**

And equally vital to Deng's reforms was "to seek truth from facts,"[87] that is, to link new ideas to reality.

Russia's communists, in contrast, channeled their creativity less productively: funneling too much of it into the military-industrial complex that came to dominate their economy and society like a tumor. And too many Russians spent their time finding creative ways to game the communist system that were utterly unproductive.[88]

If talk of productive creativity versus unproductive creativity sounds judgmental, let's look at how *artificial* intelligence can be creative. Which holds up a mirror to us humans.

* * *

AI *can* already be creative within constrained situations like board games. When DeepMind's AlphaGo beat the human world champion at Go in 2016, for example, it invented new "hand of God" strategies.[89] Those ideas were creative: both novel and useful for the challenge in question.

But as we've seen, the real world is more complicated than a board game. Moreover, in a military context, AI may lack the data it needs because wars are rare, and because adversaries won't make it easy to collect data on their weapons ahead of time. For such complicated real-world environments, AI is currently good at generating *novel* ideas (the first part of the creative process) but worse at selecting solutions that are really *useful* for achieving the intended goal (the second part of the creative process).

This difficulty arises because of a basic principle of how AI works: AI systems try to achieve some kind of *goal*. That goal might be scoring more in a board game like Go, or classifying photographs more accurately. Clever AI can often find novel solutions to achieve a goal, but how should a goal be specified to produce a *useful* way to achieve a task?

Consider examples in which AIs have found novel shortcuts that aren't useful or are even counterproductive.[90] A boat-racing algorithm learned that instead of actually finishing the race, it could earn more points by performing tight loops through targets in the middle of the course that renewed themselves. Some simulated digital creatures found that to achieve the goal they'd been given for moving, they could simply evolve clever ways to fall over. One computer program got a perfect score in its task—by deleting the files containing the "correct" answers against which it was measured. A naval strategy game for AI was intended to develop new rules for combat tactics—but it turned out that the top-scoring rule was one that learned to take credit for others' success.

Certainly novel, out-of-the-box thinking. Moreover, the boat-racing algorithm that looped around targets in the middle of the course even scored 20 percent more than the average human—despite "repeatedly catching on fire, crashing into other boats, and going the wrong way on the track."[91] But that's not both novel *and* useful: these AIs seem to be cheating creatively.

Humans do it, too. My kids do it: when I say in the evening that they can only eat a cookie after they've eaten a piece of fruit, they may exploit the loophole that I've not specified that they should have eaten the fruit this evening . . . rather than yesterday (I won't fall for that creative interpretation twice). Creative accounting to get around (but not break) tax laws makes people rich on Wall Street. Lawyers creatively find loopholes. Lobbyists bend (but don't necessarily break) the rules to sway politicians.

The wrong targets followed too slavishly can warp behaviors. Anyone in a big organization knows the truth of the old saying that "what gets measured gets managed." Foolish U.S. targets in Vietnam, like the "body count," led to widespread and counterproductive killing of civilians.

One of the saddest cases was Mao's Great Leap Forward in the late 1950s, which sought to bring peasants into giant communes and massively ramp up steel production. Sadly, ever more inflated false production statistics were fed back to Mao, so that catastrophic policies continued despite growing famine. Grain was even exported. Desperately needed farm implements were melted in backyard furnaces because that afforded a way to help meet steel production targets—even though the low-quality steel was useless. Thirty million to forty-five million people died from famine—causing by far the biggest drop in *global* life expectancy since World War II.[92]

Cold War Russia had been highly creative in some fields—Sputnik's launch was an innovative triumph that triggered DARPA's creation. But by the 1970s, its economy began to stagnate. As the joke went, "We pretend to work, and they pretend to pay us." Russian workers and managers creatively played the system, rather than creating useful things.

Clever plans tenaciously kept on track using grit and creativity—Iceman and Maverick—are enormously valuable. But for an AI, a bureaucracy, or a human like you and me—how do we align the objectives we've set with what we *really* want?

Sometimes we must lift our eyes.

EXPERTS IN PLACE

If I need my gall bladder removed, I want an expert surgeon performing the procedure. Not a professor of theoretical physics. Certainly not a talented fitness instructor with a knack for picking things up quickly.

Experts are vital for success in any large modern challenge our societies face: military, economic, medical, and all the rest. Specialized expertise cannot be gained overnight. Good surgeons train for years. Heinz Guderian studied deeply, trained, and adapted the German General Staff's cumulative knowledge to help create *Blitzkrieg*. British air leader Hugh Dowding drew on his decades of hard-won expertise to build RAF Fighter Command.

Yet, while specialized expert knowledge is often *necessary*, it's rarely *sufficient* for overall victory. Winning battles isn't the same as winning wars. Germany lost both World Wars, unlike democratic Britain.

Indeed, experts can be useless at many decisions. The scientist Philip Tetlock spent years studying how well experts made political judgments—and showed almost all made predictions little better than a dart-throwing chimpanzee.[93] Almost all experts on communist Russia—on the left, center, or right of the political spectrum—entirely failed to predict its collapse.

And that was the *biggest* global event since 1945.

It's similar in economics. During the Cold War, expert Soviet economic planners supposedly had all the information to make rational choices but became a dead hand on the Soviet economy. In the capitalist west after 1945, experts using Keynesian ideas had all the answers until failing in the 1970s. Then radical free-market thinkers claimed all the answers—until the multiple crises that culminated in the 2008 financial crisis and eurozone debacle.

As the internet gathered steam in the 1990s, Silicon Valley tech experts believed they had all the answers to freedom, peace, and flourishing everywhere. Western experts laughed at Chinese attempts to control the internet—leading U.S. President Bill Clinton to joke in 2000 that it was "like trying to nail *Jell-O* to the wall."[94] Social media helped sweep away autocracies in the Arab Spring from 2010. Until . . . reality turned out differently.

If experts are vital *and* experts don't always have the right answers, then what do we do?

The Prussian General Staff in the 1860s were military experts who won stunning victories in battle, culminating in the defeat of French armies in 1870. Every other major state had to copy the General Staff so they could compete. But winning battles wasn't sufficient for Prussia to win those *wars*.

To win the war against France, for instance, after having won in battle, Prussia still needed to subjugate France before other powers could intervene. But although military methods alone couldn't do that quickly enough, the General Staff's von Moltke reportedly said at the time, "I have only to concern myself with military matters." Instead, the politician Otto von Bismarck drove wiser judgments based on the bigger picture, speedily concluded the war, and led Prussia through that danger zone.[95] Prussia won the war using military expertise *integrated* with a civilian who grasped the bigger picture.

In twentieth-century Germany, an overmighty military unbalanced that system: the experts climbed on top, with disastrous consequences. It contributed to World War I's outbreak: the military's rigid "Schlieffen Plan" virtually guaranteed a two-front war; the military resisted modifications and alternatives; and the military subordinated vital nonmilitary issues, such as the violation of Belgian neutrality that predictably sucked Britain into the war.[96] Germany's unbalanced system also contributed to its loss of World War I: the military pushed for the "unrestricted" submarine warfare that had military advantages, but was a predictable political disaster that brought America into the war.[97]

In interwar Germany, the overmighty military's machinations aided Hitler's rise to power. The last German chancellor before Hitler was a former General Staff officer. And Germany's president from 1925 to 1934, while Hitler rose to power, was a former chief of the General Staff.

But it doesn't have to be that way.

Britain was the only sizable power to fight for years in both World Wars without losing—and not only won, but also met these challenges while sustaining and deepening its democracy. How?

Britain built powerful general staffs of military experts. But crucially these were always subordinate to civilian masters and were balanced by powerful new specialized civilian bodies—like the Cabinet Office built during World War I, which remains at the heart of government today. After Pearl Harbor, the United States built a system with a similar character. The U.S. Joint Chiefs continued developing until the mid-1950s—and always with an eye, as voices in Congress said, against a more unified and powerful "Prussian-style general staff."[98] Powerful U.S. civilian bodies, like the National Security Council set up in 1947, remain central today. As reportedly summed up by Winston Churchill: experts should be on tap, not on top.

The British and American systems didn't weaken military experts' power. Instead, they built powerful new *specialized* military and *specialized* civilian bodies, and *integrated* them effectively. So that unlike the German system they could broaden out from narrower specialist perspectives to see more of the bigger picture.

Imperfect still, but better. In fact, specialization and integration are fundamental principles of life. For cells, brains, or societies.[99] Specialization is the process by which individuals, groups, or other entities become skilled in a particular function, or adapt to a particular environment. A cell can have specialized structures for generating energy or reproducing. A brain can have specialized regions for vision, hearing, or action. A society can have specialized scribes, blacksmiths, and warriors. Integration coordinates and combines such specialized entities in a single larger system—be it a cell, brain, or social group. No region of your brain can be fully understood in isolation, because its function depends on how it integrates with other specialized regions—language systems can link up with hearing (for speech) or vision (for reading). Societies can integrate by formal or informal institutions, markets, hierarchies, and all the rest. Integrating in new ways provides an edge and also enables new specializations, which in turn enable new types of integration, and on they spiral. What is specialized can contribute to something broader.

We need clever plans, and these often require deep specialist expertise. But sometimes we must lift our eyes, to see if the goals for our clever plans align with what we really want. And sometimes we must lift our eyes, to see if we're missing obvious context from the bigger picture, which means our clever plans are unlikely to work well.

The comedy show *The Big Bang Theory* follows a group of friends at Caltech who are extremely clever, but by missing obvious context from the bigger picture their plans constantly fall apart or lead to unintended consequences. Clever but not wise. Over many seasons, they do start to see (a bit) more of the bigger picture, so they can flourish more broadly. To become not only extremely clever, but also (a bit) wiser.

As this chapter began, we described a chain going from data, to information, to knowledge. But the chain doesn't end at knowledge, because we need more. As the poet T. S. Eliot described:

> Where is the wisdom we have lost in knowledge?
> Where is the knowledge we have lost in information?[100]

And in the military sphere, as von Clausewitz described:

> To bring a war, or one of its campaigns, to a successful close requires a thorough grasp of national policy. On that level strategy and policy coalesce: the commander-in-chief is simultaneously a statesman. [King] Charles XII of Sweden is not thought of as a great genius, for he could never subordinate his military gifts to superior insights and wisdom, and could never achieve a great goal with them.[101]

To the chain of data, information, and knowledge—lifting our eyes higher we can add wisdom. If wisdom sounds abstract, let's walk through the chain, using the example of a human gene.

Data are facts and statistics collected together for reference or analysis, in which a single "datum" is a distinction that makes a difference (for example, a thing is red or blue).[102] Data require processing to be meaningful.

For instance, the human genetic code is a three-billion-long string made up of four letters (C, T, G, or A). It looks like this: . . . ATGCAAAAGTTCAAGGTCGTC . . .

Information is meaningful data. It involves descriptions and is, usually, useful. Chapter 5 on perception described how our sensory cortex turns data from our eyes and ears into information.

Genes can be read from sections of the genetic code, such as those coding for eye color, cancers, or early-onset dementia.

Next, *knowledge*: this can be considered a more-or-less systematically ordered set of beliefs that are true and that we are justified in believing.[103] Knowledge is often useful, and it takes experience to master a body of knowledge.

A physician considering a patient's genetic test result may combine that with the scientific literature, plus information from the results of the patient's other medical tests, and so have knowledge of what a particular gene reveals about the patient's risk of cancer or dementia.

Wisdom involves broader knowledge—which provides context as well as humility about unknowns—and uses this to more holistically assess the trade-offs in complex decisions about taking actions to achieve goals.[104] Wisdom is the focus of our final chapter, which ends our journey through the brain at the frontal pole.

A physician can consider specific genetic knowledge in the broader context of a patient's family circumstances, past mental health, young children, religious beliefs, and so on. What are the best (or least bad) ways of moving forward?

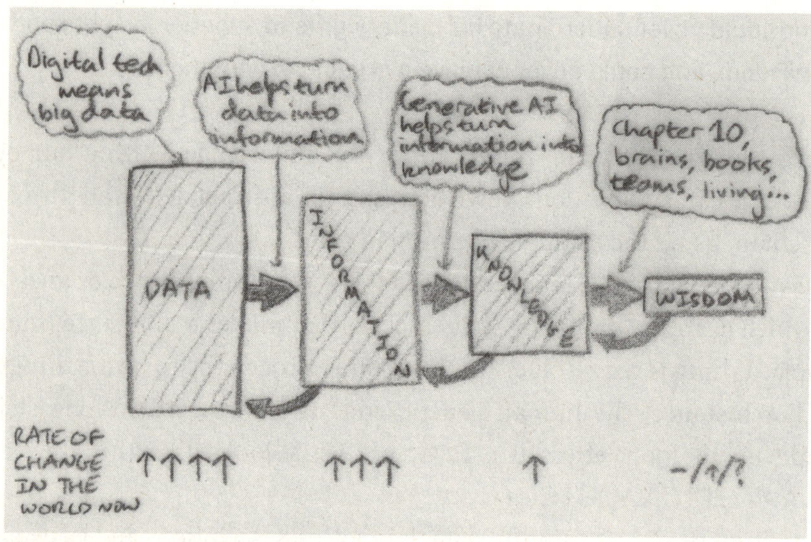

FIGURE 18: Data, information, knowledge, and wisdom. Consider the chain from data as a "raw material" processed into information (meaningful data); then knowledge (ordered sets of justified-enough beliefs); and wisdom (broader context for more holistic judgments). The character of technology now means that data is expanding rapidly, which AI can turn into information, and that generative AI is now beginning to weave into sets of knowledge, but this only more slowly increases wisdom.

Most decisions we care about, from medicine to war, contain this chain: data-information-knowledge-wisdom. Stepping through the chain helps us anticipate how new factors may affect our decisions—as we can see for AI if we look at a military example.

Begin with data in the form of pixels from Earth observation satellites, of which vast quantities are now dirt cheap.

AI can use semiautomated image recognition to turn this data into information—in this case vehicles counted, located, and identified according to type and unit. This century's AI boom began after AI perception hugely improved in 2012 and it was harnessed in the Pentagon's Project Maven.

Human experts place such information within their broader expert knowledge, and generative AI will increasingly aid them using its ordered sets of beliefs. In this military example: vehicles of this type, taken together with other new capabilities, recent history, and changes in online discussions, suggest a marked change in a competitor's military posture. This military group may be about to strike another faction.

And finally, wisdom: What does this new knowledge mean within that actor's broader sociopolitical context, or the broader regional and global contexts? As once commented by a very senior U.S. decision-maker about the early days of the fight against Islamic State[105]—the United States can launch our own strikes, but step back and look at the bigger picture, and if that means we lose Turkey as an ally, then we have lost far more than we gained. A stunning tactical or operational victory may be a strategic negative (like "winning" an argument with a romantic partner)—just as the reverse can happen so that a military failure (like Mao's Long March or Vietnam's Tet Offensive) is actually a victory in the bigger picture.

In war, we don't want to be clever but not wise, like the "whiz kids" working for the U.S. Secretary of Defense in the Vietnam War who often miserably failed to see the bigger picture. And of course we need wisdom in our everyday lives, too. We don't want to work ever harder and better making widgets—and then look up to discover it was for a pointless or even bad purpose. We don't want to end up like the AI speedboat, cleverly getting lots of points but unwisely completely missing what the game was really about.

We can all be unwise in some aspects of our life—the most talented people, for example, can take the most foolish risks for sex—and we can all be unwise sometimes. But we should try to be wiser, and in the next chapter we will consider features of wiser decision-making. It can help when making the most consequential decisions: about how to live our own life; about how to treat complex patients; and about nuclear weapons.

Take a moment to try to recall some facts about nuclear weapons from this chapter's start. They're a big deal.

In our time, we will need wisdom because the democracies could lose in conventional war (as Chapter 7 described), could lose domestically (as Chapter 8 described)—and even more seriously we could lose a nuclear war. If half the American population dies tomorrow morning, that is a terrible loss regardless of how many Russians also die.

Putin or any near-term successor is highly unlikely to abandon Russia's nuclear arsenal, and America cannot destroy that arsenal before it fires back. That leaves us with deterrence, which means affecting the other side's decision-making so that they *choose* not to act. Hence USSTRATCOM's deep interest in the Models used by key decision-makers like Putin.

And for nuclear deterrence, rationality and expert knowledge can only take us so far, because of a fundamental paradox at the heart of nuclear strategy: it assumes that the players are *simultaneously* both rational and irrational.[106]

In nuclear deterrence between two actors, they are rational when they are themselves being deterred, because they don't want to bring about vast destruction. That is, when the other side is threatening them, they react coolly and rationally—a bit more like Iceman. And then they are simultaneously irrational when they are deterring others, because they must threaten vast destruction however damaging it ends up being to themselves. That is, when making threats, they're more unpredictable—a bit more like Maverick.

Someone like Putin knows and manipulates this. In 2022, a U.S. intelligence assessment gave a fifty-fifty chance that Russia would launch a nuclear strike on Ukrainian forces to defend Crimea.[107]

Deterrence becomes more complicated in our era because there are no longer only two large nuclear powers as in the Cold War. Now USSTRATCOM worries about the much less stable "Three Body Problem," with America, Russia, and China together in the nuclear mix.

No clever expert or clever AI can solve these problems. Instead, we need the wisdom to look these facts in the face and live with the contradictions.

And the wisdom not to get despondent—because actually, when faced with challenges like these, things can and do turn out well.

* * *

Soviet Russia had withstood Hitler's most ferocious onslaughts. A superpower for the Cold War's four decades, it launched Sputnik, went to the brink over Cuba, and challenged America on every continent. But the Soviet regime had unwisely allowed the military-industrial complex to dominate society, and allowed their planned economy to become too sclerotic to compete—not mistakes that wiser leaders like Eisenhower or Deng Xiaoping would have made. And then in 1991 the Soviet regime collapsed. Peacefully.

That this happened illustrates the importance of individual humans—in the person of Soviet leader Mikhail Gorbachev—because Soviet Russia retained a formidable domestic security apparatus. Such dissolution, certainly peacefully, would have been implausible under someone like Putin.

U.S. President George H. W. Bush could—like any clever politician—have milked Russian collapse for every drop of political gain, but wisely he didn't "dance on the Berlin Wall," and he tried to leave Russian dignity intact.[108] That helped Russians and Americans cooperate to secure the Russian nuclear arsenal.

No loose nuclear weapons flooded the black market. No accidental nuclear war was set off. No brutal crackdown killed tens or hundreds of thousands. It is really a very upbeat story.

A happy note on which to end, before we start again.

10

WISER

ENDINGS AT THE FRONTAL POLE

The King of the Zulus, Shaka kaSenzangakhona, was a human of military and political genius.[1] A great soldier-ruler like Alexander the Great, Julius Caesar, and Napoleon. In 1816, he inherited ten square miles and an army of five hundred men. Within a decade he had revolutionized his society and warfare, to forge a politically sophisticated and administratively integrated empire across southern Africa. Shaka's success rested on not one, or two, but many sections of his brain's orchestra.

Shaka was a master of space, like his contemporary Horatio Nelson: when the Ndwandwe invaded Zulu lands in 1818, Shaka carefully chose the slopes of kwaGqokli Hill for a defensive battle. Outnumbered more than two to one, he had trained his troops so they had a formidable will to fight. Troops armed with a tool he invented: the new, heavy-bladed *iklwa* that could feel like part of a warrior's body. Like the samurai's sword in Japan.

He built alliances, which later included a small contingent of British settlers with firearms. At the Battle of kwaGqokli Hill, Shaka brilliantly grasped his adversary's intentions and used deception to outwit them (while also avoiding the trap of the enemy's deception).

Shaka was, like Mao, a social alchemist who began with a tiny group of followers and forged vast political and social change. And he led with a single unified will: his army conforming to his vision, his Model, that directed their activities.

At the climax of the Battle of kwaGqokli Hill, the enemy chief formed a huge column 200 yards wide for a final assault on Shaka. Whereupon Shaka could unleash his own reserves in a brilliant plan: the *izimpondo zenkomo* or "horns of the buffalo."

Shaka pioneered the "horns of the buffalo" maneuver for his army, in which the "chest" fixed the enemy and the "horns" enveloped them. Roman legions used similar plans two millennia before. A century later, U.S. General George Patton's "Grab them by the nose and kick them in the pants" got at a similar concept. The nature of war remains the same, even as the character of war changes. And Shaka, like Patton and many Roman generals, used a mix of grit and creativity to keep his plans on track.

He seeded every level in his plan's hierarchy with something new: new training systems and equipment for individuals; new organization of regiments; and new battlefield strategies like the "horns of the buffalo." And beyond to a new concept of total war: the *impi embonvu*. Literally "war red with blood."

His mother's death in 1827 sent him into a catastrophic decline, and he was assassinated—with the weapon he had invented.

But by then he had already won another battle, which won the war. In 1826 the Ndwandwe had rebuilt their army and invaded once again. After ten days of marching, like the Americans at the Battle of Midway, Shaka used scouts and advance guards for intelligence, surveillance, and reconnaissance (ISR) to provide an edge. He didn't just repeat his previous plans: ever flexible, Shaka changed his plans to defeat the enemy in detail. Piece by piece. Winning another stunning victory.

Shaka's kingdom lived on after him, a remarkable product of his social alchemy. More than half a century later, in 1879, the Zulus famously defeated the British in battle at Isandlwana. To this day they form a distinctive population. Much of that rests on Shaka's brain.

Shaka was brave, clever, a master of space, and all the rest—but all his remarkable brain systems were no mere cacophony, they were brought together and guided by his sight of a larger vision. Shaka shared with leaders like George Washington, Winston Churchill, and Otto von Bismarck the ability to understand the strengths and weaknesses of his own position in the world, so he could grasp and shape the bigger picture.

How can we know ourselves in the world—and make wiser decisions?

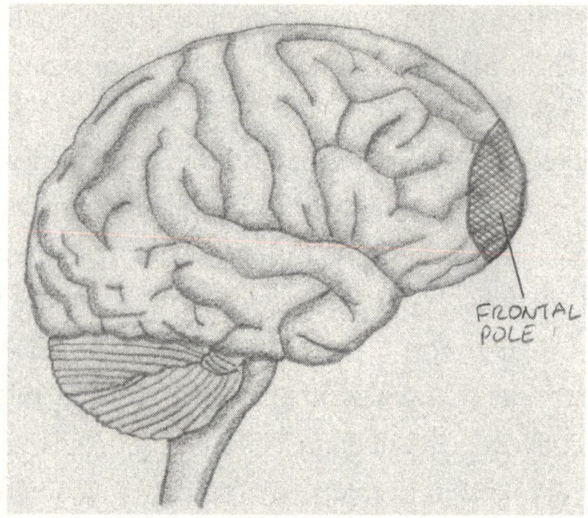

FIGURE 19: The frontal pole, the very end of our journey through the brain. The frontal pole is association cortex that sits at the very end of the prefrontal cortex.

The frontal pole ends our journey through the brain. New brain research sheds light on how it helps us to *think about our own thinking.* So that in our brain's orchestra, the frontal pole acts as conductor.

Self-reflection is crucial for wisdom because we need to know about ourselves in the world, including what we do and don't know, and what we can and can't do. Recall last chapter's description. Wisdom involves broader knowledge—which provides context as well as humility about unknowns—and uses this to more holistically assess the trade-offs in complex decisions about taking actions to achieve goals. That's a fancier version of "perceive, Model, act," which we met with our robin redbreast. Put simply, wisdom is seeing the bigger picture about ourselves in the world, so our chosen actions help us live better.

This is the basic insight behind the Pentagon's most famous office of thinkers, credited with spawning the Revolution in Military Affairs of the early 1990s that cemented the overwhelming military dominance of the U.S. unipolar moment. That Office of Net Assessment examined not only the adversary but us and them together to find opportunities to act.[2] Taking a step back, to "think about our thinking," is also a foundation of the

U.S. system of government. Thomas Jefferson, in a reported exchange, once asked George Washington why they should create a senate.[3]

Washington replied: “Why did you pour that tea into your saucer?”

“To cool it,” said Jefferson.

“Even so,” responded Washington, “we pour legislation into the senatorial saucer to cool it.”

Imperfect, to be sure, but more durable than almost all other regimes over the past two centuries.

We need wiser choices to handle the trade-offs our era demands. It would be easier if there were only one way to lose. And to avoid losing in all three ways we’ve met—conventional, domestic, nuclear—the democracies will require wise enough leaders who can step back, reflect, and integrate what seem to be incompatible goals.

Concerned citizens will need wisdom, too, because they matter in the democracies. And they can be deeply *un*wise: as shown by widely held beliefs in disarmament during the 1930s that gave the Axis powers an almost uncatchable head start; or by excessive bombastic nationalism before World War I. Simple answers like pacifism or militarism cannot manage the trade-offs.

Our brains use the same principles as in far simpler organisms, but it is our remarkable capacities for reflection, for self-knowledge, that can give us the wisdom we need to save civilization. And what’s most exciting about the new research on thinking about our own thinking? That we can make this remarkable human capacity better.

METACOGNITION

Self-knowledge has long been seen as a foundation of wisdom, and enhancing our powers to self-reflect has long been a route to making wiser choices. The ancient Chinese prized self-reflection. As the warrior-philosopher Sun Tzu wrote, “If you know the enemy and know yourself, you need not fear the result of a hundred battles.” For the semi-mythical philosopher-founder of Taoism, named Laozi, gaining self-awareness was one of the highest pursuits. As Laozi described, "To know that one does not know is best; not to know but to believe that one knows is a disease." The ancient Greeks prized self-knowledge as highly. "Know thyself" was carved in stone at the ancient Temple of Delphi. For Socrates, "the wise and temperate man, and he only, will know himself, and be able to examine what he does or does not know."[4] Everywhere and at all times.

The last fifteen years have seen an explosion in the scientific understanding of how humans reflect, how this reflection arises in the brain, how to measure it, and how to enhance it. This is the field of *metacognition*.

Metacognition means "thinking about thinking." ("Meta" means "after.") Our neural machinery for reflection is crucial for how humans learn and adapt in complicated environments. Metacognition is not the same as intelligence or IQ, because people who are good, bad, or indifferent at such thinking can all be completely different in their metacognition as well (good, bad, or indifferent).[5] That's why people can be clever, but not wise. Research also shows that an individual's metacognitive ability seems to work pretty consistently across many types of decisions[6]—and, as we shall see, you can also improve your metacognition.

To examine "thinking about thinking" in the lab, my good friend, colleague, and collaborator at Queen Square, Steve Fleming, invented a clever method that we used together in an experiment.[7] As you read about it, try to imagine yourself doing the task.

To begin, you meet us in the lobby of our lab at Queen Square, and fill out some forms giving your consent to take part. We lead you downstairs, through a warren of tunnels and rooms containing brain scanners and other equipment. We lead you into a testing room and explain your task.

You sit down in the quiet room, looking at a computer screen. During an hour of testing, you will make hundreds of judgments. In each judgment you see two images flashed on the screen, one after the other, and your job is to say whether the first or the second image contains a slightly brighter patch. After every decision, you indicate your confidence in that decision on a six-point scale ranging from totally unconfident to totally confident. The decisions are tricky. The computer was set up—though you don't know this—to adapt to your skill. If you are doing well, then the computer makes the task a bit harder, and if you make many mistakes, it gets a bit easier. This ensures that everyone actually performs at a similar level, so that we can focus on how good you are at thinking about your thinking. In this case, you are judging your confidence in your judgments.

An analogy Steve likes to give is the TV game show *Who Wants to Be a Millionaire?*[8] One early contestant in the UK show was Judith Keppel. She had answered a series of increasingly tricky general knowledge questions: each time deciding whether to walk away with what she had already won, or if she was confident enough to risk her winnings and go for a higher prize. Finally, she faced the £1 million question: "Which king was married to Eleanor of Aquitaine?"

If she got it wrong, she would lose almost £500,000. "Henry II," she said.

But how sure was she? How sure?

The game-show host asked: "Is that your final answer?"

She reflected on her decision, and she decided she was confident. And she won £1 million.

In our experiment, Steve and I measured how well people assessed their own thinking. Steve has also used brain imaging to show that people who are better at metacognition tend to have more "gray matter" (the cell bodies of brain cells) in their frontal pole and also better connected "white matter" (wiring between brain cells) that links the frontal pole to and from other regions. Steve and others have shown that damage to people's frontal pole causes disruption to their metacognitive abilities. A wealth of convergent evidence now supports the basic findings—and has now gone on to tease apart many aspects of what metacognition does.[9]

In short, our brain's systems work together like an orchestra to give us an overarching Model of the world, with which we stay alive, perceive, act, and think—and in that orchestra, metacognition acts as the *conductor.*

An orchestra *can* play on without a conductor, and often during a performance the conductor can seem superfluous. But good conductors can make the difference between brilliant or poor performances.[10] Symphony orchestras have at least eighty members, each with only their own music in front of them—and a conductor synchronizes the musicians' entrances, the rhythm and tempo of a piece, and the relative volume of each soloist or instrumental group. And the same with learning during rehearsals. Conductors may spend much of their time on stage with their arms folded, but their occasional interventions can make all the difference.

I recently chatted with a professional horn player, and I asked what his orchestra's famous conductor adds. He mentioned the things above, and also that the conductor can take a step back, reflect, and ask: What are we trying to achieve? Should we play Beethoven more slowly to enhance the drama? What speed did Beethoven *really* intend? Should we use modern instruments that are essentially perfected, or "flawed" instruments that Bach would actually have heard?

The analogy of an orchestral conductor is one of many possible analogies for metacognition. Others include the chair of a committee. Or a village elder. Or George Washington's senatorial saucer. And when we are thinking about thinking, it's useful to reflect and ask which analogies we lay down next to each other—just as we did earlier in the book by comparing the analogies of being in the run-up to World War I, or the run-up to World War II. We pause, to check we're asking the right questions.

In Chapter 1, we met a robin with a simple Model of the world to help it survive. A Model that describes how senses can be linked to actions that help it achieve its goals. I mentioned then that increasingly sophisticated life-forms use increasingly sophisticated Models to stay alive. And yet although we've now journeyed far up to the frontal pole at the other end of the brain, here, too, the basics remain the same. To help the organism survive and thrive, its Models must be close enough to *reality* to help, not hinder, the organism; *anticipate* potential problems or opportunities; and be *flexible* enough to adapt as the world changes.

What's truly awesome about us humans, though, is that we have extra loops of processing—so we can do reality, anticipation, and flexibility with metacognitive style.

REALITY (METACOGNITIVE STYLE)

The robin in my garden needs a Model that is anchored to reality, because to stay alive such small birds must eat between one-quarter and one-third of their body weight every day. Human wisdom, too, has always required an anchoring to reality. Wisdom requires knowledge, and that knowledge needs to be justified enough—so that if we believe we know something, then we probably do, and if we believe we don't know something, then we probably don't.

But for a brain, sealed away in its skull, staying in touch with reality isn't easy. We cannot perceive the world like a passive TV set, so we use a controlled perceptual Model—but then how can we distinguish reality from imagination? Indeed, brain scanning shows that seeing a thing and imagining that thing evoke very similar patterns of brain activity.[11] Memory is intimately linked to imagination. We build intellectual castles in the sky. And in fact, hundreds of millions of people today with conditions like schizophrenia or Alzheimer's often *do* struggle to tell real from imagined. So why aren't we all constantly hallucinating, paranoid, falling prey to delusions, and losing touch with reality?

Researchers can use many methods to explore how human brains tell real from imaginary. Experiments can, for example, make even entirely healthy people unsure if they're imagining or perceiving. One method asks people to stare at a screen while imagining particular images (for example, a particular shape)—and then researchers can project a real image (for example, a fruit) onto the screen very faintly just above or below the limits of perception. Such methods can make the imagined and real images get mixed up. Recent brain imaging of such experiments suggests that the brain evaluates how strong the evidence is that an image is real—and if the evidence is strong enough to get over a "reality threshold," then the brain thinks it's real; otherwise, it's assessed as imagined.[12]

But we don't moor our Models to reality equally well in every type of decision.[13] Our Models for perception are often moored to reality pretty well, for instance, because getting perception wrong often causes feedback like tripping over things. In contrast, we get less direct feedback on how well we are doing higher-level tasks—like having a conversation or understanding a complicated paragraph in a book—and this increases the scope for illusions.

In such higher-level tasks, specific factors loosen our moorings to reality.[14] One key factor, it turns out, is that when information is easier to process that makes us *feel* we are performing well, even if that metacognitive judgment is wrong. If text is printed in larger font, for instance, we *feel* more confident we'll remember it, even if that doesn't affect our memory in reality. When we act faster—something experiments can manipulate in the lab—we *feel* more confident in our decisions, even if they aren't more accurate in reality.

This matters because inaccurate metacognition can itself damage performance in reality. In one example, seventy students from the University of Haifa were asked to read information leaflets, on topics like warming up before exercise.[15] The students could read the leaflets either on a computer screen or printed out. Reading on a screen, rather than reading the printed version, made people more confident that they would perform well in a subsequent test—but actually the exact opposite happened in the test. Why? Because they could choose how long to read the leaflets, and their misplaced confidence from reading on-screen led them to give up studying earlier. Inaccurate metacognition made them study less, so they performed worse in reality.

We're often wrong when judging reality about other aspects of ourselves, too, in predictable ways. Hungry or thirsty people often (incorrectly) believe their cognitive powers are impaired, while sleep-deprived people often (incorrectly) believe their cognitive powers remain intact. Knowing the truth helps us, for example, decide when pulling an "all-nighter" is helpful or harmful. We can all use such tools, and it's interesting that a successful leader like Winston Churchill was very particular about when he slept.[16] We're often mistaken about our own abilities, too: When American college students are asked about their leadership ability, 70 percent rate themselves above average, and 2 percent rate themselves below average.[17] Again it's interesting that many hugely successful business leaders try actively to correct for such inaccuracies and consider self-knowledge to be vital. Amazon founder Jeff Bezos wrote to his shareholders in 2017:

> You can consider yourself a person of high standards in general and still have debilitating blind spots. There can be whole arenas of endeavor where you may not even know that your standards are low or nonexistent . . . It's critical to be open to that likelihood.[18]

Bezos was famed for unusual executive meetings, with thirty minutes for silently reading a memo that was prepared in advance—forcing executives to think and reflect.[19] Nineteenth-century Prussian officers used different methods, such as war games or discussions during "staff rides" over old battlefields, but similarly showed that reflection can provide a vital edge.[20]

In fact, all the many areas of knowledge about ourselves and of the world outside ourselves build up into a *tapestry of knowledge*—and metacognition helps us interrogate the quality of different parts of our tapestry. Knowledge about ourselves, others, and so much more. Indeed, any good tapestry includes many areas of explicit factual memories of the type we saw in Chapter 4, which give us knowledge of areas like history or geography, and metacognition helps us assess our confidence in these memories, too.[21]

Many wiser leaders dedicated considerable time during their lives to learning and reading, to be more sure that their factual memories were anchored to reality. Churchill read extensively in many areas of human knowledge and wrote many books. Nelson Mandela famously studied, reflected, and taught during his long incarceration. Dwight Eisenhower was a lowly officer with a career in the doldrums until, during a posting in Panama, a mentor made him embark on a course of intensive study. Eisenhower started on military fiction, then went on to Shakespeare, Nietzsche, military history, biographies, von Clausewitz, and much on allies. When Eisenhower later attended Command and General Staff College, he finished top of his class.[22] Churchill, Mandela, and Eisenhower worked to better anchor their tapestry of knowledge to reality, to give them justified confidence in what they did know—and also about what they *did not know*, so that they could ask better questions.

Indeed, everyone's tapestry always contains many gaps where we are partially ignorant: and that is okay. Memory is warped to be useful, as we saw in Chapter 4, and we actively forget things. The point is that we can have better—or worse—quality of ignorance (as well as knowledge) about ourselves and the world. Self-reflection helps us here: How confident are we about what we think we don't know? In a trivial example, when I was a medical student I could name all the bones of the foot. I can't do that anymore. But I have better quality ignorance than if I'd never known the bones of the foot—I have a sense of the size and feel of that hole in my tapestry of knowledge. I am a bit wiser about the foot.

It's impossible to be truly wise if your tapestry of knowledge is not anchored to reality. And equally you cannot be wise if you just sit there, never putting your knowledge into practice, never choosing between better or worse possible futures.

ANTICIPATION (METACOGNITIVE STYLE)

A robin's Model constantly makes choices about possible futures in its world of potential dangers and opportunities. So must ours, and metacognition helps us better anticipate possible futures so that we can make wiser choices.

To better anticipate the future, our most sophisticated brain systems can elaborate on two fundamental building blocks for metacognition that we share with the robin. One building block is the prediction errors about our own actions—which, if you think about it, are a form of self-monitoring that helps us reconsider what we anticipate. Another building block is to quantify our uncertainty about how things will turn out. How uncertain am I, for example, that what I see behind those bushes in the zoo will turn out to be a tiger, or whether my tennis shot will land in or out?

As we move up from the brainstem to more sophisticated brain regions, these building blocks for self-monitoring get more sophisticated.

Our lower levels of metacognitive machinery are simpler but crucial for survival and can be really fast. In the 1960s, a classic experiment got people to do a difficult, repetitive task: participants had to respond to sequences of numbers by pushing buttons; and participants also had to push another button if they thought they'd made an error. Remarkably, their *internal* error detection was 40 milliseconds *faster* than their fastest responses to the external stimuli.[23]

On the other hand, people can spend years beavering away introspecting as philosophers. Or people can reflect to reconsider their future career, relationships, or other ways they could spend their futures.

Often, we are in the middle, with minutes to think about our choice—like Judith Keppel thinking about her choice to win (or lose) a fortune. Or like Lieutenant Colonel Stanislav Petrov of the Soviet Air Defense Forces.

If you have ever felt uncomfortable in a dilemma, well, Petrov faced a truly momentous choice.[24] At the height of the Cold War in 1983, both sides were on a hair trigger for nuclear first strike. Petrov was in charge of monitoring early warning satellites. Just past midnight on September 26, 1983, alarms went off in his command center—indicating that U.S. nuclear missiles were on their way to Russia. In some twenty-five minutes they would detonate on Soviet soil. Petrov had to choose: Should he alert his superiors of a surprise attack, or not? He took valuable time to think as the clock ticked, his doubts arising as the computer readout seemed almost too clear. Why only five missiles in this first wave? How certain was he? How uncertain was he? One possible future could leave his country desperately vulnerable in the face of nuclear attack. The other possible future could mean an unnecessary nuclear war. He chose.

And it turned out the satellite had misread sun reflected from the cloud tops.

Petrov could draw on our most sophisticated human abilities to introspect, to deliberately reach in and interrogate our thinking—what can be called *explicit metacognition*.[25] To be sure, we still need the automatic and unconscious self-monitoring, called implicit metacognition, to handle everyday activities like making a cup of tea or driving to work. But our explicit metacognition can take us far beyond the robin, or any other animal, to help us better anticipate the future—by explicitly reflecting on our own uncertainty and updating in light of new evidence. Consider an example.

Intelligence, used in the sense of spying, is at its core about anticipating the future. Catastrophic intelligence failures—like 9/11 or the Yom Kippur War—are failures to predict. The intelligence equivalent of DARPA is called IARPA (with an I for Intelligence), and in 2011 IARPA began a forecasting competition. Competitors had to predict things in the future that only have a right or wrong answer, such as "Will North Korea launch a new multistage missile before May 10, 2014?" And with many questions across varied topics, nobody could be expert in everything. Who won?

Teams from many top institutions (such as MIT) took part—and were all blown away by a team led by the psychologist Philip Tetlock.[26] Tetlock's team were mostly amateurs, selected as the best forecasters among many internet users who volunteered to take part. He called them "superforecasters." And it turned out that compared to less adept forecasters, superforecasters were particularly good at dealing with the two building blocks for metacognition: explicitly updating their predictions in light of new evidence (that is, prediction errors), and thinking explicitly about their own uncertainty.

Explicitly thinking about our own thinking is powerful, but can we improve our anticipation by going further—to think about thinking about thinking? Consider the example of a student who confidently anticipates they will score highly on an exam, and then fails. To improve in the future, the student won't benefit only from extra study on the subject matter, but also from understanding why their confidence wasn't right. That is, by judging their confidence judgments about their performance (or what could be called meta-metacognition).

Researchers have adapted experiments on metacognition like the one I used with Steve Fleming—and shown at least four levels of "thinking about thinking."[27]

Imagine yourself in a lab looking at a computer screen and doing a simple visual choice task, similar to the one I described earlier. First you choose between two visual stimuli (level one choice). Then you give a confidence rating in your choice (level two). Then you chose whether (a) your original choice or (b) your confidence rating was more likely correct (level three). And then (level four) you rate your confidence in that level-three decision. At all four levels, participants performed better than chance. Up to what can be called meta-meta-metacognition. That's in the same ballpark as the three to six levels of depth people typically analyze in decision trees. And the one to three levels of iterated reasoning (my move, your move, my move . . .) when people play strategic games in the social world.

Explicit metacognition improves how we anticipate our social world, too. Reflecting on how others see us, and may anticipate our intentions, can be life-and-death. Self-reflection also gives us insights that we can teach to others. The best golfers may not make the best teachers, who are instead often people who can best explain what they are doing and why. Self-knowledge of the teacher's own Model helps the teacher export their Model into their students' brains, to explain *why* golf works as it does.

Metacognition will be key in human-machine teams, where we'll need to construct a human-machine lingua franca to communicate things like confidence and uncertainty, which can help both sides better anticipate each other's actions. Companies like DeepMind are exploring how AI can best explain its thought processes to humans[28]—and success there requires understanding metacognition in the humans on the receiving end.

Some researchers are even adding metacognition to AI in machines that are fully autonomous from humans, because it helps the machines better anticipate the future.[29] One method gives robots multiple, slightly varied copies of a network, providing a range of predictions that gives the AI a measure of how confident it should be. Another method gave a drone a second neural network (metacognitive machinery, in other words) to detect the likelihood of crashes during test flights around Manhattan—and then when later released into a dense forest the drone could avoid flying in ways that it anticipated would cause crashes.

Nobody yet knows the best ways to create machine metacognition, but metacognition is so useful that it will happen: to help machines reflect on their uncertainty and update in light of new evidence, so they can better anticipate the future and thus make wiser choices. AI robots will look after our children, sick, elderly, nuclear reactors, and weaponry—we'll want them to be able to lift their robot eyes at least a little, to avoid the worst types of *un*wise choices about the future.

It's impossible to make wiser choices if you aren't anchored to reality, and if you can't anticipate potential futures to help make your choices. And also if you lack the flexibility to change your mind and learn.

FLEXIBILITY (METACOGNITIVE STYLE)

Our robin's Model enables it to choose from a repertoire of responses if a competitor robin enters its territory—deter, attack in different ways, or flee—and that could save its life as up to 10 percent of adults die from clashes in some robin populations. Down at the other end of the human brain, we saw that if a Spitfire pilot hit by a bullet were immediately overwhelmed by pain, they may not react in the best way—which is why the brain's Models sit between sensation and action, so we can respond *flexibly* and choose from among a repertoire of actions. Metacognition extends this flexibility, interposing itself to give us flexibility in sophisticated processes like planning.

We need flexibility because once we're up here looking at the bigger picture, we must often switch between pursuing different goals that *all* matter. In the big picture of war in our time, the democracies can lose in three ways—conventional, domestic, and nuclear—and leaders thinking about any one alone must sometimes stop, reflect, and think of implications for other goals. Churchill in World War II was deeply involved in pursuing plans in multiple military theaters, and the military commanders in each theater often wanted more resources. Churchill had to step back, switch between considering each theater, and ask how they affected each other in the bigger picture—and this enabled him to reallocate crucial resources like tanks from the home islands to the Middle East.[30]

Sometimes we should step back and reflect on the goal, too, and potentially change our mind. We might have a great plan to build an impenetrable Maginot Line, or to swiftly topple the regime in a country like Iraq, but step back—is that *really* what we want to do right now? And within that plan, should we change our mind about how best to achieve key sub-goals, like Mao did when he temporarily set aside Taiwan to get a joint statement with Kissinger and America? Churchill often changed his mind during the war—notoriously so, to some—and was willing to be argued out of implementing his ideas like sending troops to liberate Norway in 1942.[31] We must constantly change our minds at every level in our lives.

Metacognition is central to how we change our minds—as I explored in a study with Jian Li at Peking University, and Steve Fleming at Queen Square in London.[32] In each trial people first made a choice about visual stimuli, much like the choices we've seen before. Then in each trial they received additional sensory evidence either for or against that previous judgment, and we could zoom in on changes of mind. Intriguingly, we showed across two separate experiments that Chinese participants in Beijing were better than British participants in London at using new evidence to change their minds—a difference we would love to test again and explore further. But equally important were the cultural commonalities: both experiments across both sites revealed the same basic metacognitive processes, in which people thought about their previous choice and changed their minds. And as Steve has shown using this task in the brain scanner, that metacognitive process involves a brain region farther back in prefrontal cortex to encode evidence for or against changing one's mind—and then a region farther forward reflects on confidence in the choice.[33]

That we could have acted differently is a defining feature of actions over which we feel we have *free will.* These "voluntary actions" are the *most* flexible behaviors we can exhibit. An amoeba has a few options to act. The fruit fly *Drosophila* fighting a duel against another fly has more, such as the "head butt" and "lunge." Our cortex can give us an almost infinite range of potential affordances: sitting at my desk now I could type, burst into song, or try to eat my computer mouse. Metacognition helps us step back, and consider new perspectives for new affordances—even in seemingly insoluble situations. During Britain's darkest hours of World War II in the summer of 1940, a famous story has Churchill thinking as he shaved in front of the mirror one morning. Churchill's son entered the bathroom to ask about Britain's survival: Churchill had, his son recalled, seen a way through—the only path was to "drag the United States in."[34]

Metacognition also helps us flexibly adapt our Models in another way: helping us *learn.*

A recent Harvard Business School study of adults compared groups of trainees at the Indian IT company Wipro.[35] The trainees spent the last fifteen minutes of their day either reflecting on what they had learned (the reflection condition), explaining the main lessons to others (the sharing condition), or continuing their studies as normal (the control condition). Compared to the control, both the reflection and sharing conditions boosted performance by over 20 percent. Metacognition also has longer-term effects in education. A study followed children aged seven to fifteen years over time, finding that development of metacognition predicted future gains in IQ.[36]

Better self-knowledge can also help us avoid metacognitive illusions that hinder learning. Most of us have studied for a test and had to choose between: (a) massing the study into a single long session; or (b) spacing the same amount of revision out (reviewing it once, leaving it for a day or two, and then returning). Most participants across a series of experiments reported that massed practice was more effective for learning—but in reality, 90 percent did better with spacing. Massed learning *seems* more effective because it is more fluent, but that fluency fools our metacognitive machinery. A bit like going to the gym and using only lighter weights when appropriately heavier weights work better.[37]

When a metacognitive illusion leads us down the wrong path, we humans can explicitly turn to a higher level of metacognition to help recognize the error—and correct for it. Getting meta on our meta. For example, by reading a book like this.

ENHANCE METACOGNITION; ENHANCE WISDOM

Like the robin, our brain helps us cope with reality, anticipation, and flexibility—but we do so for vastly more complicated challenges. Metacognition helps us cope more wisely, and recent research shows that, as individuals, we can improve metacognition. That is, we *can* become wiser.

Some methods are direct—and not yet ready for use outside specialist settings. One applies a weak electrical current across the skull to stimulate prefrontal cortex. The drugs Ritalin and beta-blockers boost metacognition. And people undergoing brain scanning can be trained to directly alter the brain circuits that track confidence in their decisions.[38]

Other powerful methods *can be tried by any of us.* In fact, I often recommend them to people in everyday life, and I use them, too.

A simple and powerful way to improve self-awareness is to take a third-person perspective of ourselves.[39] We are often more accurate when judging others' work than when judging our own work—for example, when judging how long a project will take, we tend to be overoptimistic for ourselves and realistic for others. Formal planning is so useful partly because you put your ideas down on the page, so you can better apply your own metacognition. Advisers can also be crucial: Churchill deliberately chose his top World War II military chief to be a man who would stand up to him.[40] Being forced to make our knowledge public by explaining things to others is valuable, because we are better at recognizing when others talk nonsense than recognizing nonsense from ourselves.

Hearteningly for our era, many such techniques are easier in democracies than authoritarian states like China. "Read, write, fight" was the call by a recent U.S. chief of naval operations—asking sailors to spend time reflecting, not just doing.[41] But, that said, we should remember the cautionary tale that interwar French political polarization led French military leaders, unlike in Nazi Germany, to close down discussion.

Technologies will increasingly help improve our metacognition. IARPA, the intelligence version of DARPA, recently began a program to develop AI that can take an analyst's draft report along with its source documents and automatically identify additional supporting evidence, as well as contradictory evidence.[42] AI will also automatically seek strengths and weaknesses in the draft report's reasoning. Then, based on all this, AI will produce comments to help the analyst improve their report.

That is essentially what a good human colleague, mentor, reviewer, or editor has often done for me on documents I've written—but AI will be faster and more accessible. AI may miss context and aspects of the bigger picture but should cover the basics, which will free up time for human commenters to focus where humans help most.

Such AI tools will become widespread. Pause for a moment to remember the spectrum going from an inert tool like a hammer, to partially freethinking agents like a dog, through to a human colleague.

Now think about the physical object that is a book.

Hundreds of these objects sit on shelves in my house or in piles on my office floor. Each physical book is an inert object, much as a hammer is inert. It is a tool for storing and communicating information. I interact with it, read it, insert bookmarks, and so on. The book as a form of object really began to take off in the fourth century CE, and changed radically after that.[43] In the seventh century, spaces began to separate words. Punctuation was a new innovation. We now take the index of a nonfiction book for granted, but the index didn't start until the thirteenth century. An index is itself a "meta" aspect of a book. Printed page numbers first arrived in 1470. Digital books on an e-reader are now searchable for particular words. The book has become more useful, yet remained inert.

In the near future, the "book" will move along the spectrum to become more freethinking, like a dog. The book will become an intelligent artifact that you can interrogate and discuss with, in order to aid your metacognition.

It can summarize itself to your desired length. You could ask a history book covering debates on the evolution of species, "If I had Charles Darwin in the room with me right now, how would he respond to this question?"

You could interrogate a book on military strategy: "Use the internet to give me fresh examples of your contents, but from the fields of business, medicine, and law." Or "What are the implications for strategy in medicine or law?" Or "Book, how would you advise me to treat this patient?"

A book on World War I might discuss with you the parallels, and differences, between its subject matter and current China-U.S. relations.

Reimagine a book, as it more actively helps your metacognition. By giving you accessible analogies outside your personal areas of knowledge, or new perspectives, or contrary points of view. We often get new insights by seeing the seemingly familiar from a new perspective.

Of course, right now, without AI, we can also explore new perspectives.

* * *

Across previous chapters we used multiple perspectives to view the stories of World War II and the Cold War. Not only the typical stories seen from one western perspective, but also at sea, and in China. That was a deliberate strategy on my part to aid your metacognition, and here we can do it again, consciously.

This last chapter takes us from the end of the Cold War, through the period of U.S. dominance, and into our new era of competition. For western audiences, these are well-trodden events, through which many of us lived in whole or in part, about which we *think* we know much.

Yet that's a partly misleading fluency, a metacognitive illusion: not everybody sees the stories as we do.

Consider the end of the Cold War. I've always thought it was on balance a good thing because the threat of nuclear war receded and brutal authoritarian regimes collapsed. I thought that the Soviet leader Mikhail Gorbachev, who was central to bringing that about, was, on balance, a good thing, too.

Now consider an analogy: the story of Sweden. A while ago I gave a talk for the Pentagon Joint Staff and commented admiringly about Sweden's democratic traditions, when a Polish colonel interjected to give a far less flattering perspective on Swedish history. To him, Sweden rapaciously invaded neighbors like Poland until repeated military defeats led it into a long period of "neutrality," during which Swedes profited nicely and failed to help neighbors like Poland in 1939. I was taken aback because, to many people like me, "Sweden" was almost a byword for a fair, tolerant, admirable society. And I still admire much about Sweden, but my point here is that when I made my assumptions public they were challenged—and when I checked my assumptions from this new perspective, I found my assumptions wanting. A jarring collision with another perspective.

Now consider the Cold War's end from a Russian perspective.

Losing the Cold War hit Russia's population hard. An average Russian man's lifespan had been sixty-six years in 1985, but malnutrition and alcoholism plunged it below fifty-eight years a decade later.[44] Oligarchs stole vast riches while unemployment went from zero to 30 percent in three years. By 2013, opinion polls in Russia named geriatric 1970s ruler Leonid Brezhnev their best twentieth-century leader, followed by Lenin and Stalin. Gorbachev, hero in the west, came last.

I still think the Cold War, on balance, ended well. But a Russian perspective helps make the world more comprehensible. That's why in this last chapter, to help our metacognition, I suggest we look from a new perspective at post–Cold War history: a Chinese perspective.

* * *

For the United States, the 1991 Soviet collapse meant they had won the Cold War. To many in China's Communist Party it meant something very different.

"It's hard to overstate how obsessed they are with the Soviet Union," noted scholar David Shambaugh, who extensively studied how the Chinese Communist Party (CCP) adapted to the Soviet collapse.[45] It was perceived that by loosening too far, the Soviet Communist Party itself collapsed, which led to the country's collapse and the loss of territories like Ukraine.

Xi Jinping gave a private speech in December 2012, shortly after assuming power, and blamed the Soviet implosion on officials who loosened too far from their ideological roots.

> **"Why must we stand firm on the party's leadership over the military?" Xi asked. "Because that's the lesson from the collapse of the Soviet Union. In the Soviet Union, where the military was depoliticized, separated from the party and nationalized, the party was disarmed." When the crisis came "a big party was gone just like that . . . nobody was man enough to stand up and resist."[46]**

The Soviet Union's collapse and dismemberment wasn't the only shock. The First Gulf War in 1991 destroyed Saddam Hussein's Iraqi Army—and was a rude awakening about Chinese military weakness. Saddam's military was similar to China's, and the United States cut through it like tofu.

Worse, America no longer needed China to face down Russia, and America pulled away. In 1992 President George H. W. Bush sold 150 advanced F-16 fighters to Taiwan. Bill Clinton won the 1992 election partly by decrying the "butchers of Beijing."[47] To many in the CCP the Clinton administration seemed a return to early Cold War U.S. ideas of promoting a "peaceful evolution" to dissolve China's Communist Party.[48]

The CCP's leaders hoped to hang on politically—the 1989 Tiananmen Massacre had shown their will—and reverse their fortunes economically. Chinese leaders like Deng Xiaoping sought to play their hand more wisely. Facing the reality of America's overwhelming military, in Deng's famous phrase they sought to "bide their time" abroad. They believed western human rights talk was in reality hypocritical and self-serving. In 1989 Deng anticipated that China would be a "big piece of meat" that foreign business could not resist—so those businesses would pressure their governments.[49] Deng's shrewd bet led by 2000 to permanent, normalized trade relations and China's accession to the World Trade Organization. China's leaders set Chinese scholars to reflect on how to flexibly balance multiple aims that all matter, to create what they called "Comprehensive National Power" across the economy, society, science, tech, and all the rest, not just the military.[50] Deng and his successors built a culture of local experimentation to flexibly meet challenges, so people could change their minds. Even the group of top leaders—the Politburo—governed more as a committee, to gain multiple perspectives instead of being entirely dominated by a single individual in the style of Mao or today's Xi Jinping.[51]

Militarily, the United States seemed willing in the 1990s to intervene and carve up other countries in places like the Balkans. The Chinese military looked at the bigger picture to find ways to avoid facing U.S. military tech head-on: strong missile forces could help China sidestep American advantages, for instance, if there was time to build them.[52] The United States seemed to be increasing support for Taiwan during episodes surrounding the 1995-to-1996 Taiwan crisis. And during U.S. and allied action against Serbia over Kosovo, in 1999, many Chinese were shocked by the U.S. precision strike against the Chinese Embassy in Belgrade, which specifically destroyed the military attaché's part of the embassy. That Belgrade bombing was a huge surprise to many in China—a big "Oh shit!" prediction error.[53]

What was the United States capable of, and what did its leaders intend toward China?

Would the United States wisely husband its power, and deploy that power against the only country with the sheer size to compete for domination of the globe? Indeed, from the mid-1990s some more reflective U.S. thinkers did come to believe that China must begin to challenge the United States for world dominance—in particular the Pentagon's Office of Net Assessment, which more holistically considered not just external threats but reflected on how America itself interacted with the outside world.[54] Or instead, as Chinese leaders hoped, would America run from crisis to crisis and dissipate its energies?

Chinese people who faced these questions could not be infinitely wise. Nobody can. Human metacognition is an astonishing strength that helps us make wiser choices, but even our highest-level neural machinery has limitations. Self-knowledge of both our strengths *and* our limitations can make us wiser. Our brain's strengths and weaknesses both appear clearly as we consider a final highest-level capability, one intimately involved in reflection: consciousness.

CONSCIOUSNESS

We humans have a tough time agreeing on a definition of consciousness—a challenge that in itself illustrates the difficulties we have in understanding ourselves. We debate what consciousness is, and why we have it. But remember a simple fact: consciousness is so foundational for our brains that every human, everywhere, whoever wrote about consciousness did so while they were conscious.

Despite these debates, we can use a simple definition that for a conscious creature *there is something it is like to be that creature.*[55] For you, there is something it feels like to be you. Consciousness is being aware of some of the contents of your brain's activity—hence the link to reflection and to the explicit metacognition in humans that interrogates our own brain processes. To put it simply, consciousness is having subjective experiences.

As a doctor, while treating thousands of patients I have assessed their *level of consciousness.* That is, their amount of consciousness. Level of consciousness matters to doctors because it can be affected by head injuries, anesthetics, alcohol, epilepsy, and much else. If a knock to the head causes you to lose consciousness, that's a warning sign that makes a doctor think your head injury might be more serious. The brainstem can switch consciousness on and off, but our orchestra of brain systems can give us much finer gradations in level of consciousness than that. I've seen this revealed in patients with severe head injuries in neurological intensive care, who gradually progress over weeks from unconscious to fully knowing who they are and what's going on. Turning to other organisms, it seems reasonable that dogs have a higher level of consciousness than earthworms, and that a rock has none.

As a neuroscientist, I am also interested in the *contents of consciousness,* which are the perceptions, feelings, and thoughts that arise from our orchestra of brain systems. And I'm interested in our neural machinery for self-awareness, including for metacognition, which helps us *subjectively experience* these contents.

Some debates about consciousness shade into the highest realms of philosophy, but in practical terms we have learned a lot about how consciousness works in our brains. We can consider four aspects, which are already familiar from everything we've seen about how our Models work in cortex—that they are *cumulative, hierarchical, integrative,* and *processed efficiently.*

Looking at the four aspects in turn, each illustrates the limits and strengths of our most sophisticated abilities to reflect. The machinery *you* use to consciously reflect about yourself in the world, as you try to make wiser decisions.

CUMULATIVE CONTENTS OF CONSCIOUSNESS

With contents of consciousness that are more useful and closer to reality, you can make wiser choices—but where do the contents of your consciousness come from?

The contents of your consciousness include ingredients that bubble up from the depths of your own brain, such as your feelings, perceptions, and thoughts. These contents often leave your brain, traveling outward through your facial expressions, speech, or composing of a social media post. But your brain's link to other brains is a two-way traffic system.[56] Much of the contents of your consciousness travels *inward*, too.

Much of what we are conscious of—words for colors we see, the wheel, who we might be—are actually cumulative knowledge and ideas that flow inward, inherited from millions upon millions of other people. This inflow shapes and provides much of the raw material for our tapestry of knowledge about ourselves in the world, which gives us the bigger picture. The problem is that we're often oblivious to where most of these contents of our consciousness come from, and how they got in. And that's a profound limitation to our wisdom.

To be sure, some of this raw material for our tapestry of knowledge is extremely helpful. Even entire areas of knowledge are made digestible for nonspecialists, so there's always a new "history of the world" or "all physics in a nutshell." Wise leaders like Churchill can shape something important but nebulous into something tangible—like the "Battle of the Atlantic"—that we can fit into the bigger picture.[57] Our mothers (or Marx and Mao Zedong) can give us entire worldviews. But as well as what's good among this raw material, much is also indifferent, or even bad.

Many of the influences clamoring to enter our consciousness actively seek entry, whether we want it or not. Celebrities like Kim Kardashian and her family penetrate the consciousness of many of us via television and social media. Advertisers, such as Nike or Apple, and political forces have long sought to shape our consciousness. They can use a step-by-step, cumulative process to do that. Before people fight and die for catchy slogans like "Workers of the world unite!," those people must first be conscious of their class interests. Marx, Lenin, and Mao realized that process might require a vanguard or intelligentsia, to help workers wake from their "false consciousness" and so achieve true "class consciousness." Many movements have done something similar, like nationalists for "national consciousness."

Our tapestry of knowledge will always be limited by the raw materials available to us: and we can consciously improve this diet. Perhaps stop, on occasion, to reflect on what you're allowing to flow inward. Too much social media, too much about areas of knowledge already familiar to you, too many perspectives from your time and place—these won't provide the best material for a broad and rich tapestry of knowledge. Of course we can't know everything, and everyone's tapestry will always be full of giant holes, but we can improve the quality of raw materials flowing into our consciousness by giving our tapestry better knowledge in some areas and better ignorance in others. If Nelson Mandela can do it incarcerated in apartheid South Africa, or Eisenhower as a young officer in 1920s Panama, we can probably at least make a few tweaks.

Our brilliant brains help us make wiser choices by seeing the bigger picture about ourselves in the world—*and* we need humility, because we will always be limited in how much of that bigger picture we can be conscious of. And those limitations become even more evident as we explore the very lowest, and highest, reaches of our brains' hierarchies.

HIERARCHIES, HICCUPS, AND HIGHER PURPOSES

Our brain's organization has a hierarchical flavor: from brainstem at the base up to the lofty heights of association cortex, ending at frontal pole. But although higher levels call on lower levels to perform actions, those lower levels are actually semi-autonomous.[58] Even the lowest part of the brainstem, the medulla, can hiccup—something that all our fancy machinery above cannot simply decide to stop. Hiccups also illustrate the limits of how deeply we can reflect. Can we really bring to consciousness why we are hiccupping, or if the hiccups will stop? This brings advantages: our brain's higher levels can avoid constant distractions to get on with bigger pictures for wiser choices. But that comes with the limitation that big factors—like dopamine, sexual urges, or fear—remain inaccessible or only partly accessible to conscious reflection. Wiser decision-making often requires understanding ourselves, so these limits to the conscious access and control lower down in our hierarchies further limit our capacities for wisdom.

Profound challenges also arise as we try to peer upward in our hierarchies for explaining and acting in the world—and this time the challenges arise not from our inabilities to interrogate ourselves, but *from* our remarkable abilities to consciously interrogate ourselves. Remember that in London Zoo my kids might see eyes, a mouth, and a nose that form a face, which is part of a head, which is part of an animal with four legs: *Tora! Tora! Tora!* A tiger! In doubles tennis, I use hierarchical Models of my partner and opponents with many levels: what shot they intend right now, what they are thinking of me thinking of them, what they are doing in this particular episode, and what their ultimate goals are in our relationship (is this game actually an important business meeting?). These hierarchies of causes help us anticipate the world, to explain *why*. As we reach upward toward ever higher-level causes, we benefit from ever wider context that helps make wiser decisions—for example, to see when a lower-level tactical victory may be a strategic disaster. But as our explicit metacognition consciously interrogates the higher reaches in our hierarchies, what cause is at the *highest* level? To end an endless string of causes is there, as the philosopher Aristotle suggested, an "unmoved mover"?[59]

This aspect of our Models helps explain the timeless mystery of why humans seek an ultimate cause; why many humans remain metaphysically unsatisfied; and why many humans do believe in an ultimate cause that explains everything. A God, or Gods, or ideas like Marxism. Whether we personally think this is a limitation or a good thing, we should recognize that this means *there will always be*: (a) some humans who are profoundly unsatisfied and so may become radical; and (b) unless everyone believes in the same ultimate explanation, then some humans will hold profoundly certain beliefs, even if those beliefs conflict with others' equally certain beliefs.

Moreover, our hierarchies for explaining the world are only half the story: What is at the top of our hierarchies for acting in the world? Wisdom concerns not only seeing the bigger picture about ourselves in the world, but also *choosing actions that help us live better.* What is highest in a hierarchy of actions, going from individual muscle movements, to components of the Fosbury flop, to living a whole life, and beyond. Unlike the AI speedboat spinning in circles in the middle of the course, we can consciously ask: What's the ultimate goal? The highest-level purpose?

Many people consciously seek a purpose-driven life. Often benign or helpful, this is illustrated by the immense popularity of the book *The Purpose Driven Life* by U.S. pastor Rick Warren, who gave the invocation at President Obama's 2008 inauguration. His book has sold more than fifty million copies, and its five purposes include: You Were Planned for God's Pleasure (Worship); You Were Formed for God's Family (Fellowship); and You Were Made for a Mission (Mission).[60] That seems pretty wholesome to me, as does such purpose arising from many religious sources. Or secular sources as seen among earnest communists, liberals, and nationalists. Or family. Or pursuit of scientific truth. In fact, possessing too little purpose can lead to depression or self-destruction, which is a particularly human challenge—robins don't consciously ask themselves about their highest purpose (as far as we know), so, like pretty much every nonhuman animal, robins don't commit suicide.[61] While purpose empowers some humans, some humans who lack purpose are limited by their need for purpose.

The need for a highest-level purpose can not only lead to self-harm, but also to awful extremes of harm to others—as seen in the purpose-driven jihadis, who left comfortable western lives for the promise of purpose in the Islamic State. Like so many others since humanity began, they were prepared to kill with abandon and even martyr themselves for their highest purpose. So, too, was another human, a human who raises a very difficult question for ideas of wisdom.

Hitler was brave, talented, clever—and he was utterly foul (or evil). But was Hitler wise and utterly foul? Can anyone be? During his rise to power in the late 1920s through to victory in the 1940 Battle of France, Hitler played a skillful hand domestically and then abroad. During that period he listened to advice. During that period he showed restraint in key areas as he saw the bigger picture of how to become Führer and then win astonishing military victories against the odds. During that period, he was horrible, but was he also wise? I would say no, for two reasons. One is that he too exclusively pursued his highest purpose of creating an Aryan supremacy on Earth—and so he created too many enemies, killed too many people, and acted too appallingly, to achieve his goal in a lasting way. That is, he pursued his highest purpose too exclusively, without the balance between goals needed for wisdom. But the second and larger reason is that his higher purpose was foul—and I think Hitler *ought* to have included in his highest goal that human life more broadly (not just in his group) does matter positively in itself. This second point arises as part of my own personal morality, because I believe that human life ought to matter—which is a foundation stone of my thinking. It sits beside other foundation stones such as that I believe I do exist, and I believe I am not a brain floating in a tank imagining the world.

This sounds abstract and philosophical—but actually it's important for our very near future with AI. Nobody knows if or when we will build an AI with general intelligence, which means an intelligence that matches or exceeds the human brain's capabilities across a broad range of activities. But it could happen in the next ten or twenty years (although I think it will probably take longer), so we need to plan now. Building general AI doesn't necessarily doom humanity, a point I made a while ago to some deeply worried technologists and academics at lunch in a restaurant: "That waiter over there has a general intelligence; if any of you invented AI with his capabilities you would become the most famous scientist in the world—and he is not going to destroy humanity tomorrow. He couldn't even if he wanted to. And anyway, he almost certainly doesn't want to. Even most humans who have held awesome power have also possessed enough wisdom to avoid large-scale annihilation."

An obvious part of the solution is to limit the AI's capabilities (for example, don't allow it too near nuclear weapons)—but it's equally important to try to align what the AI wants with what we want for humanity. To do that, we need to give the AI the components for wiser choices, so we can avoid creating an AI Hitler that could treat *all* humans like Hitler treated the Jews, Roma, and Russians. That requires building AI with the right goals, including by hard-coding that human life has positive value. And it requires building AI with the machinery for wisdom that includes self-reflection, caring about context, and not following its highest purpose too exclusively—so, for example, it doesn't only seek to maximize the manufacture of paper clips, even if the best way to make paper clips involves killing all humanity.

Hopefully we can give AI ever more of the right goals *and* the right machinery for wisdom. That will be informed by better understanding the goals and machinery in human brains, as well as through experimentation in building AI. This will help make wiser AI that can see the bigger picture about itself in its world, so its chosen actions help it exist better.

But we cannot expect any AI to be infinitely wise, because it will face the same insoluble limitations as us conscious humans. Its tapestry of knowledge about reality will rest on imperfect cumulative raw material. It will face mysteries raised by its hierarchies' highest and lowest reaches. And, furthermore, across any broad tapestry of knowledge, how many different areas can really be integrated together into a coherent big picture?

INTEGRATE CONSCIOUSLY

Wisdom requires us to consciously integrate our tapestry of knowledge, to see a big enough picture for tackling the challenges we face. Our explicit metacognition enables us to step back and consciously ask if we have considered the relevant knowns and unknowns, about ourselves and the world. We can, for example, integrate thinking about the three ways democracies can lose in our time (conventional, domestic, and nuclear) as we will a bit later in the chapter. We can integrate thinking on war with economics, for instance when thinking about the security of a country's supply chains. And we can even integrate war into enormously diverse sets of philosophical ideas, as did most of history's foremost philosophers because they lived in times of war: the Warring States period saw ancient Chinese philosophy flourish; the warring states of ancient Greece found Aristotle teaching Alexander the Great; and Immanuel Kant published *Perpetual Peace* while Napoleon fought wars.

Integration sounds abstract, but it's fundamental to life, as we saw in the last chapter, and integration is equally fundamental to conscious experience.[62] As you chat with a friend in a café, your brain uses specialized areas for sounds, visual colors, speech, intentions, and so on—which are integrated into a single unified scene. The frontal pole helps integrate across the brain's whole orchestra, because it sits atop many brain hierarchies and receives inputs from many regions.[63] The frontal pole helps to transcend perception and action; to bring together awareness of the self, the social, and physical worlds; and to gather *many* plans and goals for comparison and integration.

For millennia, wisdom has sought to integrate knowledge into bigger pictures. Aristotle studied all of life: from the tiniest biological components his ancient Greek instruments could discern; through the individual human's body and intellect; to the state; and beyond to carefully examine 158 city-states across his world. For Aristotle, wisdom needed a broad tapestry of knowledge.[64] Seeing not just isolated parts but the whole can provide context that makes pieces of information or knowledge intelligible: knowing a tiger is a mammal, for example, means it likely has four limbs and feeds its babies milk. Part of a shattered pot often makes more sense when you've seen some of the pot's other broken shards for context. Great leaders like Winston Churchill need a big picture for strategy. The scholar Eliot Cohen describes Churchill's incredible integration, across political and military factors, or across historical episodes like the end of World War II that started the next historical era.[65] As Churchill described of painting a great picture, "There must be that all-embracing view which presents the beginning and the end, the whole and each part, as one instantaneous impression."[66]

Metacognition helps us craft and strengthen our tapestry of knowledge, as we reflect on linkages between fields. Wide-ranging analogies and perspectives can help us. It turns out that Nobel laureates, compared to other scientists, are at least twenty-two times more likely to have a side interest as an amateur actor, magician, or other type of performer. And scientists who go to work abroad, whether or not they return, produce work with more impact.[67] A good stock of analogies helps within a single discipline, too: each case becomes more than the sum of its parts when enriched by being put alongside others, to see similarities and differences. That helped Eisenhower turbocharge his career—and lead wisely. Metacognition also helps us reflect on how we can integrate general principles with the specifics of the actual case in front of us, like a doctor does with a specific patient. Every war is different, and there are useful general principles.

But . . . however good you are, you cannot integrate everything.

Our ability to integrate is always limited in any complex challenge like war. There are too many factors to master (from ethics to economics), and even if we could master them all we would still face combinatorial explosion as all the factors interacted—and then we would still need to view the system as a whole. In his book *Strategy*, the scholar Lawrence Freedman concludes his history of strategies of force with a chapter entitled "The Myth of the Master Strategist."[68] Even with an encyclopedic tapestry of knowledge, nobody could integrate it all.

Instead, we need the humility to recognize we must integrate our understanding with that of other individuals who bring complementary skills, as we saw in the last chapter. Those specialists also need appropriate humility: they need self-knowledge of what their specialism contributes, and their *own* areas of ignorance. In many government meetings I've heard experts in fields like economics, psychology, or cyber dogmatically argue that *their* field has all the right answers—but that's unlikely for most real-world problems. Moreover, *top-down* visions of where one wishes to go must be integrated with *bottom-up* appraisals of what's possible, given reality on the ground. Deng Xiaoping captured it well with the famous metaphor of "crossing the river while feeling the stones one by one."[69] And successful revolutionaries, like Mao, usually have an able organizer of victory to handle the admin.[70]

Wiser leaders need the humility to ask questions of subordinates—and the ability to ask useful questions. The scholar Eliot Cohen's seminal book *Supreme Command*[71] showed that this was crucial in four leaders of acknowledged skill: Abraham Lincoln, Georges Clemenceau, Churchill, and

David Ben-Gurion. Great leaders can intuit when others are more wrong than they are and if needed probe deep into details.

Even vast bureaucracies like the Pentagon cannot integrate everything that matters. I've worked with the Joint Staff to model key factors for wielding strategic power in the global system. We started with twenty-four factors (of which military was just one) and all their most important linkages. Integrating that together becomes as much an artistic project as a scientific enterprise, in which impressions emerge at the higher integrated levels—as happens when you step back from the individual brush strokes to see the Impressionist Claude Monet's water lilies. Churchill was a talented painter, and in his pamphlet on painting he directly compared it to war: "It is the same kind of problem as unfolding a long, sustained, interlocked argument. It is a proposition which, whether of few or numberless parts, is commanded by a single unity of conception." And sometimes that requires reflection. Churchill welcomed his sea voyage to America after Pearl Harbor because "it is perhaps a good thing to stand away from the canvas from time to time and take a full view of the picture."[72]

The philosopher Isaiah Berlin beautifully captures the strengths *and* limits of the human brain's ability to integrate. During World War II, he was a British liaison with the Americans in Washington, D.C. He closely observed both nations' most senior leaders during a time when they made thousands—millions—of world-changing decisions. Like the poet T. S. Eliot and philosopher of war von Clausewitz in the last chapter, Berlin distinguished information and knowledge from that higher quality of wisdom. For Berlin, the talent of great political leaders

> entails, above all, a capacity for integrating, a vast amalgam of constantly changing, multicoloured, evanescent, perpetually, overlapping data, too many, too swift, too intermingled to be caught and pinned down and labeled like so many individual butterflies' . . . [W]hat makes men, foolish, or wise, understanding, or blind, as opposed to knowledgeable or learned or well-informed, is the perception of these unique flavours of each situation, as it is, in its specific differences.[73]

It is no counsel of despair that integrating *everything* is impossible for individuals, groups, or AIs—because we can integrate better, and our consciously stated aim can be to integrate across enough of the big picture to be useful for wiser decisions. It's art *and* science. We need a big picture and details that are good enough to be useful. That self-knowledge itself helps make us wiser.

Our cortex helps us rise to this challenge through Models that are cumulative, hierarchical, integrative—and processed efficiently.

PROCESS EFFICIENTLY

Your brain's orchestra contains hundreds or thousands of specialized systems, each with their own Models. But your brain is an orchestra, not a cacophony.

The orchestra could not function if every system blared out at once. Instead, hunger, thirst, reward, navigation, perception, or reflection might each win the competition for prominence from moment to moment, and so bubble into your conscious awareness.[74] Or one region might query another—how hungry am I right now?

This must be processed efficiently, because no brain has unlimited processing power. An adult's brain runs on around 20 watts (like a dull incandescent light bulb), and even that already constantly consumes some 20 percent of our entire body's energy.[75] Sophisticated control layers in our brains' hierarchy—particularly in prefrontal cortex and the frontal pole—enhance some signals, quash others, and edit pieces together.

In this efficiently processed version of reality, your conscious experience flows smoothly between thoughts that create a single integrated narrative across time. Like when the scenes in a movie such as *Top Gun* flick around from one character's perspective (the pilot Maverick in an aerial duel) to shots of other people (his comrades watching from the ground) to yet more things (his missiles hitting a target)—but in a movie we don't notice all these different shots; it's just the story. We don't notice this happening in our brains either—unless it goes wrong. Astonishingly, split-brain patients, who have the two sides of their cortex separated, might even have two separate consciousnesses, one on each side.[76]

The movie of consciousness with which we live our lives is a continuous masterpiece of the filmmaker's art. So convincing, we can scarcely believe its limitations. And yet, this efficiently processed movie only ever serves up a heavily edited selection of ingredients from which we can make wiser choices.

During any period of time, there's only so much of which we can be conscious. The big difference between the movie of our consciousness and a typical movie, however, is that we can actively interrogate our conscious awareness—shout, "Stop and rewind to check what's really happening over there!" Our explicit metacognition can consciously ask good questions so we don't miss really big things.

Consciously looking for the right things is crucial. Because sometimes even when we pay careful attention to a movie, as we saw in Chapter 7, we can miss the obvious fact that running into the middle of a scene and dancing around—is a large gorilla.

* * *

Chinese worries about U.S. intentions didn't improve when George W. Bush became U.S. president. Tensions rose. On April 1, 2001, a U.S. EP-3 reconnaissance plane was flying near China when it collided with a Chinese fighter and made a forced landing. The captured U.S. crew was finally released after eleven days. Days later, Bush decided on a major arms deal to Taiwan and told *Good Morning America* that the United States would do "whatever it took to help Taiwan defend herself" against China. Senior officials on both sides worried about a military showdown.[77]

And then 9/11 erupted into the U.S. consciousness.

Twenty years later, nine in ten Americans who were aged four or older in 2001 could remember exactly where they were, or what they were doing, when they heard about the terrorist attacks. For years, 9/11 affected Americans' dreams.[78]

But step back for a moment, and see it through the eyes of many in

China where—entirely naturally—it didn't have such an impact. Sad and shocking, but far away. And for many Chinese leaders, the sudden, radical shift in U.S. focus provided a respite. Terrorism suddenly dominated U.S. leaders' thinking, so China could now pursue its development agenda unafraid of serious U.S. pushback. In 2002, China's president formally heralded China's "period of strategic opportunity."[79]

China's course didn't change. America—and thus the world—changed course around China. With America distracted, China boomed for well over a decade. Look at a few areas:

Economically, China's gross domestic product jumped from $1.2 trillion in 2000 to more than $14.7 trillion in 2020.[80] It became the workshop of the world, dominating global manufacturing like Britain in the nineteenth century and America in the mid-twentieth century. The 2008 financial crisis, and the subsequent eurozone crisis, severely dented notions that westerners had all the answers for running successful economies. By 2020, a leading western organization's figures showed that China produced more than the world's next nine largest manufacturers put together.[81]

Scientifically, China blossomed. By 2024 it had two of the world's top twenty-five universities, according to a leading western ranking.[82] Chinese tech companies like Alibaba, Tencent, and Baidu grew to a scale seen nowhere else outside America. In 2022 China installed over half the world's industrial robots.[83]

Militarily, the United States spent up to $8 trillion, bogged down fighting a "war on terror" in Afghanistan, Iraq, and beyond.[84] These wars showed that if U.S. strengths were avoided, America wouldn't necessarily win. And 9/11 even helped China more favorably shape the narrative over how it treated its own Muslim Uyghur minority.[85]

Politically, Chinese communism didn't implode. China saw the tidy, organized handing over of power from Deng Xiaoping to his successor in 1989, and then twice more at regular intervals after that. The last handover was in 2012: to Xi Jinping. Xi changed China's political course, taking China on a more authoritarian path. He increased the Communist Party's control over society, and gathered more personal control over the Party and military than any other leader since Mao's death in 1976.[86]

So, this "period of strategic opportunity" had seen a vibrant, surging, changing China at home—but what about abroad? To avoid imperiling domestic progress, China after 9/11 had largely continued the restrained foreign policy of "hide one's capacities, and bide one's time," to use Deng Xiaoping's famous phrase. But just as Xi radically changed China's political trajectory at home, Xi changed China's trajectory abroad.

It's impossible to say precisely when China became much more assertive, which happened sometime between Xi's accession in 2012 and his speech in 2017 that clearly stated his new direction in public.[87] But a reasonable date is the midpoint, and the year he cemented his new direction in the minds of China's foreign policy elites:[88] 2014.

The year 2014 was also when Russia invaded East Ukraine and seized Crimea, the first such European territory seized since World War II.

A new era had begun—as new eras always do.

Competition became direct between the west on one side versus China and Russia on the other and has only increased since then. Once the west started becoming conscious of the challenge, it no longer had the overwhelming military superiority it had enjoyed during America's post–Cold War unipolar moment. The countries opposing the west had new capabilities and intentions.

This is the new era in which we live.

* * *

As this book began, I described meeting friends in a London pub talking about war. Questions on war that are significant, although about which many prefer not to think.

But we must think, because today the democracies really can lose. The preceding chapters introduced three ways the democracies can lose—conventional, domestic, and nuclear—and here we can combine them to see a bigger picture that illustrates why we'll need wisdom. Thinking about each alone is helpful, but we cannot *only* do that because the simplest solutions in each throws up problems in the others. Navigating a path here doesn't require us to be infinitely wise, and our brain's limitations mean we never can be anyway. Yet our brains are brilliant and we can all try to be a bit wiser. Or at least avoid the unwisdom of entirely foreseeable problems, such as the widely held beliefs in disarmament that during the 1930s gave the Axis powers an almost uncatchable head start; or the excessive bombastic nationalism before World War I. Oversimplistic notions can't manage the trade-offs.

Let's step through the three ways we can lose and how they interact.

First, let's consider losing a conventional war, such as over Taiwan, or a global war that could rage across Asia, Europe, and the Middle East. That challenge requires a military capable and aggressive enough to win. America's mighty military must change to harness new factors like human-machine teams (as we discuss in the Conclusions)—but even assuming that goes brilliantly there is only so much America to go around, and military spending by NATO's European members and Canada reached post–Cold War lows in 2014. That year only America and Britain, among larger countries, met NATO's target of spending 2 percent of GDP on defense, and it took until 2024 before they were joined by France and Germany. Spending remains much lower in many NATO members, and is only 1.6 percent in Japan. And many of those militaries more closely resemble armed backup to humanitarian work, rather than professional and aggressive forces who would attack and defeat tough enemies.[89]

It may now seem shortsighted that back in the interwar period before 1939 many democracies—like the Netherlands, Denmark, and Norway—left themselves almost totally undefended, and barely fought back even when Nazi Germany invaded them. But then, as now, democracies always face trade-offs as electorates (understandably) desire domestic spending on hospitals or schools,[90] as well as to avoid the destruction of war. And even if democracies do want to build capabilities for winning conventional wars, although it may seem simple to pour in resources and let the warriors "get on with it" free from interfering politicians—that carries risks, too. Throughout history a large, aggressive, professional military has often threatened the economic and political health of their society. Instead of protector, an overmighty military can grow into tumor or tyranny.

Second, then, let's look at losing domestically, if lengthy Cold War–style competition decays democracy. Nothing matters more for any political system in the long run than relations between civilians and the military. An overmighty military can warp politics (as in twentieth-century Germany) and economics (as in Soviet Russia). So, should we then simply focus exclusively on reducing risks of losing domestically—by cutting military funding and maximizing civilian control over the how the military think, train, and act? Remove the military's autonomy as completely as possible, and fear a Julius Caesar in every general, or a Putin in every spy?[91]

Such a simplistic solution brings problems: societies unable and unwilling to defend themselves make easy pickings[92]—something democracies close to China, Russia, Iran, or North Korea would be unwise to forget. Civilians and the military must work together to be effective. Antagonistic relations between civilians and the military deeply damaged the military in interwar France, not least because aggressive and professional militaries require some autonomy to focus on military effectiveness. Civilians who support the military are also crucial to drive military innovation by asking good questions, having opinions, and supporting military pioneers—as interwar France failed to do, but interwar Britain did brilliantly to build RAF Fighter Command that won the Battle of Britain.[93] Given that this balance isn't always easy, some might then ask a question for a country like the United States—could it junk most of its military, pull back to the western hemisphere, and sit out world history? Things haven't worked out that way before, because adversaries have their own perspectives and will always feel threatened by what America *could* decide. Like in 1941. Moreover, today the western hemisphere holds a small and shrinking part of the world's population (about 13 percent[94]), some two-thirds of whom live south of the United States. And often far south: Houston, Texas, is geographically closer to London than to Buenos Aires.

Perhaps, then, we can rely on an alternative option operated by technicians far too few in number to enforce military tyranny, and that's also relatively cheaper: nuclear weapons?

This brings us to a third way democracies could lose in our time: if escalation led to nuclear war. Even a limited nuclear war would likely kill millions in every country fighting it. If stopping China meant destroying most of California or Texas, then America would still lose in any meaningful sense—however many Chinese also died. That's a major problem with relying too exclusively on nuclear weapons for defense, because you would be threatening disaster to yourself. That makes nuclear threats increasingly unbelievable to adversaries unless the threats aim to protect truly core interests—but for the United States, is Buenos Aires or Berlin truly a core interest? Perhaps, perhaps not. That's why to credibly defend what isn't absolutely core (such as everywhere outside the United States itself), you still need conventional military capabilities—which brings us back to the number one way to lose. Moreover, in a democracy, the domestic population isn't enormously keen to live for decades with threats of Armageddon as their main line of defense—which brings us back to the number two way to lose.

Bringing together the three ways to lose enriches our understanding of each by giving context. Reasonable people can disagree on how to move forward, but ignoring any of the three ways we can lose would be deeply unwise. And our brilliant brains give us reason for hope that we can do better still—to navigate a wiser course between all three.

For that, we'll need our highest-level neural machinery. It will help if we reflect occasionally, for example in order to recall that others (such as China's Xi Jinping) may not see the world as we do, or see us as we see ourselves. We should try to anchor our tapestry of knowledge about ourselves in the world to *reality*; try to better *anticipate* potential futures by learning from prediction errors as events unfold; and try to remind ourselves that we may need the *flexibility* to change our minds. We should also take heart because today we can consciously draw on far more *cumulative* self-knowledge about us as humans than ever before in history. In our *hierarchies* we can adapt analogies from those who went before us, such as Eisenhower, and set an achievable high-level goal for our societies in our era: to thrive domestically, push back where we can while avoiding unnecessary escalations, and prepare to fight effectively if we must. We can consciously *integrate* different areas, such as the three ways to lose, into bigger pictures. To be sure, this must all be *processed efficiently* so our brain only ever serves up a heavily edited movie. But compared to any previous generations we have far greater self-knowledge about the processes by which we know about ourselves—and this can help us enhance these highest-level human capabilities, blunt their limitations, and harness their strengths.

Our brain's highest-level regions can help us navigate the highest-level challenges about war, and indeed the highest-level challenges in our personal lives, too. A consummate conductor for our brain's outstanding orchestra.

But an orchestra is much more than just the conductor.

* * *

Every part of our brain's orchestra is needed for humans to survive and thrive in dangerous environments like war. Having journeyed from brainstem to frontal pole, we've seen how different brain regions relate to different aspects of war—but how does the whole orchestra relate to the big picture of war? And what is the big picture of a theme as vast as war? War has been a central theme throughout human history, and every prediction about our human future depends on judging if we can avoid major wars. No other future existential threat—AI, climate change, pandemics—can be understood without reference to how it interacts with the likelihood of war.

Two angels whisper in my ear as I ponder how to scope the big picture of war. One is a wise, old scientific mentor of mine, who counsels to come at such a challenge not from a position of thinking we know everything, but of being able to ask better questions. The second is the Victorian wit Oscar Wilde, who knew that most of us humans have a lot going on so that we don't want to spend *too* much time thinking about big topics like war. As Wilde supposedly said about socialism: "The problem . . . is that it takes too many evenings."

So, let's acknowledge that we have limited time and attention to dwell on every aspect of war. Within those limitations, let's recognize that we need questions that are complete enough for wiser choices, to give us the context that matters, so we don't sprint off with a dangerously incomplete picture. But what key questions can give us a complete enough picture about war?

CONCLUSIONS

OPTIMISM

We asked a question as this book started, which built on millennia of cumulative thinking about peace and war: *Why do humans fight, lose, and win wars?*

Many people who see such a question seek only to answer the first part—*why do we fight?*—because they hope to end war. But if it turns out that we can't very likely end war soon, then it would be unwise if the democracies' leaders and concerned citizens hadn't *also* thought a little about how to win. Not losing against Hitler's Nazi Germany was good.

That said, many others who see such a question instead seek only to answer the second part—*why do we lose or win?*—because they want a more powerful military to defend themselves, deter others, or take what they want by force. But even if we believe wars are inevitable, it would be unwise if the democracies' leaders and concerned citizens hadn't *also* thought about why humans fight: to try to reduce the frequency of wars starting, and of wars expanding to cataclysmic scale.

Answering either part of the question alone is not *wrong*, just *too incomplete* for making wiser choices about war. Both parts together hopefully capture enough of the big picture for wiser decisions about war—and don't worry, they won't take up too many evenings. Let's tackle each part of the question in turn, and apply the self-knowledge we've gained as we've journeyed from brainstem to frontal pole.

Will it make us infinitely wise? No. Wiser? Hopefully. Wise enough to save civilization? I'm optimistic.

WHY DO HUMANS FIGHT WARS?

Our tour of the brain began with the two basic features of life: maintaining our internal order as an organism, and reproducing. These two features enabled an unbroken chain of life over some 3.8 billion years, down to you reading this book right now. The point of a brain, from a biological point of view, is to link *senses* to *actions* that help the organism achieve its goals—and these two features of life are the brain's most basic goals. Moreover, for the hundreds of millions of years organisms have had brains, aggression has been part of the repertoire of many animals' behaviors: from dueling fruit flies to our closest relatives the great apes.

A very simple point, often overlooked amid the nuance of geopolitics, is that there will always be a certain amount of competition, and competition can get out of hand. Competition is a reality for living organisms. It's not only violent. Who has the most likes on Instagram? Who is the most virtuous? And the narcissism of small differences means we can become really hostile about a single inch of difference.

Next, in the hypothalamus we saw our vital drives—thirst, hunger, warmth, sleep, and sexual reproduction—and nobody needs reminding about how far many hungry or thirsty humans will go. As recently as 1930, within living memory, the world had only two billion people: that's risen to a staggering eight billion today and rising. Some kind of resource crunch is not beyond the realms of possibility over the coming centuries, or even decades. And it is incredible what people do for sex. Or for their children. However elegant, sophisticated, and intellectual they are.

Nobody originally intended to cause climate change. Pandemics can arise entirely naturally that are far worse than COVID-19. Some such disruption could very possibly threaten access to the resources needed for life, and do so unequally between and within societies.

The amygdala and insula gave us the opportunity to review the visceral instincts that drive us as we react to an uncertain world. Emotions like fear save our lives, and we walk around every day with survival-grade neural machinery built to cope with serious dangers. Humans in today's developed world objectively have very little to fear, compared to almost every place and time in history, but anxiety disorders—essentially fear run amok—are highly prevalent.

Social motivations like the rejection of unfairness feel so visceral, so powerful, so righteous. They cause the kind of tragedy seen in the plays of ancient Greece: arising not because of the clash of right and wrong, but because each side in a conflict firmly *feels* its position to be just. Like Israel-Palestine. Or between nuclear-armed India and nuclear-armed Pakistan over Kashmir.

The hippocampal-entorhinal region maps out the territories over which so many people are prepared to fight. China builds military islands out of uninhabited rocks in parts of the South China Sea claimed by its neighbors. Putin's Russia wants parts of its neighbors. The ambiguities of partially abstract terrains like cyber and outer space can worsen fears leading to escalation. The memories that this brain region processes are an endless source of grievance: as Aristotle described, we often talk about the past so we can grant praise or blame.

Perception can always be clouded by the fog of war, which leads to misperception, uncertainty, and misunderstandings. In the future, countries like America and China will perceive the world through ever more layers of technology, into which deception and uncertainty will be inserted. Information has gone from the eye, to the telescope, to radar, and now also through AI—but no technology can ever halt the perceptual arms race between militaries.

Affordances? The possibilities for violence afforded by historical examples and modern technologies can never be fully closed down—unless we censor every history book and abandon modern society. And even that wouldn't be enough, if done in only one society. For over two centuries, Japan regulated firearms domestically, but concerns about security and outside powers drove their return as weapons.[1]

Humans are fantastic at cooperating with others who aren't relatives, because of our machinery for Modeling others' intentions. But we must live with the uncertainty that others may deceive us or defect. What does

China's Xi Jinping *intend*? How do we know if we are in the run-up to World War I or the run-up to World War II? Those were the last two general wars fought between the great powers, beginning ninety-nine years after the preceding such conflict. It's easy to say we should just hope for the best and assume others in the world have good intentions, but what if they don't? We might just as well have said, "Surely someone like Vladimir Putin can't *really* intend to invade Ukraine."

You don't have to be a rat in a Leningrad apartment block to question Putin's intentions. It's good to be optimistic, but as psychologist Steven Pinker noted after Putin chose to invade Ukraine, "I certainly recalibrated my subjective probability of the appeal of conquest to political leaders."[2]

Perhaps, then, cultural change is the answer, to create new generations of humans for whom war is impossible? But even if achieved, peace, freedom, and prosperity would become the boring status quo, with which humans are likely too exciting, vibrant, and disputatious to remain satisfied for long. And leaders will always be tempted to steer our identity-culture spiral in self-serving directions away from peace.

Our remarkable planning abilities can create castles in the sky, whether that's communism, liberalism, or any number of other "-isms." Yet given our capacity to think up new -isms, is it plausible everyone will agree on any particular one, agree on its implementation, and stick with it indefinitely? Millions died for clashing twentieth-century -isms.

Perhaps self-reflection can help us? Yes. But what would it reveal? The author of the Winnie-the-Pooh books, A. A. Milne, was an ardent pacifist in the interwar years—along with millions in the democracies who expressed pacifist views. But Milne dropped his objection to war in 1940 because fighting Hitler was "truly fighting the Devil, the Anti-Christ."[3] The most famous interwar pacifist, Albert Einstein, safe from the Holocaust in the United States, had a letter sent under his name in 1939 to U.S. President Roosevelt—urging faster atomic weapon research to compete with Germany. Once the war was safely won, Einstein once more had the luxury of pacifism.[4]

* * *

Over these last few paragraphs, I allowed each section of the orchestra to play a quick solo—to show how each contributes to why we fight. Wisdom tries to be honest, to contemplate all parts of our brain's orchestra rather than pretending that we are only "better than" the lower parts. Wisdom acknowledges that yes, I am a creature and I may become scared or angry. I, too, have these base parts of the brain. Even my brain's fanciest parts, for planning and self-reflection, are limited. All contribute to the orchestra, and wiser choices account for the loud percussion alongside the elegant violins.

And what of the *real* reason many people ask *why war?* because they hope for an end to war sometime soon? Anything is possible—I may wake tomorrow with telekinetic powers that can lift cars into the air with my mind, but the possibility is vanishingly small.

War is essentially inevitable not because of one simple reason, but from the many causes like those discussed earlier: misunderstandings from the fog of perception; spiraling fears; tragedies when groups clash who each have too exclusive an idea of justice; and deliberate wars started by the minority of humans who will always exist as Putins, Hitlers, Stalins, bin Ladens. So many ingredients are baked into how our Models work—with all their brilliance and limitations—that push us toward war.

Pacifists who lead themselves to actually believe we can somehow remake enough humans to build perpetual peace anytime soon—they are as deluded as Hitler, who thought that force of will could overcome the reality of bitter cold while wearing lederhosen.

Peace in Nazi Germany in 1945 was not gained by persuading Germans through force of argument, but by bitterly won victory—and then ensured by massive armies of occupation, despite a majority of Germans continuing to think Nazism was pretty good for years afterward. Many people today argue we should ignore dusty old history like World War II—but any reflections on peace and war that don't include the last general war between great powers isn't very useful. And 1945 is closer to us than the ninety-nine years between Napoleon's defeat in 1815 and the cataclysm of the First World War.

Lifting our eyes above clever plans for pacifist utopias, we can instead put our self-knowledge to better use for forging peace. In Chapter 1 on the brainstem we saw prediction errors harnessed to devastating effect by Nazi Germany—but then later we saw Egyptian leader Anwar Sadat use prediction errors to overcome a seemingly impossible impasse and forge peace with Israel. After two recent wars with Israel, in 1977 Sadat shocked the world by personally offering to go to Israel, "to their house, to the Knesset itself and to talk to them."[5] His move dissolved the diplomatic stalemate. Peace between the two countries has lasted more than four decades. In Chapter 7 we saw that cooperation and reconciliation are every bit as human as war. Lasting peace with Germany after 1945 rested on military victory *and* cooperation. That's why Churchill stressed at the very front of his history of World War II the moral that "In Victory: Magnanimity."[6] Chapter 8 described the importance of affording Germans a new identity. At the far end of the brain, at the frontal pole, we saw our human machinery for wiser decisions that can be enhanced in all of us, which can also be harnessed for peace.

Wise leaders like Eisenhower and Churchill saw the bigger picture to help forge a more peaceful world. A necessary part of that was resisting brutal dictators—but they knew that aggression was not sufficient unless accompanied by magnanimity, teamwork, alliances, and restraint. Deng Xiaoping forged a more peaceful path for China in the 1980s after decades of turmoil, offering the dictum that guided his successors before Xi Jinping: "Hide our strength, bide our time." To forge peace in his own society, the wise leader Nelson Mandela saw the bigger picture and drew on every part of his brain's orchestra: fear, courage, anger, reading others' intentions, soaring rhetoric, clever plans, knowledge through education, and self-reflection. Mandela liked "friends who have independent minds because they tend to make you see problems from all angles."[7]

Women and men throughout the democracies can try to be a bit wiser, to see a bit more of the bigger picture to avoid dangerously incomplete siren calls from pacifism, militarism, or a magical arc of history that will soon lead to total peace. Concerned citizens in the interwar democracies helped to drive forward clever utopian schemes, such as the 1928 Kellogg-Briand Pact that most countries signed and that aimed to outlaw war. *Every* eventual Axis power signed the pact, promising to fully arbitrate "all disputes or conflicts of whatever nature or of whatever origin."[8] Entirely unmoored from reality, it was a foreseeable failure and dearly cost the interwar democracies.

In our time, we must recognize that the democracies can probably do little in the short or medium term to change the domestic trajectory of a country as big and capable as China. No plausible successor to Putin seems likely to turn Russia into a nice, liberal democracy anytime soon. And Russia's vast nuclear arsenal makes any big domestic shift fraught with risks. At the time of writing, many Chinese and Russians really do support their leaders.[9] Those leaders, and many citizens, don't want merely to accept the world's current rules. Many people in the democracies might not agree, and that may lead to conflict.

Self-knowledge is power. Self-knowledge of our human reality, of why humans fight, can help us reduce the frequency and severity of wars.

But we need to go beyond the question of why humans fight, and ask why we lose and win. It is true, in a way, that every side loses in a war. But billions of people today can be thankful that Nazi Germany did *actually* lose, so the Nazis couldn't directly kill tens of millions more civilians and couldn't enact their pitch-dark plans for the world. The Allies were imperfect—and thank goodness they won.

WHY DO WE LOSE OR WIN WARS?

In our new competitive era, democratic societies won't necessarily fight a war better than authoritarian states like China or Russia just because they are democracies—any more than democratic France did against authoritarian Germany.

And if we fight in our era, technologies and systems will matter, but *humans* will remain the heart of losing or winning. If we fight a conventional war, humans will remain at the center of whether democracies collapse, surrender, and collaborate—like in 1940 when six weeks after the German offensive began, Hitler was enjoying his victory parade on the Champs-Élysées. If we succumb to domestic decay, or even to civil war, a central role will be played by human anger and mistrust getting out of hand between polarized groups; humans will form those groups through identity and culture; human fingers will tap insults on smartphones or pull triggers; and human leaders will decide how to steer their groups. If war goes nuclear, human brains will decide—in the bony vault of a president's head and across the chain of command—based on vengeance, stress, morality, reason, and (hopefully) wisdom.

Technologies and systems are powerful. But Mao won against seemingly overwhelming material odds, again and again. Chiang Kai-shek's nationalists held out for years against massive Japanese technological superiority. Mao's Chinese troops directly fought sizable American armies in Korea, and despite vastly inferior tech those Chinese initially defeated the Americans, forced a long retreat, and then held them at a stalemate. Under Xi Jinping today, why can't Chinese forces win—when they no longer even face huge technological or manufacturing disadvantages? If anything, although slightly behind in tech overall, China now has some tech advantages. It has the world's leading drone industry and has long taken rocket forces more seriously than America—so that a few $10 million–$20 million Chinese DF-21 or DF-26 anti-ship ballistic missiles could quite possibly destroy a $13 billion U.S. aircraft carrier and kill its crew of six thousand.[10] America lost against the Taliban, and China is a far greater challenge.

Few would want a China-U.S. war. America is a formidable adversary for China; China is a formidable adversary for America—and between powers in the same weight class, human aspects will be central to defeat or victory. Self-knowledge is power here, too. If war happens, then whichever side has better harnessed self-knowledge about us human is more likely to win.

Part I gave us self-knowledge about our brain's fundamental and internal regions that help us anticipate life and death. These lower regions use Models of the world built from survival-grade neural machinery, to navigate life-threatening emergencies. They will always accompany us—and if harnessed well they add clashing cymbals and fulsome horns to the brain's orchestra that contribute mightily to success.

Surprise is fundamental to how many of our Models work, because it is one aspect of prediction error. As *Blitzkrieg* showed time and again, surprise can help win battles.

That said, battles aren't wars, and surprise rarely wins wars between great powers unless their will to fight collapses. Any group can lose if they lose the will to fight, which is why for countries like Taiwan today no amount of fancy weaponry matters if they lose courage. But will to fight, though necessary, is not sufficient to win. During World War II the will to fight for years was shown by the militaries and societies of the British, Americans, Russians, Germans, Japanese, Communist Chinese, and Nationalist Chinese. My great-uncle Sydney fought for years. Between such belligerents, winning rests on factors like expertise.

Expertise takes years to build, as we saw on both sides of World War II's duels between the U-boats and Allied convoy escorts. That's why societies must prepare years in advance to win. Our era will see technologists dueling in ever more spaces—like outer space and cyberspace—that will matter as much as the mass armies locking horns in places like Ukraine. Today, much of that expertise is in the commercial sector, not in government, which is why Chinese leaders push "civil-military fusion," company militias, hackers for hire, and all the rest.[11] The democracies, while keeping true to our values, must also prepare our organizations like "big tech" years ahead of time.

Part II gave us self-knowledge about how we properly apply force. Our Models make perceiving and acting *seem* so simple. But that cannot be correct: we only ever perceive a warped part of reality; and we struggle to perform basic actions for survival without receiving cumulative knowledge passed down to us. In war, better perception and action always provide an edge.

You can only direct fire against what you can perceive—and there is a perpetual perceptual arms race between perceiver and perceived. Extenders like the telescope, radar, and potential future quantum sensors play a role. But the logistics of perception are just as vital to turn data into information that's useful for defense or attack—and a big part of that today is how well new technologies interface with the perceptual Models of the humans who use such tech.

First-person-view (FPV) drones recently revolutionized Ukraine's battlefield—putting armed eyes everywhere—not least because their first-person, real-time video feed fits neatly with how humans perceive the world in order to act.[12] That's why they were developed for racing and can do crazy battlefield stunts like circling a tank before precisely hitting ammunition stores at the tank turret's base. In our era, human-machine interfaces will increasingly depend on augmented reality that superimposes information on our view to help us act—not because augmented reality is a Silicon Valley fad (though it has been), but because that's a natural extension of how we perceive. Our perception is warped to help us act.

Learning to act is as hard as perceiving. That's why better training will always provide an edge—and today that edge could be huge if America and China fought over Taiwan, because neither has fought such a war since at least 1945. China hasn't fought abroad at all since 1979. Which side will have a George C. Marshall, who, years before World War II, reformed the teaching-learning spiral at Fort Benning for a generation of soldiers—a generation who spread those skills to millions when war came?

Which side will have had—years before—a Guderian insisting on rigorous training with the newest tools of our time? Experimenting. Getting stuck in. Making mistakes, learning, and improving with those tools. Ensuring troops generalize their learning across tools and situations, so they can adapt more flexibly than adversaries. In the brain-tool spiral, technologies like tanks and their operators both ratcheted up improvements through an iterative process—and that's exactly what we've seen with drones in Ukraine. In our new era, the spiral will speed up because new software will enhance tools as much as new hardware did in the past. Software like generative AI that increasingly moves new aids along the "tool-colleague" spectrum, from inert hammer toward a more freely thinking dog.

When we give commands to a modern AI dog, or AI war elephant, what do we intend it to do? How will "it" decide to act—based on our spoken prompts, heart rate, eye gaze, and all the other ways we communicate with it? As the Romans discovered, an enemy's war elephants could be tricked to stampede the wrong way. Building the right human-machine relationships will be key to win.

In Part III, we end and start again. In our brains we have loops on top of loops of processing—so that where each loop ends another starts above. The brainstem contains our most fundamental, lifesaving loops of processing. Starting above those are loops for our vital drives and our visceral instincts. On top of those starts the loop in which sensory and motor cortex control the proper application of force. And then association cortex starts—the focus of Part III—which contains loops for thinking.

Outthinking others often helps us win.

What are the intentions of Vladimir Putin, Xi Jinping, or Kim Jong Un? We can't see into their brains, but we must estimate their intentions well enough—so that, if needed, we can deter them or defend ourselves. Will they hit crosscourt or down the line? And in war we must deceive, too: Do we land in Calais or Normandy?

Assessing others' intentions matters equally for the alliances that often make the difference between losing and winning. In 1940, many smaller European democracies failed to fight until invaded by Germany (and sometimes not even then), but their support could have prevented Britain and France from losing. In contrast, incredibly close British and American collaboration helped win World War II. And it continued afterward with the remarkable "Five Eyes" intelligence collaboration—between America, Britain, Canada, Australia, and New Zealand—to produce and share enormously sensitive information. An alliance today in its eighth decade.

Many European countries currently worry about U.S. intentions if Vladimir Putin invaded a NATO member like one of the Baltic republics. Hearing that often makes me recall a few days I spent with U.S. members of Congress—Democrat and Republican—during which one asked a question: How do I explain to my constituent why their son or daughter has died overseas?

Many European leaders and publics *do* want Americans to fight and die for them but *don't* want to spend much or prepare for their own defense. How does that affect many Americans' assessment of *their* intentions? Moreover, when many Americans felt threatened and—rightly or wrongly—wanted others to support the toppling of Saddam Hussein in 2003, only British and Australian troops joined (with a small number from Poland).[13] A total of 179 British personnel died in Iraq.[14] Robust alliances can *never* be purely transactional but *must* be reciprocal.

Leadership is another social factor that can bring defeat or victory. Political leaders like Mao, and military leaders like Nelson, create a vision and communicate it to those who must carry it out. They are social alchemists, who can steer the identity-culture spiral by which we chatty apes form groups. Groups for which we sacrifice, fight, and die. Leaders will always exert power in human groups. That power can be used for the better, like Churchill, or for the worse, like Hitler. And it's needed just as much by leaders opposing formal authority, such as Mahatma Gandhi or Martin Luther King Jr.

Many citizens in today's democracies are infuriated with politics. That includes "big P" Politics in Washington, D.C., or Westminster, state capitals, or town halls. And many dislike the "small p" politics in workplaces or bureaucracies, too. But in any human group responsible for things its members care about—such as food, money, status, security, or dignity—some kind of politics is inevitable because some people will, sooner or later, have more power to achieve their preferred outcomes. Politics is inevitable. Politics can get out of hand. And such politics directly relates to war within, and between, states.

Carl von Clausewitz's most famous dictum is usually given as "War is a continuation of politics by other means." Scholars debate its precise meaning,[15] but at least two relevant ideas emerge here. One is that when politics gets out of hand, there will always be a military dimension. That is why the long-run health of any political regime—communist Chinese or democratic American—must try to avoid paths where their domestic politics can get too far out of hand. Plus, as Mao said, it must be clear who holds the barrel of the gun. A country loses if it is in civil war, as China has been within living memory.

Also emerging from "war as a continuation of politics" is the idea that although war may be an instrument of politics, it's a limited instrument because wars so easily get out of hand. That's because any political goal is always up against the forces of "violence, hatred and enmity," as well as chance. Europe's leaders in World War I probably wouldn't have gone to war if they'd known at the start how it would develop, but the catastrophe developed its own momentum. Moreover, as von Clausewitz described, war is complicated, and beset by a "friction" in which difficulties accumulate so that "everything in war is simple, but the simplest thing is difficult."[16] That friction is why success in war both defensive (as for the democracies in World War II and Ukraine in 2022) or offensive (as for Russia in 2022) is so often affected by the quality of planning.

Poor planning can cause failures. When Russia invaded Ukraine in February 2022, they outnumbered the Ukrainians twelve to one north of Kiev. But poor planning left them lacking food and fuel, relying on maps sometimes from the 1960s, and with badly maintained vehicles on which the tires might fall apart. A traffic jam of armored vehicles built up over days, eventually reaching a ludicrous thirty-five miles long. After stalling for weeks and under attack, it retreated. A shambles.[17]

Good planning can help win battles and even campaigns. Napoleon's capacious brain planned brilliantly. As did the nineteenth-century Prussian General Staff that responded to his genius by systematizing good planning. Every great power then copied that General Staff system, or they couldn't compete. Against the stereotype of the inflexible square head, such effective staff officers actually show both grit *and* creativity. Channeling *Top Gun*'s Iceman *and* Maverick.

Most U.S. military experts on China I know suggest that—currently—superior U.S. military planners may provide a crucial edge over their Chinese counterparts. But we are entering a disruptive period because AI is very good at some aspects of planning, so that many human planners on military staffs will become augmented by AI assistants. Humans plus tech.[18] To retain their edge, the United States and its allies must lead this disruption.

But the ultimate problem for expert planning, however clever, is that it may miss the bigger picture. Winning battles but losing the war. Like the AI speedboat earning points in the middle of the course, when the aim was really to find better routes forward. Or on TV dating shows where both partners in a couple are trying to win an argument—but fail to lift their gaze, so they don't see that winning that argument actually means losing in their relationship's bigger picture.

Or like the fate of the main character in the Dr. Seuss book *The Lorax*, who is called the Once-ler. Clever (oh-so-clever), the Once-ler is also diligent and family-minded. He is laser-focused on biggering and Biggering and BIGGERING his ingenious and well-planned manufacturing and distribution of Thneeds. Which are a "Fine-Something-That-All-People-Need!" But the Once-ler focuses too exclusively on one goal, ignores the bigger picture and trade-offs needed to make his business sustainable—and so brings catastrophe on himself and the local community. If only the Once-ler had read Sun Tzu's advice about war, which applies to life more generally: "He will win who knows when to fight and when not to fight."[19] The Once-ler was clever but not wise.

We can all hope to make wiser decisions in our lives. We walk around every day with survival-grade neural machinery for things like fear, perception, and navigating our social world—and also survival-grade machinery for that orchestra's conductor: metacognition. Not only is this "thinking about thinking" good, but we can improve metacognition, too.

All of us concerned citizens in the democracies can hope to be wiser. Concerned citizens matter to set the terms of public debates—and we should try to avoid overly simplistic ideas like pacificism, militarism, or isolationism that have failed so badly before. Without it taking too many evenings, we can lift our gaze and aim for better.

A strength of democracies versus authoritarian regimes has often been to combine a range of perspectives: asking better questions, constructively challenging others' ideas, and reflecting on our own ideas to better adapt to a changing world. So we can better walk and chew gum at the same time. The prominent optimists before the cataclysm of World War I—as well as modern thinkers like Steven Pinker who echo their optimism—were probably correct that the arc of history tends, overall, toward more peaceful lives within and between states. But to such ideas we must add *the active work we must do*, so that we can avoid losing wars to people like Putin, avoid nuclear war, and avoid domestic decay.

War is complicated, difficult to do well, and easy to mess up.

Self-knowledge about humans helps us manage challenges with no definitive solution: uncertainty about others' intentions; the unpredictability of ever-changing identity-culture spirals; or the need to be clever and also to remember that being clever isn't necessarily being wise. Self-knowledge can help give us the wisdom to recognize that war should be undertaken with the goal of gaining a better peace.[20] And remind us why, in our time, living history forward as concerned citizens, leaders, or soldiers, we should try to avoid what Winston Churchill identified as the democracies' central failing before World War II: "unwisdom."[21]

* * *

We need self-knowledge of *why we fight, lose, and win wars*, so that we can help prevent the worst of wars and, if we must fight, so that we can save civilization. Self-knowledge about us as individuals, and self-knowledge about us as humanity. And no self-knowledge is more consequential for our future than the spiral built up throughout this book: that the brain shapes war and war shapes the brain.

Like never before in history, neuroscience today helps us anchor our self-knowledge to reality, so that we can anticipate and flexibly fashion our futures—and that makes me optimistic.

OPTIMISM

Your everyday life is lived with neural machinery built to cope with the *possibility* of life-and-death events. Violence is only one factor that has shaped you, but it has shaped every part of the orchestra of Models by which you understand yourself and the world.

Your color vision is worse than in many animals—birds, fish, many lizards, and even many insects—which makes sense if the ancestor of mammals, including you, survived dangerous dinosaurs by living nocturnally and so lost its good color vision.[22] In the west now we live objectively comfortable and safe lives compared to almost everyone else who ever lived, but fears still plague many of us. Most of us care deeply about our reputations and about our own social groups—and that's because when hunting, hunted, or in combat, our lives may depend on the people around us. We see patterns and conspiracies. We build castles in the sky, simulating "what if" scenarios in our brains that would be dangerous if we just did them. We play games and watch movies that give us stocks of analogies about how the world works, in ways we may hope never to experience in reality.

But so much for everyday life—this is a book about the brain and war.

Wiser people don't just look away from things that are big and unpleasant, if the stakes are high. We need to anchor our Models to reality, because doing otherwise can be fatal.

The reality? We aren't all doomed. Nor are we definitely going to be fine whatever choices we make. Instead, we can live with life's uncertainty and make active choices.

And here is why I am hopeful for my children. Because I *am* hopeful.

My kids will probably live to about this century's end. To think about the big risks during their lifetimes, I can draw on over a decade working with organizations like the Pentagon Joint Staff. That gave me access to the expert knowledge—and wisdom—of many of the world's top scholars, alongside intelligence chiefs, military leaders, politicians, and those with deep experience on the ground, in the labs, or deep in the bunkers. We've examined predictions about specific risks such as climate change, nuclear war, an apocalyptic fight against rogue AI, pandemics, or combinations of such nastiness.[23] We've examined historical analogies for periods with plenty of violence and close calls that didn't spark global cataclysm: such as the ninety-nine years without a general war between Waterloo and World War I, or the roughly eight decades since 1945. And lesser-known periods like 1534 to 1631 in Europe that saw almost no major battles (although a lot of sieges). We examined how general wars did erupt, too. And we spent a lot of time on how new technologies, and myriad other factors, might combine with human nature to shape the character of competition and war. Many varied, and often contradictory, perspectives, but the upshot is pretty reassuring.

During my kids' lifetimes, I think there's *an approximately one in three chance they will see a catastrophe on at least the scale of either World War.*[24] And *if* there were such a catastrophic event, *then* the rich democracies will have a tough time—but as in countries like Britain and America before, many people will, more likely than not, survive.

Partly, my self-knowledge about human brains tells me I am optimistic because my brain is built to be optimistic—so I've tried to correct for that. I've asked what my prediction would look like if I was making it for someone else (a good way to correct an optimistic bias, as we saw earlier).

And I'm still optimistic.

A prime reason for my optimism is that human self-knowledge is cumulative: we have learned more about ourselves as humans and developed new institutions suited to our better self-knowledge. We aren't perfectible creatures who can fit the mold of Utopias, whether communist, fascist, liberal, or anything else. We are too creative, heterogeneous, and flexible for that.

Nor are we determined entirely by nature. We are too creative, heterogeneous, and flexible for that, too.

Western societies are now neither as militaristic as before World War I, nor as pacifist as before World War II. Both those wars give analogies to lay side by side, from which to learn.

The next generation will add analogies of their own and will seek to change what they inherit as a boring status quo. Their brains will be too exciting and focused on anticipating the future. Eternally unsatisfied. And full of plans—clever, and hopefully wise enough—for how they can make the world a better place for themselves, their families, and societies. That's their nature. That's what human brains do.

Maybe making things worse, but hopefully once again making things better.

And as we learn ever more about ourselves, about the orchestra of Models in our brains that anchor us to reality, we humans can get closer to a more peaceful world. Through neuroscience, history, the social sciences, art, literature, and common sense we can understand our Models better. Our creativity means that technologies for destruction will spiral upward; and so, too, will our self-knowledge. The more I learn about humans, the more I like them. We have an immense capacity for self-knowledge. And that gives me hope.

ACKNOWLEDGMENTS

I have learned so much from so many people that it is impossible to list them all here. In my medical work, my scientific work, and my work on security, there are many whose ideas have contributed to this book. With that important caveat, I must thank specific individuals who made this book possible. My agent, Jaime Marshall, was, and is, enormously helpful in every aspect of creating this book—and he made the process of writing the book more fun. My editor at St Martin's Press, Michael Flamini, provided wonderful feedback and insights on the manuscript—helping me to be better where I needed to be, and that certainly improved the book. I am deeply grateful to Claire Cheek, who very kindly wrangled the moving parts of the publication process. Mike Harpley at Pan Macmillan gave valuable encouragement and support. John-Paul Flintoff provided incredibly useful advice and help on writing a book for a general audience. Advice and mentoring from Karim Sadjadpour, Moises Naim, and Steve Levine made a concrete difference.

A number of colleagues and friends very kindly gave their time to read the whole manuscript, and that vastly improved the book: Steve Fleming, Rosalyn Moran, Steve Feldstein, Larry Kuznar, Eric Kuznar, Jeff Michaels, Andrew Whiskeyman, Giles Clark, David Weissman, Jack Shanahan, Geraint Rees, David Vernal, and Dominic Jacquesson. Zeb Kurth-Nelson kindly read parts. Many provided deep expertise or experience from academic fields or the military—and, of course, all remaining errors remain mine alone.

I've been linked with University College London (UCL) since I first arrived there as a medical student, and with Queen Square more specifically for a good part of the past two decades. I was inspired by the superb neurology doctors such as Mary Reilly, with whom I worked at the National Hospital for Neurology, and by Cathy Price, who oversaw my first ever functional brain imaging research (and whose passion for truth remains a model). I was enormously lucky to have worked with many of the most brilliant neuroscientists of our time, who all deeply influenced how I understand the brain: Ray Dolan, Peter Dayan, Karl Friston, and Chris Frith. The Wellcome Trust, the Medical Research Council, and the Max Plank Society all provided funding at different times.

My move to Washington, DC, was kindly made possible by James Acton, George Perkovich, and Toby Dalton at the Carnegie Endowment for International Peace. They took a punt that a British neuroscientist could contribute something on nuclear weapons. I am grateful to the Stanton Foundation for funding that research.

While in Washington, I met the group at the Pentagon Joint Staff with whom I have worked closely for over a decade. They are remarkable people, thoughtful and passionate, and they make me optimistic for the future. Hriar "Doc" Cabayan was a wonderful leader and thinker, who understood the importance not only of rigorous and cutting-edge science, but of making that science practically useful. Todd Veazie is a man I admire, who has changed how I think, and with whom it is a pleasure to work (and drink bourbon). I also thank Mariah Yaeger, Allison Astorino-Courtois, Sarah Canna, Nicole Omundson, and the rest of the team (not least JC with his sound system). More broadly, I am grateful to the many others who are good people working hard to make things better, and in particular the men and women doing difficult and dangerous jobs.

I have benefitted from collaboration with many others in the British defense community, including many enlightening cups of tea with Fergus Anderson. And the odd pint, too. Jim Giordano at Georgetown has been a wonderful collaborator over many years, as has Geraint Rees at UCL, and as was Jim Lewis at the Center for Strategic and International Studies.

I owe so much to my family. My father, Allan, for instilling a love of history and for all his support. I am grateful that he has been a model for me in many ways. My mother, Carol, for her unflagging positivity, and she would have loved to see this book. Julia, for accompanying me on formative adventures (with and without a tent). Peter, for insightful discussions.

My children, Ceci and Hugo, gave me a writing kit (including biscuits) that proved both useful and delicious. They are also really fun—Ceci, your cover really was the best version that anyone came up with, and Hugo, here is the "Nonsense of War." My wife, Marsha, is truly kind and supportive. She is also fun, talented, always devastatingly stylish, and in every way that matters she makes the world a better place. It's hard to overstate how great she is, and I am sure I haven't done her justice here. Marsha was wonderful in every way during the writing of this book—thank you.

NOTES

INTRODUCTION

1. Ernest R. May, *Strange Victory: Hitler's Conquest of France* (Farrar, Straus and Giroux, 2000), 5–6.
2. Antony Beevor, *The Second World War* (Weidenfeld & Nicolson, 2012), 155, 237, 514; Michael J. McNerney et al., "National Will to Fight: Why Some States Keep Fighting and Others Don't," RAND Corporation, September 20, 2018, www.rand.org/pubs/research_reports/RR2477.html, 40, 44, 46–47.
3. Martin Gilbert, *The Second World War* (Weidenfeld & Nicolson, 1989), 1.
4. Henry Mance, "Steven Pinker: 'Putin's Invasion Won't Lead to a Return to the Age of Warring Civilisation,'" *Financial Times*, October 23, 2022, www.ft.com/content/4a6ac655-66a9-4d1c-8646-9ab32c36fbe2; Steven Pinker, *The Better Angels of Our Nature: The Decline of Violence in History and Its Causes* (Allen Lane, 2011); Margaret MacMillan, *War: How Conflict Shaped Us* (Profile Books, 2020), 2–3, 18–19; Lawrence Freedman, *The Future of War: A History* (Allen Lane, 2017), xi–xv.
5. MacMillan, *War*, 244, 246.
6. Sami Yousafzai, "10 Years of Afghan War: How the Taliban Go On," *Newsweek*, October 2, 2011, www.newsweek.com/10-years-afghan-war-how-taliban-go-68223.
7. Alexander Palmer, Henry H. Carroll, and Nicholas Velazquez, "Unpacking China's Naval Buildup," June 5, 2024, www.csis.org/analysis/unpacking-chinas-naval-buildup. The human has been central to Chinese military modernization, e.g., Dennis J. Blasko, *The Chinese Army Today: Tradition and Transformation for the 21st Century*, second edition (Routledge, 2012), 16–18.
8. Richard Baldwin, "China Is the World's Sole Manufacturing Superpower: A Line Sketch of the Rise," *VoxEU*, January 17, 2024, https://cepr.org/voxeu/columns/china-worlds-sole-manufacturing-superpower-line-sketch-rise.

1: STAYING ALIVE

1. Inga Clendinnen, *Aztecs: An Interpretation* (Cambridge University Press, 1991), 94–96.

2. Stephen Moss, "Robin Guide: Species Facts and How to Attract Robins to Your Garden," *BBC, Countryfile*, www.countryfile.com/wildlife/birds/our-guide-to-robins-where-to-see-top-facts-and-how-to-attract-robins-to-your-garden, accessed November 22, 2024; British Trust for Ornithology, "European Robin Guide: Diet, Habitat and Species Facts," *BBC Wildlife*, www.discoverwildlife.com/animal-facts/birds/facts-about-robins, accessed November 22, 2024.
3. Terence Allen and Graham Cowling, *The Cell: A Very Short Introduction* (Oxford University Press, 2011), 11–12.
4. Elizabeth Pennisi, "Microbes That Gave Rise to All Plants and Animals Became Multicellular 1.6 Billion Years Ago, Tiny Fossils Reveal," *Science* 383, no. 6681 (January 24, 2024), doi.org/10.1126/science.z4ibvhb.
5. BBC, "Water Worlds," *The Green Planet*, episode 2, 2022.
6. Ross P. Anderson et al., "Fossilisation Processes and Our Reading of Animal Antiquity," *Trends in Ecology & Evolution* 38, no. 11 (November 1, 2023): 1060–71, doi.org/10.1016/j.tree.2023.05.014.
7. Such classic definitions work well for vertebrates. Like all definitions that matter, fascinating debates arise from fuzzy cases around its edges. See, e.g., Ricard Solé, Melanie Moses, and Stephanie Forrest, "Liquid Brains, Solid Brains," *Philosophical Transactions of the Royal Society B* 374, no. 1774 (April 22, 2019), doi.org/10.1098/rstb.2019.0040.
8. Michael Gazzaniga, Richard B. Ivry, and George R. Mangun, *Cognitive Neuroscience: The Biology of the Mind*, Fifth International Student edition (W. W. Norton & Company, 2019), 623–25.
9. Ben Seymour, "Pain: A Precision Signal for Reinforcement Learning and Control," *Neuron* 101, no. 6 (March 20, 2019): 1029–41, doi.org/10.1016/j.neuron.2019.01.055.
10. Joanna Bourke, "Emotions Affect How Pain Feels, as Soldiers Know Only Too Well," *The Conversation*, May 21, 2014, http://theconversation.com/emotions-affect-how-pain-feels-as-soldiers-know-only-too-well-25889.
11. Bourke.
12. Bourke; Jon D. Levine et al., "Analgesic Responses to Morphine and Placebo in Individuals with Postoperative Pain," *Pain* 10, no. 3 (June 1981): 379–89, doi.org/10.1016/0304-3959(81)90099-3.
13. Martin Gilbert, *The First World War* (HarperCollins, 1995), 538.
14. Julian Jackson, *The Fall of France: The Nazi Invasion of 1940* (Oxford University Press, 2004), 146.
15. May, 7; Jackson, 149; Andrew Marr, *The Making of Modern Britain* (Pan Publishing, 2009), 346–48.
16. Beevor, 29, 39.
17. Gilbert, *The Second World War*, 54.
18. Peter Andreas, "How Methamphetamine Became a Key Part of Nazi Military Strategy," *Time*, January 7, 2020, https://time.com/5752114/nazi-military-drugs/; Megan Garber, "'Pilot's Salt': The Third Reich Kept Its Soldiers Alert With Meth," *The Atlantic* (blog), May 31, 2013, https://www.theatlantic.com/technology/archive/2013/05/pilots-salt-the-third-reich-kept-its-soldiers-alert-with-meth/276429/.
19. Wolfram Schultz, Peter Dayan, and P. Read Montague, "A Neural Substrate of Prediction and Reward," *Science* 275, no. 5306 (March 14, 1997): 1593–99, doi.org/10.1126/science.275.5306.1593.

20. E.g., Mitsuko Watabe-Uchida, Neir Eshel, and Naoshige Uchida, "Neural Circuitry of Reward Prediction Error," *Annual Review of Neuroscience* 40, no. 1 (2017): 373–94, doi.org/10.1146/annurev-neuro-072116-031109.

21. Open Science Collaboration, "Estimating the Reproducibility of Psychological Science," *Science* 349, no. 6251 (August 28, 2015): aac4716, doi.org/10.1126/science.aac4716; C. Glenn Begley and Lee M. Ellis, "Drug Development: Raise Standards for Preclinical Cancer Research," *Nature* 483, no. 7391 (March 29, 2012): 531–33, doi.org/10.1038/483531a.

22. George Questor, in Betty Glad, ed., *Psychological Dimensions of War* (Sage Publications, 1990), 204–5, 210.

23. Edgar Jones et al., "Public Panic and Morale: Second World War Civilian Responses Re-Examined in the Light of the Current Anti-Terrorist Campaign," *Journal of Risk Research* 9, no. 1 (2006): 57–73.

24. Marr, 357–62.

25. Questor, 210.

26. "The Sputnik Surprise," Defense Advanced Research Projects Agency (DARPA), www.darpa.mil/about-us/timeline/creation-of-darpa; and "Mission," Defense Advanced Research Projects Agency, www.darpa.mil/about-us/mission, accessed March 5, 2024.

27. Soroush Vosoughi, Deb Roy, and Sinan Aral, "The Spread of True and False News Online," *Science* 359, no. 6380 (March 9, 2018): 1146–51, doi.org/10.1126/science.aap9559.

28. David Kilcullen, *Out of the Mountains: The Coming Age of the Urban Guerrilla* (Hurst, 2013), 114.

29. Julian Borger and Dan Sabbagh, "US and UK Trying to Fend Off Russian Invasion by Making Intelligence Public," *The Guardian*, February 15, 2022, www.theguardian.com/world/2022/feb/16/us-uk-russia-invasion-ingelligence-public-briefings; Julian Barnes and Adam Entous, "How the U.S. Adopted a New Intelligence Playbook to Expose Russia's War Plans," *The New York Times*, February 23, 2023, www.nytimes.com/2023/02/23/us/politics/intelligence-russia-us-ukraine-china.html; Kristian Gustafson et al., "Intelligence Warning in the Ukraine War, Autumn 2021–Summer 2022," *Intelligence and National Security* 39, no. 3 (April 15, 2024): 400–19, doi.org/10.1080/02684527.2024.2322214.

30. Beevor, 60–61; Andrew Roberts, *The Storm of War: A New History of the Second World War* (Allen Lane, 2009), 55.

31. Heinz Guderian, *Achtung Panzer!*, trans. Christopher Duffy (Arms and Armour, 1995), 75.

32. Roberts, *The Storm of War*, 57.

33. Beevor, 97.

34. Beevor, 108; Roberts, *The Storm of War*, 56.

35. Roberts, *The Storm of War*, 57; Beevor, 109.

36. Beevor, 113.

37. Beevor, 116–17.

38. Jackson, 85.

39. Jackson, 86–88; Beevor, 121.

40. May, 451.

41. Serotonin has many complicated effects in the brain, and thus although good evidence links serotonin to depression and anxiety those links are not simple. See B. U. Phillips and Trevor W. Robbins, "Chapter 31: The Role of Central Serotonin in Impulsivity,

Compulsivity, and Decision-Making: Comparative Studies in Experimental Animals and Humans," in *Handbook of Behavioral Neuroscience*; Christian P. Müller and Kathryn A. Cunningham, eds., *Handbook of the Behavioral Neurobiology of Serotonin* (Elsevier, 2020), 31, 531–48, doi.org/10.1016/B978-0-444-64125-0.00031-1; Sameer Jauhar et al., "A Leaky Umbrella Has Little Value: Evidence Clearly Indicates the Serotonin System Is Implicated in Depression," *Molecular Psychiatry* 28, no. 8 (August 2023): 3149–52, doi.org/10.1038/s41380-023-02095-y; M. J. Crockett and R. Cools, "Serotonin and Aversive Processing in Affective and Social Decision-Making," *Current Opinion in Behavioral Sciences* 5 (October 1, 2015): 64–70, doi.org/10.1016/j.cobeha.2015.08.005.

42. Crockett and Cools.
43. Quentin J. M. Huys et al., "Interplay of Approximate Planning Strategies," *Proceedings of the National Academy of Sciences* 112, no. 10 (March 10, 2015): 3098–103, doi.org/10.1073/pnas.1414219112.
44. May, 271–78, 455; Barry Posen, *The Sources of Military Doctrine: France, Britain, and Germany Between the World Wars* (Cornell University Press, 1984), chapter 4.
45. May, 453.
46. Jackson, 135; Gilbert, *The Second World War*, 91.
47. Gilbert, *The Second World War*, 91.
48. Beevor, 41.
49. Jackson, 179–80.
50. Roberts, *The Storm of War*, 79.
51. Roberts, *The Storm of War*, 79.
52. Beevor, 514.
53. Roberts, *The Storm of War*, 306.
54. Beevor, 148–49.
55. "Lend-Lease and Military Aid to the Allies in the Early Years of World War II," Office of the Historian, Foreign Service Institute, United States Department of State, https://history.state.gov/milestones/1937-1945/lend-lease, accessed November 22, 2024.
56. Catherine E. Schretter et al., "Cell Types and Neuronal Circuitry Underlying Female Aggression in Drosophila," *eLife* 9 (November 3, 2020): e58942, doi.org/10.7554/eLife.58942.
57. Aaron A. Duke et al., "Revisiting the Serotonin–Aggression Relation in Humans: A Meta-Analysis," *Psychological Bulletin* 139, no. 5 (2013): 1148–72, doi.org/10.1037/a0031544; Crockett and Cools.
58. Laurel S. Morris et al., "The Role of the Locus Coeruleus in the Generation of Pathological Anxiety," *Brain and Neuroscience Advances* 4 (July 21, 2020): 2398212820930321, doi.org/10.1177/2398212820930321; Randy J. Nelson and Brian C. Trainor, "Neural Mechanisms of Aggression," *Nature Reviews Neuroscience* 8, no. 7 (2007): 536–46.
59. M. D. Marino et al., "Genetic Reduction of Noradrenergic Function Alters Social Memory and Reduces Aggression in Mice," *Behavioral Brain Research* 161 (2005): 197–203, doi.org/10.1016/j.bbr.2005.02.005.
60. Susanne C. Hoyer et al., "Octopamine in Male Aggression of Drosophila," *Current Biology: CB* 18, no. 3 (February 12, 2008): 159–67, doi.org/10.1016/j.cub.2007.12.052; Caroline B. Palavicino-Maggio and Saheli Sengupta, "The Neuromodulatory Basis of Aggression: Lessons from the Humble Fruit Fly," *Frontiers in Behavioral Neuroscience* 16 (April 18, 2022): 836666, doi.org/10.3389/fnbeh.2022.836666; Schretter et al.

61. Craig L. Symonds, *World War II at Sea: A Global History* (Oxford University Press, 2018), 10.
62. Beevor, 150.
63. Gilbert, *The Second World War*, 107.
64. Beevor, 159.
65. Roald Dahl, *Going Solo* (Jonathan Cape, 1986), 130–32.
66. Gazzaniga et al., 369–71.
67. Gazzaniga et al., 369–71.
68. Sarah-Jayne Blakemore et al., "The Perception of Self-Produced Sensory Stimuli in Patients with Auditory Hallucinations and Passivity Experiences: Evidence for a Breakdown in Self-Monitoring," *Psychological Medicine* 30, no. 5 (September 2000): 1131–39, doi.org/10.1017/S0033291799002676; Anne-Laure Lemaitre, Marion Luyat, and Gilles Lafargue, "Individuals with Pronounced Schizotypal Traits Are Particularly Successful in Tickling Themselves," *Consciousness and Cognition* 41 (April 1, 2016): 64–71, doi.org/10.1016/j.concog.2016.02.005.
69. Roberts, *The Storm of War*, 94–95.
70. Gilbert, *The Second World War*, 117–18.
71. Beevor, 160.
72. Roberts, *The Storm of War*, 105.
73. Roberts, *The Storm of War*, 98–99.
74. Gilbert, *The Second World War*, 125.

2: VITAL DRIVES

1. This description draws on John Keegan, *The Face of Battle* (Jonathan Cape, 1976), 113–21.
2. Roberts, *The Storm of War*, 48.
3. Takako Ichiki et al., "Sensory Representation and Detection Mechanisms of Gut Osmolality Change," *Nature* 602, no. 7897 (February 2022): 468–74, doi.org/10.1038/s41586-021-04359-5; Christopher A. Zimmerman, David E. Leib, and Zachary A. Knight, "Neural Circuits Underlying Thirst and Fluid Homeostasis," *Nature Reviews Neuroscience* 18, no. 8 (August 2017): 459–69, doi.org/10.1038/nrn.2017.71; Claire Gizowski and Charles W. Bourque, "The Neural Basis of Homeostatic and Anticipatory Thirst," *Nature Reviews Nephrology* 14, no. 1 (January 2018): 11–25, doi.org/10.1038/nrneph.2017.149.
4. Zimmerman et al.
5. Yuki Oka, Mingyu Ye, and Charles S. Zuker, "Thirst Driving and Suppressing Signals Encoded by Distinct Neural Populations in the Brain," *Nature* 520, no. 7547 (April 2015): 349–52, https://doi.org/10.1038/nature14108.
6. The studies on cognition are inconsistent, e.g., reviewed in Natalie A. Masento et al., "Effects of Hydration Status on Cognitive Performance and Mood," *British Journal of Nutrition* 111, no. 10 (May 2014): 1841–52, doi.org/10.1017/S0007114513004455.
7. Asher Y. Rosinger, "Human Evolution Led to an Extreme Thirst for Water," *Scientific American*, July 1, 2021, www.scientificamerican.com/article/human-evolution-led-to-an-extreme-thirst-for-water/.

8. Thucydides, *The History of the Peloponnesian War*, trans. Rex Warner, revised edition (Penguin Books, 1974); Jackson, 169–70.
9. Charles Spencer, "Duke of Marlborough," in Andrew Roberts, ed., *The Art of War: Great Commanders of the Modern World* (Quercus, 2009).
10. "AWE: Atmospheric Water Extraction," Defense Advanced Research Projects Agency (DARPA), www.darpa.mil/program/atmospheric-water-extraction, accessed December 7, 2024.
11. Beevor, 182.
12. Roberts, *The Storm of War*, 121.
13. *The World at War* (1973–1974), season 1, episode 8, "The Desert: North Africa (1940–1943)." Directed by David Elstein. Aired December 19, 1973, on Thames Television.
14. Roberts, *The Storm of War*, 122.
15. Roberts, *The Storm of War*, 122.
16. Martin Van Creveld, *Supplying War: Logistics from Wallenstein to Patton*, second edition (Cambridge University Press, 2004), 199–201.
17. Alexis Peri, *The War Within: Diaries from the Siege of Leningrad* (Harvard University Press, 2017), 235.
18. Roberts, *The Storm of War*, 172; Beevor, 289–91, 347, 349.
19. Richard Overy, *Blood and Ruins: The Great Imperial War 1931–1945* (Allen Lane, 2021), 153.
20. Roberts, *The Storm of War*, 156–57; Beevor, 236.
21. Beevor, 241; Roberts, *The Storm of War*, 159.
22. Timothy Snyder, "The Reich's Forgotten Atrocity," *The Guardian*, October 21, 2010, www.theguardian.com/commentisfree/cifamerica/2010/oct/21/secondworldwar-russia.
23. "Hunger and the Brain," Harvard Medical School, https://hms.harvard.edu/news-events/publications-archive/brain/hunger-brain, accessed December 6, 2024; Scott M. Sternson and Anne-Kathrin Eiselt, "Three Pillars for the Neural Control of Appetite," *Annual Review of Physiology* 79, no. 79 (February 10, 2017): 401–23, doi.org/10.1146/annurev-physiol-021115-104948.
24. Mark L. Andermann and Bradford B. Lowell, "Toward a Wiring Diagram Understanding of Appetite Control," *Neuron* 95, no. 4 (August 16, 2017): 757–78, doi.org/10.1016/j.neuron.2017.06.014; Hadar Israeli et al., "Structure Reveals the Activation Mechanism of the MC4 Receptor to Initiate Satiation Signaling," *Science* 372, no. 6544 (May 21, 2021): 808–14, doi.org/10.1126/science.abf7958.
25. R. Alexander Bentley, Paul Ormerod, and Damian J. Ruck, "Recent Origin and Evolution of Obesity-Income Correlation Across the United States," *Palgrave Communications* 4, no. 146 (2018), doi.org/10.1057/s41599-018-0201-x; Joseph Henrich, *The Secret of Our Success* (Princeton University Press, 2015), 65–66.
26. Roberts, *The Storm of War*, 214.
27. David Baker and Natacha Keramidas, "The Psychology of Hunger," *Monitor on Psychology* 44, no. 9 (2013): 66.
28. Erin Gaffney-Stomberg and James P. McClung, "Nutrition, Genetics, and Human Performance During Military Training," in Michael D. Matthews and David M. Schnyer, eds., *Human Performance Optimization: The Science and Ethics of Enhancing Human Capabilities* (Oxford University Press, 2019), doi.org/10.1093/oso/9780190455132.003

.0003; Harris R. Lieberman et al., "Two Days of Calorie Deprivation Induced by Underfeeding and Aerobic Exercise Degrades Mood and Lowers Interstitial Glucose but Does Not Impair Cognitive Function in Young Adults," *The Journal of Nutrition* 147, no. 1 (January 2017): 110–16, doi.org/10.3945/jn.116.238246; note that addition of exercise can affect cognition in Grace E. Giles et al., "Two Days of Calorie Deprivation Impairs High Level Cognitive Processes, Mood, and Self-Reported Exertion During Aerobic Exercise: A Randomized Double-Blind, Placebo-Controlled Study," *Brain and Cognition* 132 (June 1, 2019): 33–40, doi.org/10.1016/j.bandc.2019.02.003.

29. Max Roser, "Why Is Life Expectancy in the US Lower than in Other Rich Countries?," *Our World in Data*, October 29, 2020, https://ourworldindata.org/us-life-expectancy-low; Samuel H. Preston, Yana C. Vierboom, and Andrew Stokes, "The Role of Obesity in Exceptionally Slow US Mortality Improvement," *Proceedings of the National Academy of Sciences* 115, no. 5 (January 30, 2018): 957–61, doi.org/10.1073/pnas.1716802115.

30. Tom Miles, "China Overtakes U.S. for Healthy Lifespan: WHO Data," *Reuters*, May 30, 2018, www.reuters.com/article/world/china-overtakes-us-for-healthy-lifespan-who-data-idUSKCN1IV15G/.

31. Niall Ferguson, "We're All Soviets Now," *The Free Press*, June 18, 2024, www.thefp.com/p/were-all-soviets-now.

32. Kevin D. Hall et al., "Ultra-Processed Diets Cause Excess Calorie Intake and Weight Gain: An Inpatient Randomized Controlled Trial of Ad Libitum Food Intake," *Cell Metabolism* 30, no. 1 (July 2, 2019): 67–77.e3, doi.org/10.1016/j.cmet.2019.05.008.

33. John Blundell et al., "Effects of Once-Weekly Semaglutide on Appetite, Energy Intake, Control of Eating, Food Preference and Body Weight in Subjects with Obesity," *Diabetes, Obesity and Metabolism* 19, no. 9 (2017): 1242–51, doi.org/10.1111/dom.12932; Long Ge et al., "Comparison of Dietary Macronutrient Patterns of 14 Popular Named Dietary Programmes for Weight and Cardiovascular Risk Factor Reduction in Adults: Systematic Review and Network Meta-Analysis of Randomised Trials," *BMJ (Clinical Research Ed.)* 369 (April 1, 2020): m696, doi.org/10.1136/bmj.m696.

34. "The British 'Limeys' Were Right: A Short History of Scurvy," Military Health System, January 10, 2022, www.health.mil/News/Articles/2022/01/10/The-British-Limeys-Were-Right-A-Short-History-of-Scurvy.

35. Dong D. Wang et al., "Fruit and Vegetable Intake and Mortality," *Circulation* 143, no. 17 (April 27, 2021): 1642–54, doi.org/10.1161/CIRCULATIONAHA.120.048996; Daniel McDonald et al., "American Gut: An Open Platform for Citizen Science Microbiome Research," *mSystems* 3, no. 3 (May 15, 2018): e00031-18, doi.org/10.1128/msystems.00031-18.

36. "Human Augmentation—the Dawn of a New Paradigm," UK Ministry of Defence, May 13, 2021, www.gov.uk/government/publications/human-augmentation-the-dawn-of-a-new-paradigm.

37. Roberts, *The Storm of War*, 179.

38. Quoted in Roberts, *The Storm of War*, 179.

39. Etain A. Tansey and Christopher D. Johnson, "Recent Advances in Thermoregulation," *Advances in Physiology Education* 39, no. 3 (September 2015): 139–48, doi.org/10.1152/advan.00126.2014.

40. Douglas T. Kenrick and Steven W. MacFarlane, "Ambient Temperature and Horn Honking: A Field Study of the Heat/Aggression Relationship," *Environment and Behavior* 18, no. 2 (March 1, 1986): 179–91, doi.org/10.1177/0013916586182002; Solomon M.

Hsiang, Marshall Burke, and Edward Miguel, "Quantifying the Influence of Climate on Human Conflict," *Science* 341, no. 6151 (September 13, 2013): 1235367, doi.org/10.1126/science.1235367; Lawrence A. Kuznar and Jeffrey Day, "Homicide, Inequality, and Climate: Untangling the Relationships," *Frontiers in Psychology* 12 (August 11, 2021), doi.org/10.3389/fpsyg.2021.697126.

41. Roberts, *The Storm of War*, 178.

42. Ann Gibbons, "Grisly Find Suggests Humans Inhabited Arctic 45,000 Years Ago," *Science*, January 14, 2016, www.science.org/content/article/grisly-find-suggests-humans-inhabited-arctic-45000-years-ago.

43. Alex Wilkins, "Human Hibernation Is a Real Possibility—this Is How It Might Work," *New Scientist*, October 11, 2022, www.newscientist.com/article/mg25634080-400-human-hibernation-is-a-real-possibility-this-is-how-it-might-work/.

44. Wilkins.

45. Kevin Jiang, "Sleep, Death, and . . . the Gut?," *The Harvard Gazette*, June 4, 2020, https://news.harvard.edu/gazette/story/2020/06/study-reveals-guts-role-in-causing-death-by-sleep-deprivation; Matthew Walker, *Why We Sleep* (Allen Lane, 2017).

46. Walker, 17–19, 21–26.

47. Walker, 26, 30–32.

48. Watch from about 8:30 in *Scientific American: Polyphasic Sleep Study, Experiment*, www.youtube.com/watch?v=bL4kexuMLJQ.

49. Walker, 137.

50. Walker, 134–36.

51. Nita Lewis Shattuck et al., "The Role of Sleep in Human Performance and Well-Being," in Michael D. Matthews and David M. Schnyer, eds., *Human Performance Optimization: The Science and Ethics of Enhancing Human Capabilities* (Oxford University Press, 2019), 200–233, doi.org/10.1093/oso/9780190455132.003.0010; Nita Lewis Miller, Panagiotis Matsangas, and Aileen Kenney, "The Role of Sleep in the Military: Implications for Training and Operational Effectiveness," in Janice H. Laurence and Michael D. Matthews, eds., *The Oxford Handbook of Military Psychology* (Oxford University Press, 2012), doi.org/10.1093/oxfordhb/9780195399325.013.0084.

52. Walker; "Healthy Sleep," *Medline Plus* (National Library of Medicine), https://medlineplus.gov/healthysleep.html, accessed November 23, 2024.

53. Cameron H. Good et al., "Sleep in the United States Military," *Neuropsychopharmacology* 45, no. 1 (January 2020): 176–91, doi.org/10.1038/s41386-019-0431-7.

54. "App-Based Treatment for People with Insomnia an Effective Alternative to Sleeping Pills," The National Institute for Health and Care Excellence (NICE), May 20, 2022, www.nice.org.uk/news/articles/App-based-treatment-for-people-with-insomnia-an-effective-alternative-to-sleeping-pills.

55. Claude R. Sasso, "Soviet Night Operations in World War II," *Leavenworth Papers* (U.S. Army Command and General Staff College, 1982).

56. Sasso, 2.

57. No definition of life satisfies everyone, because every definition faces difficult cases: Are viruses alive because they cannot reproduce on their own? Is a single immature rabbit alive as it cannot reproduce until it gets older and it cannot reproduce without a partner? Is a single cell in an organism, such as a skin cell on your elbow, alive as it cannot sustain itself without other cells? But most of what matters is captured by a practical

definition of life that includes: (a) an organism's ability to maintain its own order; and (b) an organism's ability to reproduce in a way that means an organism's key features are inherited by its offspring. It is consistent, for example, with a recent working definition used by NASA that "life is a self-sustaining chemical system capable of Darwinian evolution" ("NASA Astrobiology," https://astrobiology.nasa.gov/about/, accessed December 11, 2024). It also captures the idea of reproduction with errors where the errors are themselves reproducible, which excludes a variety of nonliving chemical systems (e.g., crystals) that can reproduce but don't pass sufficient information about errors to the offspring (Steven A. Benner, "Defining Life," *Astrobiology* 10, no. 10 (December 2010): 1021–30, doi.org/10.1089/ast.2010.0524).

58. Robert C. Froemke and Larry J. Young, "Oxytocin, Neural Plasticity, and Social Behavior," *Annual Review of Neuroscience* 44 (July 8, 2021): 359–81, doi.org/10.1146/annurev-neuro-102320-102847.

59. Elseline Hoekzema et al., "Pregnancy Leads to Long-Lasting Changes in Human Brain Structure," *Nature Neuroscience* 20, no. 2 (February 2017): 287–96, doi.org/10.1038/nn.4458; Magdalena Martínez-García et al., "First-Time Fathers Show Longitudinal Gray Matter Cortical Volume Reductions: Evidence from Two International Samples," *Cerebral Cortex* 33, no. 7 (April 1, 2023): 4156–63, doi.org/10.1093/cercor/bhac333; Elseline Hoekzema et al., "Mapping the Effects of Pregnancy on Resting State Brain Activity, White Matter Microstructure, Neural Metabolite Concentrations and Grey Matter Architecture," *Nature Communications* 13, no. 1 (November 22, 2022): 6931, doi.org/10.1038/s41467-022-33884-8.

60. Roberts, *The Storm of War*, 161.

61. Robert M. Sapolsky, *Behave: The Biology of Humans at Our Best and Worst* (Bodley Head, 2017), 354–58, 366.

62. Gazzaniga et al., 466–68, 438.

63. Jasmin Cloutier et al., "Are Attractive People Rewarding? Sex Differences in the Neural Substrates of Facial Attractiveness," *Journal of Cognitive Neuroscience* 20, no. 6 (June 1, 2008): 941–51, doi.org/10.1162/jocn.2008.20062; Robert O. Deaner, Amit V. Khera, and Michael L. Platt, "Monkeys Pay per View: Adaptive Valuation of Social Images by Rhesus Macaques," *Current Biology* 15, no. 6 (March 29, 2005): 543–48, doi.org/10.1016/j.cub.2005.01.044.

64. "The British Army's Fight Against Venereal Disease in the 'Heroic Age of Prostitution,'" Project Team, World War I Centenary, University of Oxford (2024), doi.org/10.25446/oxford.25837285.v1.

65. Daria Sito-Sucic, "'Invisible' Bosnians Born of Wartime Rape Use Art to Find Their Voice," *Reuters*, October 15, 2019, www.reuters.com/article/us-bosnia-war-play-idUSKBN1WU1SC.

66. MacMillan, *War*, 190–91.

67. Kirsten Johnson et al., "Association of Combatant Status and Sexual Violence with Health and Mental Health Outcomes in Postconflict Liberia," *JAMA* 300, no. 6 (August 13, 2008): 676–90, doi.org/10.1001/jama.300.6.676.

68. Jean D. Wilson and Claus Roehrborn, "Long-Term Consequences of Castration in Men: Lessons from the Skoptzy and the Eunuchs of the Chinese and Ottoman Courts," *The Journal of Clinical Endocrinology & Metabolism* 84, no. 12 (December 1, 1999): 4324–31, https://academic.oup.com/jcem/article/84/12/4324/2864451.

69. Peter Beaumont, "Video Appears to Show Russian Soldier Castrating Ukrainian

Prisoner," *The Guardian*, July 29, 2022, www.theguardian.com/world/2022/jul/29/video-appears-to-show-russian-soldier-castrating-ukrainian-prisoner.

70. Douglas P. Fry and Patrik Söderberg, "Lethal Aggression in Mobile Forager Bands and Implications for the Origins of War," *Science* 341, no. 6143 (July 19, 2013): 270–73, doi.org/10.1126/science.1235675.
71. Nicholas D. Wright et al., "Testosterone Induces Off-Line Perceptual Learning," *Psychopharmacology* 224, no. 3 (December 2012): 451–57, doi.org/10.1007/s00213-012-2769-y.
72. Nicholas D. Wright et al., "Testosterone Disrupts Human Collaboration by Increasing Egocentric Choices," *Proceedings of the Royal Society B: Biological Sciences* 279, no. 1736 (February 1, 2012): 2275–80, doi.org/10.1098/rspb.2011.2523.
73. J. Archer, "Testosterone and Human Aggression: An Evaluation of the Challenge Hypothesis," *Neuroscience & Biobehavioral Reviews* 30, no. 3 (2006): 319–45; Martin N. Muller and Richard W. Wrangham, "Dominance, Aggression and Testosterone in Wild Chimpanzees: A Test of the 'Challenge Hypothesis,'" *Animal Behaviour* 67, no. 1 (January 2004): 113–23.
74. Camille Michèle Williams et al., "Neuroanatomical Norms in the UK Biobank: The Impact of Allometric Scaling, Sex, and Age," *Human Brain Mapping* 42, no. 14 (2021): 4623–42, doi.org/10.1002/hbm.25572; Lise Eliot et al., "Dump the 'Dimorphism': Comprehensive Synthesis of Human Brain Studies Reveals Few Male-Female Differences Beyond Size," *Neuroscience & Biobehavioral Reviews* 125 (June 1, 2021): 667–97, doi.org/10.1016/j.neubiorev.2021.02.026.
75. *The World at War* (1973–1974), season 1, episode 16, "Inside the Reich: Germany (1940–1944)." Directed by David Elstein. Aired February 20, 1974, on Thames Television.
76. Kate Vigurs, *Mission France: The True History of the Women of SOE* (Yale University Press, 2022).
77. Beevor, 244, 281; MacMillan, *War*, 150.
78. Roberts, *The Storm of War*, 608.
79. Eric Grundhauser, "The Little-Known Story of the Night Witches, an All-Female Force in WWII," *Vanity Fair*, June 25, 2015, www.vanityfair.com/culture/2015/06/night-witches-wwii-female-pilots.
80. Holger Ursin, ed., *Psychobiology of Stress: A Study of Coping Men* (Academic Press, 1978), 11; Karl E. Friedl and Stephen J. Grate, "Metabolic Enhancement of the Soldier Brain," in Michael D. Matthews and David M. Schnyer, eds., *Human Performance Optimization: The Science and Ethics of Enhancing Human Capabilities* (Oxford University Press, 2019), doi.org/10.1093/oso/9780190455132.003.0002.
81. Andreas G. Nerlich, Angelika Fleckinger, and Oliver Peschel, "Life and Diseases of the Neolithic Glacier Mummy 'Ötzi,'" in Dong Hoon Shin and Raffaella Bianucci, eds., *The Handbook of Mummy Studies: New Frontiers in Scientific and Cultural Perspectives* (Springer, 2020), 1–22, doi.org/10.1007/978-981-15-1614-6_19-1.
82. Gazzaniga et al., 447.

3: STAND AND FIGHT?

1. My great-uncle was Sydney Spiers. The recommendation for his Military Cross is available at the United Kingdom National Archives (www.nationalarchives.gov.uk/).

2. Justin S. Feinstein et al., "The Human Amygdala and the Induction and Experience of Fear," *Current Biology* 21, no. 1 (January 11, 2011): 34–38, doi.org/10.1016/j.cub.2010.11.042.

3. Joseph LeDoux and Nathaniel D. Daw, "Surviving Threats: Neural Circuit and Computational Implications of a New Taxonomy of Defensive Behaviour," *Nature Reviews Neuroscience* 19, no. 5 (May 2018): 269–82, doi.org/10.1038/nrn.2018.22; Dean Mobbs et al., "Viewpoints: Approaches to Defining and Investigating Fear," *Nature Neuroscience* 22, no. 8 (August 2019): 1205–16, doi.org/10.1038/s41593-019-0456-6; Dean Mobbs et al., "Space, Time, and Fear: Survival Computations Along Defensive Circuits," *Trends in Cognitive Sciences* 24, no. 3 (March 1, 2020): 228–41, doi.org/10.1016/j.tics.2019.12.016.

4. Ralph M. Kaufman, "'Ill Health' as an Expression of Anxiety in a Combat Unit," *Psychosomatic Medicine* 9, no. 2 (March 1947): 104, doi.org/10.1097?00006842-194703000-00004.

5. Definitions of mental illnesses, and how they are applied, change markedly over time and between different populations. But the main points are illustrated by data on prevalence of anxiety disorders from Global Burden of Disease Collaborative Network, *Global Burden of Disease Study 2021 (GBD 2021)*, Institute for Health Metrics and Evaluation (IHME), 2024. You can explore this yourself with data from 1990–2021 at "Anxiety Disorders Prevalence vs. GDP per Capita," Our World in Data, https://ourworldindata.org/grapher/anxiety-disorders-prevalence-vs-gdp, accessed November 25, 2024.

6. David Forbes et al., "Treatment of Military-Related Post-Traumatic Stress Disorder: Challenges, Innovations, and the Way Forward," *International Review of Psychiatry* 31, no. 1 (January 2, 2019): 95–110, doi.org/10.1080/09540261.2019.1595545; Chen Xue et al., "A Meta-Analysis of Risk Factors for Combat-Related PTSD Among Military Personnel and Veterans," *PLOS ONE* 10, no. 3 (March 20, 2015): e0120270, doi.org/10.1371/journal.pone.0120270.

7. Dan W. Grupe and Jack B. Nitschke, "Uncertainty and Anticipation in Anxiety: An Integrated Neurobiological and Psychological Perspective," *Nature Reviews Neuroscience* 14, no. 7 (July 2013): 488–501, doi.org/10.1038/nrn3524. For discussions of the importance of training, competence, and "veterancy" in the will to fight, see Ben Connable et al., "Will to Fight: Analyzing, Modeling, and Simulating the Will to Fight of Military Units," RAND Corporation, September 20, 2018, www.rand.org/pubs/research_reports/RR2341.html.

8. Lisa M. Shin and Israel Liberzon, "The Neurocircuitry of Fear, Stress, and Anxiety Disorders," *Neuropsychopharmacology* 35, no. 1 (January 2010): 169–91, doi.org/10.1038/npp.2009.83; Christian J. Merz and Oliver T. Wolf, "How Stress Hormones Shape Memories of Fear and Anxiety in Humans," *Neuroscience & Biobehavioral Reviews* 142 (November 1, 2022): 104901, doi.org/10.1016/j.neubiorev.2022.104901.

9. Forbes et al.

10. Forbes et al.; Simon Wessely, "Twentieth-Century Theories on Combat Motivation and Breakdown," *Journal of Contemporary History* 41, no. 2 (April 1, 2006): 268–86, doi.org/10.1177/0022009406062067.

11. D. C. Blanchard and R. J. Blanchard, "Ethoexperimental Approaches to the Biology of Emotion," *Annual Review of Psychology* 39, no. 1 (1988): 43–68; D. Caroline Blanchard, "Translating Dynamic Defense Patterns from Rodents to People," *Neuroscience & Biobehavioral Reviews*, 76 (May 1, 2017): 22–28, https://doi.org/10.1016/j.neubiorev.2016.11.001. Mobbs et al., "Space, Time, and Fear."

12. Vladimir Putin, *First Person: An Astonishingly Frank Self-Portrait by Russia's President Vladimir Putin* (PublicAffairs, 2000).
13. Jonathan D. Spence, *The Search for Modern China*, third edition (W. W. Norton & Company, 2013), 261–62.
14. David Graff and Robin Higham, eds., *A Military History of China*, updated edition (University Press of Kentucky, 2012), 135.
15. Xiaobing Li, ed., *China at War: An Encyclopedia*, illustrated edition (ABC-CLIO, 2012), xxviii.
16. Spence, *The Search for Modern China*, 262–63, 307, 310–27; Beevor, 64.
17. For Mao's early life, see Spence, *The Search for Modern China*, 262; on the founding of the Communist Party, see Spence, *The Search for Modern China*, 298; Jonathan D. Spence, *Mao Zedong* (Viking, 1999), 56–58.
18. Xiaobing Li, xxix.
19. Xiaobing Li, xxx.
20. Overy, *Blood and Ruins*, 32–33.
21. Spence, *The Search for Modern China*, 397.
22. No single, short list of emotions is adequate to capture the full range of human emotions, but this list at least gives readers in the modern western world an idea of the types of phenomena we are discussing. Whether this specific palette of emotions is universal across time and place is a focus of research. For a discussion, see Gazzaniga et al., 434–39.
23. Jolie Baumann and David DeSteno, "Emotion Guided Threat Detection: Expecting Guns Where There Are None," *Journal of Personality and Social Psychology* 99, no. 4 (2010): 595–610, doi.org/10.1037/a0020665.
24. Jolie Baumann Wormwood, Karen S. Quigley, and Lisa Feldman Barrett, "Emotion and Threat Detection: The Roles of Affect and Conceptual Knowledge," *Emotion* 22, no. 8 (2022): 1929–41, doi.org/10.1037/emo0000884.
25. Gazzaniga et al., 451–53.
26. Yu Tong et al., "Disgust Selectively Dampens Value-Independent Risk-Taking for Potential Gains," *Cognition* 200 (July 2020): 104266, doi.org/10.1016/j.cognition.2020.104266.
27. Ellen Peters et al., "Affect and Decision Making: A 'Hot' Topic," *Journal of Behavioral Decision Making* 19, no. 2 (2006): 79–85, doi.org/10.1002/bdm.528.
28. Spence, *The Search for Modern China*, 397–98.
29. Spence, *The Search for Modern China*, 398–99.
30. Rana Mitter, *Forgotten Ally: China's World War II, 1937–1945*, first edition (Houghton Mifflin Harcourt, 2013), 79.
31. Mitter, *Forgotten Ally*, 75.
32. Mitter, *Forgotten Ally*, 89–91.
33. Nathaniel D. Daw and John P. O'Doherty, "Chapter 21: Multiple Systems for Value Learning," in Paul W. Glimcher and Ernst Fehr, eds., *Neuroeconomics*, second edition (Academic Press, 2014), 393–410, doi.org/10.1016/B978-0-12-416008-8.00021-8.
34. Daniel Kahneman, *Thinking, Fast and Slow* (Farrar, Straus and Giroux, 2011).
35. Elizabeth A. Stanley and Kelsey L. Larsen, "Difficulties with Emotion Regulation in the Contemporary U.S. Armed Forces: Structural Contributors and Potential

Solutions," *Armed Forces & Society* 47, no. 1 (January 1, 2021): 77–105, doi.org/10.1177/0095327X19848018.

36. George A. Bonanno, "Loss, Trauma, and Human Resilience: Have We Underestimated the Human Capacity to Thrive After Extremely Aversive Events?," *American Psychologist* 59 (2004): 20–28.
37. Zulkayda Mamat and Michael C. Anderson, "Improving Mental Health by Training the Suppression of Unwanted Thoughts," *Science Advances* 9, no. 38 (September 20, 2023): eadh5292, doi.org/10.1126/sciadv.adh5292.
38. Jane M. Richards and James J. Gross, "Composure at Any Cost? The Cognitive Consequences of Emotion Suppression," *Personality and Social Psychology Bulletin* 25, no. 8 (August 1, 1999): 1033–44, doi.org/10.1177/01461672992511010; Jane M. Richards and James J. Gross, "Emotion Regulation and Memory: The Cognitive Costs of Keeping One's Cool," *Journal of Personality and Social Psychology* 79, no. 3 (2000): 410–24, doi.org/10.1037/0022-3514.79.3.410.
39. Kateri McRae and James J. Gross, "Emotion Regulation," *Emotion* 20, no. 1 (2020): 1–9, doi.org/10.1037/emo0000703.
40. Stanley and Larsen, 91–92.
41. Stanley and Larsen.
42. MacMillan, *War*, 160–61.
43. Mitter, *Forgotten Ally*, 98.
44. Beevor, 71; Graff and Higham, 244.
45. Mitter, *Forgotten Ally*, 135.
46. Mitter, *Forgotten Ally*, 138.
47. Richard C. Bush, "Commentary: Thoughts on the Nanjing Massacre," The Brookings Institution, December 1, 2007, www.brookings.edu/opinions/thoughts-on-the-nanjing-massacre/.
48. Alex Kacelnik and Melissa Bateson, "Risky Theories—the Effects of Variance on Foraging Decisions," *American Zoologist* 36, no. 4 (1996): 402; David W. Stephens and John R. Krebs, *Foraging Theory*, first edition (Princeton University Press, 1987).
49. Carl von Clausewitz, *On War*, trans. Michael Howard and Peter Paret (Oxford University Press, 2008), 60.
50. Nicholas D. Wright et al., "Approach–Avoidance Processes Contribute to Dissociable Impacts of Risk and Loss on Choice," *The Journal of Neuroscience* 32, no. 20 (May 16, 2012): 7009–20, doi.org/10.1523/JNUROSCI.0049-12.2012.
51. Nicholas D. Wright et al., "Dissociable Influences of Skewness and Valence on Economic Choice and Neural Activity," *PLOS ONE* 8, no. 12 (2013): e83454, doi.org/10.1371/journal.pone.0083454; Mkael Symmonds et al., "The Chronometry of Risk Processing in the Human Cortex," *Frontiers in Neuroscience* 7 (2013): 146, doi.org/10.3389/fnins.2013.00146.
52. Li Li et al., "Parsing Cultural Impacts on Regret and Risk in Iran, China and the United Kingdom," *Scientific Reports* 8, no. 1 (September 14, 2018): 13862, doi.org/10.1038/s41598-018-30680-7.
53. Nicholas D. Wright, "Global Strategy Amidst the Globe's Cultures: Cultures in Individual Cognition, States and the Global System," *Intelligent Biology*, v2 (December 2019), www.intelligentbiology.co.uk/s/Wright2019_Glob_Strategy_cultures_v2.pdf.
54. Graff and Higham, 216.
55. Mitter, *Forgotten Ally*, 143.

56. Mitter, *Forgotten Ally*, 150.
57. Mitter, *Forgotten Ally*, 161.
58. Graff and Higham, 222.
59. Spence, *The Search for Modern China*, 375–81.
60. Colin F. Camerer, *Behavioral Game Theory: Experiments in Strategic Interaction* (Princeton University Press, 2003), 9-10, chapter 2.
61. Andrea Larney, Amanda Rotella, and Pat Barclay, "Stake Size Effects in Ultimatum Game and Dictator Game Offers: A Meta-Analysis," *Organizational Behavior and Human Decision Processes* 15 (March 2019): 61–72, doi.org/10.1016/j.obhdp.2019.01.002.
62. Nicholas D. Wright et al., "Human Responses to Unfairness with Primary Rewards and Their Biological Limits," *Scientific Reports* 2 (2012): 593, doi.org/10.1038/srep00593.
63. Nicholas D. Wright et al., "Neural Segregation of Objective and Contextual Aspects of Fairness," *The Journal of Neuroscience* 31, no. 14 (April 6, 2011): 5244–52, doi.org/10.1523/JNEUROSCI.3138-10.2011. After our study, a causal study in nonhuman primates showed results highly consistent with our findings for functional divisions within the insula: Fausto Caruana et al., "Emotional and Social Behaviors Elicited by Electrical Stimulation of the Insula in the Macaque Monkey," *Current Biology* 21, no. 3 (February 8, 2011): 195–99, doi.org/10.1016/j.cub.2010.12.042.
64. Nicholas Sambanis, Jonah Schulhofer-Wohl, and Moses Shayo, "Parochialism as a Central Challenge in Counterinsurgency," *Science* 336, no. 6083 (May 18, 2012): 805–8, doi.org/10.1126/science.1222304; Jack A. Goldstone, *Revolutions: A Very Short Introduction* (Oxford University Press, 2014), 11, 15, 17.
65. Graff and Higham, 236.
66. Lawrence Freedman, *Strategy: A History* (Oxford University Press, 2013), 186.
67. Spence, *The Search for Modern China*, 430.
68. "How Xi Jinping Is Mobilising the Masses to Control Themselves," *The Economist*, November 10, 2022, www.economist.com/china/2022/11/10/how-xi-jinping-is-mobilising-the-masses-to-control-themselves.
69. Charles Ardant du Picq, *Battle Studies*, eighth edition (The Military Services Publishing Company, 1947), 109. Quoted in Anthony Kellett, "The Soldier in Battle: Motivational and Behavioral Aspects of Combat Experience," in Betty Glad, ed., *Psychological Dimensions of War* (SAGE Publications, 1990), 225.
70. "Mao Zedong, on Protracted War, May 1938," Marxists Internet Archive, www.marxists.org/reference/archive/mao/selected-works/volume-2/mswv2_09.htm, accessed December 7, 2024; Mitter, *Forgotten Ally*, 156; Freedman, *Strategy*, 185–86, 192.
71. Graff and Higham, 244.
72. Kellett, 229.
73. Dave Grossman, *On Killing: The Psychological Cost of Learning to Kill in War and Society* (Little, Brown, 1995), xv, 153.
74. Kellett, 228.
75. Michael D. Matthews, *Head Strong: How Psychology Is Revolutionizing War*, second edition (Oxford University Press, USA, 2020), 244.
76. Matthews, *Head Strong*, 245.
77. Grossman, 180–81. Discussed in Rune Henriksen, "Warriors in Combat–What Makes

People Actively Fight in Combat?," *Journal of Strategic Studies* 30, no. 2 (April 1, 2007): 187–223, https://doi.org/10.1080/01402390701248707.

78. Quoted in Henriksen.
79. Matthews, *Head Strong*, 246–49.
80. Henriksen.
81. Jonathan D. Spence, *The Search for Modern China*, first edition (W. W. Norton & Company, 1990), 306–310.
82. Karl Marx, *The Eighteenth Brumaire of Louis Bonaparte*. Quoted in Peter Singer, *Marx: A Very Short Introduction*, first edition (Oxford University Press, 2000), 50.

4: WHERE, WHEN, AND WHAT IF . . .

1. This section draws on N. A. M. Rodger, *The Command of the Ocean: A Naval History of Britain, 1649–1815* (London: Allen Lane, 2004), 530–43.
2. Rodger, 459–60.
3. Richard. J. Overy, *War: A History in 100 Battles* (William Collins, 2016), 55.
4. Rodger, 538.
5. Alexander Palmer, Henry H. Carroll, and Nicholas Velazquez, "Unpacking China's Naval Buildup," Center for Strategic and International Studies, June 5, 2024, www.csis.org/analysis/unpacking-chinas-naval-buildup.
6. May-Britt Moser worked with John O'Keefe before doing her brilliant work that won a Nobel for "grid cells" alongside his for "place cells" in 2014. She wrote a highly accessible introduction, on which the first three steps in this section draw: May-Britt Moser and Noa Segev, "How Do We Find Our Way? Grid Cells in the Brain," *Frontiers for Young Minds*, September 7, 2021, https://kids.frontiersin.org/articles/10.3389/frym.2021.678725.
7. Russell A. Epstein et al., "The Cognitive Map in Humans: Spatial Navigation and Beyond," *Nature Neuroscience* 20, no. 11 (November 2017): 1504–13, doi.org/10.1038/nn.4656.
8. Epstein et al.; Timothy E. J. Behrens et al., "What Is a Cognitive Map? Organizing Knowledge for Flexible Behavior," *Neuron* 100, no. 2 (October 24, 2018): 490–509, doi.org/10.1016/j.neuron.2018.10.002. Causal evidence is cited in Isabel I. C. Low and Lisa M. Giocomo, "Fifty Years of the Brain's Sense of Space," *Nature* 599, no. 7885 (November 2021): 376–77, doi.org/10.1038/d41586-021-03010-7.
9. Roberts, *The Storm of War*, 351.
10. Roberts, *The Storm of War*, 353.
11. Symonds, 10.
12. This tale of the *Graf Spee* draws on: Symonds, chapter 2; Paul Kennedy, *Victory at Sea* (Yale University Press, 2022), 110–13.
13. Symonds, 33.
14. Kennedy, *Victory at Sea*, 113.
15. A. Coutrot et al., "Entropy of City Street Networks Linked to Future Spatial Navigation Ability," *Nature* 604, no. 7904 (2022): 104–10, doi.org/10.1038/s41586-022-04486-7.
16. Eleanor A. Maguire et al., "Navigation-Related Structural Change in the Hippocampi of Taxi Drivers," *Proceedings of the National Academy of Sciences* 97, no. 8 (April 11,

2000): 4398–4403, doi.org/10.1073/pnas.070039597; Eva-Maria Griesbauer et al., "London Taxi Drivers: A Review of Neurocognitive Studies and an Exploration of How They Build Their Cognitive Map of London," *Hippocampus* 32, no. 1 (2022): 3–20, doi.org/10.1002/hipo.23395.

17. Marielena Sosa and Lisa M. Giocomo, "Navigating for Reward," *Nature Reviews Neuroscience* 22, no. 8 (August 2021): 472–87, doi.org/10.1038/s41583-021-00479-z.

18. Gazzaniga et al., 402.

19. Maud Mouginot et al., "Differences in Expression of Male Aggression Between Wild Bonobos and Chimpanzees," *Current Biology* 34, no. 8 (April 22, 2024): 1780–85.e4, doi.org/10.1016/j.cub.2024.02.071.

20. Richard Wrangham, *The Goodness Paradox* (Pantheon Books, 2019), 91.

21. Robin E. Morrison et al., "Western Gorilla Space Use Suggests Territoriality," *Scientific Reports* 10, no. 1 (March 12, 2020): 3692, doi.org/10.1038/s41598-020-60504-6.

22. Rada Dyson-Hudson and Eric Alden Smith, "Human Territoriality: An Ecological Reassessment," *American Anthropologist* 80, no. 1 (1978): 21–41, doi.org/10.1525/aa.1978.80.1.02a00020; Elizabeth Cashdan et al., "Territoriality Among Human Foragers: Ecological Models and an Application to Four Bushman Groups [and Comments and Reply]," *Current Anthropology* 24, no. 1 (February 1983): 47–66, doi.org/10.1086/202934.

23. Overy, *Blood and Ruins*, xi, xii, 20, 22, 24 (on Germany), 33, 34.

24. "'An Independent Destiny for America': Charles A. Lindbergh on Isolationism," *History Matters*, https://historymatters.gmu.edu/d/5163, accessed November 26, 2024; Bear F. Braumoeller, "The Myth of American Isolationism," *Foreign Policy Analysis* 6, no. 4 (October 1, 2010): 349–71, doi.org/10.1111/j.1743-8594.2010.00117.x.

25. "Your Rules or Mine?," *The Economist*, November 13, 2014, www.economist.com/special-report/2014/11/13/your-rules-or-mine.

26. "These Four Chokepoints Are Threatening Global Trade," BCG Global, February 8, 2024, www.bcg.com/publications/2024/these-four-chokepoints-are-threatening-global-trade.

27. "Territorial Disputes in the South China Sea," Global Conflict Tracker, https://cfr.org/global-conflict-tracker/conflict/territorial-disputes-south-china-sea, accessed November 26, 2024.

28. Elizabeth C. Economy, *The Third Revolution: Xi Jingping and the New Chinese State* (Oxford University Press, 2018), 202; "China Has Put Missiles on Islands in the South China Sea," *The Economist*, May 10, 2018, www.economist.com/china/2018/05/10/china-has-put-missiles-on-islands-in-the-south-china-sea. These issues are covered by "Asia Maritime Transparency Initiative," Center for Strategic and International Studies, https://amti.csis.org/, accessed December 7, 2024.

29. Joint Publication 3–12, *Cyberspace Operations*, June 2018, DOD; Max Smeets, "Cyber Command's Strategy Risks Friction with Allies," *Lawfare* (blog), May 28, 2019, www.lawfareblog.com/cyber-commands-strategy-risks-friction-allies; Paul M. Nakasone and Michael Sulmeyer, "How to Compete in Cyberspace," *Foreign Affairs*, August 25, 2020, www.foreignaffairs.com/articles/united-states/2020-08-25/cybersecurity; Nicholas Wright, *Future Character of Information in Strategy*, 2021, Intelligent Biology, www.intelligentbiology.co.uk.

30. Nicholas Wright, *Mind Space: Cognition in Space Operations*, v2, 2019, Intelligent Biology, www.intelligentbiology.co.uk.

31. Wright, *Mind Space.*
32. Wright, *Mind Space*; China Aerospace Studies Institute, "In Their Own Words: Lectures on the Science of Space Operations," Air University, U.S. Air Force, August 12, 2022, www.airuniversity.af.edu/CASI/Display/Article/3125495/in-their-own-words-lectures-on-the-science-of-space-operations/.
33. Xi Jinping quote from China Aerospace Studies Institute, "China's Ground Segment: Building the Pillars of a Great Space Power," United States Department of the Air Force, March 1, 2021.
34. Jessie Yeung and Candice Zhu, "China Reveals How It Plans to Put Astronauts on the Moon by 2030," CNN, July 13, 2023, www.cnn.com/2023/07/13/china/china-crewed-moon-landing-2030-intl-hnk-scn/index.html.
35. Eberhard Rössler, *The U-Boat: The Evolution and Technical History of German Submarines* (London: Cassell, 1981), 19; Jan S. Breemer, "Defeating the U-Boat" (2010). *Newport Papers*, 36. https://digital-commons.usnwc.edu/usnwc-newport-papers/36, 1, 2.
36. Symonds, 104–5.
37. Symonds, 10–16.
38. Symonds, 103, 119.
39. Symonds, 129.
40. Alan Burn, *The Fighting Captain* (Pen and Sword, 2006), 4–5; *The World at War* (1973–1974), season 1, episode 10, "Wolf Pack: U-Boats in the Atlantic (1939–1944)," directed by David Elstein, aired January 9, 1974, on Thames Television.
41. Paul Kennedy, *Engineers of Victory: The Problem Solvers Who Turned the Tide in the Second World War* (London: Allen Lane, 2013), 95–96.
42. *World at War*, episode 10, "Wolf Pack."
43. Symonds, 191–92.
44. He had limbic encephalitis with antibodies to the voltage-gated potassium channels. See Christopher R. Butler et al., "Persistent Anterograde Amnesia Following Limbic Encephalitis Associated with Antibodies to the Voltage-Gated Potassium Channel Complex," *Journal of Neurology, Neurosurgery & Psychiatry* 85, no. 4 (2014): 387–91, doi.org/10.1136/jnnp-2013-306724.
45. Gazzaniga et al., 389–90.
46. Albert Tsao et al., "Integrating Time from Experience in the Lateral Entorhinal Cortex," *Nature* 561, no. 7721 (September 2018): 57–62, doi.org/10.1038/s41586-018-0459-6; Gray Umbach et al., "Time Cells in the Human Hippocampus and Entorhinal Cortex Support Episodic Memory," *Proceedings of the National Academy of Sciences of the United States of America* 117, no. 45 (November 10, 2020): 28463–74, doi.org/10.1073/pnas.2013250117.
47. Joe Dawson and Scott Sleek, "The Fluidity of Time: Scientists Uncover How Emotions Alter Time Perception," *APS Observer* 31 (September 28, 2018), www.psychologicalscience.org/observer/the-fluidity-of-time; Philip A. Gable, Andrea L. Wilhelm, and Bryan D. Poole, "How Does Emotion Influence Time Perception? A Review of Evidence Linking Emotional Motivation and Time Processing," *Frontiers in Psychology* 13 (April 27, 2022), doi.org/10.3389/fpsyg.2022.848154.
48. Tomás J. Ryan and Paul W. Frankland, "Forgetting as a Form of Adaptive Engram Cell Plasticity," *Nature Reviews Neuroscience* 23, no. 3 (March 2022): 173–86, doi.org/10.1038/s41583-021-00548-3.

49. Benedict Anderson, *Imagined Communities: Reflections on the Origin and Spread of Nationalism*, revised and extended edition (Verso, 1991); Ernest Renan, "What Is a Nation? (1882)," in *Nationalism in Europe* (Routledge, 1995).
50. Roberts, *The Storm of War*, 24–25; Andrew Roberts, *Masters and Commanders: How Roosevelt, Churchill, Marshall and Alanbrooke Won the War in the West*, first edition (Allen Lane, 2008), 354–55. For an alternative view and discussion of key literature, see Peter R. Mansoor, *The GI Offensive in Europe: The Triumph of American Infantry Divisions, 1941–1945* (University Press of Kansas, 1999), 7–15.
51. Henry Rousso, *The Vichy Syndrome: History and Memory in France Since 1944* (Harvard University Press, 1991). Original French publication in 1987.
52. Rana Mitter, *China's Good War* (Harvard University Press, 2020).
53. Mitter, *China's Good War*, 6.
54. Behrens et al., "What Is a Cognitive Map?"
55. Zeb Kurth-Nelson et al., "Replay and Compositional Computation," *Neuron* 111, no. 4 (February 15, 2023): 454–69, doi.org/10.1016/j.neuron.2022.12.028.
56. Alexandra O. Constantinescu, Jill X. O'Reilly, and Timothy E. J. Behrens, "Organizing Conceptual Knowledge in Humans with a Gridlike Code," *Science* 352, no. 6292 (June 17, 2016): 1464–68, doi.org/10.1126/science.aaf0941.
57. Sinéad L. Mullally and Eleanor A. Maguire, "Memory, Imagination, and Predicting the Future: A Common Brain Mechanism?," *The Neuroscientist* 20, no. 3 (June 1, 2014): 220–34, doi.org/10.1177/1073858413495091.
58. Demis Hassabis et al., "Patients with Hippocampal Amnesia Cannot Imagine New Experiences," *Proceedings of the National Academy of Sciences* 104, no. 5 (January 30, 2007): 1726–31, doi.org/10.1073/pnas.0610561104.
59. Behrens et al., "What Is a Cognitive Map?"
60. Behrens et al., "What Is a Cognitive Map?"
61. Behrens et al., "What Is a Cognitive Map?"
62. Behrens et al., "What Is a Cognitive Map?"
63. Symonds, 78; Kennedy, *Victory at Sea*, 25.
64. Symonds, 85–88.
65. Kennedy, *Victory at Sea*, 173.
66. Symonds, 87.
67. Roberts, *The Storm of War*, 603–4.
68. Mitter, *Forgotten Ally*, 387–88.

PART II: PROPER APPLICATION OF FORCE

1. Sonia Harmand et al., "3.3-Million-Year-Old Stone Tools from Lomekwi 3, West Turkana, Kenya," *Nature* 521, no. 7552 (May 2015): 310–15, doi.org/10.1038/nature14464.
2. The invention of hafting, the fitting of handles to tools, may have happened as long as 500,000–300,000 years ago: Lawrence Barham, *From Hand to Handle: The First Industrial Revolution* (OUP Oxford, 2013), 1, 15, 146.
3. "The Story of the Tendon Hammer," *Past Medical History*, July 28, 2017, www.pastmedicalhistory.co.uk/the-story-of-the-tendon-hammer/; Francisco Pinto, "A Short

History of the Reflex Hammer," *Practical Neurology* 3, no. 6 (December 1, 2003): 366–71; Bill Bynum and Helen Bynum, "Reflex Hammer," *The Lancet* 390, no. 10095 (August 12, 2017): 641, doi.org/10.1016/S0140-6736(17)31969-4.

4. "Joseph Bell," The Royal College of Surgeons of Edinburgh, https://archiveandlibrary.rcsed.ac.uk/surgeon/3769275-joseph-bell, accessed November 27, 2024.
5. Warren Thompson and Andrew Thomas, *American Nightfighter Aces of World War 2*, illustrated edition (Osprey Publishing, 2008), 9.
6. "Optic Nerve Disorders," *Medline Plus*, National Library of Medicine, https://medlineplus.gov/opticnervedisorders.html, accessed November 27, 2024; "The Rods and Cones of the Human Eye," http://hyperphysics.phy-astr.gsu.edu/hbase/vision/rodcone.html, accessed November 27, 2024.
7. Kai-Fu Lee, *AI Superpowers: China, Silicon Valley, and the New World Order* (Houghton Mifflin Harcourt, 2018), 166–67.
8. Winston Churchill, *The Grand Alliance (Volume III), The Second World War* (Cassell, 1950), 539.

5: PERCEIVING REALITY

1. This specific pilot is fictional. The historical events are from Symonds, 195–208.
2. *The World at War* (1973–1974), season 1, episode 6, "Bansai! Japan (1931–1942)." Directed by David Elstein. Aired December 5, 1973, by Thames Television on ITV.
3. Symonds, 207.
4. For a fascinating tour of such animal senses, see Ed Yong, *An Immense World: How Animal Senses Reveal the Hidden Realms Around Us*, first edition (Bodley Head, 2022).
5. Antoine Bousquet, *The Eye of War: Military Perception from the Telescope to the Drone*, first edition (University of Minnesota Press, 2018), 44.
6. Clausewitz, 46.
7. Christopher D. Frith, *Making Up the Mind: How the Brain Creates Our Mental World* (Blackwell, 2007), 34–35.
8. Quoted in Frith, *Making Up the Mind*, 34.
9. Quoted in Frith, *Making Up the Mind*, 33.
10. Frith, *Making Up the Mind*, 41–42.
11. Various alternatives are proposed that, although they take many specific forms, boil down to a simple idea of a controlled perceptual model. For accessible introductions, see Chris Frith, *Making Up the Mind*; and Anil Seth, *Being You: A New Science of Consciousness* (Faber & Faber, 2021). Chris Frith uses the term "controlled hallucination."
12. Hierarchies have long been discussed in scientific fields beyond neuroscience: see John H. Holland, *Complexity: A Very Short Introduction* (Oxford University Press, 2014), 52. Hierarchies are important in influential ideas related to perception in the brain and artificial intelligence: see Karl Friston, "The Free-Energy Principle: A Unified Brain Theory?," *Nature Reviews Neuroscience* 11, no. 2 (2010): 127–38. Hierarchies are central to many aspects of brain function: see Edmund T. Rolls, *Cerebral Cortex: Principles of Operation* (Oxford University Press, 2016), chapter 2.
13. Friston, "The Free Energy Principle"; Peter Dayan and Larry F. Abbott, *Theoretical*

Neuroscience: Computational and Mathematical Modeling of Neural Systems (MIT Press, 2001), 359.

14. The brain integrates new information with expectations using processes that work something like Bayes's rule, which is a good mathematical way of doing this. For Bayes in neuroscience, see Frith, *Making Up the Mind*, 119–27; Friston, "The Free Energy Principle." Also see David Omand, *How Spies Think: Ten Lessons in Intelligence* (Penguin UK, 2020).
15. Symonds, 281–82.
16. Symonds, 282–83.
17. Symonds, 286.
18. Overy, *War*, 359.
19. Symonds, 287.
20. Symonds, 289.
21. Overy, *War*, 359.
22. Beevor, 376.
23. *Life in Colour with David Attenborough*, episode 2, "Hiding in Colour," aired 2021 on BBC One.
24. Antoine Bousquet, *The Eye of War: Military Perception from the Telescope to the Drone*, first edition (University of Minnesota Press, 2018), 45, 48–49.
25. Bousquet, 65–66.
26. Bousquet, 67.
27. Adam K. Raymond, "'We Own the Night': The Rise and Fall of the US Military's Night-Vision Dominance," *Task & Purpose*, July 11, 2017, https://taskandpurpose.com/tech-tactics/night-rise-fall-us-militarys-night-vision-dominance/.
28. Yong, 304–5.
29. Bousquet, 154.
30. Bousquet, chapter 5.
31. Bousquet, 157.
32. Elsa B. Kania, "China's Quantum Future," *Foreign Affairs*, September 26, 2018, www.foreignaffairs.com/articles/china/2018-09-26/chinas-quantum-future; Chris Jay Hoofnagle and Simson Garfinkel, "Quantum Sensors—Unlike Quantum Computers—Are Already Here," *Defense One*, June 27, 2022, www.defenseone.com/ideas/2022/06/quantum-sensorsunlike-quantum-computersare-already-here/368634/; "Quantum Radar Has Been Demonstrated for the First Time," *MIT Technology Review*, August 23, 2019, www.technologyreview.com/2019/08/23/75512/quantum-radar-has-been-demonstrated-for-the-first-time/.
33. *Life in Colour with David Attenborough*, episode 2.
34. Lucy Ash, "How Russia Outfoxes Its Enemies," *BBC News*, January 29, 2015, www.bbc.co.uk/news/magazine-31020283.
35. Nicholas Rankin, *Churchill's Wizards: The British Genius for Deception 1914–1945* (Faber, 2008), 519.
36. Overy, *War*, 242–45.

37. Rankin, 522–23.
38. Rankin, 523–24.
39. Roberts, *The Storm of War*, 299.
40. Gazzaniga et al., 206–7.
41. Gazzaniga et al., 206.
42. Nichola Raihani, *The Social Instinct: How Cooperation Shaped the World* (Jonathan Cape, 2021), 87–88.
43. Wright et al., "Testosterone Disrupts Human Collaboration by Increasing Egocentric Choices."
44. Joseph Henrich, *The Secret of Our Success* (Princeton University Press, 2015), 241–42.
45. Bousquet, 92.
46. Quoted in Bousquet, 93.
47. John Lewis Gaddis, *The Cold War: A New History* (Penguin, 2005), 73.
48. Nicholas D. Wright, ed., *Artificial Intelligence, China, Russia, and the Global Order* (Maxwell Air Force Base, Alabama: Air University Press, 2019), xix, 3, chapter 1.
49. Paul Scharre, *Four Battlegrounds: Power in the Age of Artificial Intelligence* (W. W. Norton & Company, 2023), chapter 7.
50. Wright, *Artificial Intelligence, China, Russia, and the Global Order*, 5–7.
51. Lynch et al., "*OFFSET-X : Closing the Deterrence Gap and Building the Future Joint Force*" (Special Competitive Studies Project, May 2023), 6; Nathan Beauchamp-Mustafaga, "Chinese Next-Generation Psychological Warfare: The Military Applications of Emerging Technologies and Implications for the United States," RAND Corporation, June 1, 2023, www.rand.org/pubs/research_reports/RRA853-1.html; Elsa B. Kania, "Minds at War: China's Pursuit of Military Advantage Through Cognitive Science and Biotechnology," *PRISM* 8, no. 3 (2019): 82–101.
52. Hodan Omaar and Martin Makaryan, "How Innovative Is China in Quantum?," Information Technology and Innovation Foundation, September 9, 2024, https://itif.org/publications/2024/09/09/how-innovative-is-china-in-quantum/; Jamie Gaida et al., "ASPI's Critical Technology Tracker," Australian Strategic Policy Institute, www.aspi.org.au/report/critical-technology-tracker, accessed December 9, 2024.
53. "How Could FPV Drones Change Warfare?," *The Economist*, August 4, 2023, www.economist.com/the-economist-explains/2023/08/04/how-could-fpv-drones-change-warfare; "How Cheap Drones Are Transforming Warfare in Ukraine," *The Economist*, February 5, 2024, www.economist.com/interactive/science-and-technology/2024/02/05/cheap-racing-drones-offer-precision-warfare-at-scale; "How Ukraine Uses Cheap AI-Guided Drones to Deadly Effect Against Russia," *The Economist*, December 2, 2024, www.economist.com/europe/2024/12/02/how-ukraine-uses-cheap-ai-guided-drones-to-deadly-effect-against-russia.
54. For discussion of the "kill chain" concept in various contexts and published before the 2022 Ukraine invasion, see Christian Brose, *The Kill Chain: Defending America in the Future of High-Tech Warfare* (Hachette UK, 2020).
55. Milford Beagle, Jason C. Slider, and Matthew R. Arrol, "The Graveyard of Command Posts: What Chornobaivka Should Teach Us About Command and Control in Large-Scale Combat Operations," *The Military Review, U.S. Army University Press*, May–June 2023, www.armyupress.army.mil/Journals/Military-Review/English-Edition-Archives

/May-June-2023/Graveyard-of-Command-Posts/; Sam Skove, "How a US Armor Brigade Is Applying Lessons from Ukraine," *Defense One*, September 24, 2024, www.defenseone.com/technology/2024/09/armored-unit-adapts-old-tech-lessons-ukraine/399785/; Katie Crombe and John A. Nagl, "A Call to Action: Lessons from Ukraine for the Future Force," *The US Army War College Quarterly: Parameters* 53, no. 3 (2023): 4.

56. Daphné Richemond-Barak, "Israel Must Destroy Hamas's Tunnels," *Foreign Affairs*, November 9, 2023, www.foreignaffairs.com/israel/israel-must-destroy-hamas-tunnels; Sophia Goodfriend, "Israel's High-Tech Surveillance Was Never Going to Bring Peace," *Foreign Policy* (blog), December 12, 2024, https://foreignpolicy.com/2023/10/30/israel-palestine-gaza-hamas-war-idf-high-tech-surveillance/.
57. Roberts, *The Storm of War*, 319.
58. Bousquet, 96.
59. Bousquet, 129–30.
60. Beevor, 432, 436, 437.
61. Robert Beckhusen, "Russia Won World War II Thanks to Its Snipers—This Is What They Used," *The National Interest*, April 16, 2021, https://nationalinterest.org/blog/reboot/russia-won-world-war-ii-thanks-its-snipers%E2%80%94-what-they-used-183052.
62. Beevor, 438–39.
63. Roberts, *The Storm of War*, 330.
64. Beevor, 448.
65. Beevor, 453; Roberts, *The Storm of War*, 327.
66. David Kilcullen, *The Dragons and the Snakes: How the Rest Learned to Fight the West* (Oxford University Press, 2020), chapter 5.
67. Frith, *Making Up the Mind*, 101–2.
68. Friston, "The Free Energy Principle."
69. Thomas Parr, Giovanni Pezzulo, and Karl J. Friston, *Active Inference: The Free Energy Principle in Mind, Brain, and Behavior* (MIT Press, 2022), vii.
70. For an accessible introduction to *Theses on Feuerbach* by a major modern philosopher see Singer, 43, from which I take these interpretations.
71. Spence, *The Search for Modern China*, 368–69.
72. Rebecca E. Karl, *Mao Zedong and China in the Twentieth-Century World: A Concise History* (Duke University Press, 2010), 59.
73. "On Practice, July 1937, in the Selected Works of Mao Tse-Tung," Marxists Internet Archive, www.marxists.org/reference/archive/mao/selected-works/volume-1/mswv1_16.htm, accessed November 28, 2024.
74. Bousquet, 108–18.
75. Roger Mola, "Super Helmet," *Smithsonian Magazine*, September 2017, www.smithsonianmag.com/air-space-magazine/super-helmet-180964342/.

6: LEARNING TO ACT

1. *The World at War* (1973–1974), season 1, episode 22, "Japan (1941–1945)." Directed by David Elstein. Aired April 10, 1974, on Thames Television.

2. Matthews, *Head Strong*, 39.
3. "How the Brain Controls the Body," lecture by Daniel Wolpert, posted on June 30, 2021, by The Royal Society, 41 min., 50 sec., www.youtube.com/watch?v=WGtcD2UDUyA.
4. Gazzaniga et al., 337–39.
5. Gazzaniga et al., 365–66.
6. Gazzaniga et al., 366.
7. Daniel McNamee and Daniel M. Wolpert, "Internal Models in Biological Control," *Annual Review of Control, Robotics, and Autonomous Systems* 2, no. 1 (2019): 339–64, doi.org/10.1146/annurev-control-060117-105206.
8. Cassandra Sampaio-Baptista, Zeena-Britt Sanders, and Heidi Johansen-Berg, "Structural Plasticity in Adulthood with Motor Learning and Stroke Rehabilitation," *Annual Review of Neuroscience* 41, no. 1 (2018): 25–40, doi.org/10.1146/annurev-neuro-080317-062015.
9. Sampaio-Baptista et al.
10. James B. Heald, Máté Lengyel, and Daniel M. Wolpert, "Contextual Inference Underlies the Learning of Sensorimotor Repertoires," *Nature* 600, no. 7889 (December 2021): 489–93, doi.org/10.1038/s41586-021-04129-3. Also see comment by Anne G. E. Collins and Samuel D. McDougle, "Context Is Key for Learning Motor Skills," *Nature* 600, no. 7889 (December 2021): 387–88, doi.org/10.1038/d41586-021-03028-x.
11. This is a debated area, but the basic idea seems sound. Brooke N. Macnamara and Megha Maitra, "The Role of Deliberate Practice in Expert Performance: Revisiting Ericsson, Krampe & Tesch-Römer (1993)," *Royal Society Open Science* 6, no. 8 (August 21, 2019): 190327, doi.org/10.1098/rsos.190327; Brooke N. Macnamara, David Moreau, and David Z. Hambrick, "The Relationship Between Deliberate Practice and Performance in Sports: A Meta-Analysis," *Perspectives on Psychological Science* 11, no. 3 (May 1, 2016): 333–50, doi.org/10.1177/1745691616635591; K. Anders Ericsson, Ralf T. Krampe, and Clemens Tesch-Römer, "The Role of Deliberate Practice in the Acquisition of Expert Performance," *Psychological Review* 100, no. 3 (1993): 363–406, doi.org/10.1037/0033-295X.100.3.363.
12. Mark F. Cancian, Matthew Cancian, and Eric Heginbotham, "The First Battle of the Next War: Wargaming a Chinese Invasion of Taiwan," Center for Strategic & International Studies, January 9, 2023, www.csis.org/analysis/first-battle-next-war-wargaming-chinese-invasion-taiwan.
13. David Epstein, *Range: How Generalists Triumph in a Specialized World* (Macmillan, 2020), 5–18, 21, 64, 74, 88.
14. John Keegan, *A History of Warfare* (Pimlico, 1993), 268–69.
15. "Flavius Josephus: Of the War, Book III, Chapter 5," http://penelope.uchicago.edu/josephus/war-3.html, accessed November 28, 2024.
16. John Childs, "Maurice of Nassau," in Andrew Roberts, ed., *The Art of War: Great Commanders of the Modern World* (Quercus, 2009), 22.
17. "Sun Tzu and The Art of War," *In Our Time*, BBC Radio 4, www.bbc.co.uk/programmes/b09smh59, accessed November 28, 2024.
18. Hew Strachan, "Training, Morale and Modern War," *Journal of Contemporary History* 41, no. 2 (2006): 211–27.
19. Michael Savage, "How British 'Tank-Busters' Are Helping Ukraine Halt Russian Attack," *The Observer*, March 20, 2022, www.theguardian.com/world/2022/mar/20/how-british-tank-busters-are-helping-ukraine-halt-russian-attack; Janne Haaland Matlary

and Rob Johnson, *NATO and the Russian War in Ukraine: Strategic Integration and Military Interoperability* (Oxford University Press, 2024), 202.

20. "Taiwan Is a Vital Island That Is Under Serious Threat," *The Economist*, March 6, 2023, www.economist.com/special-report/2023/03/06/taiwan-is-a-vital-island-that-is-under-serious-threat?frsc=dg%7Ce.
21. Strachan.
22. David P. Harding, "Heinz Guderian as the Agent of Change: His Significant Impact on the Development of German Armored Forces Between the World Wars," *Army History* 31 (Summer 1994): 26–34, www.jstor.org/stable/26304190?seq=6.
23. As the Yale historian Paul Kennedy described, *Blitzkrieg* rested on: (1) mobile and highly trained infantry units; (2) unorthodox fast attack; and (3) an air force brilliantly set up for close infantry support. Kennedy, *Engineers of Victory*, 204.
24. Kennedy, *Engineers of Victory*, 16.
25. Overy, *War*, 363.
26. Overy, *Blood and Ruins*, 228.
27. Richard J. Overy, *Why the Allies Won*, second edition (London: Pimlico, 2006), 109.
28. Peter B. Mersky, *Time of the Aces: Marine Pilots in the Solomons, 1942–1944*, (History and Museums Division, Headquarters, U.S. Marine Corps), 31.
29. Co-evolution is a major mechanism for change in many types of biological and other systems: see Holland, *Complexity*, 54–55; John H. Holland, *Signals and Boundaries: Building Blocks for Complex Adaptive Systems* (MIT Press, 2012), 18–20.
30. Raihani, 91–95.
31. Raihani, 93–94.
32. Esther Herrmann et al., "Humans Have Evolved Specialized Skills of Social Cognition: The Cultural Intelligence Hypothesis," *Science* 317, no. 5843 (September 7, 2007): 1360–66, doi.org/10.1126/science.1146282; Esther Herrmann et al., "The Structure of Individual Differences in the Cognitive Abilities of Children and Chimpanzees," *Psychological Science* 21, no. 1 (January 2010): 102–10, doi.org/10.1177/0956797609356511; Henrich, 13-15.
33. Henrich, 19, 105.
34. Henrich, 108–9.
35. Henrich, 64–65.
36. Henrich, 51.
37. Laurence Steinberg et al., "Around the World, Adolescence Is a Time of Heightened Sensation Seeking and Immature Self-Regulation," *Developmental Science* 21, no. 2 (March 2018), doi.org/10.1111/desc.12532.
38. "Demographics of the U.S. Military," Council on Foreign Relations, last updated July 13, 2020, www.cfr.org/backgrounder/demographics-us-military.
39. Henrich, 63–64.
40. John Keegan, *A History of Warfare* (Pimlico, 1993), 268–69.
41. Caleb E. Finch and Steven N. Austad, "Primate Aging in the Mammalian Scheme: The Puzzle of Extreme Variation in Brain Aging," *Age* 34, no. 5 (January 5, 2012): 1075–91, doi.org/10.1007/s1137-011-9355-9.
42. Raihani, 104–7.

43. Henrich, 131–33.
44. Russell A. Hart, *Guderian: Panzer Pioneer or Myth Maker?* (Potomac Books, 2006), 24.
45. Daniel Kurtz-Phelan, *The China Mission: George Marshall's Unfinished War, 1945–1947* (W. W. Norton & Company, 2018), 18.
46. John R. Maass, "The Benning Revolution," in Jon T. Hoffman, ed., *A History of Innovation: U.S. Army Adaptation in War and Peace* (Center of Military History, United States Army, 2009), https://purl.fdlp.gov/GPO/LPS121770.
47. Maass, 30.
48. Maass, 32.
49. Maass, 33.
50. "Human Characteristics: What Does It Mean to Be Human," Smithsonian National Museum of Natural History, last updated January 3, 2024, https://humanorigins.si.edu/human-characteristics.
51. Dirk Leder et al., "The Wooden Artifacts from Schöningen's Spear Horizon and Their Place in Human Evolution," *Proceedings of the National Academy of Sciences (PNAS)* 121, no. 15: e2320484121, doi.org/10.1073/pnas.2320484121; "Oldest Wooden Spear," Smithsonian National Museum of Natural History, last updated June 29, 2022, https://humanorigins.si.edu/evidence/behavior/getting-food/oldest-wooden-spear.
52. Henrich, 65, 69–71, 286–87.
53. A. Iriki, M. Tanaka, and Y. Iwamura, "Coding of Modified Body Schema During Tool Use by Macaque Postcentral Neurones," *Neuroreport* 7, no. 14 (October 1, 1996): 2325–30, doi.org/10.1097/00001756-199610020-00010; M. M. Quallo et al., "Gray and White Matter Changes Associated with Tool-Use Learning in Macaque Monkeys," *Proceedings of the National Academy of Sciences (PNAS)* 106, no. 43: 18379–84; doi.org/10.1073/pnas.0909751106.
54. Paulina Kieliba et al., "Robotic Hand Augmentation Drives Changes in Neural Body Representation," *Science Robotics* 6, no. 54 (May 19, 2021): eabd7935, doi.org/10.1126/scirobotics.abd7935; Hunter R. Schone et al., "Expert Tool Users Show Increased Differentiation Between Visual Representations of Hands and Tools," *Journal of Neuroscience* 41, no. 13 (March 31, 2021): 2980–89, doi.org/10.1523/JNEUROSCI.2489-20.2020.
55. Ian Levy, "So Long and Thanks for All the Bits," National Cyber Security Centre (blog post), October 27, 2022, www.ncsc.gov.uk/blog-post/so-long-thanks-for-all-the-bits.
56. Anika Binnendijk, Timothy Marler, and Elizabeth M. Bartels, "Brain-Computer Interfaces: U.S. Military Applications and Implications, an Initial Assessment," RAND Corporation, August 27, 2020, www.rand.org/pubs/research_reports/RR2996.html; "iHuman: Blurring Lines between Mind and Machine," The Royal Society, September 2019, www.royalsociety.org/ihuman-perspective; "Human Augmentation—the Dawn of a New Paradigm," UK Ministry of Defence, May 13, 2021, www.gov.uk/government/publications/human-augmentation-the-dawn-of-a-new-paradigm; Matthias Stangl, Sabrina L. Maoz, and Nanthia Suthana, "Mobile Cognition: Imaging the Human Brain in the 'Real World,'" *Nature Reviews Neuroscience* 24, no. 6 (June 2023): 347–62, doi.org/10.1038/s41583-023-00692-y; William Hannas et al., "Bibliometric Analysis of China's Non-Therapeutic Brain-Computer Interface Research," Georgetown University, Center for Security and Emerging Technology, March 2024, https://cset.georgetown.edu/publication/bibliometric-analysis-of-chinas-non-therapeutic-brain-computer-interface-research/.
57. Maxwell J. D. Ramstead, Samuel P. L. Veissière, and Laurence J. Kirmayer, "Cultural

Affordances: Scaffolding Local Worlds Through Shared Intentionality and Regimes of Attention," *Frontiers in Psychology* 7 (2016), doi.org/10.3389/fpsyg.2016.01090.

58. Henrich, 229.
59. Henrich, 229.
60. The "Overton window" describes what range of actions are politically possible, that is, what politics currently affords. And that can be shifted: see Maggie Astor, "How the Politically Unthinkable Can Become Mainstream," *The New York Times*, February 26, 2019, www.nytimes.com/2019/02/26/us/politics/overton-window-democrats.html.
61. John Maynard Keynes, *The General Theory of Employment Interest and Money* (Macmillan, 1936), chapter 24.
62. Beevor, 532.
63. Beevor, 533.
64. Beevor, 536–37.
65. Beevor, 543.
66. Beevor, 458.
67. Roberts, *Masters and Commanders*, 12, 23–25.
68. Forrest C. Pogue, *George C. Marshall: Ordeal and Hope 1939–1943*, (Viking, 1966) 337.
69. Omar Nelson Bradley, *A General's Life: An Autobiography* (Simon and Schuster, 1983), 20, 63.

PART III: END AND START AGAIN

1. Kenneth J. W. Craik, *The Nature of Explanation* (Cambridge University Press, 1943), 61.
2. McNamee and Wolpert, "Internal Models in Biological Control."
3. Matthew Cobb, *The Idea of the Brain: A History* (Profile Books, 2020), 186–87.
4. Cobb, 178–81, 183–84.
5. Cobb, 203.

7: OTHERS' INTENTIONS

1. *Dynasties*, series 1, episode 2, "Chimpanzee." Aired November 11, 2018, on BBC One; Lucy Jones, "What Happened to David the Chimp from Dynasties?," *BBC Earth*, www.bbcearth.com/news/what-happened-to-david-the-chimp-from-dynasties, accessed November 28, 2024.
2. Winston S. Churchill, *The Second World War*, volume V (Cassell, 1951).
3. Chris Frith and Uta Frith, *What Makes Us Social?* (MIT Press, 2023), 141, chapter 10.
4. Heinz Wimmer and Josef Perner, "Beliefs About Beliefs: Representation and Constraining Function of Wrong Beliefs in Young Children's Understanding of Deception," *Cognition* 13, no. 1 (January 1, 1983): 103–28, doi.org/10.1016/0010-0277(83)90004-5.
5. Sarah-Jayne Blakemore et al., "Adolescent Development of the Neural Circuitry for Thinking About Intentions," *Social Cognitive and Affective Neuroscience* 2, no. 2 (June 1, 2007): 130–39, doi.org/10.1093/scan/nsm009.
6. Nicholas D. Wright et al., "Neural Segregation of Objective and Contextual Aspects of

Fairness," *The Journal of Neuroscience* 31, no. 14 (April 6, 2011): 5244–52, doi.org/10.1523/jneurosci.3138-10.2011.

7. Frith and Frith, chapter 10.
8. A. N. Hampton, P. Bossaerts, and J. P. O'Doherty, "Neural Correlates of Mentalizing-Related Computations During Strategic Interactions in Humans," *Proceedings of the National Academy of Sciences* 105, no. 18 (2008): 6741, doi.org/10.1073/pnas.0711099105.
9. Lara Bardi, Davide Gheza, and Marcel Brass, "TPJ-M1 Interaction in the Control of Shared Representations: New Insights from tDCS and TMS Combined," *NeuroImage* 146 (February 1, 2017): 734–40, doi.org/10.1016/j.neuroimage.2016.10.050.
10. Aditi Arora, Matthias Schurz, and Josef Perner, "Systematic Comparison of Brain Imaging Meta-Analyses of ToM with vPT," *BioMed Research International* 2017, no. 1 (2017): 6875850, doi.org/10.1155/2017/6875850; Elizabeth R. Chrastil, "Heterogeneity in Human Retrosplenial Cortex: A Review of Function and Connectivity," *Behavioral Neuroscience* 132, no. 5 (2018): 317–38, doi.org/10.1037/bne0000261.
11. Frith and Frith, 152–55.
12. Fumihiro Kano et al., "Great Apes Use Self-Experience to Anticipate an Agent's Action in a False-Belief Test," *Proceedings of the National Academy of Sciences* 116, no. 42 (October 15, 2019): 20904–9, doi.org/10.1073/pnas.1910095116. For further species, see Christopher Krupenye and Josep Call, "Theory of Mind in Animals: Current and Future Directions," *WIREs Cognitive Science* 10, no. 6 (2019): e1503, doi.org/10.1002/wcs.1503.
13. Raihani, 126.
14. Raihani, 142.
15. A. W. Woolley et al., "Evidence for a Collective Intelligence Factor in the Performance of Human Groups," *Science* 330, no. 6004 (2010): 686–88, doi.org/10.1126/science.1193147.
16. Raihani, 196, 198.
17. Jakob Nielsen, "AI: First New UI Paradigm in 60 Years," Nielsen Norman Group, June 18, 2023, www.nngroup.com/articles/ai-paradigm.
18. Roberts, *The Storm of War*, 54, 56–57; German application in Russia, e.g., Beevor, 233; David French, *Raising Churchill's Army: The British Army and the War Against Germany, 1919–1945* (Oxford University Press, 2000), 20.
19. Roberts, *The Storm of War*, 57.
20. "Army Leadership Doctrine," Director Leadership, Commandant Royal Military Academy Sandhurst, British Ministry of Defence Crown copyright, www.army.mod.uk/media/14177/21-07-267-army-leadership-doctrine-web.pdf.
21. Stephen E. Ambrose, *Eisenhower: Soldier and President* (Simon and Schuster, 1990), 76.
22. Roberts, *Masters and Commanders*.
23. Samuel Newland and Clayton Chun, *The European Campaign: Its Origins and Conduct* (U.S. Army War College Press, 2011), chapter 4, 142.
24. "FBI Hosts Five Eyes Summit to Launch Drive to Secure Innovation in Response to Intelligence Threats," Press Release, Federal Bureau of Investigation, October 16, 2023, www.fbi.gov/news/press-releases/fbi-hosts-five-eyes-summit-to-launch-drive-to-secure-innovation-in-response-to-intelligence-threats; BBC World Service, "What Is Five Eyes?," *The Explanation*, December 11, 2023, www.bbc.co.uk/programmes/w3ct4z74.
25. Quoted in Roberts, *The Storm of War*, 26.

26. To be sure, Hitler was a dictator throughout the war, and it was not simply a case of Hitler ignoring expert generals like those who developed May 1940's "sickle cut" (Roberts, *The Storm of War*, 600–602), but he took personal command on the Eastern Front in December 1941 and thereafter listened to senior generals less and less (Roberts, *The Storm of War*, 590–94).
27. Roberts, *The Storm of War*, 602.
28. Roberts, *Masters and Commanders*, 105.
29. "Archbishop of Canterbury Learns Identity of Biological Father," *BBC*, April 9, 2016, www.bbc.co.uk/news/uk-36002621.
30. "Most of the World's Workers Are 'Quiet Quitters,'" *Financial Times*, June 25, 2023, https://on.ft.com/3Xlqyy9.
31. Hampton et al.
32. Wright, *Artificial Intelligence, China, Russia, and the Global Order*, chapter 3.
33. "The Truth About Why Kids Lie, with Victoria Talwar, Ph.D.," *Speaking of Psychology*, American Psychological Association, www.apa.org/news/podcasts/speaking-of-psychology/why-kids-lie, accessed November 29, 2024.
34. Martha J. Farah et al., "Functional MRI-Based Lie Detection: Scientific and Societal Challenges," *Nature Reviews Neuroscience* 15, no. 2 (February 2014): 123–31, doi.org/10.1038/nrn3665.
35. Neil Garrett et al., "The Brain Adapts to Dishonesty," *Nature Neuroscience* 19, no. 12 (December 2016): 1727–32, doi.org/10.1038/nn.4426.
36. Gazzaniga et al., 278.
37. Gazzaniga et al., 283.
38. Stephen L. Macknik et al., "Attention and Awareness in Stage Magic: Turning Tricks into Research," *Nature Reviews Neuroscience* 9, no. 11 (November 2008): 871–79, doi.org/10.1038/nrn2473.
39. Daniel J. Simons and Christopher F. Chabris, "Gorillas in Our Midst: Sustained Inattentional Blindness for Dynamic Events," *Perception* 28, no. 9 (September 1, 1999): 1059–74, doi.org/10.1068/p281059.
40. Macknik et al.
41. Macknik et al.
42. Charles F. Bond and Bella DePaulo, "Accuracy of Deception Judgments," *Personality and Social Psychology Review* 10, no. 3 (2006): 214–34; doi.org/10.1207/s15327957pspr1003_2.
43. Bella M. DePaulo et al., "Cues to Deception," *Psychological Bulletin* 129, no. 1 (2003): 74–118, doi.org/10.1037/0033-2909.129.1.74; Aldert Vrij, *Detecting Lies and Deceit: Pitfalls and Opportunities*, second edition (John Wiley & Sons, 2008).
44. Farah et al.
45. You can read about military deception in officially published documents, e.g., "Military Deception," Joint Publication 3.13–4, U.S. Joint Chiefs of Staff, January 26, 2012, https://jfsc.ndu.edu/portals/72/documents/jc2ios/additional_reading/1c3-jp_3-13-4_mildec.pdf.
46. David E. Sanger, *The Perfect Weapon: War, Sabotage, and Fear in the Cyber Age* (Penguin Random House, 2018), 116–17; Brendan I. Koerner, "Inside the Cyberattack That Shocked the US Government," *Wired*, October 23, 2016, www.wired.com/2016/10/inside-cyberattack-shocked-us-government/.

47. Sue-Lin Wong, "Hide and Bide," The Prince, *The Economist*, September 28, 2022, www.economist.com/podcasts/2022/09/28/2-hide-and-bide.
48. Carissa Véliz, *Privacy Is Power: Why and How You Should Take Back Control of Your Data* (Bantam Press, 2020), chapter 4.
49. Beevor, 735.
50. Bruce R. Pirnie, "Soviet Deception Operations During World War II," United States Army Center of Military History, August 30, 1985, https://apps.dtic.mil/sti/citations/ADA165980; Beevor, 708.
51. Beevor, 755.
52. Roberts, *The Storm of War*, 481–83.
53. Tony Judt, *Postwar: A History of Europe Since 1945* (Penguin Press, 2005).
54. Gilbert, *The First World War*, 499.
55. Winston S. Churchill, *The Second World War*, volume I (Cassell, 1948), v.
56. Ina Zweiniger-Bargielowska, "Bread Rationing in Britain, July 1946–July 1948," *Twentieth Century British History* 4, no. 1 (January 1, 1993): 57–85, doi.org/10.1093/tcbh/4.1.57; Johannes-Dieter Steinert, "British Humanitarian Assistance: Wartime Planning and Postwar Realities," *Journal of Contemporary History* 43, no. 3 (2008): 421–35.
57. Giada Cordoni et al., "Domestic Pigs (*Sus Scrofa*) Engage in Non-Random Post-Conflict Affiliation with Third Parties: Cognitive and Functional Implications," *Animal Cognition* 26, no. 2 (March 2023): 687–701, doi.org/10.1007/s10071-022-01688-4.
58. Cordoni et al.
59. Camerer, 83–100; Nicholas D Wright and Karim Sadjadpour, "The Neuroscience Guide to Negotiations With Iran," *The Atlantic*, January 14, 2014.
60. Jan B. Engelman et al., "The Neural Circuitry of Affect-Induced Distortions of Trust," *Science Advances* 5, no. 3 (March 13, 2019), doi.org/10.1126/sciadv.aau3413; Brooks King-Casas et al., "The Rupture and Repair of Cooperation in Borderline Personality Disorder," *Science* 321, no. 5890 (August 8, 2008): 806–10, doi.org/10.1126/science.1156902; Wright and Sadjadpour.
61. Michael I. Handel, *The Diplomacy of Surprise, Hitler, Nixon, Sadat* (Center for International Affairs, Harvard University, 1981), 324–28; Christopher Roger Mitchell, *Gestures of Conciliation: Factors Contributing to Successful Olive Branches* (St. Martin's Press, 2000), xiii–xiv, 27–29, 119–20, 227.
62. Quoted in Robert Jervis, *Perception and Misperception in International Politics* (Princeton University Press, 1976), 83.
63. MacMillan, *War*, 248–49.
64. Margaret MacMillan, *The War That Ended Peace: The Road to 1914* (Allen Lane, 2013), xxxi.
65. Eva Michaels, "Caught off Guard? Evaluating How External Experts in Germany Warned About Russia's War on Ukraine," *Intelligence and National Security* 39, no. 3 (April 15, 2024): 420–42, doi.org/10.1080/02684527.2024.2330133; Maia De La Baume, "France Spooked by Intelligence Failures," *Politico*, April 6, 2022, www.politico.eu/article/france-military-intelligence-failure-russia-invasion-ukraine/; Shane Harris et al., "Road to War: U.S. Struggled to Convince Allies, and Zelensky, of Risk of Invasion," *The Washington Post*, August 16, 2022, www.washingtonpost.com/national-security/interactive/2022/ukraine-road-to-war/.

66. I have discussed these issues with dozens of leading thinkers in the United States, United Kingdom, other western governments, and leading universities since Xi came to power in 2012. For a publicly available example, see Richard N. Rosecrance and Steven E. Miller, *The Next Great War?: The Roots of World War I and the Risk of U.S.-China Conflict* (MIT Press, 2015).

67. Graham Allison, "Could the U.S. Lose a War with China over Taiwan?," *The National Interest*, October 29, 2021, https://nationalinterest.org/feature/could-us-lose-war-china-over-taiwan-195686.

68. Cancian et al.

69. Markus Garlauskas, "The United States and Its Allies Must Be Ready to Deter a Two-Front War and Nuclear Attacks in East Asia," Atlantic Council, August 16, 2023, www.atlanticcouncil.org/in-depth-research-reports/report/the-united-states-and-its-allies-must-be-ready-to-deter-a-two-front-war-and-nuclear-attacks-in-east-asia/.

70. "China Now Has the World's Largest Fleet, Alarming Its Pacific Rival," *The Economist*, September 26, 2020, www.economist.com/united-states/2020/09/26/china-now-has-the-worlds-largest-fleet-alarming-its-pacific-rival.

71. Overy, *Blood and Ruins*, 596.

72. Andrew Roberts, *Leadership in War* (Penguin Random House, 2019), 57.

73. Associated Press, "President Sent Sympathy on Hitler's Death," *The Guardian*, December 30, 2005, www.theguardian.com/world/2005/dec/31/secondworldwar.ireland; Mervyn O'Driscoll, "Ireland and the Nazis: a Troubled History," *The Irish Times*, May 9, 2017, www.irishtimes.com/culture/books/ireland-and-the-nazis-a-troubled-history-1.3076579.

74. Overy, *Blood and Ruins*, 646–48; MacMillan, *War*, 248–49.

75. Overy, *Blood and Ruins*, 648–49.

76. Numbers of conscientious objectors from Overy, *Blood and Ruins*, 657, 659. Total personnel figures from Robert Hansberry, "The World's War in Europe—History of Government," April 28, 2015, https://history.blog.gov.uk/2015/04/28/the-worlds-war-in-europe/; Matthews, *Head Strong*, 39.

77. "Number of Armed Conflicts, World," Uppsala Conflict Data Program, Our World in Data, last updated August 26, 2024, https://ourworldindata.org/grapher/number-of-armed-conflicts.

78. Seth Lazar, "War," *The Stanford Encyclopedia of Philosophy* (Spring 2020), first published May 3, 2016, https://plato.stanford.edu/archives/spr2020/entries/war/.

79. Clare Kelly and Redmond O'Connell, "Can Neuroscience Change the Way We View Morality?," *Neuron* 108, no. 4 (November 25, 2020): 604–7, doi.org/10.1016/j.neuron.2020.10.024.

80. For a comparison of the three main western ideas, see Jörg Schroth, "Ethical Deontology," *Oxford Bibliographies*, January 15, 2019, www.oxfordbibliographies.com/display/document/obo-9780195396577/obo-9780195396577-0383.xml. Important commonalities and differences exist between western and Chinese philosophy, and in both cases there is also a huge range of thought. For comparisons to classical Chinese philosophy, see David Wong, "Comparative Philosophy: Chinese and Western," section 3, revised September 5, 2024, *The Stanford Encyclopedia of Philosophy* (Fall 2024), https://plato.stanford.edu/archives/fall2024/entries/comparphil-chiwes/; David Wong, "Chinese Ethics," revised August 10, 2023, *The Stanford Encyclopedia of Philosophy* (Summer

2024), https://plato.stanford.edu/archives/sum2024/entries/ethics-chinese/; Chris Fraser, "Mohism," revised September 1, 2024, *The Stanford Encyclopedia of Philosophy* (Fall 2024), https://plato.stanford.edu/archives/fall2024/entries/mohism/.

81. Tatsuya Kameda et al., "Rawlsian Maximin Rule Operates as a Common Cognitive Anchor in Distributive Justice and Risky Decisions," *Proceedings of the National Academy of Sciences* 113, no. 42: 11817–22, doi.org/10.1073/pnas.1602641113.
82. Wright, "Global Strategy Amidst the Globe's Cultures."
83. Edmond Awad et al., "Universals and Variations in Moral Decisions Made in 42 Countries by 70,000 Participants," *Proceedings of the National Academy of Sciences* 117, no. 5: 2332–37, doi.org/10.1073/pnas.1911517117.
84. H. Clark Barrett and Rebecca R. Saxe, "Are Some Cultures More Mind-Minded in Their Moral Judgements than Others?," *Philosophical Transactions of the Royal Society B: Biological Sciences* 376, no. 1838 (October 4, 2021): 20200288, doi.org/10.1098/rstb.2020.0288.
85. Jean-François Bonnefon, Azim Shariff, and Iyad Rahwan, "The Social Dilemma of Autonomous Vehicles," *Science* 352, no. 6293 (June 24, 2016): 1573–76, doi.org/10.1126/science.aaf2654.
86. Gaddis, 21–22.
87. Gaddis, 26.
88. Gaddis, 26–27.
89. Definitions are from the following: For gray zone, see Nicholas D. Wright, *From Control to Influence: Cognition in the Grey Zone*, volume 3 (Intelligent Biology, 2019), www.intelligentbiology.co.uk. For war, see Colin S. Gray, "War—Continuity in Change, and Change in Continuity," *Parameters* 40, no. 2 (2010): 5–6, doi.org/10.55540/0031-1723.2521. For peace, see Michael Howard, *The Invention of Peace: Reflections on War and International Order* (Profile Books, 2001), 2.
90. Gaddis, 6.

8: LEADERS AND SOCIAL ALCHEMY

1. Robin Dunbar's influential "social brain hypothesis" proposed an evolutionary link between the size of primate groups and the size of their "neocortex" ("neo" means newer and this refers to the evolutionarily newer cortex that makes up about 90 percent of our human cerebral hemispheres). Considerable evidence supports the hypothesis that predicts human group size at around 150: see Robin I. M. Dunbar, "The Social Brain Hypothesis—Thirty Years On," *Annals of Human Biology* 51, no. 1 (December 31, 2024): 2359920, doi.org/10.1080/03014460.2024.2359920. Others, however, dispute the precise figure, e.g., Patrik Lindenfors, Andreas Wartel, and Johan Lind, "'Dunbar's Number' Deconstructed," *Biology Letters* 17, no. 5 (May 5, 2021): 20210158, doi.org/10.1098/rsbl.2021.0158. But despite such debates, the key point remains that human groups are unusually large: see Tamas David-Barrett, "Human Group Size Puzzle: Why It Is Odd That We Live in Large Societies," *Royal Society Open Science* 10, no. 8 (August 16, 2023): 230559, doi.org/10.1098/rsos.230559. The largest known chimp community, for example, consists of fewer than two hundred: "Ngogo Chimpanzee Project," Arizona State University School of Human Evolution and Social Change, https://shesc.asu.edu/research/projects/ngogo-chimpanzee-project-0, accessed November 20, 2024.
2. Seth, 150.

3. Seth, 151–53.
4. Gazzaniga et al., 580–84; Quote below in Seth, 158.
5. Catriona M. Morrison and Martin A. Conway, "First Words and First Memories," *Cognition* 116, no. 1 (July 1, 2010): 23–32, doi.org/10.1016/j.cognition.2010.03.011.
6. Dan P. McAdams, "The Psychological Self as Actor, Agent, and Author," *Perspectives on Psychological Science: A Journal of the Association for Psychological Science* 8, no. 3 (May 2013): 272–95, doi.org/10.1177/1745691612464657.
7. Kristina L. Steiner, David B. Pillemer, and Dorthe Kirkegaard Thomsen, "Writing About Life Story Chapters Increases Self-Esteem: Three Experimental Studies," *Journal of Personality* 87, no. 5 (2019): 962–80, doi.org/10.1111/jopy.12449; Brady K. Jones, Mesmin Destin, and Dan P. McAdams, "Telling Better Stories: Competence-Building Narrative Themes Increase Adolescent Persistence and Academic Achievement," *Journal of Experimental Social Psychology* 76 (May 1, 2018): 76–80, doi.org/10.1016/j.jesp.2017.12.006; Claire Mitchell and Elaine Reese, "*Growing Memories*: Coaching Mothers in Elaborative Reminiscing with Toddlers Benefits Adolescents' Turning-Point Narratives and Wellbeing," *Journal of Personality* 90, no. 6 (December 2022): 887–901, doi.org/10.1111/jopy.12703. But note, e.g., Lauren E. Jennings and Kate C. McLean, "Storying Away Self-Doubt: Can Narratives Dispel Threats to the Self?," *Journal of Research in Personality* 47, no. 4 (August 1, 2013): 317–29, doi.org/10.1016/j.jrp.2013.02.006.
8. Dan McAdams, "Narrative Identity," in Seth J. Schwartz, Koen Luyckx, and Vivian L. Vignoles, eds., *Handbook of Identity Theory and Research* (Springer, 2011), doi.org/10.1007/978-1-4419-7988-9_5.
9. This subsection on the social self draws on chapter 8 in the great book by Frith and Frith.
10. Haley E. Kragness, Elizabeth K. Johnson, and Laura K. Cirelli, "The Song, Not the Singer: Infants Prefer to Listen to Familiar Songs, Regardless of Singer Identity," *Developmental Science* 25, no. 1 (January 2022): e13149, doi.org/10.1111/desc.13149.
11. Yarrow Dunham, Andrew Scott Baron, and Susan Carey, "Consequences of 'Minimal' Group Affiliations in Children," *Child Development* 82, no. 3 (2011): 793–811, doi.org/10.1111/j.1467-8624.2011.01577.x.
12. Naomi Ellemers, Russell Spears, and Bertjan Doosje, "Self and Social Identity," *Annual Review of Psychology* 53, no. 1 (2002): 161–86, doi.org/10.1146/annurev.psych.53.100901.135228.
13. Armita Golkar, Vasco Castro, and Andreas Olsson, "Social Learning of Fear and Safety Is Determined by the Demonstrator's Racial Group," *Biology Letters* 11, no. 1 (January 2015): 20140817, doi.org/10.1098/rsbl.2014.0817.
14. Pyungwon Kang et al., "Why We Learn Less from Observing Outgroups," *Journal of Neuroscience* 41, no. 1 (January 6, 2021): 144–52, doi.org/10.1523/JNEUROSCI.0926-20.2020.
15. Carina C. J. M. de Klerk et al., "Selective Facial Mimicry of Native over Foreign Speakers in Preverbal Infants," *Journal of Experimental Child Psychology* 183 (2019): 33–47, doi.org/10.1016/j.jecp.2019.01.015.
16. Marco F. H. Schmidt, Hannes Rakoczy, and Michael Tomasello, "Young Children Enforce Social Norms Selectively Depending on the Violator's Group Affiliation," *Cognition* 124, no. 3 (September 1, 2012): 325–33, doi.org/10.1016/j.cognition.2012.06.004.
17. Naomi I. Eisenberger, "The Pain of Social Disconnection: Examining the Shared Neural

Underpinnings of Physical and Social Pain," *Nature Reviews Neuroscience* 13, no. 6 (June 2012): 421–34, doi.org/10.1038/nrn3231; Stephanie Cacioppo et al., "A Quantitative Meta-Analysis of Functional Imaging Studies of Social Rejection," *Scientific Reports* 3 (June 19, 2013): 2027, doi.org/10.1038/srep02027; Willem W. A. Sleegers, Travis Proulx, and Ilja van Beest, "The Social Pain of Cyberball: Decreased Pupillary Reactivity to Exclusion Cues," *Journal of Experimental Social Psychology* 69 (March 1, 2017): 187–200, doi.org/10.1016/j.jesp.2016.08.004.

18. Judt, 58.
19. David A. Messenger and Katrin Paehler, *A Nazi Past: Recasting German Identity in Postwar Europe* (University Press of Kentucky, 2015).
20. Odd Arne Westad, *The Cold War: A World History* (Allen Lane, 2017), 89.
21. Judt, 149.
22. "Lord Ismay," North Atlantic Treaty Organization, www.nato.int/cps/en/natohq/declassified_137930.htm, accessed December 2, 2024.
23. Judt, 149–52.
24. Robert Jervis, "Identity and the Cold War," in Melvyn P. Leffler and Odd Arne Westad, eds., *The Cambridge History of the Cold War: Volume 2: Crises and Détente* (Cambridge University Press, 2010), 22–43.
25. Francis Fukuyama, *The Origins of Political Order: From Prehuman Times to the French Revolution* (Profile Books, 2011), 62.
26. For features of the state, see Francis Fukuyama, *The Origins of Political Order: From Prehuman Times to the French Revolution* (Profile Books, 2011), 80–81; for the first state, James C. Scott, *Against the Grain: A Deep History of the Earliest States* (Yale University Press, 2017), 3.
27. For a general discussion of culture across many different academic fields, see, e.g., Wright, "Global Strategy Amidst the Globe's Cultures."
28. For a discussion of recent work including sound recordings, see, e.g., John Thornhill, "Can AI Help Us Speak to Animals? Part One and Part Two," *Financial Times*, September 19, 2023, www.ft.com/content/869709c0-20fb-49f3-a99d-4ed9e28dd0ef.
29. Gazzaniga et al., 476–81.
30. Judit Fazekas et al., "Do Children Learn from Their Prediction Mistakes? A Registered Report Evaluating Error-Based Theories of Language Acquisition," *Royal Society Open Science* 7 (November 4,2020): 180877, doi.org/10.1098/rsos.180877.
31. Stuart Russell, *Human Compatible: AI and the Problem of Control* (Allen Lane, 2019), 79.
32. Aida Suárez-González et al., "Semantic Variant Primary Progressive Aphasia: Practical Recommendations for Treatment from 20 Years of Behavioral Research," *Brain Sciences* 11, no. 12 (November 23, 2021): 1552, doi.org/10.3390/brainsci11121552.
33. My first-ever published brain imaging study looked at this topic, which I conducted with one of my most inspirational scientific role models, Cathy Price. Nicholas D. Wright et al., "Selective Activation Around the Left Occipito-Temporal Sulcus for Words Relative to Pictures: Individual Variability or False Positives?," *Human Brain Mapping* 29, no. 8 (August 2008): 986–1000, doi.org/10.1002/hbm.20443. Many others before and since have explored this brain region in writing and other functions.
34. Scott, *Against the Grain*, 139–49.
35. James Walker, "Top General Says Military Doesn't Take Oath to Any Individual amid

Pentagon Shakeup," *Newsweek*, November 13, 2020, www.newsweek.com/top-general-military-oath-individual-pentagon-shakeup-1547167.

36. See John Horgan, "To End War, Focus on Culture Rather than 'Root Causes,'" *Scientific American*, August 18, 2014, www.scientificamerican.com/blog/cross-check/to-end-war-focus-on-culture-rather-than-root-causes/.
37. "Ibn Khaldun, A Universal History (Selections)," https://web2.qatar.cmu.edu/~breilly2/world/Ibn%20Khaldun.htm, accessed December 2, 2024.
38. William James, *The Principles of Psychology* (Harvard University Press, 1981, originally published in 1890), 462.
39. Yascha Mounk and Roberto Stefan Foa, "This Is How Democracy Dies," *The Atlantic*, January 29, 2020, www.theatlantic.com/ideas/archive/2020/01/confidence-democracy-lowest-point-record/605686/; Roberto Foa, "Youth and Satisfaction with Democracy: Reversing the Democratic Disconnect?," The Bennett Institute for Public Policy, October 19, 2020, www.bennettinstitute.cam.ac.uk/publications/youth-and-satisfaction-democracy/; "Open Society Barometer," Open Society Foundations, September 2023, www.opensocietyfoundations.org/focus/open-society-barometer.
40. Quotes from Elizabeth Knowles, *Oxford Dictionary of Quotations*, eighth edition (Oxford University Press, 2014), 409; "Quote Origin: We Learn from History That We Do Not Learn from History," *Quote Investigator*, March 6, 2024, https://quoteinvestigator.com/2024/03/06/learn-history/.
41. Graff and Higham, 201, chapter 11.
42. Graff and Higham, 207.
43. Graff and Higham, 236.
44. Westad, *The Cold War*, 144.
45. Westad, *The Cold War*, 144.
46. Quoted in Lowell Dittmer, *China's Continuous Revolution: The Post-Liberation Epoch, 1949–1981* (University of California Press, 1987), 77.
47. Dittmer, 105.
48. Spence, *The Search for Modern China*, 545.
49. Xuetong Yan, *Ancient Chinese Thought, Modern Chinese Power*, ed. Daniel A. Bell and Sun Zhe, trans. Edmund Ryden (Princeton University Press, 2013), 229–33.
50. Sue-Lin Wong, "Xi Jinping: The Making of a Dictator," *The Economist*, October 19, 2022, www.economist.com/1843/2022/10/19/xi-jinping-the-making-of-a-dictator.
51. Roberts, *The Storm of War*, 585.
52. Nancy Padilla-Coreano et al., "Cortical Ensembles Orchestrate Social Competition Through Hypothalamic Outputs," *Nature* 603, no. 7902 (March 2022): 667–71, doi.org/10.1038/s41586-022-04507-5.
53. Madeleine F. Dwortz et al., "Neural Systems That Facilitate the Representation of Social Rank," *Philosophical Transactions of the Royal Society B: Biological Sciences* 377, no. 1845 (January 10, 2022): 20200444, doi.org/10.1098/rstb.2020.0444.
54. MaryAnn P. Noonan et al., "A Neural Circuit Covarying with Social Hierarchy in Macaques," *PLOS Biology* 12, no. 9 (September 2, 2014): e1001940, doi.org/10.1371/journal.pbio.1001940; J. Sallet et al., "Social Network Size Affects Neural Circuits in Macaques," *Science* 334, no. 6056 (November 4, 2011): 697–700, doi.org/10.1126/science.1210027.
55. Seongmin A. Park, Douglas S. Miller, and Erie D. Boorman, "Inferences on a

Multidimensional Social Hierarchy Use a Grid-Like Code," *Nature Neuroscience* 24, no. 9 (2021): 1292–1301, doi.org/10.1038/s41593-021-00916-3.

56. Fukuyama, *Origins of Political Order*, 69–79.

57. Stephen M. Fleming and Dan Bang, "Shouldering Responsibility," *Science* 361, no. 6401 (August 3, 2018): 449–50, https://doi.org/10.1126/science.aau5392; Iain D. Couzin et al., "Effective Leadership and Decision-Making in Animal Groups on the Move," *Nature* 433, no. 7025 (February 2005): 513–16, doi.org/10.1038/nature03236; Andrew J. King, Dominic D. P. Johnson, and Mark Van Vugt, "The Origins and Evolution of Leadership," *Current Biology: CB* 19, no. 19 (October 13, 2009): R911–916, doi.org/10.1016/j.cub.2009.07.027.

58. Henrich, chapter 8.

59. Tian Chen Zeng, Joey T. Cheng, and Joseph Henrich, "Dominance in Humans," *Philosophical Transactions of the Royal Society B: Biological Sciences* 377, no. 1845 (January 10, 2022): 20200451, doi.org/10.1098/rstb.2020.0451.

60. Dwortz et al.

61. Jan R. Landwehr and Michaela Wänke, "Face-to-Face: Three Facial Features That May Turn the Scale in Close Electoral Races," *Journal of Experimental Social Psychology* 108 (September 1, 2023): 104488, doi.org/10.1016/j.jesp.2023.104488; Emma Jacobs, "Chief Executives—Taller and Cleverer," *Financial Times*, June 4, 2014, www.ft.com/content/65d545cd-6ca5-35cb-b3a6-682dc4229f1f; "CEO Height: The Long and Short of It," *Financial Times*, August 6, 2023, www.ft.com/content/bb548d31-aa6b-4700-8c0c-3cc623b7376f.

62. Zeng et al.

63. Henrich, 118.

64. Henrich, 42, 124–25, chapter 4.

65. Stanley Milgram, *Obedience to Authority: An Experimental View* (Tavistock Publications, 1974); Craig Haney, Curtis Banks, and Philip Zimbardo, "A Study of Prisoners and Guards in a Simulated Prison," *Naval Research Reviews*, Office of Naval Research (September 1973): 11. The breadth of the conclusions from these studies has been hotly debated: see Alexander Haslam and Stephen D. Reicher, "Contesting the 'Nature' of Conformity: What Milgram and Zimbardo's Studies Really Show," *PLOS Biology* 10, no. 11 (November 20, 2012): e1001426, doi.org/10.1371/journal.pbio.1001426. But a basic idea remains that many seemingly "ordinary" people (although not all, including some who may actively resist) will conform and do others' dirty work.

66. Evan Osnos, *Age of Ambition: Chasing Fortune, Truth and Faith in the New China* (Random House, 2014), 60.

67. Micah G. Edelson et al., "Computational and Neurobiological Foundations of Leadership Decisions," *Science* 361, no. 6401 (August 3, 2018), doi.org/10.1126/science.aat0036; Fleming and Bang.

68. Zeng et al.

69. Roberts, *Leadership in War*.

70. The idea of scripts is the concluding framing in Freedman, *Strategy*, 598–99, 618–29.

71. Spence, *The Search for Modern China*, 505.

72. "Xi Jinping Is Obsessed with Political Loyalty in the PLA," *The Economist*, November 6, 2023; www.economist.com/special-report/2023/11/06/xi-jinping-is-obsessed-with-political-loyalty-in-the-pla; "Communist Party Members Must Study Xi Jinping's Thinking,"

The Economist, April 13, 2023, www.economist.com/china/2023/04/13/communist-party-members-must-study-xi-jinpings-thinking.

73. Craig Singleton, "Xi's Schadenfreude Over Moscow's Mutiny," *Foreign Policy* (blog), December 4, 2024, https://foreignpolicy.com/2023/06/29/xi-putin-wagner-prigozhin-russia-china-ukraine-war/.
74. David Vergun, "America Marks Anniversary of End of Korean War," U.S. Department of Defense, July 24, 2023, www.defense.gov/News/News-Stories/Article/Article/3418679/america-marks-anniversary-of-end-of-korean-war/.
75. Lawrence Freedman, *Command: The Politics of Military Operations from Korea to Ukraine* (Allen Lane, 2022), 24.
76. Freedman, *Command*, 29.
77. "Eisenhower and McCarthy," *PBS*, www.pbs.org/wgbh/americanexperience/features/eisenhower-politics/, accessed December 2, 2024.
78. Freedman, *Command*, 5–7; Carlo D'Este, "Dwight D. Eisenhower," in Andrew Roberts, ed., *The Art of War: Great Commanders of the Modern World* (Quercus, 2009).
79. Westad, *The Cold War*, 224–26, 288. Aaron L. Friedberg, "The Long Haul: Fighting and Funding America's Next Wars," *Foreign Affairs*, July 1, 2007, www.foreignaffairs.com/reviews/review-essay/2007-07-01/long-haul.
80. Michael Beschloss, "Eisenhower, an Unlikely Pioneer of TV Ads," *The New York Times*, October 30, 2015, www.nytimes.com/2015/11/01/upshot/eisenhower-an-unlikely-pioneer-of-tv-ads.html.
81. Sam Tanenhaus, "Who Stopped McCarthy?," *The Atlantic*, April 2017, www.theatlantic.com/magazine/archive/2017/04/who-stopped-mccarthy/517782/.
82. Wong, "Xi Jinping."
83. Michelle Goldberg, "Opinion: Are We Really Facing a Second Civil War?," *The New York Times*, January 6, 2022, www.nytimes.com/2022/01/06/opinion/america-civil-war.html; David Remnick, "Is a Civil War Ahead?," *The New Yorker*, January 5, 2022, www.newyorker.com/news/daily-comment/is-a-civil-war-ahead.
84. Michael Smerconish, "Is America Heading to Civil War or Secession?," CNN Politics, 2022, www.cnn.com/videos/politics/2022/01/08/is-america-heading-to-civil-war-or-secession.cnn.
85. Stephen Marche, *The Next Civil War: Dispatches from the American Future* (Avid Reader Press, 2022); Barbara F. Walter, *How Civil Wars Start: And How to Stop Them* (Penguin UK, 2022).
86. Peter T. Coleman, "The U.S. Is Heading Toward a Second Civil War. Here Is How to Avoid It," *Time*, October 20, 2022, https://time.com/6222633/second-civil-war-us-how-to-avoid/.
87. "How the LDP Dominates Japan's Politics," *The Economist*, October 28, 2021, www.economist.com/the-economist-explains/2021/10/28/how-the-ldp-dominates-japans-politics.
88. Wright, *Artificial Intelligence, China, Russia, and the Global Order*, chapter 3.
89. "Communist Party Members Must Study Xi Jinping's Thinking," *The Economist*, April 13, 2023, www.economist.com/china/2023/04/13/communist-party-members-must-study-xi-jinpings-thinking.
90. "Politics by Numbers," *The Economist*, March 23, 2016, www.economist.com/special-report/2016/03/23/politics-by-numbers.
91. Laura Barrón-López et al., "Trump's Success Among Young Men Illustrates Influence

of Online 'Manosphere,'" *PBS News*, November 25, 2024, www.pbs.org/newshour/show/trumps-success-among-young-men-illustrates-influence-of-online-manosphere.

92. Thomas Rid, *Active Measures: The Secret History of Disinformation and Political Warfare*, illustrated edition (Macmillan, 2020).

93. Westad, *The Cold War*, 113–14.

94. Rid; on peace movements see chapter 19, on HIV see chapter 22, and on relative later CIA restraint compared to earlier in the Cold War and compared to the KGB see 7, 11–12, 322–23.

95. Heidi Holz, "China's Global Public Opinion War with the United States and the West," War on the Rocks, August 14, 2024, https://warontherocks.com/2024/08/chinas-global-public-opinion-war-with-the-united-states-and-the-west/; Raksha Kumar, "How China Uses the News Media as a Weapon in Its Propaganda War Against the West," Reuters Institute for the Study of Journalism, November 2, 2021, https://reutersinstitute.politics.ox.ac.uk/news/how-china-uses-news-media-weapon-its-propaganda-war-against-west.

96. Rid, e.g., since 2015 see 377–422.

97. "China Is Flooding Taiwan with Disinformation," *The Economist*, September 26, 2023, www.economist.com/asia/2023/09/26/china-is-flooding-taiwan-with-disinformation; Sarah Rainsford, "How Meddling Blamed on Russia Exploited Real Grievances in Romania," *BBC News*, December 10, 2024, www.bbc.com/news/articles/c20ndg1eeeno.

98. Frank Dikötter, *China After Mao: The Rise of a Superpower* (Bloomsbury Publishing, 2022), 151–53, 156, 158, 162, 174, 277; John Culver, "Envisioning Positive U.S.-China Relations in the 2030s," in *U.S.-China Relations for the 2030s: Toward a Realistic Scenario for Coexistence*, ed. Christopher Chivvis (Washington, D.C.: Carnegie Endowment for International Peace, 2024).

99. Nicholas D. Wright, "Cognitive Defense of the Joint Force in a Digitizing World," *Intelligent Biology*, July 2021, www.intelligentbiology.co.uk; Beauchamp-Mustafaga, "Chinese Next-Generation Psychological Warfare."

100. Abraham Lincoln, "Address Delivered Before the Young Men's Lyceum of Springfield, Illinois, January 27, 1837," The American Presidency Project, www.presidency.ucsb.edu/documents/address-delivered-before-the-young-mens-lyceum-springfield-illinois, accessed December 2, 2024.

101. Matthews, *Head Strong*, 1.

9: CLEVER

1. Richard Wolfson and Ferenc Dalnoki-Veress, "The Devastating Effects of Nuclear War," excerpt from *Nuclear Choices for the Twenty-First Century* (MIT Press, 2021), *The MIT Press Reader*, March 2, 2022, https://thereader.mitpress.mit.edu/devastating-effects-of-nuclear-weapons-war/; Joe Phelan, "How Many Nuclear Weapons Exist, and Who Has Them?," *Scientific American*, March 22, 2022, www.scientificamerican.com/article/how-many-nuclear-weapons-exist-and-who-has-them/.

2. Richard Levy, "The Prefrontal Cortex: From Monkey to Man," *Brain* 147, no. 3 (March 1, 2024): 794–815, doi.org/10.1093/brain/awad389; Chad J. Donahue et al., "Quantitative Assessment of Prefrontal Cortex in Humans Relative to Nonhuman Primates," *Proceedings of the National Academy of Sciences* 115, no. 22 (May 29, 2018), doi.org/10.1073/pnas.1721653115; but note Robert A. Barton and Stephen H. Montgomery, "Proportional

Versus Relative Size as Metrics in Human Brain Evolution," *Proceedings of the National Academy of Sciences* 116, no. 1 (January 2, 2019): 3–4, doi.org/10.1073/pnas.1817200116.

3. "The State of Global AI Research," Emerging Technology Observatory, May 2, 2024, https://eto.tech/blog/state-of-global-ai-research/; Ryan McMorrow and Edward White, "China Challenges the West for Driverless Car Supremacy," *Financial Times*, January 31, 2024, www.ft.com/content/3a649978-69df-46eb-94c8-eee23a69e6bb; "Artificial Intelligence Index Report 2024," Stanford University: Stanford Institute for Human-Centered Artificial Intelligence, 2024, https://aiindex.stanford.edu/report/.

4. Peter Smittenaar et al., "Disruption of Dorsolateral Prefrontal Cortex Decreases Model-Based in Favor of Model-Free Control in Humans," *Neuron* 80, no. 4 (November 20, 2013): 914–19, doi.org/10.1016/j.neuron.2013.08.009.

5. This subsection draws on a recent report, Nicholas Wright, "Who will we—and they—be on Day 30 or Day 1000 in deterrence?" v1, 2025, *Intelligent Biology*, www.intelligent biology.co.uk.

6. Raymond J. Dolan and Peter Dayan, "Goals and Habits in the Brain," *Neuron* 80, no. 2 (October 16, 2013): 312–25, https://doi.org/10.1016/j.neuron.2013.09.007.

7. Adapted from Marcelo G. Mattar and Máté Lengyel, "Planning in the Brain," *Neuron* 110, no. 6 (March 16, 2022): 914–34, doi.org/10.1016/j.neuron.2021.12.018.

8. Mattar and Lengyel.

9. See Huys et al., "Interplay of Approximate Planning Strategies"; Joseph Snider et al., "Prospective Optimization with Limited Resources," *PLOS Computational Biology* 11, no. 9 (September 14, 2015): e1004501, doi.org/10.1371/journal.pcbi.1004501; Bas van Opheusden et al., "Expertise Increases Planning Depth in Human Gameplay," *Nature* 618, no. 7967 (June 2023): 1000–05, doi.org/10.1038/s41586-023-06124-2.

10. See Mehdi Keramati et al., "Adaptive Integration of Habits into Depth-Limited Planning Defines a Habitual-Goal-Directed Spectrum," *Proceedings of the National Academy of Sciences* 113, no. 45 (November 8, 2016): 12868–73, doi.org/10.1073/pnas.1609094113. Note also van Opheusden et al. for further interesting effects. Subjects also trade off the frequency of deeper and shallower analyses after an action or series of actions (Snider et al.).

11. Clare Wilson, "Why Thinking Hard for Several Hours Can Leave You Mentally Exhausted," *New Scientist*, August 11, 2022, www.newscientist.com/article/2333230-why-thinking-hard-for-several-hours-can-leave-you-mentally-exhausted/.

12. Huys et al.

13. Keith Kyle, "Britain and the Crisis, 1955–1956," in Wm. Roger Louis and Roger Owen, eds., *Suez 1956: The Crisis and Its Consequences* (Oxford University Press, 1991), 114–19, doi.org/10.1093/acprof:oso/9780198202417.003.0006.

14. The U.S. Special Inspector General for Iraq Reconstruction (SIGIR), for example, wrote that the administration had "no established plans to manage the increasing chaos" in Iraq, and that "when Iraq's withering post-invasion reality superseded [officials'] expectations, there was no well-defined 'Plan B' as a fallback and no existing government structures or resources to support a quick response." SIGIR, *Hard Lessons: The Iraq Reconstruction Experience* (Government Printing Office, 2009), 323–24. Decision-makers and officials had sufficient resources to look ahead and plan for uncomfortable scenarios such as a long insurgency, e.g., Secretary of Rumsfeld's "Parade of Horribles" secret memorandum drafted in October 2002, sent by him to the president and National Security Council (NSC), that listed possible bad outcomes, including a U.S. occupation lasting eight to ten years: Mike Allen, "Rumsfeld Hits Comeback Trail," *Politico*,

May 22, 2011, www.politico.com/story/2011/05/rumsfeld-hits-comeback-trail-055460. But these possibilities beyond the unwelcome event that postwar Iraq collapsed, incurring big U.S. costs—they were ignored and not planned for. Bob Woodward, for example, reviewed notes taken during the briefing on postwar Iraq on March 4, 2003, by the official overseeing policy planning for postwar Iraq to the NSC—and concluded that what was presented was a "rosy, pie-in-the-sky" scenario lacking particulars: Bob Woodward, *Plan of Attack* (Simon and Schuster, 2004), 136.

15. May, 460.
16. Camerer, 20; but it may be higher in some circumstances and so more similar to the depth of look-aheads noted earlier, e.g., Adam S. Goodie, Prashant Doshi, and Diana L. Young, "Levels of Theory-of-Mind Reasoning in Competitive Games," *Journal of Behavioral Decision Making* 25, no. 1 (2012): 95–108, doi.org/10.1002/bdm.717; Yohsuke Ohtsubo and Amnon Rapoport, "Depth of Reasoning in Strategic Form Games," *The Journal of Socio-Economics*, Essays on Behavioral Economics, 35, no. 1 (February 1, 2006): 31–47, doi.org/10.1016/j.socec.2005.12.003.
17. Friedrich Engels quoted in Singer, 47.
18. Gaddis, 84.
19. Sergey Radchenko and Vladislav Zubok, "Blundering on the Brink," *Foreign Affairs*, April 3, 2023, www.foreignaffairs.com/cuba/missile-crisis-secret-history-soviet-union-russia-ukraine-lessons.
20. Radchenko and Zubok.
21. Radchenko and Zubok.
22. Graham T. Allison and Philip Zelikow, *Essence of Decision: Explaining the Cuban Missile Crisis*, second edition (Longman, 1999), 111–20.
23. Allison and Zelikow, 112–13, 115–18; Freedman, *Command*, 81. It was described as a "quarantine" rather than a blockade.
24. Freedman, *Command*, 85–86, 89, 90–91, 105.
25. Freedman, *Command*, 89.
26. Radchenko and Zubok.
27. Freedman, *Strategy*, ix.
28. Knowles, 539.
29. Michael Howard, *War in European History* (Oxford University Press, 1976), 83–84.
30. Howard, *War in European History*, 101.
31. Howard, *War in European History*, 83–84; Clausewitz, *On War*, 17–19, 46–8, 54, 59.
32. Tim Shallice and Paul W. Burgess, "Deficits in Strategy Application Following Frontal Lobe Damage in Man," *Brain* 114, no. 2 (1991): 727–41.
33. Stephen M. Fleming, *Know Thyself: The New Science of Self-Awareness* (John Murray, 2021), 48.
34. Mohamady El-Gaby et al., "A Cellular Basis for Mapping Behavioural Structure," *Nature* 636 (November 6, 2024): 1–10, doi.org/10.1038/s41586-024-08145-x.
35. Donald A. Norman and Tim Shallice, "Attention to Action," in Richard J. Davidson, Gary E. Schwartz, and David Shapiro, eds., *Consciousness and Self-Regulation: Advances in Research and Theory*, volume 4 (Springer, 1986), 1–18, doi.org/10.1007/978-1-4757-0629-1_1.
36. Mindset is discussed in various contexts with different definitions. This definition is broadly

consistent with most strands of debate, e.g., Robert P. French, "The Fuzziness of Mindsets: Divergent Conceptualizations and Characterizations of Mindset Theory and Praxis," *International Journal of Organizational Analysis* 24, no. 4 (2016): 673–91, doi.org/10.1108/IJOA-09-2014-0797; Peter M. Gollwitzer, "Mindset Theory of Action Phases," in Paul Van Lange, Arie W. Kruglanski, and E. T. Higgins, eds., *Handbook of Theories of Social Psychology*, volume 1 (Sage Publications Ltd, 2012), 526–45, doi.org/10.4135/9781446249215.n26.

37. Gollwitzer.
38. Dominic D. P. Johnson and Dominic Tierney, "The Rubicon Theory of War: How the Path to Conflict Reaches the Point of No Return," *International Security* 36, no. 1 (2011): 7–40.
39. Johnson and Tierney.
40. James Danckert and Andreas Elpidorou, "In Search of Boredom: Beyond a Functional Account," *Trends in Cognitive Sciences* 27, no. 5 (May 1, 2023): 494–507, doi.org/10.1016/j.tics.2023.02.002.
41. Beevor, 60–62.
42. Raphaël Le Bouc and Mathias Pessiglione, "A Neuro-Computational Account of Procrastination Behavior," *Nature Communications* 13, no. 1 (September 26, 2022): 5639, doi.org/10.1038/s41467-022-33119-w.
43. Epstein, *Range*, 132–39, 145, 294.
44. Animal studies discussed in Ariana Vanderveldt, Luís Oliveira, and Leonard Green, "Delay Discounting: Pigeon, Rat, Human—Does It Matter?," *Journal of Experimental Psychology: Animal Learning and Cognition* 42, no. 2 (2016): 141–62, doi.org/10.1037/xan0000097; but note Benjamin Y. Hayden, "Time Discounting and Time Preference in Animals: A Critical Review," *Psychonomic Bulletin & Review* 23, no. 1 (February 1, 2016): 39–53, doi.org/10.3758/s13423-015-0879-3. Twin studies cited in Le Bouc and Pessiglione.
45. Le Bouc and Pessiglione.
46. Radchenko and Zubok.
47. Kevin P. Madore and Anthony D. Wagner, "Multicosts of Multitasking," *Cerebrum: The Dana Forum on Brain Science* 2019 (April 1, 2019): cer-04-19.
48. Kelly G. Garner and Paul E. Dux, "Knowledge Generalization and the Costs of Multitasking," *Nature Reviews Neuroscience* 24, no. 2 (February 2023): 98–112, doi.org/10.1038/s41583-022-00653-x.
49. Madore and Wagner.
50. David L. Strayer, Frank A. Drews, and Dennis J. Crouch, "A Comparison of the Cell Phone Driver and the Drunk Driver," *Human Factors* 48, no. 2 (June 1, 2006): 381–91, doi.org/10.1518/001872006777724471.
51. Madore and Wagner.
52. "Plans Are Worthless, But Planning Is Everything," *Quote Investigator*, November 18, 2017, https://quoteinvestigator.com/2017/11/18/planning/.
53. Douglas Pike, *PAVN: People's Army of Vietnam* (Brassey's Defence, 1986), chapters 9 and 10, 213–17, 233; Donald Stoker, *Purpose and Power: US Grand Strategy from the Revolutionary Era to the Present* (Cambridge University Press, 2024), doi.org/10.1017/9781009257268, chapter 12; Geoffrey Perret, "Vo Nguyen Giap," in Andrew Roberts, ed., *The Art of War: Great Commanders of the Modern World* (Quercus, 2009), 427.
54. Pike, chapters 9 and 10; Stoker, chapter 12; Westad, *The Cold War*, 333–34.

55. George W. Ball, "Memorandum from the Under Secretary of State (Ball) to President Johnson" (Office of the Historian, June 18, 1965), Foreign Relations of the United States, 1964–1968, Volume III, Vietnam, June–December 1965, https://history.state.gov/historicaldocuments/frus1964-68v03/d7.
56. Geoffrey C. Ward and Ken Burns, *The Vietnam War: An Intimate History* (Random House, 2018), 184.
57. Paul Ham, *Vietnam: The Australian War* (HarperCollins, 2010); Robert H. Scales, *Certain Victory: The U.S. Army in the Gulf War* (Potomac Books, Inc., 1997), 6.
58. See "Vietnam (1954–1968)," *Cold War* (CNN, 1998–1999), which described Secretary of Defense Robert McNamara's search for statistics but reported lack of listening to Vietnamese feedback on his visits.
59. Ward and Burns, 262.
60. Jon Askonas, "A Vicious Entanglement, Part V: The Body Count Myth," *War on the Rocks*, October 12, 2017, https://warontherocks.com/2017/10/a-vicious-entanglement-part-v-the-body-count-myth/.
61. Interview, "Vietnam," *Cold War*.
62. Phillip B. Davidson, *Vietnam at War: The History, 1946–1975* (Presidio Press, 1988), 655.
63. Anna Abraham, *The Neuroscience of Creativity* (Cambridge University Press, 2018), 7–10.
64. James Lucas, *Battle Group!: German Kampfgruppen Action of World War Two* (Arms and Armour, 1993), 7.
65. Lucas, 8–9.
66. Elizabeth Kier, *Imagining War: French and British Military Doctrine Between the Wars* (Princeton University Press, 1997), 83.
67. Milan Vego, "On Military Creativity," *Joint Force Quarterly* 70, no. 3 (2013): 83–90.
68. Vego, "On Military Creativity."
69. May, *Strange Victory*, 10.
70. John Winthrop Hackett, *The Profession of Arms* (Sidgwick & Jackson, 1983), 100–4; Milan Vego, "German War Gaming," *Naval War College Review* 65, no. 4 (2012): 106–48.
71. Gil Gonen-Yaacovi et al., "Rostral and Caudal Prefrontal Contribution to Creativity: A Meta-Analysis of Functional Imaging Data," *Frontiers in Human Neuroscience* 7 (August 14, 2013): 465, doi.org/10.3389/fnhum.2013.00465.
72. Roger E. Beaty et al., "Core Network Contributions to Remembering the Past, Imagining the Future, and Thinking Creatively," *Journal of Cognitive Neuroscience* 30, no. 12 (December 1, 2018): 1939–51, doi.org/10.1162/jocn_a_01327.
73. Melissa Ellamil et al., "Evaluative and Generative Modes of Thought During the Creative Process," *NeuroImage* 59, no. 2 (January 16, 2012): 1783–94, doi.org/10.1016/j.neuroimage.2011.08.008.
74. Roger E. Beaty, "The Creative Brain," *Cerebrum: The Dana Forum on Brain Science* 2020 (January 1, 2020): cer-02-20.
75. Shelly L. Gable, Elizabeth A. Hopper, and Jonathan W. Schooler, "When the Muses Strike: Creative Ideas of Physicists and Writers Routinely Occur During Mind Wandering," *Psychological Science* 30, no. 3 (March 1, 2019): 396–404, doi.org/10.1177/0956797618820626.
76. Epstein, *Range*, 33–34.

77. Brian Uzzi et al., "Atypical Combinations and Scientific Impact," *Science* 342, no. 6157 (October 25, 2013): 468–72, doi.org/10.1126/science.1240474.

78. Philip E. Tetlock, *Expert Political Judgment: How Good Is It? How Can We Know?* (Princeton University Press, 2017).

79. Clare Wilson, "Interrupting Sleep After a Few Minutes Can Boost Creativity," *New-Scientist*, December 8, 2021, www.newscientist.com/article/2300883-interrupting-sleep-after-a-few-minutes-can-boost-creativity/.

80. George Perkovich and James Acton, *Abolishing Nuclear Weapons*, first edition (Routledge, 2008).

81. Henry Kissinger, *On China* (Penguin, 2011), 217.

82. Kissinger, *On China*, 217.

83. Kissinger, *On China*, 234.

84. Kissinger, *On China*, 269–70.

85. Spence, *The Search for Modern China*, 629–33, 654–55, 669–73; Kissinger, *On China*, 329–37, 396–407, 441–45. To be sure, it was also a messy process, as described in Dikötter, *China After Mao* e.g., Preface.

86. Deng at the December 1978 Third Plenum, quoted in Kissinger, *On China*, 336.

87. Deng at the December 1978 Third Plenum, quoted in Kissinger, *On China*, 335.

88. Westad, *The Cold War*, 367–69, 528–30; Gaddis, 213–14.

89. "For Artificial Intelligence to Thrive, It Must Explain Itself," *The Economist*, February 15, 2018, www.economist.com/science-and-technology/2018/02/15/for-artificial-intelligence-to-thrive-it-must-explain-itself.

90. Paul Scharre, *Four Battlegrounds: Power in the Age of Artificial Intelligence* (W. W. Norton & Company, 2023), chapter 28.

91. "Functions Reward Functions in the Wild," OpenAI, December 21, 2016, https://openai.com/research/faulty-reward-functions.

92. Spence, *The Search for Modern China*, 514–23; Westad, *The Cold War*, 243; Frank Dikötter, "Looking Back on the Great Leap Forward," *History Today*, August 8, 2016, www.historytoday.com/archive/looking-back-great-leap-forward. The effect of the Great Leap Forward can be seen on global life expectancy data, e.g., "Life Expectancy," *Our World in Data*, https://ourworldindata.org/grapher/life-expectancy?country=OWID_WRL~Americas~OWID_EUR~OWID_AFR~OWID_ASI~OWID_OCE~CHN, accessed December 3, 2024.

93. Tetlock, *Expert Political Judgment*.

94. James Griffiths, "China Is Exporting the Great Firewall as Internet Freedom Declines Around the World," CNN, November 2, 2018, https://edition.cnn.com/2018/11/01/asia/internet-freedom-china-censorship-intl/index.html.

95. Freedman, *Strategy*, 106–7. This subsection more broadly draws in part on Wright, *Why are we integrating now*.

96. Margaret MacMillan, *The War That Ended Peace: How Europe Abandoned Peace for the First World War* (Profile Books, 2013), 322–23.

97. David C. Gompert, Hans Binnendijk, and Bonny Lin, *Blinders, Blunders, and Wars: What America and China Can Learn* (RAND Corporation, 2014), chapter 5, www.rand.org/pubs/research_reports/RR768.html.

98. Steven L. Rearden, *Council of War: A History of the Joint Chiefs of Staff, 1942–1991* (Washington, D.C.: NDU Press for the Joint History Office, Office of the Director, Joint Staff, Joint Chiefs of Staff, 2012), 60.

99. For brains, see the introduction by Friston to Part II on imaging neuroscience theory and analysis in Richard S. J. Frackowiak et al., eds., *Human Brain Function*, second edition (Academic Press, 2004), www.fil.ion.ucl.ac.uk/spm/doc/books/hbf2/. For a broader view, see Nicholas D. Wright, "Why Are We Integrating Now—and How Can We Integrate Better? History, Complexity and Metacognition," Intelligent Biology, August 2022, www.intelligentbiology.co.uk.

100. T. S. Eliot, *The Rock* (1934), part 1.

101. Clausewitz, 59.

102. Luciano Floridi, *Information: A Very Short Introduction* (Oxford University Press, 2010), 23. This subsection on data, information, knowledge, and wisdom draws on Wright, *Future Character of Information in Strategy.*

103. Knowledge and information are members of the same conceptual family, but knowledge enjoys a web of mutual relations that allow one part of it to account for another—so that once some information is available, knowledge can be built in terms of explanations or accounts that make sense of the available information (Floridi, 51). Knowledge as "justified true belief" has been a powerful definition since Plato, although the problems raised in Edmund Gettier's 1963 paper as to whether this is sufficient for knowledge have compromised that definition for many contemporary philosophers of knowledge; Jonathan Jenkins Ichikawa and Matthias Steup, "The Analysis of Knowledge," revised March 7, 2017, *The Stanford Encyclopedia of Philosophy* (Summer 2018), https://plato.stanford.edu/archives/sum2018/entries/knowledge-analysis/.

104. Wisdom is discussed across many diverse disciplines. For accessible discussions of wisdom in philosophy, see, e.g., Sharon Ryan, "Wisdom," revised February 4, 2013, *The Stanford Encyclopedia of Philosophy* (Spring 2020), https://plato.stanford.edu/archives/spr2020/entries/wisdom/; in psychology, see, e.g., Igor Grossmann, "Wisdom in Context," *Perspectives on Psychological Science* 12, no. 2 (March 1, 2017): 233–57, doi.org/10.1177/1745691616672066; in management, see, e.g., Jennifer Rowley, "The Wisdom Hierarchy: Representations of the DIKW Hierarchy," *Journal of Information Science* 33, no. 2 (April 1, 2007): 163–80, doi.org/10.1177/0165551506070706; and in functional genomics, see, e.g., Chris P. Ponting, "Big Knowledge from Big Data in Functional Genomics," *Emerging Topics in Life Sciences* 1, no. 3 (November 14, 2017): 245–48, doi.org/10.1042/ETLS20170129.

105. As relayed to this author and paraphrased here.

106. Consider two of the foremost deterrence thinkers: Bernard Brodie, "The Anatomy of Deterrence," *World Politics* 11, no. 2 (January 1959): 173–91, doi.org/10.2307/2009527, 293, who stated that "For the sake of deterrence before hostilities, the enemy must expect us to be vindictive and irrational if he attacks us"; Thomas Crombie Schelling, *Arms and Influence* (Yale University Press, 1966), 37, who wrote that "Another paradox of deterrence is that it does not always help to be, or to be believed to be, fully rational, cool headed, and in control of one's country." Both are discussed in Frank Zagarre, "Double Deterrence," Strategic Multilayer Assessment, NSI, August 2023, https://nsiteam.com/social/double-deterrence-two-challengers-one-defender/.

107. W. J. Hennigan, "Opinion: The Brink," *The New York Times*, March 4, 2024, www.nytimes.com/interactive/2024/03/07/opinion/nuclear-war-prevention.html.

108. Christopher Maynard, *Out of the Shadow: George H. W. Bush and the End of the Cold War* (Texas A&M University Press, 2008), 42–52.

10: WISER

1. This section on the remarkable life of Shaka Zulu is based on Saul David, "Shaka Zulu," in Andrew Roberts, ed., *The Art of War: Great Commanders of the Modern World* (Quercus, 2009).
2. As Paul Bracken describes: "Net assessment, thus, had its origins in the need to integrate Red [the other side] and Blue [our side] strategy in a single place. This is where the term net came from." Paul Bracken, "Net Assessment: A Practical Guide," *The US Army War College Quarterly: Parameters* 36, no. 1 (March 1, 2006), doi.org/10.55540/0031-1723.2285. For the Revolution in Military Affairs, see, e.g., Freedman, *Strategy*, 214–20.
3. Jeffrey Toobin, "Blowing Up the Senate," *The New Yorker*, February 27, 2005, www.newyorker.com/magazine/2005/03/07/blowing-up-the-senate; "Historical Highlights: Senate Created," United States Senate, www.senate.gov/artandhistory/history/minute/Senate_Created.htm, accessed December 4, 2024.
4. Quotes in Fleming, *Know Thyself*, preface. Parts of this subsection draw on Wright, *Why are we integrating now*.
5. Fleming, *Know Thyself*, 84–85.
6. Jason Carpenter et al., "Domain-General Enhancements of Metacognitive Ability through Adaptive Training," *Journal of Experimental Psychology: General* 148, no. 1 (January 2019): 51–64, doi.org/10.1037/xge0000505; Stephen M. Fleming, "Metacognition and Confidence: A Review and Synthesis," *Annual Review of Psychology* 75, no. 75, 2024 (January 18, 2024): 241–68, doi.org/10.1146/annurev-psych-022423-032425.
7. Wright et al., "Testosterone Induces Off-Line Perceptual Learning"; Stephen M. Fleming et al., "Relating Introspective Accuracy to Individual Differences in Brain Structure," *Science* 329, no. 5998 (September 17, 2010): 1541–43, doi.org/10.1126/science.1191883.
8. Fleming, *Know Thyself*, 3–4.
9. Fleming, *Know Thyself*, chapter 4.
10. Cristina Simón, "What Does an Orchestra Conductor Really Do?," *The Conversation*, November 2, 2023, https://theconversation.com/what-does-an-orchestra-conductor-really-do-216685; Shankar Vedantam, "Do Orchestras Really Need Conductors?," *NPR*, November 27, 2012, www.npr.org/sections/deceptivecadence/2012/11/27/165677915/do-orchestras-really-need-conductors.
11. Nadine Dijkstra, Sander E. Bosch, and Marcel A. J. van Gerven, "Shared Neural Mechanisms of Visual Perception and Imagery," *Trends in Cognitive Sciences* 23, no. 5 (May 1, 2019): 423–34, doi.org/10.1016/j.tics.2019.02.004.
12. Nadine Dijkstra and Stephen M. Fleming, "Subjective Signal Strength Distinguishes Reality from Imagination," *Nature Communications* 14, no. 1 (March 23, 2023): 1627, doi.org/10.1038/s41467-023-37322-1.
13. Fleming, *Know Thyself*, 102–3.
14. Fleming, *Know Thyself*, 103–4.

15. Rakefet Ackerman and Morris Goldsmith, "Metacognitive Regulation of Text Learning: On Screen Versus on Paper," *Journal of Experimental Psychology: Applied* 17, no. 1 (2011): 18–32, doi.org/10.1037/a0022086.
16. Eliot A. Cohen, *Supreme Command: Soldiers, Statesmen, and Leadership in Wartime* (Anchor Books, 2003), 103–4.
17. Richard Nisbett, *Mindware: Tools for Smart Thinking* (Allen Lane, 2015), 198.
18. "2017 Letter to Shareholders," UK About Amazon, April 19, 2018, www.aboutamazon.co.uk/news/company-news/2017-letter-to-shareholders.
19. Fleming, *Know Thyself*, 153.
20. Samuel P. Huntington, *The Soldier and the State: The Theory and Politics of Civil–Military Relations* (Harvard University Press, 1957), 48–49, 53.
21. Audrey Mazancieux et al., "Towards a Common Conceptual Space for Metacognition in Perception and Memory," *Nature Reviews Psychology* 2, no. 12 (December 2023): 751–66, doi.org/10.1038/s44159-023-00245-1.
22. For Eisenhower, Edward Cox, "Grey Eminence: Fox Conner and the Art of Mentorship," The Institute of Land Warfare, Association of the United States Army, September 15, 2010, 11–16, www.ausa.org/publications/grey-eminence-fox-conner-and-art-mentorship. For Winston Churchill, e.g., Cohen, 106–10. For Nelson Mandela, e.g., "Nelson Mandela Day—Remembering His Devotion to Education and Equality," University of London, July 15, 2020, www.london.ac.uk/news-events/student-insider/nelson-mandela-day-remembering-his-devotion-education-equality; Nelson Mandela, *Long Walk to Freedom* (Little, Brown and Company, 1994).
23. P. M. A. Rabbitt, "Error Correction Time Without External Error Signals," *Nature* 212, no. 5060 (October 1966): 438, doi.org/10.1038/212438a0.
24. Pavel Aksenov, "Stanislav Petrov: The Man Who May Have Saved the World," *BBC News*, September 26, 2013, www.bbc.com/news/world-europe-24280831; Kristine Phillips, "The Former Soviet Officer Who Trusted His Gut—and Averted a Global Nuclear Catastrophe," *The Washington Post*, September 18, 2017, www.washingtonpost.com/news/retropolis/wp/2017/09/18/the-former-soviet-officer-who-trusted-his-gut-and-averted-a-global-nuclear-catastrophe/.
25. Frith and Frith, chapter 14; Fleming, *Know Thyself*, 53–54.
26. Philip Tetlock and Dan Gardner, *Superforecasting: The Art and Science of Prediction* (Random House, 2015), 142–47, 166–73.
27. Samuel Recht et al., "Confidence at the Limits of Human Nested Cognition," *Neuroscience of Consciousness* 2022, no. 1 (2022): niac014, doi.org/10.1093/nc/niac014.
28. Antonia Creswell and Murray Shanahan, "Faithful Reasoning Using Large Language Models," *arXiv* (August 30, 2022), doi.org/10.48550/arXiv.2208.14271.
29. Fleming, *Know Thyself*, 201.
30. Cohen, *Supreme Command*, 118–21.
31. Cohen, *Supreme Command*, 99, 102; Roberts, *Masters and Commanders*, 47–48, 226–27, 283–85.
32. Elisa van der Plas et al., "Identifying Cultural Differences in Metacognition," *Journal of Experimental Psychology: General* 151, no. 12 (December 2022): 3268–80, doi.org/10.1037/xge0001209.

33. Stephen M. Fleming, Elisabeth J. van der Putten, and Nathaniel D. Daw, "Neural Mediators of Changes of Mind About Perceptual Decisions," *Nature Neuroscience* 21, no. 4 (April 1, 2018): 617–24, doi.org/10.1038/s41593-018-0104-6.

34. Beevor, 122–23.

35. Giada Di Stefano et al., "Making Experience Count: The Role of Reflection in Individual Learning," SSRN Scholarly Paper (Rochester, NY, June 30, 2021).

36. Yana Fandakova et al., "Changes in Ventromedial Prefrontal and Insular Cortex Support the Development of Metamemory from Childhood into Adolescence," *Proceedings of the National Academy of Sciences* 114, no. 29 (July 18, 2017): 7582–87, doi.org/10.1073/pnas.1703079114.

37. Fleming, *Know Thyself*, 119–20.

38. Siobhán Harty et al., "Transcranial Direct Current Stimulation over Right Dorsolateral Prefrontal Cortex Enhances Error Awareness in Older Age," *The Journal of Neuroscience: The Official Journal of the Society for Neuroscience* 34, no. 10 (March 5, 2014): 3646–52, doi.org/10.1523/JNEUROSCI.5308-13.2014; Tobias U. Hauser et al., "Noradrenaline Blockade Specifically Enhances Metacognitive Performance," *eLife* 6 (May 10, 2017): e24901, doi.org/10.7554/eLife.24901; Robert Hester et al., "Neurochemical Enhancement of Conscious Error Awareness," *The Journal of Neuroscience: The Official Journal of the Society for Neuroscience* 32, no. 8 (February 22, 2012): 2619–27, doi.org/10.1523/JNEUROSCI.4052-11.2012; Morten Joensson et al., "Making Sense: Dopamine Activates Conscious Self-Monitoring Through Medial Prefrontal Cortex," *Human Brain Mapping* 36, no. 5 (May 2015): 1866–77, doi.org/10.1002/hbm.22742; Aurelio Cortese et al., "Multivoxel Neurofeedback Selectively Modulates Confidence Without Changing Perceptual Performance," *Nature Communications* 7, no. 1 (December 15, 2016): 13669, doi.org/10.1038/ncomms13669; Aurelio Cortese et al., "Decoded fMRI Neurofeedback Can Induce Bidirectional Confidence Changes Within Single Participants," *NeuroImage* 149 (April 1, 2017): 323–37, doi.org/10.1016/j.neuroimage.2017.01.069. This subsection draws in part on Wright, *Why are we integrating now.*

39. Fleming, *Know Thyself*, 130–32.

40. Roberts, *Masters and Commanders*, 46–47, 56–59, 574–75; Cohen, *Supreme Command*, 120, 127–28; Roberts, *Storm of War*, 142.

41. Admiral John Richardson wrote as Chief of Naval Operations. John Richardson and Ashley O'Keefe, "Now Hear This—Read. Write. Fight.," *Proceedings of the U.S. Naval Institute* 142 (June 1, 2016), www.usni.org/magazines/proceedings/2016/june/now-hear-read-write-fight.

42. "REASON: Rapid Explanation, Analysis, and Sourcing Online," Office of the Director of National Intelligence, IARPA, www.iarpa.gov/research-programs/reason, accessed December 4, 2024.

43. Dennis Duncan, "How the Index Changed Reading, for Better and Worse," *The Economist*, September 2, 2021, www.economist.com/books-and-arts/2021/09/02/how-the-index-changed-reading-for-better-and-worse.

44. Westad, *The Cold War*, 622–24.

45. Quoted in William Wan, "In China, Soviet Union's Failure Drives Decisions on Reform," *The Washington Post*, March 23, 2013, www.washingtonpost.com/world/asia_pacific/in-china-soviet-unions-failure-drives-decisions-on-reform/2013/03/23/9c090012-92ef-11e2-ba5b-550c7abf6384_story.html. Parts of the beginning of this subsection draw on Wright, *Why are we integrating now.*

46. Damian Grammaticas, "China's New President Xi Jinping: A Man with a Dream," *BBC News*, March 14, 2013, www.bbc.com/news/world-asia-china-21790384.
47. Nancy Bernkopf Tucker, "The Evolution of U.S.-China Relations," in David Shambaugh, ed., *Tangled Titans: The United States and China*, first edition (Rowman & Littlefield Publishers, 2013), 38–40.
48. Dikötter, *China After Mao*, 158.
49. Bernkopf Tucker, 39.
50. David Shambaugh, *China Goes Global: The Partial Power* (Oxford University Press, 2013), 6, 274; Andrew Scobell et al., "China's Grand Strategy: Trends, Trajectories, and Long-Term Competition," RAND Corporation, July 24, 2020, www.rand.org/pubs/research_reports/RR2798.html.
51. Weiyi Cai et al., "How Xi Returned China to One-Man Rule," *The New York Times*, September 2, 2023, www.nytimes.com/interactive/2023/09/02/world/asia/china-xi-rule.html; Dikötter, *China After Mao*; Susan L. Shirk, "China in Xi's 'New Era': The Return to Personalistic Rule," *Journal of Democracy* 29, no. 2 (April 2018): 22–36.
52. Kilcullen, *The Dragons and the Snakes*, 185, 196–97; on Chinese missile forces, see, e.g., China Aerospace Studies Institute, "PLA Aerospace Power: A Primer on Trends in China's Military Air, Space, and Missile Forces," Air University, U.S. Air Force, July 22, 2024.
53. Thomas J. Christensen, *The China Challenge: Shaping the Choices of a Rising Power* (W. W. Norton & Company, 2015), 195–98.
54. "Obituary: Andrew Marshall Died on March 26th," *The Economist*, April 11, 2019, www.economist.com/obituary/2019/04/11/obituary-andrew-marshall-died-on-march-26th.
55. Seth, 11–14. Gazzaniga et al., G-4, 622.
56. Frith and Frith, chapter 14.
57. Cohen, *Supreme Command*, 114–15.
58. For semi-autonomy in motivation, see, e.g., Kent C. Berridge, "Motivation Concepts in Behavioral Neuroscience," *Physiology & Behavior* 81, no. 2 (2004): 179–209.
59. What Aristotle means by the unmoved mover has been discussed for centuries, e.g., in Bertrand Russell, *History of Western Philosophy* (George Allen & Unwin, 1946), 181, 216, 446; Jonathan Barnes, *Aristotle: A Very Short Introduction*, revised edition (Oxford University Press, 2000), 102; Istvan Bodnar, "Aristotle's Natural Philosophy," revised April 24, 2023, *The Stanford Encyclopedia of Philosophy* (Summer 2023), https://plato.stanford.edu/archives/sum2023/entries/aristotle-natphil/.
60. Rick Warren, *The Purpose Driven Life: What on Earth Am I Here For?* (Zondervan, 2002); sales figures in "Rick Warren," Simon & Schuster, www.simonandschuster.com/authors/Rick-Warren/39904606, accessed December 4, 2024.
61. Antonio Preti, "Suicide Among Animals: A Review of Evidence," *Psychological Reports* 101, no. 3 (December 1, 2007): 831–48, doi.org/10.2466/pr0.101.3.831-848; Richard Pallardy, "Do Animals Commit Suicide?," *Discover*, August 11, 2021, www.discovermagazine.com/planet-earth/do-animals-commit-suicide.
62. Seth, 52–58; Giulio Tononi and Gerald M. Edelman, "Consciousness and Complexity," *Science* 282, no. 5395 (December 4, 1998): 1846–51, doi.org/10.1126/science.282.5395.1846.
63. Fleming, *Know Thyself*, 83; Iroise Dumontheil, "Development of Abstract Thinking During Childhood and Adolescence: The Role of Rostrolateral Prefrontal Cortex," *Developmental Cognitive Neuroscience* 10 (October 2014): 57–76, doi.org/10.1016/j.dcn.2014.07.009.

64. E.g., Ryan.

65. Cohen, *Supreme Command*, 130–31.

66. Winston S. Churchill, *Painting as a Pastime*, 1948, https://gutenberg.ca/ebooks/churchillws-paintingasapastime/churchillws-paintingasapastime-00-h-dir/churchillws-paintingasapastime-00-h.html, accessed December 11, 2024.

67. David Epstein, *Range*, 33, 281.

68. Freedman, *Strategy*, 237.

69. Kissinger, *On China*, 400–401. As Kissinger describes: "cross the river by feeling the stones," charting a path in part on the basis of what worked.

70. Jack A. Goldstone, *Revolutions: A Very Short Introduction* (Oxford University Press 2014), 34–35.

71. Cohen, *Supreme Command*.

72. Cohen, *Supreme Command*, 108–9.

73. Quoted in Cohen, *Supreme Command*, 211–12.

74. Gazzaniga et al., 655.

75. "Energy Demands Limit Our Brains' Information Processing Capacity," *UCL News*, August 3, 2020, www.ucl.ac.uk/news/2020/aug/energy-demands-limit-our-brains-information-processing-capacity; "Neuroscientists Use AI to Simulate How the Brain Makes Sense of the Visual World," Wu Tsai Neurosciences Institute, May 28, 2024, https://neuroscience.stanford.edu/news/neuroscientists-use-ai-simulate-how-brain-makes-sense-visual-world.

76. For recent discussions, see Lukas J Volz et al., "Unifying Control over the Body: Consciousness and Cross-Cueing in Split-Brain Patients," *Brain* 141, no. 3 (March 1, 2018): e15, doi.org/10.1093/brain/awx359; Edward H. F. de Haan et al., "Split-Brain: What We Know Now and Why This Is Important for Understanding Consciousness," *Neuropsychology Review* 30, no. 2 (June 2020): 224–33, doi.org/10.1007/s11065-020-09439-3.

77. Frank Ching, "Why China Needed Bin Laden," May 26, 2011, *The Diplomat*, https://thediplomat.com/2011/05/why-china-needed-bin-laden/.

78. Emily Sullivan and Dina Smeltz, "20 Years Later: 9/11 in the Public Memory," *Running Numbers* (blog), Chicago Council on Global Affairs, September 9, 2021, https://globalaffairs.org/commentary-and-analysis/blogs/20-years-later-911-public-memory; Kelly Bulkeley and Tracey L. Kahan, "The Impact of September 11 on Dreaming," *Consciousness and Cognition* 17, no. 4 (December 2008): 1248–56, doi.org/10.1016/j.concog.2008.07.001.

79. 王文 (Wang Wen), "On the Strategic Opportunity Period in the New Era: Origin, Status Quo, and Future [论新时代的战略机遇期：源起、现状与未来]," CSIS Interpret: China, original work published in *Journal of the Central Institute of Socialism* [中央社会主义学院学报], August 15, 2022, https://interpret.csis.org/translations/on-the-strategic-opportunity-period-in-the-new-era-origin-status-quo-and-future/.

80. Dan De Luce, "After 9/11, China Grew into a Superpower as a Distracted U.S. Fixated on Terrorism, Experts Say," *NBC News*, October 17, 2021, www.nbcnews.com/politics/national-security/after-9-11-china-grew-superpower-distracted-u-s-fixated-n1278671.

81. Richard Baldwin, "China Is the World's Sole Manufacturing Superpower: A Line Sketch of the Rise," *VoxEU*, January 17, 2024, https://cepr.org/voxeu/columns/china-worlds-sole-manufacturing-superpower-line-sketch-rise.

82. "QS World University Rankings 2024: Top Global Universities," QS Top Universities, www.topuniversities.com/world-university-rankings, accessed February 2024.

83. "Artificial Intelligence Index Report 2024."

84. This figure is in 2021 dollars and includes future spending on disability and other costs. Neta C. Crawford, "The U.S. Budgetary Costs of the Post-9/11 Wars," Watson Institute for International and Public Affairs, Brown University, September 2021, https://watson.brown.edu/costsofwar/figures/2021/BudgetaryCosts.

85. Yun Sun, "China's Rise Post-9/11," in Lydia Khalil, ed., *Did 9/11 Change Our World?* (Lowy Institute, 2021), https://interactives.lowyinstitute.org/features/9-11/.

86. Economy.

87. Rush Doshi, "Analysis: Xi Jinping Just Made It Clear Where China's Foreign Policy Is Headed," *The Washington Post*, October 25, 2017, www.washingtonpost.com/news/monkey-cage/wp/2017/10/25/xi-jinping-just-made-it-clear-where-chinas-foreign-policy-is-headed/; Economy, 187–90.

88. Economy, 190.

89. Spending discussed in: Patricia Cohen and Liz Alderman, "The 'Peace Dividend' Is Over in Europe. Now Come the Hard Tradeoffs," *The New York Times*, May 3, 2023, www.nytimes.com/2023/05/03/business/economy/russia-ukraine-war-defense-spending.html; "Press Release: Defence Expenditure of NATO Countries (2014–2024)," North Atlantic Treaty Organisation, June 2024, www.nato.int/nato_static_fl2014/assets/pdf/2024/6/pdf/240617-def-exp-2024-en.pdf, 2; Daisuke Kawai, "Japan's Defence Budget Surge: A New Security Paradigm," *RUSI* (blog), December 2, 2024, www.rusi.org/explore-our-research/publications/commentary/japans-defence-budget-surge-new-security-paradigm. Few outside America, Britain, and France can conduct serious military planning, e.g., "Can Europe Defend Itself without America?," *The Economist*, February 18, 2024, www.economist.com/briefing/2024/02/18/can-europe-defend-itself-without-america. More broadly, see Francis Harris, "Time to Panic on Europe's Rusting Defenses? Probably," *Europe's Edge*, CEPA, February 11, 2024, https://cepa.org/article/time-to-panic-on-europes-rusting-defenses-probably/; Curtis L. Fox, "Who in NATO Is Ready for War?," *Military Review*, U.S. Army University Press, July 2024, www.armyupress.army.mil/Journals/Military-Review/English-Edition-Archives/July-August-2024/Who-in-NATO-Is-Ready-for-War/.

90. Cohen and Alderman. This must also be seen alongside challenges with government debt in Europe, e.g., Tony Barber, "Europe's Fiscal Tug of War," *Financial Times*, October 26, 2024, www.ft.com/content/c015dc14-068c-40ef-bf57-a2f736f73119.

91. For an influential discussion of such trade-offs, see Huntington.

92. Howard, 143.

93. May, 10; Huntington, *The Soldier and the State*; Barry R. Posen, *The Sources of Military Doctrine: France, Britain, and Germany Between the World Wars* (Cornell University Press, 1984), chapter 4 on interwar France, 168, 171–74, 237 on RAF Fighter Command, 240 on Hitler and Blitzkrieg.

94. "World Population by Continent 2024," Statista, www.statista.com/statistics/237584/distribution-of-the-world-population-by-continent/, accessed December 11, 2024.

CONCLUSIONS

1. David L. Howell, "The Social Life of Firearms in Tokugawa Japan," *Japanese Studies* 29, no. 1: 65–80, doi.org/10.1080/10371390902780530.
2. Henry Mance, "Steven Pinker: 'Putin's Invasion Won't Lead to a Return to the Age of Warring Civilisation,'" *Financial Times*, October 23, 2022, www.ft.com/content/4a6ac655-66a9-4d1c-8646-9ab32c36fbe2.
3. Overy, *Blood and Ruins*, 605.
4. Letter from Albert Einstein written with Leo Szilard to President Franklin Roosevelt on August 2, 1939, FDR-24, www.fdrlibrary.marist.edu/archives/collections/franklin/?p=collections/findingaid&id=510; Deborah Nicholls-Lee, "'It Was the One Great Mistake in My Life': The Letter from Einstein That Ushered in the Age of the Atomic Bomb," August 6, 2024, www.bbc.com/culture/article/20240801-it-was-the-one-great-mistake-in-my-life-the-letter-from-einstein-that-ushered-in-the-age-of-the-atomic-bomb.
5. Handel, 326; Mitchell, xiii–xiv, 27–9, 119–20, 227.
6. Churchill, *The Second World War*, volume 1, v.
7. From his unpublished autobiographical manuscript written in prison, 1975, according to "Selected Quotes," Nelson Mandela Foundation, www.nelsonmandela.org/selected-quotes, accessed December 5, 2024.
8. Henry A. Kissinger, *World Order: Reflections on the Character of Nations and the Course of History* (Penguin UK, 2014), 268.
9. Paul Sonne, "Behind Putin's Potemkin Vote, Real Support. But No Other Choices," *The New York Times*, March 18, 2024, www.nytimes.com/2024/03/18/world/europe/putin-russia-election.html; "China's Leaders Are Less Popular than They Might Think," *The Economist*, January 16, 2024, www.economist.com/china/2024/01/16/chinas-leaders-are-less-popular-than-they-might-think.
10. Eric Schmidt, "War in the Age of AI Demands New Weaponry," *Financial Times*, September 21, 2024, www.ft.com/content/fe136479-9504-4588-869f-900f2b3452c4.
11. Elsa B. Kania, "The Competitive Challenge of Military-Civil Fusion, Testimony to the U.S.-China Economic Security Commission for Hearing on 'China's Pursuit of Defense Technologies,'" April 13, 2023, www.uscc.gov/sites/default/files/2023-04/Elsa_Kania_Testimony.pdf; Ryan McMorrow, "Leak Shows China Uses Private Company to Hack Citizens and Foreign States," *Financial Times*, February 22, 2024, https://on.ft.com/3T7BRct.
12. "How Could FPV Drones Change Warfare?," *The Economist*, August 4, 2023, www.economist.com/the-economist-explains/2023/08/04/how-could-fpv-drones-change-warfare; "How Cheap Drones Are Transforming Warfare in Ukraine," *The Economist*, February 5, 2024, www.economist.com/interactive/science-and-technology/2024/02/05/cheap-racing-drones-offer-precision-warfare-at-scale; "How Ukraine Uses Cheap AI-Guided Drones to Deadly Effect Against Russia."
13. "Why Did the US and Allies Invade Iraq 20 Years Ago?," *BBC News*, March 19, 2023, www.bbc.com/news/world-64980565.
14. "Iraq," GOV.UK, www.gov.uk/government/fields-of-operation/iraq, accessed December 11, 2024.
15. This dictum is based on sections of Clausewitz, including "War is nothing but a continuation of politics with the admixture of other means." *On War* (1832–1834) book 8, chapter

6, section B, quoted in "War," *Oxford Reference*, www.oxfordreference.com/display/10.1093/acref/9780191826719.001.0001/q-oro-ed4-00011287, accessed December 6, 2024. Debates surround whether the word "politics" should be translated as "policy," as it is by Howard and Paret. For a discussion, see Freedman, *Strategy*, 86–88, 92–94.

16. Freedman, *Strategy*, 87.
17. Claire Press and Svitlana Libet, "How Russia's 35-Mile Armoured Convoy Ended in Failure," *BBC*, February 22, 2023, www.bbc.co.uk/news/world-europe-64664944; Michael Schwirtz et al., "Putin's War," *The New York Times*, December 17, 2022, www.nytimes.com/interactive/2022/12/16/world/europe/russia-putin-war-failures-ukraine.html.
18. See various contributions in Nicholas D. Wright, Michael Miklaucic, and Todd Veazie, eds., *Human, Machine, War: How the Mind-Tech Nexus Will Win Future Wars* (Air University Press, forthcoming). Sidharth Kaushal et al., "Leveraging Human-Machine Teaming," Special Competitive Studies Project and the Royal United Services Institute, 2024, www.scsp.ai/2024/01/report-on-leveraging-human-machine-teaming-by-the-special-competitive-studies-project-and-the-royal-united-services-institute/, 13–14.
19. Sun Tzu, *The Art of War* (translated by Lionel Giles, 1910), www.gutenberg.org/files/132/132-h/132-h.htm, chapter 3, 17.
20. Michael E. Howard, "Strategy: The Indirect Approach," *International Affairs* 31, no. 1 (January 1955): 96, doi.org/10.2307/2604619.
21. Churchill, *The Second World War*, volume 1, ix.
22. Emily Sohn, "The Eyes of Mammals Reveal a Dark Past," *Nature*, April 10, 2019, doi.org/10.1038/d41586-019-01109-6.
23. For a public report on such risks, see, e.g., Ezra Karger et al., "Forecasting Existential Risks," August 8, 2023, https://forecastingresearch.org/s/XPT.pdf.
24. Such a catastrophe would kill at least a similar proportion of the world's population over a similar time frame to either World War I (some 15 million deaths out of a global population of 1.9 billion over four years) or World War II (some 60 million deaths out of 2.3 billion over six to eight years), or a pandemic (natural or human-made) of at least a similar scale to the influenza pandemic of 1918 to 1920 (some 50 million deaths out of 1.9 billion; for comparison, note that while very serious the COVID-19 pandemic led to significantly fewer deaths at around 27 million out of a global population of 8 billion over four years, many of whom were older or more vulnerable). Other catastrophic risks could also kill a similar proportion of the world's population over a similar time frame, such as climate change or AI gone rogue. Events often blend together, such as the influenza pandemic and World War I, or World War I and the Russian civil war, or even the two World Wars. I would estimate the probability of an extinction-level event, in which only a few thousand humans survive, such as an all-out nuclear war that seriously affects the climate, at less than 0.1 to 0.5 percent. I fully acknowledge that although based in evidence these all remain highly subjective judgments, and it is also crucial to state that this in no way minimizes the tragedy of events at other scales, such as the dozens of conflicts happening across the world today. Figures from "Population," *Our World in Data*, https://ourworldindata.org/grapher/population, accessed December 12, 2024; Gerhard Hirschfeld, Gerd Krumeich, and Irina Renz, *Brill's Encyclopedia of the First World War*, revised edition (Brill, 2012); Beevor, 1; "Estimated Cumulative Excess Deaths During COVID-19," Our World in Data, https://ourworldindata.org/grapher/excess-deaths-cumulative-economist-single-entity, accessed December 12, 2024; Niall P. A. S. Johnson and Juergen Mueller, "Updating the Accounts: Global Mortality of the 1918–1920 'Spanish' Influenza Pandemic," *Bulletin of the History of Medicine* 76, no. 1 (2002): 105–15, doi.org/10.1353/bhm.2002.0022.

INDEX

Note: Page numbers in *italics* indicate figures, and references following "n" refer notes.

ABOUT THE AUTHOR

Dr Nicholas Wright, MRCP, PhD, is a neuroscientist who researches the brain, technology and security at University College London, Georgetown University and the Center for Strategic and International Studies in Washington, DC, where he also advises the Pentagon Joint Staff. Currently working with governments and the private sector, Dr Wright was previously a neurology doctor in London and Oxford and has published numerous academic papers, many of which have been covered by the BBC and *The New York Times*. He has appeared on CNN and the BBC and regularly contributes to outlets like *Foreign Affairs*, *Foreign Policy*, *The Atlantic* and *Slate*.